Julian Barnes from the Margins

Julian Barnes from the Margins

Exploring the Writer's Archives

Vanessa Guignery

BLOOMSBURY ACADEMIC
LONDON • NEW YORK • OXFORD • NEW DELHI • SYDNEY

BLOOMSBURY ACADEMIC
Bloomsbury Publishing Plc
50 Bedford Square, London, WC1B 3DP, UK
1385 Broadway, New York, NY 10018, USA
29 Earlsfort Terrace, Dublin 2, Ireland

BLOOMSBURY, BLOOMSBURY ACADEMIC and the Diana logo are trademarks of
Bloomsbury Publishing Plc

First published in Great Britain 2020
This paperback edition published in 2021

Copyright © Vanessa Guignery, 2020

Vanessa Guignery has asserted her right under the Copyright, Designs and Patents Act, 1988, to be identified as Author of this work.

For legal purposes the acknowledgements on page x constitute an extension of this copyright page.

Cover design: Eleanor Rose
Cover image: Julian Barnes Archives. Harry Ransom Center.
The University of Texas at Austin

All rights reserved. No part of this publication may be reproduced or transmitted in any form or by any means, electronic or mechanical, including photocopying, recording, or any information storage or retrieval system, without prior permission in writing from the publishers.

Bloomsbury Publishing Plc does not have any control over, or responsibility for, any third-party websites referred to or in this book. All internet addresses given in this book were correct at the time of going to press. The author and publisher regret any inconvenience caused if addresses have changed or sites have ceased to exist, but can accept no responsibility for any such changes.

A catalogue record for this book is available from the British Library.

A catalog record for this book is available from the Library of Congress.

ISBN: HB: 978-1-3501-2501-8
PB: 978-1-3502-4318-7
ePDF: 978-1-3501-2502-5
eBook: 978-1-3501-2503-2

Typeset by Newgen KnowledgeWorks Pvt. Ltd., Chennai, India

To find out more about our authors and books visit www.bloomsbury.com and sign up for our newsletters.

To Ryan

Contents

List of Figures	ix
Acknowledgements	x
Note on the Text	xii
Introduction	1
1 *Metroland*: Everything that got away	11
1. Faltering starts	13
2. 'Petty Gripes' and 'Oua, oua, oua'	17
3. The Death Chapter	21
4. Return to Metroland	29
2 The case for/The case against	39
1. Reviewing and being reviewed	39
2. The case of *Before She Met Me*	45
a. Julian Barnes's reButs to Hermione Lee's Buts	45
b. Finding the right title	54
3 A chronology (of sorts)	59
4 *Flaubert's Parrot* from ignition to composition	75
1. Flaubert Stories	76
2. The fictional narrator	87
5 The Barnes apocrypha	95
1. *A Literary Guide to Oxford*: The itinerary of a book that was never published	95
2. The unwritten books which tantalize	103
6 *Staring at the Sun*: A novel of forking roots and paths	117
1. Multiple roots and titles	117
2. Early starts	126

7	Fragments of stories: *A History of the World in 10½ Chapters*	131
	1. Planning, naming and arranging chapters	131
	2. Not so simple stories	136
	3. 'Parenthesis'	140
	4. With a little help from my friends	143
8	*The Porcupine* in the making: Writer and translator	147
	1. An outsider's view	148
	2. Is and is not	151
	3. The ending of the novel	154
	4. The libel risks	161
9	A dictionary of Julian Barnes	165
10	*Arthur & George*: Beginnings and endings	177
	1. First and final steps	177
	2. The blind spots of research	180
	3. The art of beginning	185
	4. Finding a JB title	192
	5. Working out tenses	196
11	*Nothing to Be Frightened Of* as an echo chamber	201
	1. The obsession with death: From the early notebooks to *Nothing to Be Frightened Of*	202
	2. This is not an autobiography	204
	3. Fictionalizing memory in *The Only Story*	212
12	*The Sense of an Ending*: Time in reverse	215
	1. Prequels in real life	216
	2. A sequel to *Metroland*?	219
	3. Getting started: The title and the incipit	223
	4. A denser text	230
Conclusion		237
Works Cited		239
Index		251

Figures

1	*Metroland* – handwritten notes (1.10.5)	37
2	*Flaubert's Parrot* – 'Flaubert Completion Scheme' (1.5.3)	84
3	*Arthur & George* – early draft of the first page (2.2.5A)	187

Acknowledgements

My deepest and warmest thanks go to Julian Barnes for being such a thoughtful and generous friend over the years. He offered help and encouragement for this book, patiently answering my queries, giving me access to unarchived material, authorizing me to quote from it and providing invaluable information on his writing process. I thank him for his trust and for his great benevolence in reading a near-final draft of this book and adding comments.

I am very grateful to Dame Professor Hermione Lee for her constant support, friendship and precious advice over the years and particularly in relation to this book, and to Ryan Roberts, webmaster of Julian Barnes's website, meticulous book collector and great friend, who tirelessly provided help with the most obscure references only he could find.

Many thanks to my loyal friend and first reader, Emma Cypher-Dournes, for her keen eye and useful suggestions, always offered with a welcome touch of humour, to Rachel Cugnoni for her helpful advice on publication and to Gary Fisketjon for his enthusiasm for the book.

I am grateful to Stephen Enniss, director of the Harry Ransom Center, for generously providing me with the very best conditions under which to conduct my research at the University of Texas at Austin. I would also like to thank the staff of the Harry Ransom Center for their kindness and generosity over the years, more particularly Gil Hartman, Pat Fox, Kelly Kerbow Hudson, Jim Kuhn, Elizabeth Garver, Michael Gilmore and Kathryn Millan.

The research for this book was conducted thanks to funding from the Institut Universitaire de France, the Fleur Cowles Fellowship of the Harry Ransom Center and the programme 'soutien à la mobilité internationale-2018' of the InSHS-CNRS.

The author and publisher gratefully acknowledge the permission granted by United Agents LLP on behalf of Julian Barnes and by Random House to reproduce the copyright material in this book. Every effort has been made to trace copyright holders and to obtain their permission for the use of copyright material. The publisher apologizes for any errors or omissions in the list below and would be grateful if notified of any corrections that should be incorporated in future reprints or editions of this book.

'From *Metroland* by Julian Barnes published by Jonathan Cape. Reproduced by permission of The Random House Group Ltd. ©1980'

'From *Before She Met Me* by Julian Barnes published by Jonathan Cape. Reproduced by permission of The Random House Group Ltd. ©1982'

'From *Flaubert's Parrot* by Julian Barnes published by Jonathan Cape. Reproduced by permission of The Random House Group Ltd. ©1984'

'From *Staring at the Sun* by Julian Barnes published by Jonathan Cape. Reproduced by permission of The Random House Group Ltd. ©1986'

'From *A History of the World in 10½ Chapters* by Julian Barnes published by Jonathan Cape. Reproduced by permission of The Random House Group Ltd. ©1989'

'From *Talking It Over* by Julian Barnes published by Jonathan Cape. Reproduced by permission of The Random House Group Ltd. ©1991'

'From *The Porcupine* by Julian Barnes published by Jonathan Cape. Reproduced by permission of The Random House Group Ltd. ©1992'

'From *Cross Channel* by Julian Barnes published by Jonathan Cape. Reproduced by permission of The Random House Group Ltd. ©1996'

'From *England, England* by Julian Barnes published by Jonathan Cape. Reproduced by permission of The Random House Group Ltd. ©1998'

'From *The Lemon Table* by Julian Barnes published by Jonathan Cape. Reproduced by permission of The Random House Group Ltd. ©2004'

'From *Arthur & George* by Julian Barnes published by Jonathan Cape. Reproduced by permission of The Random House Group Ltd. ©2005'

'From *Nothing to Be Frightened Of* by Julian Barnes published by Jonathan Cape. Reproduced by permission of The Random House Group Ltd. ©2008'

'From *Pulse* by Julian Barnes published by Jonathan Cape. Reproduced by permission of The Random House Group Ltd. ©2011'

'From *The Sense of an Ending* by Julian Barnes published by Jonathan Cape. Reproduced by permission of The Random House Group Ltd. ©2011'

'From *Through the Window* by Julian Barnes published by Vintage. Reproduced by permission of The Random House Group Ltd. ©2012'

'From *Levels of Life* by Julian Barnes published by Jonathan Cape. Reproduced by permission of The Random House Group Ltd. ©2013'

'From *Keeping an Eye Open* by Julian Barnes published by Jonathan Cape. Reproduced by permission of The Random House Group Ltd. ©2015'

'From *The Noise of Time* by Julian Barnes published by Jonathan Cape. Reproduced by permission of The Random House Group Ltd. ©2016'

'From *The Only Story* by Julian Barnes published by Jonathan Cape. Reproduced by permission of The Random House Group Ltd. ©2018'

Note on the Text

Julian Barnes's papers were acquired by the Harry Ransom Center in 2002, 2006 and 2015. Extracts from the first acquisition, identified as 'Papers. 1971–2000' in the library's catalogue, will be referenced as number one followed by box and folder numbers. Extracts from 'Addition to His Papers. 1996–2006' will be referenced as number two followed by box and folder numbers. Extracts from 'Addition to his Papers II', the third acquisition which has not yet been catalogued, will be referenced as number three followed by the box number. The contents of the first two acquisitions are listed in the Finding Aids of the Harry Ransom Center website. The yet uncatalogued third acquisition is organized in six different boxes, five of which are open to the public. Each box includes a broad reference to its contents and a number (Box 1: Miscellaneous; Box 2: *Levels of Life* and *Through the Window*; Box 3: *The Sense of an Ending* and *Keeping an Eye Open*; Box 4: *Pulse*; Box 5: *Nothing to Be Frightened Of*).

Julian Barnes annotated a near-final draft of this book in March 2018. Quotations from his annotations will be referenced as 'Annotations, 22–27 March 2018'.

Introduction

On the front cover of the first British edition of Julian Barnes's *The Only Story* (2018), the title in red printed letters has been crossed out and replaced by a handwritten version in black; on the back cover, the sentence 'It is better to have loved and lost than never to have loved at all' appears twice, the first time crossed[1]; on the front cover of the first American edition, the words 'Love is' are printed more than twenty times, each crossed out in different ways. Such erasures are usually not presented to the reader who is offered the published version of a text from which early thoughts and hesitations have been sorted out and removed. In the late 1920s, Heidegger perceived the benefit of crossing out a word and leaving both the deletion and the (still legible) word in place to suggest the difficulty of conveying meaning within the constraints of language. The process of placing terms under erasure allows one to read the discarded words and therefore be aware of not only what has been deemed inadequate but also what has been retained among a set of possibilities. Such an enhanced perception of the different layers of the palimpsest is what is offered by a writer's archives which still bear the marks of the various stages of composition.

In 1996, Julian Barnes went on a wine pilgrimage to the Rhone Valley. At Château Rayas, he looked at the soil, the stones, the vines, the grapes, but refused to meet the winemaker. Looking back on his decision, he explained: 'I'm glad that someone, somewhere, knows which cuvées went into the final blend, what percentage of new oak was used, and what the fermentation temperature might have been; but as long as the maker himself knows, that's all I care about.'[2] Transferred to literature, this might mean that the reader should refrain from trying to know the writer's fabrication secrets. As Barnes remarked:

> Either you want to know everything about a writer you admire – you grab the biography, listen for the gossip, go to the book-signing, discover how rough notes and hard research become blended into the final *assemblage* – or you say, there is something better, purer about not knowing all this stuff.[3]

---

[1] This sentence is twice written and crossed out in the narrator's notebook in the novel. Julian Barnes, *The Only Story* (London: Jonathan Cape, 2018), 165.
[2] Julian Barnes, 'Pilgrimage to Rayas', *Appellation Magazine* 6, no. 6 (November 1998–31 December 1998): 34.
[3] Ibid.

Or, in the words of Geoffrey Braithwaite in *Flaubert's Parrot*, 'the real distinction between people' is 'between those who want to know everything and those who don't'.[4] The present book is written by a reader leaning towards the first category, who is, however, not so much interested in the biography and gossip as in the 'rough notes and hard research' which pave the way for the final text.[5] What is proposed here is therefore a journey through Julian Barnes's papers, holograph notebooks, drafts, manuscripts, typescripts, miscellaneous notes, letters and emails which have been preserved at the Harry Ransom Center of the University of Texas at Austin. As noted by the narrator of *Flaubert's Parrot*, directness confuses: 'The full-face portrait staring back at you hypnotises' (102). Rather than the full-face portrait, this book offers a view from the margins, from scraps of paper and scribblings, from words under erasure, false starts and discarded thoughts. The method consists in focusing on what is not directly visible to the reader who is already familiar with Barnes's oeuvre (the preliminary research, the discarded material, comments by friends, translators and editors, ideas for books never written or written differently), a perspective which authorizes the reader to temporarily look away from the published text the better to rediscover it anew.[6] The result is an investigation and a *mélange*, neither an academic literary analysis of the published work[7] nor a book of the strictest kind of genetic criticism, neither a pure story nor an exhaustive guide.

The book mainly focuses on the processes at work in eight of Barnes's novels from *Metroland* (1980) to *The Sense of an Ending* (2011) – the latest novel whose archives are stored at the Harry Ransom Center – because this is the genre for which the examination of archives seems the most enlightening and also because the author himself once said that his main interest is fiction.[8] The genesis of the non-fictional book *Nothing to Be Frightened Of* is also scrutinized as it contains thoughts and ideas which had been hoarded by the writer for several decades, some of which found their way into his fiction. The short stories, non-fictional individual pieces and collections of essays are sometimes briefly alluded to for their parallels with the novels. In homage to the formal audacity of *Flaubert's Parrot* and *A History of the World in 10½ Chapters*, the book also makes a foray into the Barnes apocrypha and offers interludes in the form of an unconventional chronology and a dictionary to provide yet more oblique vistas into

---

[4] Julian Barnes, *Flaubert's Parrot* (London: Picador, [1984] 1985), 127.
[5] Whenever the word 'final' is used in this book, it does not suggest an unalterable text or version, but refers to the text as it was published.
[6] This method entails exploring what Jean Bellemin-Noël and other geneticists have called the 'avant-texte' or 'foretext', that is, 'the documents that come before a work when it is considered a *text*'. Although the concept is not uniformly employed by geneticists, it 'carries with it the assumption that the material of textual genetics is not a given but rather a critical construction elaborated in relation to a postulated terminal – so-called definitive – state of the work'. Jed Depmann, Daniel Ferrer and Michael Groden, ed., *Genetic Criticism: Texts and Avant-Textes* (Philadelphia: University of Pennsylvania Press, 2004), 8.
[7] Several monographs already exist by Merritt Moseley (1997), Matthew Pateman (2002), Vanessa Guignery (2006), Frederick Holmes (2008) and Peter Childs (2011), as well as collections of essays (Guignery 2009; Groes and Childs 2011; Tory and Vesztergom 2014) and countless individual articles.
[8] Interview by Mark Lawson, 'Mark Lawson Talks to Julian Barnes', BBC Four Television, 30 March 2014.

Barnes's work in relation to the literary context in which it was produced and – as this reader is not a purist – into some aspects of his life.

In a short essay about the genesis of the chapter entitled 'Shipwreck' in *A History of the World in 10½ Chapters*, Barnes wrote:

> There is something so certain, so authoritative in a great painting (novel, piece of music …) that the work almost bullies us into believing that this, and only this, was what the artist initially planned. Even when advised that he or she started off in a completely opposite direction, we half don't believe the evidence: we persuade ourselves that surreptitiously, subconsciously, they always knew exactly what they were after.[9]

The examination of Barnes's archives reveals that the writer sometimes knew exactly what he was after but more often struggled to decide on the suitable structure, the adequate narrative voice, the befitting plot developments or the appropriate style. The novelist remarked: 'You start off with different possible tonalities and the right one only gradually comes into play.'[10] Genetic criticism confirms that 'the work … stands out against a background, and a series, of potentialities'[11] and that 'we should consider the text as a *necessary possibility*, as one manifestation of a process which is always virtually present in the background'.[12] The narrator of 'Shipwreck' in *A History of the World in 10½ Chapters* attempts to find out how Géricault came to paint what became known as 'The Raft of the Medusa'. He analyses what Géricault borrowed from the original catastrophe by comparing the work of art to historical documents and examines the preliminary sketches; the discarded ideas and near-misses; what he did not paint, very nearly painted and did paint; what he readjusted, raised or lowered, cut, cropped or stretched. Barnes explained what he himself was aiming at in 'Shipwreck': 'What I wanted to do … was reassert the living process – one involving intention, to be sure, but also doubt, chance, underconfidence, overconfidence, false starts, false middles, and so on.'[13] This 'living process' and all the twists and turns it involves are also what the present book seeks to examine through its exploration of the genesis of Barnes's novels.

However, one should be wary of adopting what Barnes, under the *New Review*'s pseudonym of Edward Pygge, playfully called the 'Bone Theory' in 1977.[14] Barnes/

---

[9] Julian Barnes, 'Short Story/Essay. Shipwreck', in *The Writer in You: A Writing Process Reader*, ed. Barbara Lounsberry (New York: HarperCollins, 1992), 174.
[10] John Freeman, 'How the Writer Edits: Julian Barnes', *Literary Hub*, 26 May 2016, http://lithub.com/how-the-writer-edits-julian-barnes/. Accessed on 19 January 2019.
[11] Michel Contat, Denis Hollier and Jacques Neefs, 'Editors' Preface', in *Drafts*, ed. Michel Contat, Denis Hollier and Jacques Neefs, special issue of *Yale French Studies* 89 (1996): 2.
[12] Louis Hay, 'Does "Text" Exist?', trans. Matthew Jocelyn and Hans Walter, *Studies in Bibliography* 41 (1988): 75.
[13] Barnes, 'Short Story/Essay', 174.
[14] For more information on Edward Pygge, see Ryan Roberts, 'Edward Pygge: Authors in Search of a Character', *Pseudonym as Character: The Development of Julian Barnes's Multiple Aliases* (MA diss., Department of English, University of Illinois at Springfield, 2011), 15–22.

Pygge was satirically referring to the questions interviewers typically ask novelists and what they entail:

> How did such-and-such start? What gave you the idea for your novel? What, in a quotable formula of not more than 20 words, is it *about*? Such questions usually presuppose a mechanical view of literature: that the novelist starts with a shiny idea, a particular apercu, and then, sly dog that he is, buries it in a lot of padding. The task of the reader/critic is then to scrabble away in the mound which the writer has thrown up, and piece together a summary.[15]

Barnes's papers show that no such process is taking place at composition or writing stage and that it is a delusion to think that the literary critic-turned-sleuth can unearth the unique bone or idea which will encapsulate the whole book. Despite this early distrust of adherents to the Bone Theory, after he became a novelist, Barnes agreed to satisfy the curiosity of critics and readers by disclosing that when he starts thinking of a book, what comes first is always the situation: 'I never start by making up a bunch of characters and then wonder what might happen to them. I think of a situation, an impossible dilemma, a moral or emotional quandary, and then wonder to whom it might happen and when and where.'[16] This situation then needs to be inscribed within a specific form. Thus, five or six years before writing *Talking It Over*, Barnes heard a piece of gossip about two best friends in school, one of whom got married, and during the wedding his best friend fell in love with his wife and wooed her away. At first, Barnes did not think of this news (or situation) as an idea for a story, let alone a novel, but when he thought of the narrative technique of juxtaposed monologues, he could start developing the story. He remarked: 'this germ of a story about wife theft … only became a possibility of a novel when I thought of the formal device that I then employed'.[17]

Among the early steps also features the choice of structure. Barnes remarked: 'Very early on, I have a sense of the structure of the book, of where it should break. It is like those animals which have exoskeletons. We can think of the novel as armadillo, with head, body, tail.'[18] The archives often contain planning sheets or notes which indicate the main structure of the books, especially for those organized in clearly distinguished main parts (*Staring at the Sun*, *England, England*, *Arthur & George*, *The Sense of an Ending*). As for the characters, Barnes does not need to visualize them early in the composition:

---

[15] Julian Barnes [Edward Pygge, pseud.], 'Untitled', *New Review* 4, no. 38 (May 1977): 64.
[16] Rachel Cooke, 'Julian Barnes: "Flaubert could have written a great novel about contemporary America"', *Guardian*, 29 January 2018, https://www.theguardian.com/books/2018/jan/29/julian-barnes-interview-the-only-story. Accessed on 19 January 2019.
[17] 'Audio Discussion: Julian Barnes and Jay McInerney', 7 March 2001, New York Public Library, http://movies2.nytimes.com/books/01/04/01/specials/barnes.html. Accessed on 19 January 2019.
[18] Interview by Hermione Lee, 'An Evening with Julian Barnes, Talking to Hermione Lee', 8 December 2011, The Institute of Engineering and Technology, London. Partly transcribed in Lauren Collins, 'An Evening with Julian Barnes', *New Yorker*, 12 December 2011, https://www.newyorker.com/news/lauren-collins/an-evening-with-julian-barnes#ixzz1gPFJqR4o. Accessed on 19 January 2019.

Novelists vary in how much, and how soon, they need to 'see' their characters. Some work 'outside in', unable to begin without a full physical presence; others (like me) tend to work 'inside out', starting from functional or moral significance. In the latter case, a character may be active in a novel without yet having a settled outline; then, at some point – even, with a minor figure, fairly late in the writing – the question of appearance needs attending to. Hair colour? Eyes? Stooping or erect of carriage? And so on.[19]

Barnes's papers show indeed that he usually lists down the functional and psychological characteristics of his main protagonists but rarely their physical features.

The archives for each novel reveal a composition pattern which starts with various notes about what to include, followed by several drafts containing longhand revisions and deletions, until a complete draft is sent to Barnes's friend Dame Hermione Lee for comments, which leads to more revisions.[20] In 2000, Barnes told an interviewer: 'normally I type on an IBM 196c, then hand correct again and again until it's virtually illegible, then clean type it, then hand correct again and again. And so on'.[21] The novelist firmly believes that writing is in the rewriting. Therefore, 'Writing the first draft is usually a great illusion. The first draft makes you think that the telling of this story, whatever it is, is a fairly blithe and easy business. Then you realise you've fooled yourself yet again. Then the work, the real writing starts'.[22] The numerous corrections on Barnes's manuscripts and typescripts attest to how carefully and relentlessly he hones his style and concurs with Flaubert's famous sentence which he likes to quote: 'prose is like hair – it shines with combing'.[23] Therefore, as he points out, 'quite substantial things can be changed ... even quite late in the day' – be it the name of the characters, the use of tenses or even part of the structure – and 'the book can always be improved'.[24]

In some cases, Barnes deconstructs his own text to make sure the scattered elements about a character make a coherent story. Thus, after finishing a first draft of *Flaubert's Parrot*, he wrote a note to himself: 'read through the Braithwaite bits and see if they make a narrative' (1.5.3). He used a similar method for *Talking It Over* when he feared Gillian's voice was being 'drowned out' by the voices of the male characters in the competing monologues: 'I simply took all the pages out and read her story as her story all the way through. ... it's good to feel the novel physically coming apart like that and then laying it back in place'.[25] He adopted the same technique for the story of

---

[19] Julian Barnes, 'The Case of Inspector Campbell's Red Hair', in *The Anthology of New Writing, Volume 15*, ed. Maggie Gee and Bernardine Evaristo (London: Granta Books, 2007), 289.
[20] For a typology of genetic documents, see Pierre-Marc de Biasi, 'What Is a Literary Draft? Towards a Functional Typology of Genetic Documentation', in *Drafts*, ed. Michel Contat, Denis Hollier and Jacques Neefs, special issue of *Yale French Studies* 89 (1996), 26–58.
[21] Interview by Shusha Guppy (2000), in *Conversations with Julian Barnes*, ed. Vanessa Guignery and Ryan Roberts (Mississippi: University of Mississippi Press, 2009), 81.
[22] Interview by Vanessa Guignery, in *Novelists in the New Millennium. Conversations with Writers*, ed. Vanessa Guignery (Basingstoke: Palgrave Macmillan, 2013), 22.
[23] Julian Barnes, *Something to Declare* (London: Jonathan Cape, 2002), 149. Barnes noted that when he quoted this sentence once in public, someone said, 'No, it shines with brushing, not combing'. Annotations, 22–27 March 2018.
[24] Interview by Guppy, in *Conversations*, ed. Guignery and Roberts, 81.
[25] Interview by the *Observer* (1998), in *Conversations*, ed. Guignery and Roberts, 29–30.

Martha Cochrane in *England, England* in order to achieve the right balance 'between the personal intimate life realistically treated, and the large, semi-farcical story of the island': 'When I wasn't sure whether it was working or not, I simply extracted from the draft of the book all the sections dealing with Martha's personal life, and then rewrote them as a sort of individual story. Then put them back into the book and made the necessary adjustments.'[26] Asked when he feels he has reached the final version of the book, he replies: 'When I find that the changes I'm making are dis-improving my text as much as improving it. Then I know it's time to wave good-bye.'[27]

Barnes's ninth and eleventh novels, *Love, etc* and *The Sense of an Ending*, were written by hand for the first draft, which, according to the novelist, 'probably makes you more concise',[28] but his more frequent method of composing fiction is the electric typewriter. He explained: 'I think you need the technology that suits the way your brain works. Sometimes you need your thoughts to go down your arm in what feels like a direct feed via pencil or felt-tip to paper, sometimes you require a more formal "sit up and address a machine".'[29] He works on a typewriter which is no longer manufactured, owns three in case one breaks down (one of them was bought new around 1983, the others secondhand) and has had them repaired in the same south London shop by the same person for decades. Barnes always relies 'on having a rather free first draft', and when he was forced to use a computer due to all his electric typewriters breaking down at once, he expected to find himself 'getting much more prolix and windy' but found he was 'over-correcting on the first draft': 'I was getting something that was too compact and too tight. It didn't really work. It didn't represent what I was thinking, what I needed as a writer.'[30] According to him, word processors 'tend to make things look finished sooner than they are' and he believes in 'a certain amount of physical labor'.[31] In that respect, Barnes differs from his friend Ian McEwan who was 'a grateful convert to computers' as he believes word processing parallels the way the brain works, whereas the typewriter is 'a gross mechanical obstruction'. McEwan notes: 'Word processing is more intimate, more like thinking itself. ... I like the provisional nature of unprinted material held in the computer's memory – like an unspoken thought.'[32]

Some novels are more meticulously planned than others. Thus Barnes recalls that for *Talking It Over*, 'which involved a lot of intricate interweaving of voices, I tried to plan 100 per cent of the action. As I went on, it was coming out differently, so I ended up having only planned about 80–85 per cent of it'.[33] Ten years later, for its sequel, *Love,*

---

[26] Ibid., 29.
[27] Interview by Guppy, in *Conversations*, ed. Guignery and Roberts, 81.
[28] Interview by Will Gompertz, 'Barnes: "Novels Tell Truth about Life"', BBC Arts, 2 November 2012, https://www.bbc.com/news/entertainment-arts-20179787. Accessed on 19 January 2019.
[29] Lisa Allardice, 'Barnes, Lively, Holroyd, Moggach and Self Talk about their Relationships with Their Typewriters', *Guardian*, 1 December 2009, https://www.theguardian.com/books/2009/dec/01/barnes-authors-typewriters. Accessed on 19 January 2019.
[30] Interview by Margaret Crick (2007), in *Conversations*, ed. Guignery and Roberts, 155.
[31] Interview by Guppy, in *Conversations*, ed. Guignery and Roberts, 81.
[32] McEwan also remarks: 'The chapter that is in the computer, but not yet printed, has the same – or the equivalent – virtual quality as an idea in your head that you've not committed to paper yet.' Ryan Roberts, ed. *Conversations with Ian McEwan* (Mississippi: University of Mississippi Press, 2010), 94, 82.
[33] Interview by the *Observer*, in *Conversations*, ed. Guignery and Roberts, 30.

etc, Barnes wrote down in longhand eight pages that detail with great precision what the novel should include and give helpful information about the characters (1.9.5). More frequently however, Barnes does not list down all the particularities of his books before getting down to writing and sometimes 'just sort of start[s]'. However, he points out: 'I never start at the beginning. I tend to start at a central moment and often circle round'.³⁴ Thus, most often, the first lines, paragraphs and sometimes pages of his novels were not originally there in the first draft. According to Barnes, 'novel-writing isn't architecture: you don't make a plan and then build to it; sometimes you just build, and then the plan begins to suggest itself'.³⁵ As the narrator of 'Shipwreck' in *A History of the World in 10½ Chapters* points out, when presented with the final result of a work of art, the 'progress towards it seems irresistible', the conclusion seems inevitable, but we should not forget the trials and errors and '[w]e must try to allow for hazard, for lucky discovery, even for bluff'.³⁶ The exploration of Barnes's archives suggests a balance between careful planning – what Louis Hay has called 'écriture à programme' which relies on a pre-established plan of writing – and a dose of instinctive freedom which can lead to unexpected deviations – which would correspond to 'écriture à processus', when a writer proceeds without an entirely preconceived destination.³⁷

The two books which were first written in longhand in notebooks (*Love, etc* and *The Sense of an Ending*) are the ones whose progress can be traced with the greatest accuracy in the archive. More generally, drafts and typescripts are neither dated nor identified by number and, except for the last versions, neither page-numbered nor always organized chronologically or sequentially so that it is sometimes difficult to reconstitute the order in which they were written, although a close examination of additions and deletions usually helps in the process. The distinction between the various drafts and typescripts will therefore often be fluid in this book as references will be made to early or later drafts, drawing from my own understanding of the chronology of the archives.

Writers' papers prove particularly interesting when an author comments on his own work in progress, on what he should develop, what he should cut, how he sees a character or what he considers as the core of his novel. In the archive, Barnes appears as the first critic of his own work, and often its most severe, when he takes up this role in response to remarks by an editor (Liz Calder about *Metroland*), a translator (Dimitrina Kondeva about *The Porcupine*) or a friend (Hermione Lee about all his books since *Before She Met Me*), or in notes to himself while the work is being drafted. Sometimes, he participates in a 'case against' debate in which he makes his own books stand trial, thus resembling the narrator in *Flaubert's Parrot*, who, in the chapter entitled 'The Case against', alternately plays the roles of Flaubert's accuser and defendant. Pages of handwritten notes as well as remarks in the margins testify to the questions the novelist relentlessly asked himself about specific passages and attempted to answer in later drafts. His notes and correspondence thus give invaluable indications as to what he was aiming for in his fictional work.

---

[34] Ibid.
[35] Barnes, 'The Case of Inspector Campbell', 292.
[36] Julian Barnes, *A History of the World in 10½ Chapters* (London: Picador, [1989] 1990), 134–5.
[37] Louis Hay, *La littérature des écrivains. Questions de critique génétique* (Paris: José Corti, 2002), 74–5.

In the draft of an article about writers' manuscripts dating from 1988, Barnes recalls reading a 'harmless statement' about himself:

> Barnes, Julian 1946–
> Julian Barnes intends to keep his manuscripts and typescripts in his own possession for the foreseeable future [information supplied by the author, March 1987]

He then comments:

> I thought that sounded a bit pompous. Who does this guy think he is? Who cares about his scraps and scribblings? To my relief, I discovered that this stuffy information turns out to be a standard cataloguing expression in the Location Register of Twentieth Century English Literary Manuscripts, recently published by the British Library. (2.5.3)

This register covers 'twentieth-century British literary authors whose manuscripts are held in publicly-owned collections in the British Isles', with notes of holdings in foreign libraries (2.5.3), and Barnes ponders it with 'welling unease', first because of 'the haphazardness of manuscript survival' (what survives of a writer's correspondence depends on the recipients' decision to keep it or not) and second because of what literary biographers might expose by looking through personal papers. This risk of exposure is what leads some writers to destroy (or give instructions to destroy) their diaries, letters or even manuscripts.

In 2002, Barnes decided to place his papers with the Harry Ransom Center at the University of Texas at Austin. This collection offers a fairly complete record of Barnes's writings from the 1970s to 2015 (the date of the third and most recent acquisition of his papers) as he has kept most of what he put down on paper:

> From the beginning I was a complete squirreler away of everything I wrote, of every draft, and I have a collecting nature to me […].[38]

> Everything I do from the moment I am faced by what I recognize as the possibility – or pre-possibility – of a novel is contained within the archive. I have never thrown away more than the occasional (more or less duplicate) page of typescript. My archive therefore contains 98 or 99% of all the marks I make on paper as a novelist.[39]

It should be noted, however, that the archive contains only a few of the writer's notebooks and very little correspondence, Barnes having decided not to include letters from people who are still alive. Barnes has also chosen to keep his diaries and said in

---

[38] Interview by Vanessa Guignery and Ryan Roberts (2007), in *Conversations*, ed. Guignery and Roberts, 178.
[39] Megan Barnard, ed. *Collecting the Imagination: The First Fifty Years of the Ransom Center* (Austin: University of Texas Press, 2007), 112.

an interview in 2014 that he had no present intention to publish them although he is aware that things may change: 'the possibilities are I publish some of them before I die, I burn them before I die, they're published after my death, or, to the irritation of many people, I put an embargo on them so they're published after everyone who's in them dies'.[40]

Because an archive can never be whole (especially for a living writer) and because a view from the margins entails selection, this book is necessarily partial and subjective in its choices of what to examine and what to include. Thus, it has been decided not to go into the details of fabrication of three novels dating from Barnes's mid-career – *England, England* (1998) and the diptych *Talking It Over* (1991) and *Love, etc* (2001) – but to focus instead on the early and later books because they offer an opportunity to examine a variety of writing procedures over a period of thirty years. In addition to drawing from what the novelist has agreed to make public, either through publication in books, articles or interviews or by allowing it to be stored at the University of Texas at Austin and therefore made accessible to scholars, this study benefited from Julian Barnes's great generosity in answering queries or reacting to emails sent while I was conducting research at the Harry Ransom Center. Sometimes, Barnes only had a vague memory of what he had discarded from early drafts. He commented in 2017: 'It's odd how as you proceed towards the final version of the book your mind/memory seems to wipe out all the false starts you made and blind alleys you went up. So they come as a complete surprise when a French Professor turns them up.'[41] This study seeks to shed light on these false starts, forked paths and blind alleys in order to better understand how Barnes ended up marching along the bright avenues that led to the published versions of his novels.

The structure of the book mostly follows the order of publication of Barnes's novels in order to highlight evolutions and continuities in his writing processes. Barnes adapted his ways of sketching, planning, writing and revising his books to the singularity of each one (and to the reactions of his editors, publishers and friends), and as a result, his working methods have varied throughout his career. Thus, the novels examined at each extremity (*Metroland* and *The Sense of an Ending*) are related in that the 2011 Booker Prize winning novel was initially conceived as a sequel to Barnes's first book, published some thirty years earlier. However, the composition of *Metroland*, written on and off over a period of seven or eight years, and whose original drafts were thoroughly revised and slimmed down, greatly differs from that of *The Sense of an Ending*, seemingly written in a free flow with relatively few corrections, thus testifying to the mature writer's greater assurance. While Barnes paid close attention to comments by editors and friends at the start of his career, writing letters to 'defend' his choices in *Before She Met Me*, *Flaubert's Parrot* and later on in *The Porcupine*, as years went by, he gained in confidence and no longer needed to justify his decisions so adamantly. The mainly chronological approach adopted in this book helps identify the early roots of some of Barnes's interests (in death, memory, time, love, etc.), which regularly crop up in fragmented or tentative form in his unpublished notebooks and

---

[40] In Lawson, 'Mark Lawson'.
[41] Private email correspondence with the author, 10 January 2017.

the drafts of his early novels, and observe how they achieve full development in later novels.

The examination of the archives reveals that each novel starts with a distinct beginning and is characterized by a particular procedure so that it is not possible to generalize and homogenize Barnes's modes of writing; instead, it is necessary to examine the specificity of each book's trajectory while remaining attentive to resonances. Each chapter therefore adopts a different angle and method to examine the crucial stages of composition, such as the extensive use of biographical and historical research (for *Arthur & George*), the relentless search for the right incipit (in *The Sense of an Ending*), the subtle ordering of chapters (in *A History of the World in 10½ Chapters*), the difficult choice of titles (for *Before She Met Me*, *Staring at the Sun* and *Arthur & George*) or the quest for the adequate genre(s) (in *Flaubert's Parrot* and *Nothing to Be Frightened Of*). Barnes's papers offer a unique perspective on the writer's craft and art, and the aim of this book is to accompany him in his creative voyages and bring back to the surface of the palimpsest layers that had been erased or hidden but which can still be recovered.

1

Metroland: Everything that got away

Julian Barnes published his first novel *Metroland* in 1980 with Jonathan Cape (with an advance of £750), five years after he (and twelve other contestants among several thousand applicants) had won a ghost story competition sponsored by the *Times* and Cape. The judges of the competition were Kingsley Amis, Patricia Highsmith and actor Christopher Lee, along with John Higgins of the *Times* and Tom Maschler of Jonathan Cape.[1] Not only was Barnes's winning story 'A Self-Possessed Woman' published in *The Times Anthology of Ghost Stories* (1975)[2] – along with Penelope Fitzgerald's first published story, 'The Axe', at the age of 61 years – but another requirement was that the author submit his first novel to Cape.

Metroland provides one of the most interesting opportunities for archival research not only because of the many revisions and deletions to which the novel was subject but also because in 2007 and 2012, Barnes annotated the copy he had given his parents upon its publication in 1980 before handing it to the literary charity English PEN.[3] The copy was sold (along with fifty other annotated first editions by Kazuo Ishiguro, Graham Swift, David Lodge, Tom Stoppard, Nick Hornby, J. K. Rowling, Margaret Atwood, Seamus Heaney and others) at an auction at Sotheby's on 21 May 2013. It was bought by the Morgan Library & Museum in New York which displayed it (along with Hilary Mantel's *Wolf Hall* and Ian McEwan's *Amsterdam*) in a show called *In the Margins* in May 2015. On the first page of Chapter One in that annotated copy, Barnes wrote down a series of questions which had guided him during composition:

> You write the first section of the first part of your first novel. What questions does – & must – it therefore ask?
> What effect does any art – not just the one you have begun to practise – have on someone who comes into its orbit?
> And further, if it does have an effect, is that effect measurable?
> Or if not measurable, at least observable?

---

[1] First prize was awarded to Michael Kernan for 'The Doll Named Silvio' and second prize to Francis King for 'A Scent of Mimosa'.
[2] Julian Barnes, 'A Self-Possessed Woman', in *The Times Anthology of Ghost Stories* (London: Jonathan Cape, 1975), 132–49.
[3] Most annotations in red were made in 2007 but Barnes added a few more in black in 2012 when PEN finally got around to organizing the sale.

And if so, what signs of its effects can we look out for?[4]

These pressing questions could have been daunting for a budding writer and Barnes worked on *Metroland* for seven to eight years (between 1972 and 1979 when he was between the ages of 26 and 32), with long periods of time when he put it aside.[5] He recalls: 'it was a long and greatly interrupted process, full of doubt and demoralization … I had absolutely no confidence in it. Nor was I convinced of myself. I didn't see that I had any right to be a novelist.'[6] He showed the typescript to his friends, the poets Craig Raine and Christopher Reid. The former said Barnes should 're-read *Great Expectations* and put in a wanking scene' – Barnes did not confess he had never read Dickens's novel the first time – while the latter advised him to 'put it away in a drawer as [he] would feel differently about it in a year's time'.[7] Such lukewarm reactions were hardly going to boost Barnes's morale and may have reminded the young writer of Flaubert's own experience when, at the age of 27 in 1849, he read the manuscript of his first book to his friends, an episode Barnes later recorded in *Flaubert's Parrot*: 'Gustave reads his first full-length adult work, *La Tentation de saint Antoine*, to his two closest friends, Bouilhet and Du Camp. The reading takes four days, at the rate of eight hours per day. After embarrassed consultation, the listeners tell him to throw it on the fire' (29). The book would only be published twenty-five years later in 1874 and Flaubert's first novel, *Madame Bovary*, eight years later in 1857 when the author was 35 years old.[8]

Metroland itself might never have been published. On 3 October 1978, the first reader at Jonathan Cape concluded it was 'worth going into it' as the author might be 'able to rewrite it', but on 17 November 1978, the second reader, despite praising many aspects of the book, recommended to 'pass this one up', advising the young writer to 'put it aside, as achieved intention, and get on with the next one'.[9] Fortunately, editor Liz Calder overrode the second reader's advice and asked for substantial revisions

---

[4] Julian Barnes, *Metroland* (London: Jonathan Cape, 1980. The Morgan Library & Museum, New York. PML 194959. Gift of Alyce Toonk, 2013), 11. This annotated copy of *Metroland* is quoted with the kind permission of Julian Barnes and the Morgan Library & Museum in New York. Quotations from the annotations will be identified by the mention 'Morgan Library' followed by the page number of the annotations. All quotations from *Metroland* also come from this edition.

[5] The first typescript was submitted to Jonathan Cape on 3 October 1978 but was then thoroughly revised. In the introduction to the 2016 Vintage edition of *Metroland*, Barnes mentions that he worked on the novel on and off for seven to eight years. Julian Barnes, 'Introduction', *Metroland* (London: Vintage, [1980] 2016), 1. In interviews, Barnes referred to seven, eight or nine years. Guignery and Roberts, eds, *Conversations*, 22, 23, 30.

[6] Interview by Guppy, in *Conversations*, ed. Guignery and Roberts, 66–7.

[7] Nicholas Wroe, 'Literature's Mister Cool', *Guardian*, 29 July 2000, 7. In his introduction to the 2016 Vintage edition of *Metroland*, Barnes gave a slightly different version, saying that Reid (unnamed in that piece) 'was substantially evasive, while telling a mutual friend that I should suppress the book now as otherwise I'd "regret it" later' (1–2). In the annotated copy of *Metroland* (Morgan Library 148), Barnes wrote in 2012 that the first (unnamed) friend told him to reread *David Copperfield* (rather than *Great Expectations* in the two other versions) and that the second friend, although he told Barnes to put the novel away in a drawer for a year, praised a sentence uttered by Toni after the 30-year-old Christopher asks him if he and his girlfriend have 'some modern arrangement': 'Modern, old, don't mind what you call it – anything except your soiled old Judaeo-Christian rubbish topped up with Victorian wankers' sex-hatred' (148).

[8] The book had first been serialized in the *Revue de Paris* from 1 October 1856.

[9] 'From the archive', *Metroland*, by Julian Barnes (London: Vintage, 2016), items 2 and 3.

before publication. In his acceptance speech for the David Cohen Prize for Literature in 2011, Barnes recalled his first encounter with the editor: 'I date the start of my literary career from an evening in late 1978 or early 1979, at Tuttons wine bar in Covent Garden, where I met Liz Calder for the first time. She was then at Gollancz but about to move to Cape, and she told me that she was willing to publish my first novel, *Metroland*' (3.1).

Barnes's miscellaneous notes and the various annotated drafts at the Harry Ransom Center reveal how many careful revisions went into this first novel and how much material was discarded. In the process, the novelist resembles the biographer as defined in *Flaubert's Parrot*: 'The trawling net fills, then the biographer hauls it in, sorts, throws back, stores, fillets and sells. Yet consider what he doesn't catch … think of everything that got away' (38). Concentrating on 'everything that got away', this chapter proposes to exhume some of the deleted passages or chapters from *Metroland* to try and understand what led the young novelist to end up with a much denser text than the original.[10]

1. Faltering starts

In an interview in 2014, Barnes said that 'the passage that probably gets most work in any novel is the first page but very often the first page is nowhere near the first page that you write'.[11] The examination of the writer's papers reveals that this was particularly true for *Staring at the Sun*, *Arthur & George* and *The Sense of an Ending* whose original incipits greatly differed from the final version. *Metroland* is no exception to the rule as the original drafts did not include the first two pages of the book – an untitled prelude describing Christopher and Toni's visits to the National Gallery (11–12) – but different versions of what was to become the start of Chapter One. In the annotated copy of the book, Barnes wrote in 2012 next to the first sentence of Chapter One: 'when I think of the book (which I occasionally do) I always remember this as being its first line' (Morgan Library 13), that is, 'Cut privet still smells of sour apples, as it did when I was sixteen' (13). One isolated page of an early draft of the novel reveals an essential narratological difference in the formulation of that sentence. Indeed, while the published text uses the present tense and the first-person pronoun, the early draft page employed the past tense and the third-person pronoun: 'Cut privet still *smelt* of sour apples, as it had done when *he* was sixteen' (1.10.8, my emphasis).

Whereas *Metroland* is written in first-person narration and gives direct access to Christopher Lloyd's voice and thoughts as he reminisces about his past and reflects on the present, this early draft page offered a drastically different option through the choice of a third-person narration and an inner focalization through the mind of a character named 'Paul Battersby', the unique occurrence of this first name and family name in the various drafts (with such phrases as 'Paul thought this', 'Paul stopped', 'Paul Battersby's mother').[12] This is the unique page in the whole archive which is

---

[10] The various drafts and notes for *Metroland* are in folders 1.10.5–8 and 1.11.1–2.
[11] In Lawson, 'Mark Lawson'.
[12] Paul is also the name of Martha Cochrane's boyfriend in *England, England* and most importantly of the first-person narrator in *The Only Story*, Paul Roberts, who, in some aspects and particularly in his

written in the third person, thereby suggesting that Barnes experimented with both narratological possibilities at a very early stage of composition and swiftly opted for the first person which suited the tone of this Bildungsroman better. More than forty years later, Barnes would take the reverse option for his novel about the composer Dmitri Shostakovich, *The Noise of Time* (2016), which he started writing in the first person but had to stop after four pages: 'I didn't know why it wasn't working, it just wasn't working at all, and I had just done it in the wrong person. I went back to it about nine months later, and started in the third person.'[13]

In an interview in 2013, Barnes revealed that he had planned to experiment with various narrative voices in his first three novels:

> at the very beginning I had a rough plan that I'd write my first book in the first person, the second book in the third person, and the third book from the point of view of a woman. That got slightly derailed and that third book became my fourth book. But that was really just a plan to instruct myself in the various technical skills necessary to write a novel.[14]

His second novel *Before She Met Me* is indeed written in the third person and *Staring at the Sun* which was pushed aside for a while by *Flaubert's Parrot* is written from a woman's point of view. The choice of first person for *Metroland* may be explained by the fact that Barnes said in several interviews that the book was partly autobiographical,[15] especially in the first part, and that he had a friend called Toni (like Chris's closest friend in the novel) to whom he sent the book but who did not like it.[16] On the annotated copy of the book, he wrote at the beginning of Part Two: 'Part One was – topographically & spiritually – very close to home. Proper invention starts (or begins to start) here' (Morgan Library 73). In a handwritten note in the archives, Barnes reminded himself to make '[e]arly physical descriptions of *me*, Toni' (1.10.6, my emphasis), the first-person pronoun thus confirming the parallels between the fictional Chris and Barnes himself. Some thirty years later in *Nothing to Be Frightened Of*, when referring to his first novel, Barnes mentioned 'the (at times all too convincingly autobiographical)

---

grudging relation to the world of adults and to suburbia as a 19-year-old, bears some resemblance to 16-year-old Christopher who, together with his friend Toni, 'spent a hefty amount of time … being bored' (*Metroland* 66). In *The Only Story*, when Paul comes back home (a suburb situated fifteen miles south of London) after his first year at university, he is 'visibly and unrepentantly bored' and determined not to 'end up in suburbia with a tennis wife and 2.4 children' (6).

[13] Freeman, 'How the Writer Edits'.
[14] Interview by Mark Lawson, 'Front Row. *Levels of Life*', BBC Radio 4, 3 April 2013.
[15] He told Ronald Hayman: 'the spirit of it was autobiographical, and the topography was autobiographical, but the actual incidents were invented.' *Conversations*, ed. Guignery and Roberts, 3. He also said to Craig Brown: 'I found moving from pure autobiography to fiction disarmingly simple. You believe yourself to be reasonably honest, then you surprise yourself by how quickly and easily you swing from fact to fiction. But then, in a way, it is all still autobiographical – you just imagine alternative futures for yourself.' Craig Brown, 'The Critic Has Three Lives', *Over21*, August 1980, 88.
[16] In the annotated copy of *Metroland*, Barnes wrote: 'I had a close schoolfriend of (Polish) (Jewish maybe not?) origin, called, would you believe it, Tony – indeed, Toni. But he wasn't like this (& even less did he turn out as Toni does at the end of the novel). He didn't like the book – I think he hated it – & I was naively surprised by this' (Morgan Library 32).

narrator'.[17] Going further, one may suggest that a thread could be woven between the voices of Chris in *Metroland*, Tony in *The Sense of an Ending*, Paul in *The Only Story* and Barnes himself in *Nothing to Be Frightened Of*.

In regard to *Metroland*, Barnes's shift of names from Paul Battersby to Christopher Lloyd occurred as the novel developed in the writer's mind. On a page of random notes, the author wrote: 'names earlier surname – ordinary m-class: Finlay?', and underneath 'Christopher?' (1.10.5). The final choice of family name must have come fairly late as that same page of notes already includes the titles of all chapters for Part One (as well as the epigraphs for each part, although these could have been added later),[18] thus suggesting that Barnes was still undecided about his hero's family name at that stage.[19] In a first-person novel, the narrator's first name usually only appears in dialogue when used by other characters, hence its relatively late appearance in *Metroland*, in Chapter Three, when the protagonist's mother, after her son asks her 'Mummy, what's an oonuch?', tells his father: 'Christopher wants to know what a eunuch is' (22).[20] His surname is revealed in Chapter Five when Chris refers to his family's origins: 'The Lloyds (well, our Lloyds, my father's Lloyds at least) came from Basingstoke' (32) – a name which may sound ironical (as suggested by the comment between brackets) given the Lloyd's of London insurance market (to which Barnes devoted an essay, reproduced in *Letters from London*)[21] but is an ordinary lower to middle-class surname of the type Barnes had in mind (just like Battersby in the first version).

When comparing the only page of the early draft written in the third person and the published version of the first two paragraphs of Chapter One, one notes that the original version was twice longer than the final one and gave more space to the protagonist's thoughts about the differences in perception between when he was 16 and the time of narration which is identified in the draft (but not that early in the published book) as being 'fifteen years' later. In terms of structure, content and mode, both versions are fairly similar, with the opening reference to the smell of sour apples being followed by a reflection on the fact that at the age of 16 there were 'more meanings, more interpretations', and by a second paragraph focusing on the reversible coat of the protagonist's mother (13). On the other hand, another draft composed of only two paragraphs differs greatly from these two versions in tone as it does not start with any meditation on changes over time but more concretely and bluntly starts with an intriguing and possibly erotic teaser: 'In the cupboard underneath the stairs there was a woman. For all the vital, formative years of my adolescence she stayed there, waiting, available' (1.10.8). Then follows a long list of the varied objects also stored in the spacious cupboard – an anticipation of the chapters entitled 'Object Relations' at the

---

[17] Julian Barnes, *Nothing to Be Frightened Of* (London: Jonathan Cape, 2008), 192.
[18] Barnes remembers that he 'struggled to find an epigraph for Part 3' (a quote by Bishop Butler) whereas those 'for parts 1 & 2 followed one another so perfectly' (the first by Rimbaud, the second by Verlaine). He adds: 'In those days books had to have epigraphs, it seemed. Nowadays I do without them – they seem to be instructing the reader in advance rather too much' (Morgan Library 131).
[19] Almost all the names of the first draft were later modified: Chris's brother was Ollie (later Nigel) and his sister Evie (later Mary); his wife was Miriam (later Marion) and his daughter Ada (later Amy) (1.11.1).
[20] Barnes recalls: 'I had just such an exchange with my parents (tho' did not myself mispronounce the word)' (Morgan Library 22).
[21] Julian Barnes, 'The Deficit Millionaires', in *Letters from London* (London: Picador, 1995), 192–240.

end of each part in which Chris sums up important periods of his life by enumerating the objects that surround him – and the list concludes with the same puzzling item it started with, except for the now definite article: 'and the woman'. The second paragraph reveals that this cupboard is also Chris's darkroom where he 'could be safely alone for anything up to an hour', but the enigma of the alluring woman in the cupboard is left unsolved.[22]

Yet another draft of Chapter One does not start with the reference to a mysterious woman but, as in the published book, with a nostalgic longing for the greater scope of interpretations and meanings which existed in youth: 'When I was sixteen, everything seemed much more open to interpretation than it does now' (1.10.8). The second paragraph (both in late draft and final book) focuses on the mother's coat and proves unambiguous about the identity of the woman in the cupboard: 'Under the stairs she kept a dressmaker's dummy' (1.10.8). While the published version remains deliberately elusive about the attributes of the dummy which 'told you everything and nothing about the female body (see what I mean?)' (13), the draft included a long comic paragraph with many more details as to Chris's 'clandestine actions' in the cupboard where he was developing his photographs and keeping people out thanks to 'a peremptory note sellotaped to the door ("Kodak SDP 4 costs 5d a sheet: Keep Out")'.[23] Although the dummy 'had none of the advantages of a present-day rubber woman and her unyielding tits were covered in a sort of rough, sack-line material', since she had 'no fleshier rivals' at that time, Chris 'had few complaints'. The uninterrupted privacy offered by the cupboard allowed the teenager to run 'a disbelieving hand over her pinpricked flesh' or, if he felt more aggressive, to 'square up to her and rap in a couple of straight leads before dancing out of range'. While Chris prides himself on never giving the female dummy a name, he also reflects: 'that may have been because I was merely treating her as a sex-object'. This humorous opening might have been deleted because it was too much of a digression too early in the book, as noted self-reflexively at the beginning of the next paragraph in the draft – 'Anyway, I seem to be digressing rather' – but also because the topic of the teenager's frustrating lack of sexual experience would be more extensively developed in the third chapter entitled 'Rabbit, Human'. In the margin at the beginning of the passage on the dummy, Barnes wrote 'transfer to sex section' and even if he did not shift that passage to the third chapter, this note to himself reveals his awareness that this development might have to come later.

The condensation of this comic paragraph in later versions already alerts the reader to Barnes's wish for a denser and tauter text, which led him to remove two chapters from the first part.

---

[22] After rereading this early draft in 2018, Barnes commented: 'lots of good bits in what I cut! but a correct decision'. Annotations, 22–27 March 2018.
[23] In *Nothing to Be Frightened Of*, Barnes recalls: 'In my teens, I had my own photographic period, which included modest home processing: the plastic developing tank, orange darkroom light, and contact printing frame' (28). In the Preface to *Something to Declare*, he remembers the family's first trip to France in 1959 during which he was 'the official photographer'. Julian Barnes, *Something to Declare* (London: Picador, 2002), xii.

2. 'Petty Gripes' and 'Oua, oua, oua'

The handwritten list of chapters for Part One reveals that there were originally fifteen (in addition to the prelude) against thirteen in the published version. All chapters bore the same titles as in the final version except for Chapter Ten, 'Arguments Against God',[24] which was changed to 'Tunnels, Bridges' in the last draft (a title more explicitly evocative of Chris's daily train journeys), and Chapter Thirteen, 'Turning Out' (a reference to how the teenagers would 'turn out'),[25] which was crossed out on the handwritten list and replaced by 'Hard and Low' (the vigorous advice shouted out at the School's rugby players). The two deleted chapters, entitled '12: Petty Gripes' and '14: Oua, oua, oua' in the early table of contents, feature in the archives although no title is typed at the top of these pages (1.10.8). The two pages from 'Petty Gripes' record a conversation between Chris and his mother who reproves him for his sloppy habit of picking his teeth, thus provoking the teenager's sneering question: 'But what's the intellectual basis for your case, mummy?'. This specific memory leads him on to the memory of other frustrations: 'Gripes which seem petty now, but which were matters of principle then.' What fascinates Chris is that his 'childhood memories are full of not doing things. Don't eat sweets in the street. Don't push the ice cream down into the cornet. Don't go to the cinema in jeans' or, to say it differently: 'Behaviour was directed not by positive ordinances and moral examples, but was channelled by a series of negatives.' With the benefit of hindsight, Chris confirms that the distinctive aspect was that 'the guiding principles had no philosophical or moral backup – only a vague social one'. The passage was probably deleted because in the published version, Chris's parents are precisely not 'disciplinarian' like Toni's, thus making it difficult for Chris to rebel against them: '[W]hen I was destructive, petulant or obstinate, my parents, shamefully well-heeled in tolerance, would merely identify my condition for me ("It's always a tricky time, Christopher, growing up")' (41–2). In *Nothing to Be Frightened Of*, Barnes indicates that neither he nor his brother have any memory of 'specific instructions or advice laid down by [their] mother', apart from general dicta such as '[never wear] brown shoes with a blue suit; never move the hands of a clock or watch backwards; don't put cheese biscuits in the same tin as sweet ones' (158) – and his brother considers this '*not* offering advice or instruction' as 'a mark of a good parent' (159).

In a note to himself about 'Petty Gripes' in *Metroland*, Barnes wrote: 'not doing things – reuse at start of?14' (1.10.5). Chapter Fourteen, 'Oua, oua, oua' (1.10.8), is the second chapter which was deleted from the final draft and the two pages from 'Petty Gripes' were not 'reused' there. 'Oua, oua, oua' consists of two-and-a-half pages and focuses on senses, a very early anticipation of the five short stories related to the five senses collected in the second part of *Pulse*, published in 2011. A first paragraph

---

[24] This expression appears when Chris and Toni ride on a train which goes over the viaduct at Kilburn and notice thousands of people, which leads Toni to state: 'Well, it's an argument against God, isn't it?' (61).

[25] Chris and Toni pride themselves on not being grown up yet: 'no one knew how we would "turn out". … We hadn't yet turned out' (66).

compares the 'sensuous texture' of Chris's early life with that of his adulthood: as a 30-year-old, his experience of the world is mainly visual while at 16, it had 'a larger proportion of sound and smell'. The other two senses are only given a passing mention: 'The pleasures of touch, which are pretty minimal to me, have remained probably constant; while the experiences of taste seem to have been greatly enlarged.' The next paragraph is devoted to smells through a list, which is a characteristic mode of writing for Chris in the novel:

> The stale smell of fine chalk-dust hovering like a precipitate in the air before maths lessons; the acid reek of piss in the bogs, where anything might happen to you though nothing ever did; the chlorine from the swimming bath, one whiff of which would make your balls huddle together high and tight in fear of icy water; the smell of blanco, dubbin, dried-out inkwells, rancid gym-kit, wet mackintoshes hanging by the hundred.

This selection of smells, so vividly evocative of a schoolboy's past and of a gone era (as suggested by the details of the chalk-dust, the blanco, the dubbin and the inkwells), could be compared to the incipit of *The Sense of an Ending* in which an elderly protagonist remembers his youth through six precise items related to liquid elements, reflecting the fluid nature of his memories. Chris's own recollection is untainted by nostalgia as the smells are either unpleasant – 'stale', 'acid reek', 'rancid' – or reminiscent of fear and apprehension. Although this passage was deleted, one recalls that the first chapter of the novel starts with a Proustian reference to the smell of 'sour apples' which has remained constant since 1963 (13).

Just like smells, sounds in the deleted chapter are distinctly remembered and 'mingled into the experience of school: desk lids being dropped en masse …; the animal babble of the playground; the embarrassing echo of your steel heel-quarters down the stone corridor'.[26] However, the narrator interrupts his list to focus on other sounds, 'the decorative ones, the ones we used for commentary on life rather than being part of life itself'. The decorative sounds which become a language of their own are actually defined as 'noises', deliberately produced for a specific effect (usually comic), whose finest exponent is a schoolboy named Gilchrist,[27] known for being 'slightly damp. Not greasy-damp like Middleton … more clean-damp, scrubbed and pink and salivating healthily, with a light beading of sweat on his palms which was never disgusting like Middleton's runny paws'. While Middleton's 'sebacity' makes him the victim of incessant jokes, 'Gilchrist's wetness was acceptable because it was essential to his noises' – an early and humorous example of Barnes playing with liquid imagery.

The narrator's entertaining description of Gilchrist's noises is extremely precise and detailed, and makes them appear as the boy's own idiosyncratic mode of expression:

---

[26] When annotating the draft of this book, Barnes judged the assonance of 'steel' and 'heel' 'bad'. Annotations, 22–27 March 2018.
[27] This was the real name of one of Barnes's schoolfriends (*Metroland*, Morgan Library 169).

No-one could match his range of lip-pops, from a gentle, hazy sound like a soap-bubble breaking, up to a series of hard, repeated, explosive cracks …. His tongue-clicks could start from any chosen point on his soft or hard palate, could be modulated by saliva, and could be worked into an extended and decorated musical phrase. His finger-in-cheek pulls could be heard from twenty yards; he could do an owl-hoot by blowing into cupped palms; his wolf-whistle sounded as if it would crack double-glazing. His speciality was a squelchy, squeaky, farty noise which he made by joining damp palms, trapping a little air between them, and squeezing it out between the knuckles.

The extensive use of adjectives and the joyful play on sonorities – more specifically alliterations as in 'bubble breaking', 'wolf-whistle', 'squelchy, squeaky … squeezing' – make the noises almost audible and the gestures to produce them distinctly visible to the reader. In the published version of *Metroland*, Gilchrist is only briefly referred to twice in relation to his talent for noises, thus pointing to the drastic condensation of the original chapter. In Part One, Chris recalls the school cry, ' "RoooOOOOOOOOOiiiiined …" '; 'drawn out and modulated in the way we imagined hyenas to howl' and adds: 'Gilchrist did the screechiest, most fearing version' (21). In Part Three, when Chris is about to go to the school's annual dinner, he wonders what his schoolfriends would look like: 'Would Gilchrist still be making damp, squelchy noises with his hands (had he gone into the BBC sound effects department?)' (164).[28]

In the deleted draft, Barnes, who was to publish *The Noise of Time* several decades later, has Chris remark: 'Noises now are all either talk or music. Noises then were often no more than noises, funny, pleasant, anarchic, and used regardless of the context from which they originally came.' Noises appear as a shared language among the schoolboys (friends greet each other with whinnies of 'M-i-i-n-n-n-n')[29] and are a frequent cause for smug giggles. Victims are either weakling masters or twitchy boys marked for mild persecution. The deleted chapter ends with a description of the noise especially devised for a persecuted boy named Bradshaw, which provides an explanation for the mysterious title of that chapter. The Bradshaw noise derives from the boy's idiosyncrasy of making 'a slight humming noise of nervous origin before he began to speak':

> As he approached, you would start to hum gently, alerting anyone around who knew the noise. When he got close enough to realise you were doing his Noise …, you would pull forward the lapel of your jacket, sneeze three times into the

---

[28] Another real name of one of the boys at the City of London School employed in the course of this annual dinner is that of Barton: 'Who would be there, whom would I recognise? Would Barton, who sat at the desk in front of me for a whole year when I was fourteen, still have that gristly knob above his left ear; or would it all be camouflaged by blown-dry layer-cutting?' (164). Stephen Barton wrote a humorous letter to Barnes on 4 December 1989 to 'categorically state that no gristly left lump is on record' (1.16.4).

[29] Barnes thinks this came from the Goon show, a radio comedy programme broadcast by the BBC Home Service from 1951 to 1960, which was marked by surreal humour, puns and bizarre sound effects. The series was devised and written by Spike Milligan and starred Harry Secombe, Peter Sellers and Michael Bentine.

armhole of your jacket, stare at Bradshaw, and then, flapping your wrist from side to side, shake the sneeze out of your sleeve while going 'Oua, oua, oua, oua'.[30]

While the chapter started with the potentially wistful tone of retrospective narration – 'Looking back I see my early life as having not just a greater depth and uncertainty of feeling, but also a completely different sensuous texture' – and moved on to a comic recollection of sounds, it ends on a farcical and almost absurd note which leaves the reader pleasantly baffled. In a note to himself, Barnes wrote 'school sounds & smells – work in?' (1.10.5), but he apparently could not find the appropriate place to work the passage in and cut it, depriving the reader of a most entertaining and stylistically elaborate chapter.

In an interview with Ronald Hayman, Barnes gave interesting information about the writing process for Part One, which helps to understand why he removed so many passages:

> In the first version I did of the first part I think I set myself one topic per chapter. I had one chapter where they're doing parents, and one where they're doing sex, and then I thought: 'My God this is much too bald, and if not exactly preachy, at least a bit over-instructive to the reader'. Then I worked at smoothing over the joins and taking bits out – like with pastry. Scenes were all cut up neatly, and then I pushed it all together again, and made it a more plausible shape.[31]

While the suppressions of passages or chapters from Part One took place at a relatively early stage in composition, a passage from Part Two which still appeared on the final draft was cut on the printer's typescript, the last step before proofs. In the second chapter entitled 'Demandez Nuts', Chris explains in just a few lines that instead of 'methodically working out [his] life' as a 21-year-old in Paris, he spent his first few weeks loafing, 'without much trouble or guilt' (85). Until the final draft, two paragraphs remained which attempted to rationalize the way one can find a solution to a problem (here, what to do with one's life): 'There is this problem, x, with which we are faced; let us therefore apply your brain, y, to it, until we come up with the answer, z; if this fails, we add further brains, a, b, c. and so on, until z occurs' – a passage which may have found a later echo in Adrian's mysterious algebra in his diary in *The Sense of an Ending* (85).[32] After some more 'schemes full of algebra to obfuscate the issue', a third

---

[30] Bradshaw is briefly referred to in Part Three when Christopher joins the annual dinner and refers to the colour of his former friends' faces: 'mostly they were the worn, indeterminate colour which comes from being surrounded by high buildings, earthed up like asparagus. Over there, wasn't that Bradshaw?' (168). In the annotated copy of the book, Barnes recalls a scene in the early 1980s: 'I was working in my office in the New Statesman when the internal phone went. It was the downstairs reception. "There's someone here for you. Shall I put him on?" "Yes." The phone was transferred. "Hello – it's asparagus-faced Bradshaw", said a voice. I hadn't changed the name (ditto Penny, Gilchrist, Pook, Leigh ...) & thought guiltily that I must have singled him out in M/land for being asparagus-faced' (Morgan Library 168).

[31] Interview by Hayman, in *Conversations*, ed. Guignery and Roberts, 3–4.

[32] 'Thus how might you express an accumulation containing the integers b, a^1, a^2, s, v? / $b = s - v \times a^1$ / or $a^2 + v + a^1 \times s = b$?' Julian Barnes, *The Sense of an Ending* (London: Jonathan Cape, 2011), 85.

paragraph concluded to the impossibility of coming to a decision about one's life for the next seventy years 'in a few weeks' solitary contemplation', hence Chris's guiltless loafing (1.11.2). It is only on the printer's typescript (1.11.3) that Barnes deleted this slightly technical passage, revealing how relentless and attentive he remained until the very last stages of composition.

3. The Death Chapter

While the first drafts for Parts One and Two contain many marks of revision and several deleted passages, the most heavily revised is the third part, set in 1977 when Chris, aged 30, is back in suburbia, married to Marion and the father of a child. For Barnes, this part was 'the hardest to do and the last to come right'[33] and his editor at Jonathan Cape, Liz Calder, asked him to revise it substantially. Barnes cut twenty-two pages out of the original fifty-four and added nine so that the published version contains six chapters against eight in the original (1.10.6). A comparison of the tables of contents in an early draft and the published book reveals changes in the titles and the order of chapters:

Draft		Published version	
Chapters	Titles	Chapters	Titles
	Prelude		[Prelude (*untitled*)]
1	Five o' clock shadow	1	Nude, Giant Girls[34]
2	The Skater [the Death Chapter]	4	*Partly deleted and partly transferred to* Is Sex Travel?
3	Preston Road, Northwick Park		*Deleted*
4	Running Costs	2	Running Costs
5	Joining up		*Deleted*
6	Stiff petticoat	3	Stiff Petticoat
7	Paying dues	5	The Honours Board
8	Object relations	6	Object Relations

The second chapter in the left column ('The Skater') was partly cut and partly transferred to the fourth chapter entitled 'Is Sex Travel?'. It comprised several passages

---

[33] Interview by Hayman, in *Conversations*, ed. Guignery and Roberts, 4.
[34] The phrase is a reference to the pylons Chris and his family used to drive past when he was a child. Chris would whisper to his brother: 'Look, nude, giant girls' (136), an unidentified reference to lines from the 1933 poem 'The Pylons' by Stephen Spender: 'Pylons, those pillars / Bare like nude, giant girls that / have no secret.'

about death following the passing of Uncle Arthur. In his notes, Barnes referred to that chapter as the 'Death Chapter' (followed by the question: 'cut & replace with no-sweat?'). It exists in three different drafts in the archives, one of them entitled 'White Posts, Black Labels' (but Barnes wrote 'Preachy' next to this title), and the other two 'The Skater'. The first draft is seven pages long and contains a fair number of corrections in longhand (1.11.1).[35] The second is seven-and-a-half pages long and bears almost no signs of revisions but has integrated the corrections from the previous draft (1.10.6). The third is five-and-a-half pages long and heavily annotated (1.10.5). In the third version, the title 'The Skater' has been crossed out and replaced in longhand by 'Four: Sex is Travel' and above, underlined, 'Is sex travel?' This third version starts with a recollection (which is absent from the first two drafts and from the published version) of how the teenagers Chris and Toni, who were mainly surrounded by people older than them, would often sarcastically shout out 'Hwaa, hwaa, you'll die first!' With the benefit of hindsight, Chris as an older narrator comments: 'That cry was one of the balms of adolescence. The pain of death could be eased by the thought that almost everyone you hated would have to go through dying before you did.' In *The Only Story* published almost forty years later, the narrator remembers a scene when, as a 19-year-old, he told an older driver who had just hooted and shouted at him at the zebra crossing: 'You'll be dead before I will' (18, 209), which he saw as a potential reason for the old to envy the young.

The first draft of the 'Death Chapter' in *Metroland* opens for its part on a ten-line paragraph which was condensed to two lines in the second and third drafts and was cut in the published version. The first sentences are the following: 'All this artificial dating of maturity. Sixteen, it's not illegal any more; eighteen, old enough to die in uniform and old enough to vote; twenty-one, key of the door.' In longhand, Barnes not only made the following changes: 'Sixteen, sex time; eighteen, votes for women', but also wrote in the margin: 'Rachel Papers!' (1.11.1). And indeed, the first page of Martin Amis's 1973 novel, which features an arrogant and lecherous young man, Charles Highway, includes the narrator's following comment: 'Sixteen, eighteen, twenty-one: these are arbitrary milestones, enabling you only to get arrested for H.P.-payment evasion, get married, buggered, executed, and so on.' For Amis's narrator, twenty 'is the real turning-point': 'Twenty may not be the start of maturity but, in all conscience, it's the end of youth.'[36] These echoes of *Rachel Papers* easily explain why Barnes deleted the passage.[37] However, Barnes's opening was more developed than the incipit to Amis's novel as it included the 30-year-old narrator's musings on the 'real dates', those which give 'a sense of proportion, a sense of context, a sense of the proportional expectation of joy', and

---

[35] The order of drafts has been deduced from the way corrections in longhand have been typed and integrated in the next draft.

[36] Martin Amis, *The Rachel Papers* (London: Jonathan Cape, 1973), 7. In his review of *Metroland*, John Sutherland wrote: 'The plot of *Metroland*, what there is of it, is reminiscent of Martin Amis's *The Rachel Papers*: virginity lost amid cool, egotistic wisecracking. But Barnes's hero is nicer and his tone more humane than Amis's.' John Sutherland, 'Looking Back', *London Review of Books* 2, no. 10 (22 May 1980): 27.

[37] In his unpublished *Literary Guide to Oxford*, Barnes provides 'a list of novels about Oxford, with descriptive comments'. The last entry is '1973: Martin Amis: *The Rachel Papers*. Contains a brief, but very funny, account of the terrors of a scholarship interview' (1.9.1).

which some miss. These dates are highlighted in the two-line opening paragraph of the second draft: 'Age doesn't count towards maturity, we know that. But what are the dates that clutch? First love? First falling out of love? First stab of parenthood? First death?' (1.10.6). This enumeration echoes some of the questions which appear at the end of Part One in the published book (which might explain why the passage was deleted in Part Three): 'How does adolescence come back most vividly to you? What do you remember first? The quality of your parents; a girl; your first sexual tremor; success or failure at school …?' (71). The list does not include death and it is only in maturity (in Part Three) that Chris remembers his first death, that of Uncle Arthur.

All drafts for the 'Death Chapter' comically record (at various lengths) Arthur's last years and petty eccentricities, passages which were revised and included in the published version (158–60). What disappeared, however, was the detailed description of Arthur's actual death as the published version only laconically refers to 'a fatal heart attack' (160):

> Arthur fulfilled the old euphemism 'He fell asleep …' He was watching television one evening in his wing chair with the lights off (cheaper) and the curtains drawn back (waste of time, he always said, though I suspect that it was so that he could annoy the prim neighbours with some prolonged bouts of scratching). He died in the chair, but the wing kept his head propped up, so that he still sat there looking like an old man asleep. The television played on for five days while the neighbours failed to notice, or thought he was dozing, or decided he was a telly addict, or hoped he was dead (they never said which). There was no Ferdinand [the dog] any more; Arthur was known not to answer the phone even if he was in; and he had never become involved with what he referred to as the social security commissars. The neighbours eventually called the police; they always do. (1.10.6)

While this paragraph includes comic asides between brackets, the description of a vulnerable elderly man dying unnoticed opens onto a perspective and tone which contrast with the previous unflattering portrait of Arthur, thus granting the disreputable uncle the opportunity to arouse compassion. The published version leaves out that ambivalent paragraph to concentrate instead on 'the pathos of objects', with Chris's prevailing feeling being one of 'melancholy at the half-finished things which a death persuades you to focus on' (160).

The funeral service itself and Chris's meditation about death as they are driving away from the crematorium after the ceremony were reduced to two paragraphs in the published version (160–1), while they amounted to five typescript pages in the first and second drafts and two-and-a-half typescript pages in the third. What deserves particular attention is Chris's detailed description of the images thrown up by 'the deep, gutty part of [his] brain' and evocative of death – a passage which was deleted and interestingly contains the germ for Barnes's third novel *Staring at the Sun*. Referring to these mental images, Chris notes in the third draft: 'They aren't profoundly original images: they don't suddenly illuminate the grand issues of living and dying in a way which makes you see things differently. … We can no more stare at death, said some old writer (was he French?) than we can stare at the sun. But we can stare at pictures of the sun' (1.10.5). The seventeenth-century French aphorist La Rochefoucauld was named in the first draft but not subsequently, just as he remains unnamed in *Staring at the Sun*.[38]

The description of Chris's mental images is more developed in the first and second drafts of *Metroland* than in the third which condenses them to a single paragraph consisting of a crisp enumeration of scenes: 'First came the Skater', 'Second image is the Night Sky', 'Third image is the Posts' (1.10.5). The capital letters may evoke titles of paintings, all the more as the single Skater is presented as 'formal, elegant, poised, as in the Raeburn picture' – a reference to the 1790s oil painting 'The Skating Minister' by Scottish artist Sir Henry Raeburn – while a large group of skaters is imagined in 'an Avercamp snowscape' – an allusion to the seventeenth-century Dutch artist Hendrick Avercamp who specialized in painting people ice skating on frozen lakes. In addition, the ice is said to be 'cracked, patterned finely like the tired glaze on a painting'. The fact that death comes to Chris's mind through the sense of sight is characteristic of adulthood for him. In a deleted passage from Part One referred to in the previous section, Chris had remarked that his experience of the world as an adult was more visual than when he had been at school: 'Now, things have a largely visual cast to them; which seems confirmed by the fact that I find myself looking at buildings, landscapes, photographs and so on much more than I used to' (1.10.8). This probably explains the pictorial quality of his mental projections in Part Three.

In the third draft of the 'Death Chapter', each image is followed by factual details between brackets, with nominal sentences reminiscent of the sharp style of film scripts: 'First came the Skater (scene, a frozen lake, branches of tinsel in the top corner …)' (1.10.5). In the first and second drafts on the other hand, the images are neither introduced with capital letters nor followed by brisk parenthetical indications. Instead, the narrator devotes a whole leisurely paragraph to the description of the first scene, using anaphoras to convey the swirling movement of the skaters: 'Sometimes there is just one skater …. Sometimes there are several …. Sometimes the sky is grey …; sometimes it is a summer's day …. Sometimes the ice is cracked …; sometimes there are potholes.' The premonition of death is chillingly conveyed in the last ominous sentence: 'The skaters never notice the cracks or the holes; only I do' (1.10.6).

The second image of the night sky is very briefly described in the three drafts and is said to move 'slowly, at an even pace', thus contrasting with the sometimes 'fierce' gliding of the skaters on the lake. The scene is more directly evocative of death because of the eerie absence of light and the relentless soundtrack: 'A deep purple, night-time skyscape, thousands of stars, though none of them twinkling. They have an artificial evenness to them, as if they were plugged in somewhere. Occasionally, slow, remorseless music' (1.10.6). This music contrasts with the 'eighteenth-century rondo' which accompanies the image of the skater in the second draft, a musical form which is usually vivacious.[39] In the chapter entitled 'Big D' in the first part of the published *Metroland*, the young Chris listed as a 'part-visual, part-intellectual' intimation of 'non-existence' '[a] picture

---

[38] Julian Barnes, *Staring at the Sun* (London: Picador, [1986] 1987), 155. See pp. 122–3.
[39] 'First comes the skater. This takes various forms, is always in colour, always has movement, sometimes has music (an eighteenth-century rondo, for instance)' (1.10.6).

of endlessly retreating stars, taken I expect – with the crass bathos of the unconscious – from the opening credits of a Universal Pictures film' (54), maybe a prosaic explanation for the odd 'artificial evenness' of the stars in the second scene.

The last image of the posts completes the progression by cancelling movement altogether, but paradoxically retains the reference to the filmic medium in the third draft: 'black and white, grainy texture like an old film, no movement'. In the three drafts, the syntax is mainly nominal and sharp:

> Mid-grey concrete, a row of white posts, a black label on each; you can't read the label. Subsequent appearances have shown minor modifications: black posts with white labels; white posts, white labels with a black deckle-edge to them; concrete laid in separate slabs, making a grid of lines. (1.10.6)

This uncanny frozen snapshot of implacable vertical and horizontal lines is striking for its sheer desolation and bleakness, and could evoke a prison-like environment, a morgue (with labels for corpses), or graves and tombstones, except for the slim shape of the posts. The sequence begins simply – visually, lexically and syntactically, with a predominance of monosyllables and disyllables – and then becomes more complex, as if the landscape was coming into sharper focus and revealing variations in details. The inaccessibility of the inscriptions on the labels might reflect Chris's own inability to interpret the vision and the sense that meaning will remain hidden.

At this point the first and the second (much longer) drafts greatly differ from the third whose last but one paragraph emphasizes the change brought about by Uncle Arthur's death in Chris's disposition. In that last version, while the three dismal images make their familiar way through Chris's mind, he insists that what differs this time is his lack of fear. There seems to be 'nothing to be frightened of' (a phrase which does not, however, appear in this early draft of *Metroland*): 'Nothing happened. No panic, no terror, no sudden urge to act crazily simply to forget. Nothing' (1.10.5). The recurrence of the negative forms, literally meant to convey the comforting absence of fear, cannot help but evoke simultaneously the void or nothingness that follows death and upon which Barnes meditates in *Nothing to Be Frightened Of*, a book in which the words 'panic' and 'terror' frequently appear to qualify the fear of death.

In the first and second drafts of *Metroland*, the receding of fear is not evoked but the chapter continues for, respectively, three and two-and-a-half pages which include Chris's reflections on the images, a discussion with his wife Marion about them and quotes from several people about the way they think of death. Chris first contrasts his death visions to other imagery in life, which always comes from outside the self:

> The insights of my adolescence, which was awash with significances strained from unlikely places, were really only outsights. But when the Skater and his two companions come, they do not come to evoke emotion and they do not come to explain things. They come with their own emotions attached.
>
> They do not explain experience, they are experience. You do not look at them – though for convenience I have explained them like conventional images – they envelop you. You are trapped by them, bound round with silken rope (set an image

to catch an image), consumed by them. They induce true fear, true sadness, and true concentration; oddly, they make you feel very alive. (1.10.6)

What is striking about this passage (and maybe the reason why it was deleted) is that the voice sounds more like Barnes's than Chris's, more like the voice of a writer who intertwines philosophical reflections with comments on the art of writing and handling images, and who weaves repetitions into a binary or ternary rhythm which lets his thoughts unfold at a steady pace. However, Chris's facetious mood reappears in the next paragraph in which he tones down the relative solemnity of the previous sentences through the use of a mundane and comic simile when he declines to say that the death images 'brought [him] romping into a new gravity, browned [him] into maturity like toast under grill'. The last sentence of the paragraph – 'It's not that these things come, and you ripen: rather that you ripen, then these things come' – reverts to the symmetrical alternation typical of logical reasoning, but with the type of vocabulary that more closely fits Chris's own voice.

The second stage of Chris's reflections in the first and second drafts veers towards the way in which such intimations of mortality are potentially alienating because your companion (in this case, Marion) fails to understand the meaning of your private iconography. This awareness leads Chris to another revelatory moment conveyed in a similar binary structure: 'In my glummer moments I am persuaded that growing up is not a matter of realizing (and accepting) that you die, but realizing (and accepting) that you die alone' (1.10.6). The last part of Chris's musings is triggered off by the following question in the second draft: 'Is it solemn to be shocked by the frivolity with which people view their own extinction?' The last part of the chapter (in the first and second drafts) consists in an enumeration of six perspectives from inhabitants of Metroland, whose flippancy about their own death Chris resents. Each quote is introduced by 'There's' at the end of a paragraph and followed by a blank, while the next one starts with the person's opinion in direct speech, each sounding like a matter-of-fact cliché, followed, after a dash, by 'this from' and a whimsical presentation of the speaker and his/her background. Here are three examples:

> There's
>
> 'Well, all I can say is, when the time comes, I'd like to know a bit in advance, so that I can make my preparations' – this from busty, bustling Mary Langton, clockwork Catholic, whose jamjars bulge with silver paper for guide-dogs, who never misses a bus or a train or a backhand volley at the net. There's
>
> 'No point worrying, we'll find out what's behind the whole shooting-match in the end, won't we?' – this from retired, gardening Arthur Shepster, the man who never talks about his past but lets you infer one from his semi-military phrases, who never seems to look back and certainly doesn't look forward beyond the next planting season. Or there's
>
> ...
>
> 'I don't see that it's all that frightful – it's rather like going off to sleep, isn't it?' – this from the lumpish, dog-owning widow whose name I can never remember

and who always buys British ('Is this Empire?' she will toot out across a crowded Sainsbury's on a Saturday morning). (1.10.6)

The latter response echoes a line from 'Big D' in Part One (which probably explains its deletion from the published version) when the narrator wrote: 'Few fallacies depressed me more than the line: "I don't mind being dead; it's just like being asleep …"' (54). In the first and second drafts, comedy arises from the accumulation of those 'bland, hopeful, practical' statements and incongruous details about speakers, thus placing the morbid subject in a lighter context. Chris, for his part, is unable to be so frivolous with the 'paralysing horror of Big D' as he called it in the first part (53). As an adult, the panic persists: 'It's not the problem I find unbearable, it's the answer I know to be true that I find unbearable.' To circumvent the intolerable, Chris resorts once again to logical reasoning:

> Years ago, I used to struggle endlessly with the formula 'Since death is final, then …', twisting it around, shaking it up and down, knocking it on hard surfaces as if an answer would eventually come out which obviously, obviously fitted. Since death is final, <u>carpe diem</u>; since death is final, apathy is justified; since death is final, selfish greed is justified; since death is final, work to forget it; since death is final, then let the fear of it be subsumed in a greater pity and love for suffering man; since death is final, it doesn't actually make any difference. (1.10.6)

After the humorous image of assault on the postulate 'Since death is final, then …', the anaphoras and what the narrator calls 'the slick answers' amount to an insistent form of self-persuasion which nevertheless fails to conceal Chris's persisting anxiety. In *Nothing to Be Frightened Of*, Barnes confesses that 'it's hard to hold constantly to the knowledge that death is final' (192). However, Uncle Arthur's death – which is Chris's first death – changes the young man's perspective and the three drafts end with a calming down of the protagonist's fears:

> If death is indeed like the sun, then the nearer you get to it, the more you turn away from the brightness of the image. You pass out of the realm of thought; some instinct for action takes over. You work harder, you love your family. It's not that you've come up with some metaphysical answer; merely that you've become instilled with a sense of context, of scale; not a sense of insignificance, but rather of ordinariness. The deeply ambitious, it seems to me, are those with an improper understanding of what it means to die. (1.10.6)

The narrator comes full circle by repeating the analogy between death and the sun, with which he had introduced his musings. His calmer responses to death imply a closer contact with the concrete realities of everyday life and a receding of introspective ruminations. Barnes clearly hoped to retain the last sentence about the deeply ambitious as he made a note in longhand to transfer it to the conversation with Marion, and on one of the drafts for the last chapter of the book 'Object Relations' wrote: '? use here the ambitious are those who fear † more' (1.10.6),[40] but the aphorism did not pass on to the published version in either chapter. The few lines relating to the subject of death in Chapter Four of *Metroland* testify to a radical condensation of the two drafts:

> I mused lightly about Arthur's death, about him simply not existing any more; then let my brain idle over my own future non-existence. I hadn't thought about it for years.[41] And then I suddenly realised I was contemplating it almost without fear. I started again, more seriously this time, masochistically trying to spring that familiar trigger for panic and terror. But nothing happened; I felt calm. (161)

The detailed images and the practical opinions of the original drafts, the grandiloquence of the negations in the third draft ('Nothing happened') and the overall meditative tone have been replaced by a passing mention of a calm reconciliation with the idea of death, which suffices to indicate Chris's change of attitude. The only sentence from the third draft which remained identical in the published book is an original way of qualifying this moment of tranquillity after the fading out of fear: 'It was like the moment when the Indians go away' (161) – an unexpected reference to Westerns which defuses any gravity there might have been to the subject.

Thirty years later, in an early draft of *Nothing to Be Frightened Of*, Barnes referred to his fictional narrator's calm acceptance of death in *Metroland* and quoted the image of the Indians going away (in a passage that was removed from the final version of the book):

> In my first novel, the protagonist experiences, as an adolescent, a réveil mortel much like my own. By the end of the book, now married with a small child, he becomes suddenly aware that he hasn't thought about death for years, and can no longer even kick-start its terrors. If life, and its inevitable ending, had once made him feel like a beleaguered cowboy trapped in a box canyon, this is 'like the moment when the Indians go away.'
>
> Angela Carter, reviewing the novel, … praised its handling of 'aspects of maturity, like the acceptance of death.' I was flattered, of course, but part of me simultaneously also thought: 'Well, <u>that</u> fooled you – so clearly, fiction does work. If you believed that I was once that schoolboy, which I more or less was, then you must also have believed I am now that calm, unfearful adult, which I am very much not.' (3.5)

Angela Carter had indeed praised Barnes's first novel in the terms quoted above,[42] and this had impressed the novelist so much that he still remembered it more than twenty years later and included a reference to that review in the blurb he proposed

---

[40] In Barnes's notes, the symbol of the cross usually refers to death and not to religion.

[41] In the annotated copy of *Metroland*, Barnes wrote next to that sentence: 'How unlike the author' (Morgan Library 161).

[42] Carter wrote in her review: 'There's a great deal of art in this novel; its crisp one-liners, cultural jokes and lyrical *aperçus* are organized with the tension of poetry and the apparently airy structure is quite solid enough to contain with great dignity aspects of maturity, like the acceptance of death'. Angela Carter, 'Love in Two Climates', *Vogue* 1980, 21–2. This review is in Barnes's bound volume of clippings (1.18).

for *Nothing to Be Frightened Of*, which contains the following sentence: 'When Angela Carter reviewed Barnes's first novel, *Metroland*, she praised the mature way he wrote about death' (3.5).

There can be several ways of justifying the eventual deletion or condensation of the arresting pages on death in the third part of *Metroland*: the topic had already been treated fairly extensively (although from a different perspective) in 'Big D' in the first part; the lengthy discussion might have slowed down the pace of the chapter which was otherwise brisk and sharp; the lingering on death might have upset the balance of comedy and gravity which characterizes the fourth chapter of Part Three; finally, one may suggest that the philosophical content of some passages would be better suited to the authorial voice in *Nothing to Be Frightened Of* some thirty years later.

In addition to the 'Death Chapter', Barnes deleted an isolated page from the third part which focused on Chris's Sunday night activity of settling down to his scrapbook. Next to 'literary obituaries', one of the categories for his cuttings of newspaper articles for which he claims some originality is that of 'Odd Deaths':

> The Man who committed suicide by boring holes in his head with a Black-and-Decker drill. The man who committed suicide by making a grand piano fall and crush him. Bodies found without finger-ends and teeth. Crucifixions. People killed by lightning, by unlikely forms of poisoning, by heart attacks while having sex. Some, I know, will come in useful in my detective stories. (1.11.1)

Such ghastly acts could have found their way into Dan Kavanagh's detective stories and the last sentence encourages the reader to perceive a parallel between Chris (who is only dreaming of becoming a writer of detective fiction) and Barnes's pseudonymous alter ego Dan Kavanagh who published his first work of detective fiction (*Duffy*) in 1980, in the same year as Barnes's *Metroland*. The page was removed from the next draft but is significant for the way it portrays Chris as having settled in a quiet and contented life in suburbia with his wife and child, even if he admits to feeling 'a bit guilty about this particular pleasure' of keeping a scrapbook, which 'seemed rather, somewhat, anti-life: the sort of thing that children and old men engage in, when the process of living is either before or behind them' (1.11.1). This was not the only passage about Chris's embrace of his middle-class life in suburbia which Barnes discarded as he more generally revised his portrayal of the character's return to Metroland in the third part.

4. Return to Metroland

When revising Part Three upon the request of his editor Liz Calder, Barnes deleted two full chapters which focused on Chris's evolution since adolescence as the adult narrator happily returns to live in the middle-class suburb of Metroland he used to sneer at as a teenager.[43] In his heavily amended draft letter to Calder (1.10.5), Barnes justified

---

[43] In the first chapter of Part Three, the older narrator does not name the town where he lives but merely states: 'It's certainly ironic to be back in Metroland' (135). In an early draft, the name of

his revisions to the third part in terms of structure: 'I've tried to make Part Three less relentless in its parallels to Part One, less crudely reflective.' He also judged the original draft of Part Three 'too much of a Suburban Surrender' (Morgan Library 131) and too much of a 'solipsistic monologue' (1.10.5). In an interview upon publication of the novel, Barnes noted that it was hard to make 'Christopher's character-change plausible': 'The first time I did it, I made him amazingly complacent and changed, and it was just wrong for that kind of time-structure. He couldn't have sunk into as deep a rut as I made him fall into.'[44]

Barnes therefore deleted Chapter Three, entitled 'Preston Road, Northwick Park',[45] which includes a section where, according to the novelist in his letter to Calder, Chris's daily commute was made to parallel his adolescent vision in a rather 'crude and implausible' way. The chapter, which consists of four-and-a-half typescript pages, starts with Chris's quotidian walk from home to the station in which the iterative use of the present tense emphasizes the repetition of the very same gestures every day: 'Each morning I'm out of the house by eight. To a healthy squelch of gravel, I swing my brolly at the hedge, making the overnight raindrops leap up before they fall.' Of the detailed description of the houses he passes every day, only the reference to three houses with their names carved on wood has been kept in the first chapter of Part Three when Chris describes his Sunday morning walk (135).

The third paragraph of the draft, rather than relying on the habitual present, is then composed of sharp nominal sentences that confirm the comforting sense of regularity brought about by habits:

> A paper from the news-stand (I don't need to speak – my face is familiar); a ticket from the refurbished booking-office after a necessary bellow through the Hygienephone window; the barrier, the steps, past the waiting-room (just one for both sexes nowadays), and halt at my usual spot, a third of the way between the last two posts supporting the platform roof.

The deleted chapter continues with a wonderfully comic passage about Chris's quotidian 'petty worries' as to whether his platform place would be available – 'The sense of relief at finding my platform place empty (even though it has never been occupied) amounts to congratulation' – and whether the train would be late or cancelled. He begins to worry at 8.09, but the train always draws in at 8.11, and then a new anxiety arises, which makes for another humorous passage:

> Next comes the problem of the seat.
> Every commuter has a favourite seat. However carelessly you start, with however much <u>hauteur</u> you initially regard travel, you will eventually own up to

---

'Northwood' (1.10.6) was used, an authentic town in Metroland where Barnes himself grew up, while it was 'Eastwold' in another draft (1.10.8). In the first part of the published book, the town where the teenagers live is the fictional 'Eastwick' (33).

[44] Interview by Hayman, in *Conversations*, ed. Guignery and Roberts, 4.
[45] This chapter exists in two fairly similar drafts (the first in 1.11.1, the second in 1.10.6). The following quotes come from the second draft.

a certain type of seat. Smoker or anti-smoker. Then, which way you want to face. Then pro- or anti-heater. Then window side or inside. Then a two- or a three-person seat (always a tricky decision: the three-seaters give more room as long as there are only two of you, but you can end up squashed between two slack-thighed bloatards).

Having made your decisions, and having placed yourself on the platform at the exact spot you need to be at for when you arrive, you remember that in the section of the train which will stop in front of you, there will be only one seat which fits your requirements. Only one! Imagine the twitching and pawing at the platform's whitened edge when the rails begin to vibrate. Is there a rival on the platform? Is there already a regular on the train with the same preference as you? Is there perhaps some wild card, an early-morning mid-week shopper off to Barkers for the sales? Worst of all, will there be an untidy dandruffy schoolboy (some of them quite big) carrying a lethal cricket bag full of smelly rugger-boots wrapped in newspaper? A smirking, swotting, smelly space-taker on a half-fare season-ticket? Or a grouchy little monster in a khaki uniform, lurching against you on the way out and leaving blanco on your coat?

Comedy is triggered by the disparity between the first short isolated sentence and the next two extremely detailed paragraphs based on symmetrical constructions, either through anaphoras ('However', 'Then', 'Is there') or through binary structures as in the description of the different types of seats. Such an elaborate development testifies to Chris's immoderate preoccupation with a trivial element and to his laughable fastidiousness, as suggested not only by such expressions as 'always a tricky decision', 'at the exact spot' or 'Worst of all', but also by the series of rhetorical questions which get more and more specific as to the characteristic features of potential rivals. The description of other passengers is particularly precise and comically visual. The hyperbolic alliterative accumulation of qualifying adjectives at the end of the second paragraph reveals Chris's sheer repugnance of 'untidy dandruffy' schoolboys and 'smirking, swotting, smelly' space-takers.

This comic description of Chris's commuting angst echoes a passage from Part One in the published book (which is probably why Barnes deleted the one above in Part Three), when the teenager plays subversive games on the train, one of them consisting in frustrating 'old fuggers' by making a dash for their favourite seats. The description of the scene in Part One is as comic as the deleted scene but more focused on the boy's mischievousness and mode of operation than on the men's anxiety for their seats although one finds a precise and humorous portrayal of them: 'The pinstripes and the chalkstripes always forced themselves to get their favourite place without appearing to care where they sat, yet casually sticking out their fatty hips and metal-cornered attaché cases in an attempt to grab pole position' (59). The use of the third-person plural to refer to the fastidious men and the distancing and dehumanizing effect of the opening synecdoche ('The pinstripes and the chalkstripes') emphasize the teenager's smirking tone and contrast with the use of the second-person pronoun 'you' in the deleted passage, which espouses the point of the view of the adult commuter who thereby attempts to engage the reader in a greater complicity.

In the deleted chapter, 30-year-old Chris's concern about having a schoolboy occupy his favourite seat leads him to recall a specific conversation with his doppelgänger (a young version of himself from the same school) on the train. A farcical dialogue covers two pages in which Chris pedantically attempts to draw the schoolchild into banal conversation, which the insolent boy takes as evidence of him being 'queer', 'a poof'. When Chris retorts that he is happily married, the cheeky teenager snaps back: 'Only the old shagbag doesn't work, does it? Find yourself looking at boys again, don't you?' Comedy is triggered off by the contrast between Chris's formal language to the boy as he vainly tries to clear up the misunderstanding ('I beg your pardon?', 'Certainly not', 'I think I should explain') and the (almost) uncensored colloquial turn of his indignant inner voice ('The little cocksu ... (well, maybe not)', 'These confident little sods nowadays'). If Chris has enough self-awareness to draw a parallel with similar situations from when he was a boy and to gradually understand the schoolchild's distrustful reaction, he is still dumbfounded by the latter's confidence and patronising tone. As the boy murmurs 'Bumfucker' upon exiting the train, Chris's reaction is comically ineffective: 'Were it not for my self-restraint, I would have – I would have ... well, I certainly wouldn't have restrained myself.'

Barnes probably deleted this passage because of its too obvious parallel with a similar scene in Part One when a commuter talks to the 16-year-old Chris about the history of the Metropolitan Line (35–8).[46] The 1963 commuter's first words, 'Verney Junction', are echoed fourteen years later by older Chris's (then deleted) question 'Did you know this line once ran to Verney Junction?'. The main difference between the two scenes is that while the 1977 boy rudely refuses to listen to Chris and throws sexual insults at him, the 1963 teenager did not dare interrupt the older man and even took a polite interest in the conversation while his inner voice was simultaneously calling the commuter 'an old sod', 'dead bourgeois', 'rickety old fugger' and imagined him to be a ravisher: 'What was he after? Rape, abduction?', 'He must be a rapist; anyone who spoke to kids on trains obviously was, *ex hypothesi*' (35–6).

Another reason for deleting the doppelgänger passage in Part Three is that Barnes decided to 'conflate boy meeting & girl at party' as he wrote in one of his notes to himself. Indeed, in the chapter entitled 'Stiff Petticoat', 30-year-old Chris meets a 20-year-old girl who bluntly tells him 'OK so we go and fuck?' (154) and then accuses him of being a 'cunt-teaser' (155) when he turns down her offer. More than thirty years after composition, Barnes wrote in his annotated copy of *Metroland*: 'a fairly improbable scene, I now think' (Morgan Library 155). The balance of power between the young girl with her 'detached zest' turning to 'aggression' (155), her crude vocabulary and condescending tone, and a panicked and mumbling Chris who is desperately trying to maintain some degree of formality (while wondering 'Is that how they talk nowadays?', 155) is quite similar to the tense relationship between the confident boy on the train and the helpless adult character, thus justifying the decision to conflate the two scenes. In an early draft, Chris explicitly connected the two scenes when he reflected on misunderstandings about sex: 'First I was a child rapist, then a cunt-teaser, when all

---

[46] In the annotated copy of *Metroland*, Barnes wrote that he 'never had such an encounter' (Morgan Library 35).

I wanted to do was to make love to my lawful wife two or three times a week.' In his letter to Liz Calder, Barnes explained the removal of the train episode in the following terms: 'the thrust of this scene (Chris's realisation of being outflanked by a younger generation; his surprise at their sexual attitudes) can be borne by a slightly expanded version of the scene where he meets the girl at the party.'

Among the deleted passages of the third part is also Chapter Five, 'Joining Up',[47] which deals with Chris joining a community group called 'ZAC – the Zebra Action Committee', whose aim is to ask the Council to put a zebra crossing on a dangerous bend of one of the neighbourhood roads. While his wife shows no interest in this type of 'public-spirited communal exercise', Chris takes it as an example of what he would have despised in his youth, but now seems worthwhile to him in his new status as 'reformed' adult, husband and father. He smugly argues that having a daughter has changed his relationship with the world: 'she gives you a sense of being a citizen of the world, of having bonds with other parents, of having an inheritance from the past and a duty to the future. Or even a Duty to the Future – but that may be overdoing it a bit.' Although that last remark and the capital letters show he is comically aware of his complacency, he later adopts a similar tone when he remarks that 'if you have a job, a family, a social life', '[t]he acute self-consciousness of adolescence, which the idle and the unmarried continue to display, becomes toned down into reasoned self-awareness'.

The deleted chapter's comic dimension largely derives from the description of the first meeting of ZAC and the pseudo-democratic election of a chairman, with each neighbour's behaviour revealing their personality (genial and manipulative, pushy, silent, shy or pretending to look embarrassed). After discussing such issues as 'fund-raising, meeting-places, stationery, a title for the committee, and how to attract new members', they decide to leave '[s]erious matters of strategy' to the next meeting and all of them eventually chat away on a 'well-I-was-thinking-of-sending-ours-to-St-Godfrey's and a but-don't-you-think-too-much-peat-encourages-the-foliage-at-the-expense-of-the-flowers basis'. When Chris relates their self-congratulatory discussions to Marion on coming home, she shows herself to be unimpressed and sarcastic, especially when her husband facetiously imagines an example of direct action from ZAC: 'They'll probably have all the pregnant women in the area lying down in the road and inviting juggernauts to run over them.' Marion's unflustered reaction in this deleted chapter is emblematic of what Barnes saw as her 'purely practical thinking', 'anti-romanticism, self-assurance & strength of character', aspects that he meant to clarify and sharpen in the new draft and which also characterize Tony's ex-wife Margaret in *The Sense of an Ending*.

In addition to the suppression of these two chapters from the final draft, Barnes deleted several isolated passages. One of them originally appeared in Chapter Four ('Is Sex Travel?') and focused on the way adult life changes one's perspective. While the published version ends with Chris and Marion making love after their discussion on infidelity, an early draft continued with two pages of Chris's musings about decisions of moral principle: 'Why is it, I sometimes wonder, that there seems to be fewer moral

---

[47] This chapter exists in two fairly similar drafts (the first in 1.11.1, the second in 1.10.6). The following quotes come from the second draft.

decisions in adult life than I'd anticipated?' Referring to his flirting with the girl at the party, he notes: 'the moral element seems more diffuse that I'd expected, more watered down by overriding practical considerations'. He then takes the example of selling a house which you can do 'with almost no intervention from the moral faculty' because you need to remain within the limits of the law so that there is no room for immoral action. Chris wonders again, apparently with some regret: 'Isn't it strange that morality has been so squeezed out of life?' His third and more developed example concerns charity and comes in the form of a comic dialogue during dinner at his sister's house. As Chris wonders why the meal only consists of eggs and cheese, his sister Mary explains: 'Phil and I decided we ought to live off eggs and milk and cheese for one week in four, and give the money we save to Oxfam.' When a puzzled Chris asks why they don't simply send money instead of starving themselves, Mary explains that it is symbolic and that it makes the children more conscious of other people. This argument is what leads Chris to think that what could have been a moral decision is actually an egotistic one, as he petulantly tells Mary: 'Saving the starving millions is just a by-product of making your kids into better citizens?', 'Does the ratio 1:4 reflect some inner harmony between conscience and allowable selfishness?' The whole passage was probably uncompleted and deleted because Chris's meditation and truculent questions to his sister, despite their comic undertones, were maybe slightly too didactic. However, the passage efficiently highlighted Chris's perplexed sense of a waning of morality, which had been triggered off by the earlier discussion of adultery.

In contrast to the deletion of mostly comic passages about everyday life in suburbia, Barnes added in his final draft of Part Three Chris's trip to the National Gallery (164) to echo Toni and Chris's roguish visits as teenagers in Part One (11–12). He also kept a reference to a 'sodium lamp' giving off an orange light in the street (175) and turning his pyjamas 'muddy brown' (176), which recalls a similar reference in Part One about the 'first months of sodium lighting', which turned brown anything red (14) and led the young Chris to lament: 'They even fug up the spectrum' (14). According to Barnes in his letter to Calder, such an echo sufficiently 'brings the story full circle' and justifies the suppression of the chapters and passages referred to above.

Several readers were unsure as to how to interpret the evolution of Chris in the third part and his moving back to the suburbia he despised as a teenager, with '[w]ife, baby, reliable job, mortgage, *flower* garden' (167). As Barnes remarked in an interview, the ambiguity as to whether Chris has 'become mature, sensible, wise, or has completely sold out and tuned all his values to those of wider society'[48] was deliberate and that is why he rewrote Chris 'from the inside', as noted in his letter to Calder:

> he's still as self-aware as in Parts One & Two, a bit complacent, but ready to defend himself (against Toni); the main point I'm trying to put across about him is not that he's become a smug bourgeois, etc, (which he hasn't), but that he's semi-gracefully, if sometimes ironically, submitting to the onset of happiness & the recognition of various realities (re what he believes re art, love, materialism). It's not just that he thinks he's lost some & won some; you're meant to think that too. The novel turns

---

[48] Interview by Rudolf Freiburg (1999), in *Conversations*, ed. Guignery and Roberts, 33–4.

on his loss of the spirit of adventure (hence, for instance, the changing bits of luggage at the end of each Part); but you're not meant to think that this doesn't have genuine compensations. He may be regretful but he's still observant & doesn't need patronising (chapter 6).[49] I think this character development is wholly plausible. Getting it across in a first-person narrative has been the problem: the first draft verged too much on a sort of contented solipsistic elegy for himself; this time I've tried to make it sharper, clearer, more self-aware. At the same time, since it is first-person, the sassy, cocky elan of Part One wd be out of place; it's deliberately written in [a] way that is a bit more measured; but it's still, I hope, funny. (1.10.5)

Barnes has thus worked towards a more ambivalent ending which is, at the same time, more balanced and poised, in which Chris is 'less resigned, more positive – self-aware'. In handwritten pages of notes to himself about the manuscript, the author listed what he needed to emphasize about Chris's new self in the third part: 'tone of enthusiasm for his life if poss.', 'justify change in his attitude to language', 'bring out point about primacy of life', 'make it sound enjoyable'. Referring to Chris's meeting with a reproachful Toni, Barnes wrote: 'Stress Chris's regret more & justify it better. Touches of rebellion.' He thus insisted on not making Chris's return to Metroland a synonym of defeat and resignation but the result of a maturation leading to some nuanced happiness.[50]

Barnes's painstaking revisions and numerous cuts in his very first novel reveal how relentless he was (and still is) as a critic of his own work. His random notes on separate pages (for *Metroland* but also all later novels) highlight this careful attention to detail: he typically writes down a page number to identify a specific passage in the typescript, followed by remarks or questions such as 'keep?', 'don't overdo if used in ch.1 – maybe cut, though', 'shouldn't this be justified?', 'detail this?', '<u>liven</u> and retype', 'retype and sharpen', '<u>rewrite</u>', 'improve?', 'decide metaphor', 'better word?'. Comments about Part One of *Metroland* include such indications as 'Sharpen Toni. Look at tenses. Family scene – introduce better', 'establish bro & sis earlier on. Describe parents', 'Introduce characters more firmly'. Concerning Part Three, he wrote down: 'Sharpen Marion', 'More dialogue' and 'Try & liven up the complacent chapters'. The notion which keeps recurring in the handwritten notes and in the letter to Calder is that of writing 'more sharply' and dealing with some aspects 'briefly', merely through 'passing mentions'. The verbs 'chop', 'conflate', 'compress', 'cut' and 'abbreviate' all appear on the same page of notes about Part Three. The last handwritten comment on the draft letter to his editor is 'tauter, neater, more plausible' and the self-advice which is underlined at the top of a page of handwritten notes is '<u>Don't fear making it shorter overall</u>'. *Metroland*

---

[49] Chapter Six ('Object relations') starts with a memory of Toni's reproachful remark: ' "So this is it?" Toni had said as he stood slyly quizzing my vegetable patch' (174), an echo of Toni's earlier visit when he had uttered those very same words (144).

[50] However, in an interview in 2000, Barnes said *Metroland* was 'about defeat': 'I wanted to write about youthful aspiration coming to a compromised end. I wanted to write a novel that was un-Balzacian, in that, instead of ending with the hero looking down from a hill onto a city that he knows, or at least believes, he is going to take, it ended with the non-hero *not* having taken the city, and accepting the city's terms.' Interview by Guppy, *Conversations*, ed. Guignery and Roberts, 68–9. He confirmed this interpretation in his introduction to the 2016 Vintage edition of the novel. Barnes, 'Introduction', *Metroland*, 5.

ended up being a slim book of 176 pages, as were his next two (*Before She Met Me* and *Flaubert's Parrot*), a tendency that was repeated some thirty years later with *The Sense of an Ending*, *Levels of Life* and *The Noise of Time*. The examination of the various drafts and notes for *Metroland* has shown that Barnes's preference for condensation, sharpness and precision already characterized his work from the very outset of his career and continued to be a guiding principle in later years.

Coda: In February 2016, Julian Barnes read a first draft of this chapter and commented: 'How odd to be confronted with the misgivings, half-thoughts and uncertainties of 40 or so years ago. I remember almost nothing of what I left out, and yet am strangely impressed a) by the acceptable quality of much that I cut; and b) by my own rigour towards my prose.'[51]

---

[51] Private email correspondence with the author, 6 February 2016.

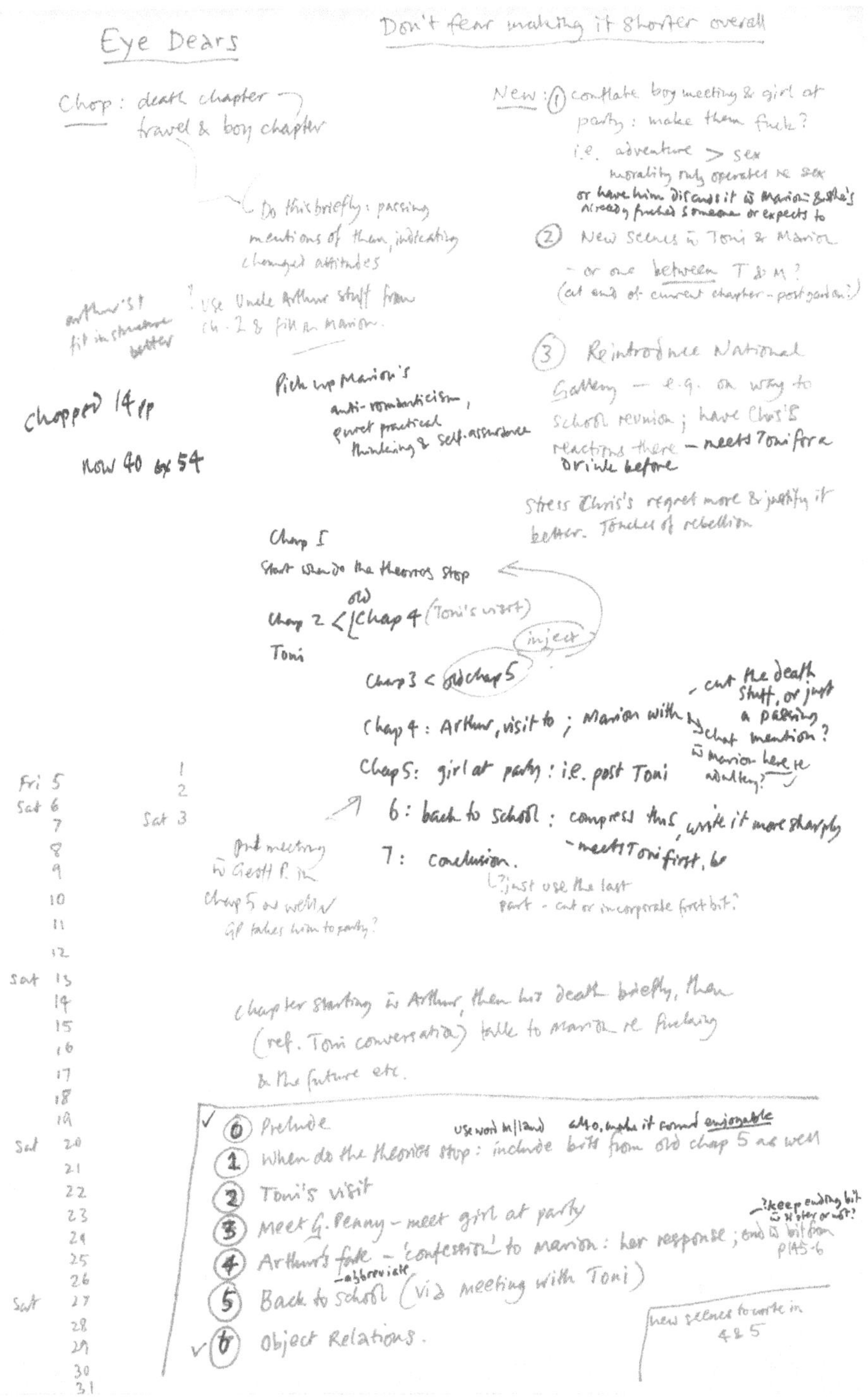

Figure 1 *Metroland* – handwritten notes (1.10.5). Harry Ransom Center. The University of Texas at Austin.

2

The case for/The case against

1. Reviewing and being reviewed

The old style critic treated a book like a hotel which he has chosen, paid for, & expects to enjoy; his presence there, he feels, is slightly conditional, slightly resented, but he does his best to have a good time. The new style structuralist critic treats a book like a house abandoned by its former occupier & to which he now has sole rights: even if the former owner only decamped a few days ago, he feels no sense of recent occupation, no sentimentality. He wanders round thinking how the layout of the rooms reflects the previous owner's nature, noting the old-fashionedness of his decorative scheme, imagining that the previous owner must have been taken in by the bits of fakery he observes. He doesn't ring up the previous owner (who is in the telephone book) because that would prejudice the scientific nature of his enquiries.
 Both these attitudes are wrong. (1.1.1)

This extract from Julian Barnes's first notebook dating from the late 1970s and early 1980s proposes a very apt metaphor to refer to two different types of criticism ('old style' vs. 'new style structuralist'), neither of which is satisfactory. A writer is bound to feel dismayed by the treatment his work receives at the hands of critics, be they academics or reviewers, as criticism entails simplification which cannot do justice to the complexities and subtleties of the work. Depending not only on the personality of writers but also on the potential evolution of their attitude to critical judgements on their work, their responses may vary from despondency, indignation or outrage to indifference, amusement or satisfaction.
 More than a century after Robert Southey called reviewing 'the ungentle craft', Kingsley Amis was famously credited with the dismissive statement: 'A bad review may spoil your breakfast but you shouldn't allow it to spoil your lunch.'[1] John Updike wrote a favourable review of *Flaubert's Parrot*,[2] and several of his books were reviewed

---

[1] Elizabeth M. Knowles, *The Oxford Dictionary of Quotations* (Oxford: Oxford University Press, 1999), 14.
[2] John Updike, 'A Pair of Parrots', *New Yorker*, 22 July 1985, 86–7.

by Barnes,[3] but the American writer said in a self-interview with his own character (Henry Bech) that he found reviews 'humiliating' as '[a]ll the little congruences and arabesques you prepared with such delicate anticipatory pleasure are gobbled up as if by pigs at a pastry cart'.[4] Barnes himself is wary of critics who position themselves between book and reader. He wrote in his second notebook: 'Criticism is like some dense French letter rolled on to the writer, & which interferes w[ith] him [sic] intercourse w[ith] the reader. Sensitivity & pleasure are decreased. The Russian slang for French letters is "galoshes": criticism is a galosh – thick, rubbery, impermeable, sensible, and killing' (1.1.2). This most original image did not make it to any published piece but could have been penned by Gustave Flaubert himself who famously vilified journalistic critics to the point of wanting them all exterminated.[5] It could also have found its way into *Flaubert's Parrot* in which the narrator opens the fifth chapter with an uncompromising declaration: 'Let me tell you why I hate critics' (74) – by which he meant academic critics rather than journalists and reviewers –, and in 'Examination Paper', he quotes a letter from Flaubert to Louise Colet of 28 June 1853 in which the French writer was just as blunt: 'Criticism occupies the lowest rung in the hierarchy of literature' (173). The Finnish composer Jean Sibelius had the same misgivings about criticism and Barnes likes to quote his remark when he was consoling a young colleague for a bad review: 'Always remember, there is no city in the world which has erected a statue to a critic.'[6]

In 1977, when Barnes was penning pieces under the pseudonym of Edward Pygge for *The New Review* (what the writer referred to as '[n]ews, publishing gossip, light interviews'),[7] the magazine sent a questionnaire to twenty-three novelists (including Kingsley and Martin Amis, Margaret Drabble, John Fowles, David Lodge, Paul Theroux and John Wain, among others) to ask them what they thought of their reviewers. Pygge remarked that the novelists had 'an accurate enough picture of the average reviewer – callow, ignorant, naturally vicious, and innocent of the problems of writing fiction' but mostly reacted 'with a sort of benign pity'.[8] The next month, Edward Pygge sardonically

---

[3] Julian Barnes, 'Grand Illusion', review of *In the Beauty of the Lilies*, by John Updike, *New York Times*, 28 January 1996, section 7, 9; 'A Game which Demands a Saintly Letting Go', review of *Golf Dreams*, by John Updike, *Literary Review*, May 1997, 43–4; 'Flights', review of *My Father's Tears and Other Stories, Endpoint and Other Poems* and *The Maples Stories*, by John Updike, *New York Review of Books* 56, no. 10 (11 June 2009): 8, 10; 'Running Away', review of *Rabbit Angstrom*, by John Updike, *Guardian*, 17 October 2009, R20. The two writers exchanged letters between 1995 and 2002, praising each other's work (archives 3). Barnes published a tribute to Updike after his death (Julian Barnes, 'Remembering Updike', *New Yorker*, 27 January 2009, http://www.newyorker.com/online/blogs/books/2009/01/remembering-upd.html. Accessed on 19 January 2019) and wrote a short story entitled 'Sleeping with John Updike', collected in *Pulse* (London: Jonathan Cape, 2011), 33–47.

[4] Henry Bech, 'Henry Bech Redux', *The New York Times Book Review*, 14 November 1971, section 3, 3.

[5] Letter to Louise Colet, 16 November 1852. Gustave Flaubert, *Correspondance III. 1859–1868*, ed. Jean Bruneau (Paris: Gallimard, 1991), 148.

[6] The quote appears in Barnes's short story 'The Silence', in *The Lemon Table* (London: Jonathan Cape, 2004), 211, and in his essay 'Where Sibelius Fell Silent', *The Economist 1843*, January/February 2012, https://www.1843magazine.com/content/arts/house-sibelius-fell-silent. Accessed on 19 January 2019.

[7] Julian Barnes, 'The Bitter Lemon Days', *Another Round at the Pillars: Essays, Poems, & Reflections on Ian Hamilton*, ed. David Harsent (Tregarne, Manaccan: Cargo Press, 1999), 19.

[8] Julian Barnes [Edward Pygge, pseud.], 'Greek Street', *The New Review* 4, no. 42 (September 1977): 1.

referred to the reviewers of *Times* newspapers and noted that no imitator manages to be simultaneously as stodgy and as lightweight. He then gave the example of a *Times* review of Margaret Drabble's new novel by Jan Morris 'whose qualifications for the job were 1) that she's never read Drabble before, and 2) that she'd never reviewed fiction before'.[9] Barnes himself was a regular literary reviewer at the time (and not yet a published novelist) and the severity he later imposed upon his own work as well as his causticity and irony are perceptible in some of his early pieces. In March 1974, he draws attention to 'appallingly lazy' sentences in Peter Prince's second novel *Dogcatcher*: after quoting 'I switched the Buick's motor on. It ... purred, there's no other word for it', Barnes comments: 'Yes, there is, and Mr Prince might have found it if he had bothered to look.'[10] A 1976 review of three now-forgotten novels starts with the following corrosive sentence: 'Not a deepening, or even a flashy, read to be had this week, but enough modest competence, grammatical correctness, and A1 punctuation to ward off the wilder excesses of malice.'[11] Jennifer Beckett and her first novel, *The Trap*, then fall prey to Barnes's devastating irony: the reviewer finds the prose 'spotty with conjunctivitis' but notes that 'the author is married to the publisher of *Country Life*, so at least the fittings and fixtures are authentic'. About Molly Parkin, he writes in 1977: 'Molly is a jolly lady who writes jolly bad books.'[12] In the same year, he takes Tom Sharpe to task for having established himself as a 'genuine farceur' without being actually funny: 'he sets up promising comic situations with some ingenuity, and then delivers the goods in a doggedly limp way',[13] and the year after compares reading Sharpe's novel *The Throwback* to 'watching a boxer with very fast footwork and very short arms'.[14]

In an interview in 2008, Barnes said: 'I've reviewed hundreds of novels in my time and I think I've only ever written one review that I would reprint. It was a review of Philip Roth's *The Counterlife* – which I think is his best book – and it took me three or four weeks to write.'[15] Barnes's 1987 laudatory review of Roth's novel starts with the disclaimer: '[M]ore than with most novels, to review it is to betray it',[16] which highlights Barnes's wariness of the genre. Unlike writers who include some of their reviews of contemporary books in collections of essays, Barnes has only reprinted some of his

---

[9] Julian Barnes [Edward Pygge, pseud.], 'Greek Street', *The New Review* 4, no. 43 (October 1977): 1.
[10] Julian Barnes, 'The Big Yawn', *Times Literary Supplement*, 29 March 1974, 313.
[11] Julian Barnes, 'Conservational', *New Statesman*, 9 January 1976, 45.
[12] Julian Barnes, 'Rousing Stuff', *New Statesman*, 1 July 1977, 22.
[13] Julian Barnes, 'Decent Exposure', *New Statesman*, 22 April 1977, 537.
[14] Julian Barnes, 'Farce Talking', *New Statesman*, 24 March 1978, 407. In 2000, Barnes started an essay on influences with the following remarks: 'Most British writers of my generation, when promoting their books in Spain, have been asked the following question: "Can you describe, please, the exact influence on you of the works of Tom Sharpe?" Mr Sharpe, it may need explaining, is a writer of jocose farce (student, embarrassed by acquiring large quantities of condoms, inflates them with gas, stuffs them up his chimney, someone lights the fire, the chimney explodes – that sort of thing), who in some Spanish eyes holds a central and dominating position in English literature. The trick is to keep a polite expression on your face while wondering whether translation has greatly improved Mr Sharpe's work or sabotaged your own.' Julian Barnes, 'Influences – Single-Handed', *New Yorker*, 25 December 2000–1 January 2001, 114.
[15] Scarlett Baron, '*Nothing to Be Frightened Of*: An Interview with Julian Barnes', *The Oxonian Review of Books* 7.3 (Summer 2008), http://www.oxonianreview.org/wp/nothing-to-be-frightened-of-an-interview-with-julian-barnes/. Accessed on 15 October 2019.
[16] Julian Barnes, 'Philip Roth in Israel', *London Review of Books* 9, no. 5 (5 March 1987): 3.

longer pieces on dead writers' work (in *Something to Declare* and *Through the Window*), the exceptions being his 1998 review of Lorrie Moore's *Birds of America*[17] and his 2010 review of diaries of widowhood, Joyce Carol Oates's *A Widow's Story: A Memoir* and Joan Didion's *The Year of Magical Thinking*, both collected in *Through the Window*.[18]

As a young novelist, Barnes felt little confidence in his own work and did not relish exposure to the general reading public. He wrote in 1989:

> In general, beginning a novel isn't difficult – at least, compared to finishing a novel; while finishing a novel isn't difficult – at least, compared to publishing a novel. It's not so much fear of bad reviews, but something wider and more nugatory: fear of being exposed, fingered, pinned down; fear of getting caught out in some piercing manner.[19]

At the beginning of his career, Barnes would read every review of his books and from 1980 to 1991, he pasted the clippings of these reviews into a volume which is archived at the Harry Ransom Center (1.18). In *The Noise of Time*, Barnes points out that Shostakovich, who had never kept reviews beforehand, started pasting every article about him and his work in a large scrapbook after the publication of the devastating review of his opera *Lady Macbeth of Mtsensk* in the *Pravda*: 'He noted how critics who had consistently praised *Lady Macbeth of Mtsensk* over the past two years suddenly found no merit at all in it'[20] – thus showing how fickle the press could be (and in the case of Russia, subject to the whims of political power). Barnes's novels did not suffer the fate of Shostakovich's opera, and yet, for his first two books, the author wrote in advance 'the most extravagantly damning review[s]' they might possibly receive. These self-reviews have not been included in the archives but Barnes reveals part of them in his introduction to the 2016 Vintage archive edition of *Metroland*. The review of Barnes's first novel by 'Mack the Knife' in the *Daily Sniveller* started thus:

> Once upon a time there was a creature called the sensitive young man. Often he was awarded capital letters, thus: the Sensitive Young Man. He flourished at the time, in the shadow, and sometimes tucked into the shoulder, of Oscar Wilde. He wrote novels not because he had anything to say, but because he wanted to be a novelist. Being a novelist was, he thought, a fine thing.[21]

As recalled by Barnes,

> Mack the Knife then went to work on the book, on its unoriginality, its disregard of Modernism, its blandness. Patronisingly, he admitted that Barnes 'does not write

---

[17] Julian Barnes, 'The Wise Woman', *New York Review of Books* 45, no. 16 (22 October 1998): 15, reproduced as 'Lorrie Moore Takes Wing', in Julian Barnes, *Through the Window: Seventeen Essays and a Short Story* (London: Jonathan Cape, 2012), 193–7.
[18] Julian Barnes, 'For Sorrow There Is No Remedy', *The New York Review of Books* 58, no. 6 (7 April 2011): 10–14, reproduced as 'Regulating Sorrow', in Barnes, *Through the Window*, 215–27.
[19] Julian Barnes, 'Diary. Ambushed in Streets of the Sneaky Pun', *Guardian*, 17 June 1989.
[20] Julian Barnes, *The Noise of Time* (London: Jonathan Cape, 2016), 39.
[21] The quotes below are all taken from Barnes, 'Introduction', *Metroland*, 3–4.

inelegantly' and 'occasionally turns a sprightly phrase', while pointing out that 'A smattering of French cannot conceal the poverty of the author's imagination, and the novel's brevity is, alas, no guarantee against tedium.'

The ruthless reviewer concluded thus:

> In the old days, the Sensitive Young Man, after producing 'his novel', would slide back into the obscurity of book-reviewing and hock-and-seltzer; he would in middle age be much taken with writing letters to the newspapers; and in old age, chairbound in his club, he would reveal himself to be the unremitting philistine which his earlier manifestation had sought to conceal. We must wish Mr Barnes well as he sets off on this inevitable journey.

Barnes's 'plan' was that 'if any reviewer identified all the faults that Mack had, [he] would give up writing fiction'. None of the reviews proved as harsh as Mack the Knife's and most of them were very favourable. However, Barnes repeated the same exercise for his second novel, *Before She Met Me*: 'When Mr Barnes isn't being sensitive, he is being vulgar, seemingly obsessed on this occasion with lower-bowel noises; he seems unable to appreciate that most of life takes place in the middle ground between "being sensitive" and "farting".'[22] Barnes's anticipation of what critics might say can also be found in an undated letter to Hermione Lee:

> I can just hear E Lucie-Smug[23] saying 'Of course, he isn't really a novelist, he's just a fairly good TV critic'[24] .... Actually, what would be worse than being dumped on is what is more likely: lukewarm praise, an avuncular pat on the back, a swift agreement on moderate talent before passing on to the big show of the week, a collection of Afghan bus-tickets at the Whitechapel. (1.1.4)

The novel includes a sly reference to a critic through the fictional character of Bailey, a colleague of the main protagonist's at London University, who 'always tried to look as shabby as possible, and usually succeeded' (147). Barnes humorously confided to Hermione Lee:

> He only exists because I wanted to revenge myself on Paul Bailey for his hypocritical behaviour when reviewing Metroland, in the course of which review he said that my fiction – unlike, say, well, just for instance, his own – didn't have enough deeply fuck[ed]-up old people in it. Bailey has a thing – privately and fictionally – about

---

[22] Ibid., 5.
[23] This is a satirical distortion of the name of Edward Lucie-Smith, writer, poet and critic. Lucie-Smith was often on *Critics' Forum*, a weekly radio show on BBC Radio 3, in which four critics reviewed different art forms (cinema, books, theatre, broadcasting and the visual arts), hence the reference to the 'collection of Afghan bus-tickets' at the end of the passage.
[24] Julian Barnes was television critic for the *New Statesman* from 1978 to 1980 and then for the *Observer* from 1982 to 1986, taking up the position from his friend Clive James who had occupied it for the previous ten years.

old men. So I thought, I'll have a really shabby loon called Bailey, and make him a gerontologist. (1.1.4)

Barnes recalls that Bailey had gone to see his editor Liz Calder before reviewing *Metroland* and told her 'how terrific he thought it was', but he then went on to write an unsympathetic review in the *Times Literary Supplement*, later telling Calder that when he reread the book, he 'realized after all that it was not as good as he first thought'.[25] Bailey noted in his review that what enlivened the book was the character of Uncle Arthur, described by his nephew as a 'humorous old fugger – cunning, stingy and usually lying' (46), who became 'more insultingly mendacious' as he grew older (158).[26]

In his annotated copy of *Metroland*, Barnes refers to the review his first novel received from Auberon Waugh who noted that Chris's first sexual excitement was 'provided by second-hand copies of the News of the World' and doubted that such a newspaper could provide any sexual solace.[27] However, Waugh's memory was inaccurate as in *Metroland*, Chris is attracted to Uncle Arthur's 'neatly strung bundles of the *Daily Express*' in which he reads the 'juiciest column' called 'This America', 'with at least one sex story a day', as well as the gossip column – 'posh adulteries got me going', he remarks in an aside – and 'cases of rape, incest, exposure and indecent behaviour' (50). A less fortunate schoolfriend is given the *News of the World* to read by his father 'in the hope that this would let him out of telling his son the facts of life' (50). Barnes recalls his encounter with Waugh a few months later:

> When I met him, some time in the following year, I couldn't refrain myself from pointing out this massive error. 'Oh, how interesting,' he replied (infuriatingly), 'I wonder why I did that?' Whereas I had been expecting him to apologize, he had turned the error into an amusing eccentricity about himself. It – that is to say, my failure to control the exchange – made me determined <u>never</u> to complain to a reviewer (& as far as possible never to write a letter of complaint to the literary pages). (*Metroland*, Morgan Library 50–1)

Such comments by Barnes only apply to his early novels, probably because, as he wrote in his annotated copy of *Metroland* – which he remembers had been praised by Kingsley Amis but disliked by his wife Elizabeth Jane Howard –, 'writers always remain grateful for the first encouragements they received. And perhaps the first slights never go away either' (Morgan Library 141). Therefore, Barnes treasured Philip Larkin's encouraging letter of 20 April 1980 about *Metroland* which the poet thought 'original in having a decent chap for a hero, consistently amusing (I liked Uncle Arthur), and all very illuminating on social mores etc' and much enjoyed 'despite [his] prejudice against novels with people under the age of 21 in them'. On the envelope of Larkin's letter, Barnes wrote: 'BLOODY MARVELLOUS' (1.17.2), and more than twenty years

---

[25] Annotations, 22–27 March 2018.
[26] For Paul Bailey, Arthur's 'viewpoint, however jaundiced, provides some welcome shade'. Paul Bailey, 'Settling for Suburbia', *Times Literary Supplement*, 28 March 1980, 345.
[27] Auberon Waugh, 'Pseuds' Progress.' *Evening Standard*, 1980. This review is in Barnes's bound volume of clippings (1.18).

later, he reflected: 'This unexpected praise was the most gratifying moment of the strange passage of first publication' (Morgan Library, n.p., last page).

Less than two decades later, Barnes decided to stop reading reviews. He dates that decision from 1998 when *England, England* came out and he read the first review of the novel in the *Sunday Times* by John Carey[28] who not only praised the novel but, more importantly, 'described it exactly', which, as Barnes remarks, 'increasingly is what you want more even than praise'. He adds: 'I knew no one would describe it better, so there was no point reading the others.'[29] Barnes realized at that point that '[c]riticism doesn't help you practically as a writer, so all you get is an emotional lifting-up or an emotional lowering-down. Really you ought to be mature enough not to need the praise after a certain point'.[30] What proved more useful than reviews were comments by readers and friends before the work was published, at a time when it could therefore still be amended. Barnes's archives include fascinating comments by his most faithful and helpful reader, Hermione Lee, who started giving her detailed opinions on the drafts of his books from his second novel, *Before She Met Me*.

2. The case of *Before She Met Me*

a. Julian Barnes's reButs to Hermione Lee's Buts

Since 1981, Julian Barnes's first reader has been the renowned critic and biographer Dame Professor Hermione Lee. Although they overlapped in Oxford in 1964–8 when Barnes read modern languages and philosophy at Magdalen College and Lee read English at St Hilda's College, they did not meet there, but in 1975 when Barnes was assistant literary editor at the *New Statesman* and asked Lee to do some reviewing for him. Since *Before She Met Me*, Lee has been reading and commenting on the drafts of Barnes's novels, short stories and essays, sending long letters, faxes or emails with very careful indications, annotating the typescripts in great detail or sending pages of typed comments. Lee's intimate familiarity with Barnes's work over the years as well as her expertise in literary matters make her comments extremely valuable. Her status as close friend allows her to be both frank and considerate in her criticism of Barnes's production.

One of the rare pieces of correspondence from Barnes in his archives is a copy of his four-page letter (dating from 24 March 1982) to Lee responding to her comments about *Before She Met Me*, or rather, as Barnes wrote on the document, 'defending BSMM' – a defence which started with the following words: 'Now for your Buts, and my reButs.'[31] Lee's own letter is absent from the archives, but it can be partly reconstituted thanks to Barnes's selective quotes from it as well as his detailed responses and refutations which offer an interesting insight into the book. Barnes's explanations in the letter

---

[28] John Carey, 'Land of Make-Believe', *Sunday Times*, 23 August 1998, section 8, 1–2.
[29] Annotations, 22–27 March 2018.
[30] Interview by Freiburg, in *Conversations*, ed. Guignery and Roberts, 33.
[31] All quotes from the archives in this section are from 1.1.4, except when indicated.

can be complemented by the notes he took in the first notebook archived at the Harry Ransom Center in which he wrote down the main plot of the novel over four right-hand pages, beginning with 'Try this', and using left-hand pages for miscellaneous notes about point of view, characterization, various strands, quotes and details, some of them retained, others discarded (1.1.1).

In his letter to Lee and before justifying some of his contested choices, Barnes declares himself 'glad you found it as funny as you did, and glad about the bits you liked'. He also gives interesting information about the character of Jack Lupton: Graham's friend is presented in the novel as a self-indulgent novelist and eccentric womanizer, 'uncompromisingly amiable, ... noisily open and ... physical' (42), often seen with 'a smouldering cigarette lodged in the side of his beard' (42), wearing 'an old leather waistcoat' (70) and famous for his 'rowdy, worked-at, middle-aged farts' (44). While revising the novel, Barnes seemed to find his characterization of Jack a bit exaggerated: 'Jack's character overdone – less sexist banter and gung-ho – less farting?'; 'Jack: bit over the top, occas. too much "boyo"'. On a list of physical traits for his characters, he describes Jack as 'squat, brown, bearded, dressed like Sillitoe' and in his notebook as 'chunky, brown-suited, cynical, worldly' (1.1.1). In his letter to Lee, Barnes asserts that Jack 'isn't really anyone' while simultaneously admitting that the fictional creation is a mix of several writers he knows:

> the idea is more, say, a cynical version of someone like Sillitoe. I made him look a bit like Craig, I suppose ... but I gave him Sillitoe's leather waistcoat, ... a description of farting from Kingsley, and so on. The chunk of his novel is Braine-ish, but not particularly; maybe a bit Melvish; generally, just getting at post-Lawrence humourlessness ... Oh yes, there was a touch of Mervyn Jones in Jack (physically).

Jack thus appears as this comic patchwork of writers belonging to several generations, a *mélange* which might be a reflection of what was taking place at the time – the early 1980s – on the British literary scene. 'Craig' is the (bearded) poet Craig Raine (born in 1944) who has known Barnes since the 1970s when they both contributed to the *New Review*, while 'Melvish' is a reference to Melvyn Bragg (born in 1939). Bragg started his career as a radio and television arts presenter as well as a novelist and his book *Kingdom Come* was reviewed in some newspapers together with Barnes's first novel, *Metroland*, to one or the other's advantage. In 1993, for a 'Letter from London' published in the *New Yorker* and later collected in *Letters from London*, Barnes interviewed Bragg about his being a Lloyd's Name, an unexpected choice for a loyal member of the Labour Party. In *Nothing to Be Frightened Of*, Barnes recalls the embarrassing episode when, registering his father's death with his mother, the latter asked the registrar: '"Julian Barnes, have you heard of him?" But the registrar had not; and instead we found common literary ground by discussing the television adaptation of Melvyn Bragg's *A Time to Dance*' (202).

Next on the list as an inspiration for the character of Jack in *Before She Met Me* is the (bearded) journalist and novelist Mervyn Jones (1922–2010), who worked at the *New*

Statesman as a reporter at the same time as Barnes in the 1970s.[32] As for John Braine (1922–86), Kingsley Amis (1922–95) and Alan Sillitoe (1928–2010),[33] they were all part of the informal group of Angry Young Men in the 1950s and 1960s, continued to publish novels in the 1980s and were not quite ready to offer the 'room at the top' to the new generation of novelists, to which Barnes, Martin Amis and Ian McEwan belonged. Barnes once remarked: 'It's always the job of the next generation of critics to try to assassinate the earlier generation of writers. When I was a critic on the New Statesman the idea that John Braine should be still publishing novels offended me.'[34]

Indeed, Amis and Barnes quite often 'assassinated' novels by the social realists of the 1950s and 1960s, including John Braine whose novel, *Waiting for Sheila*, Barnes reviewed in the *New Statesman* in 1976. The younger writer had read in the *Sunday Times* that Braine's wife threw out all the nasty and mean reviews of his husband's work, and therefore felt he could more openly state what he thought about Braine's novel. He presented *Waiting for Sheila* as a 'straight novel', produced by 'John Braine (Bingley) Ltd, the company which turns out hand-crafted copies of ambitious working-class materialists', and added that the novel seemed to applaud rather than query the protagonist's 'hardhat philosophy'.[35] What Barnes did not anticipate was that Braine read the review and the next week, the *New Statesman* published the latter's vitriolic letter to the editor, accusing Barnes of having failed to see that his novel was mainly about love, a subject the young writer supposedly knew nothing about: 'How could he, since never in the whole of his life has he had a thought which wasn't based upon his own material advancement?' Braine concluded firmly: 'I'm not going to be reproved for materialism by a thoroughgoing middle-class materialist.'[36] Such cutting exchanges are indicative of the apparently unbridgeable chasm between the old order which was still producing social realist novels and an emerging generation of writers yearning for change and nurturing ambitions for innovation. Six months later, Alan Sillitoe received slightly better treatment when Barnes reviewed his novel *The Widower's Son*, 'a tale of painful progress from a Nottinghamshire pit village'. Barnes remarked that Sillitoe's 'prose still tends to confuse awkwardness with integrity' and pointed to 'a miscalculated eight-page reworking of the tired metaphor of love as warfare', but he also praised the 'gritty drive behind the narrative' and found that the novel had 'both individuality and resilience'.[37] Barnes finally met Sillitoe in the late 1990s and found him 'a nice man'.[38]

In *Before She Met Me*, Barnes includes an (invented) extract from a politico-sexual novel by Jack Lupton, *Out of the Dark* (160–1), meant to be a bit 'Braine-ish' and a bit

[32] For the *New Statesman*, Barnes reviewed Jones's *Scenes from Bourgeois Life* which focuses on the 'voluntary sleepiness' of bourgeois life and the 'jogging half-awareness of the bourgeois mind'. Julian Barnes, 'Any Old Irony', *New Statesman*, 30 July 1976, 152.
[33] Mark Lawson remarks that in one of his scrapbooks (not archived at the Harry Ransom Center), Barnes keeps weird newspaper cuttings, 'one reporting that the novelist Alan Sillitoe had been fined £25 for giving his age as 100 on a census form'. Mark Lawson, 'A Short History of Julian Barnes', *Independent Magazine*, 13 July 1991, 34.
[34] Henry Porter, 'The Heart of a Man of Letters', *Independent on Sunday*, 2 April 1995, 6.
[35] Julian Barnes, 'Nice and Nasty', *New Statesman*, 18 June 1976, 822.
[36] John Braine, 'Letters to the Editor', *New Statesman*, 25 June 1976, 848.
[37] Julian Barnes, 'Many a Snip', *New Statesman*, 10 December 1976, 846.
[38] Annotations, 22–27 March 2018.

'Melvish': this love scene between two characters would certainly deserve a very bad review if taken literally, but is a brilliant comic pastiche. Braine also indirectly features when Jack tells Graham about his first wife Valerie with whom he used to have rows in the late 1950s and early 1960s: 'Not your sort of milieu, old cunty; it was all *Room at the Top* and *A Kind of Loving* stuff' (50). Braine's 1957 novel and Stanley Barstow's 1960 book (turned into a film starring June Ritchie in 1962) are emblematic of the kind of 'kitchen sink realism' which focused on the life trajectories of working-class characters. Valerie's rows with Jack justify the echo with the Angry Young Men, although her anger was domestic rather than social and political, while the name of the eccentric and promiscuous middle-class novelist Jack Lupton (who lives at Repton Gardens) ironically parodies that of ambitious working-class Joe Lampton, the protagonist of *Room at the Top*. *A Kind of Loving* – the story of two working-class lovers in 1960s Lancashire – had already been referred to in *Metroland* as one of the schoolboys venerates his 'signed portrait of June Ritchie in *A Kind of Loving*' (16).[39]

In his response to Lee, Barnes also comments upon his characterization of the female protagonists – Barbara (Graham's first wife), Ann (his second wife) and Sue (Jack's second wife) – as his friend seems to have had some reservations (or 'Buts') about the first two. In his notebook, Barnes wrote: 'make the 3 women more strongly characterized – esp. Sue' and 'firm up characters – tastes, origins, looks' (1.1.1), but in his letter to Lee, he proves quite confident about his coherent characterization of Barbara:

> First wife – 'though very funny, a crude cut-out'. Actually, I didn't write her as funny at all; I wrote her as chilling, and that's how she still strikes me. A sort of refined, disappointed version of part of my mother. It's true that she's always in the same key, but then a) She is a peripheral character, there for (among other things) contrast with Ann; and b), more importantly, we only see her – in person, and then in memory – at the end of a long and soured relationship. People stick in grooves at that sort of time, it seems to me – especially with those they hold responsible for their situation. Barbara is quite jolly at coffee mornings (so I'm told), but would hate Graham to know that; she insists on turning towards him the most guilt-inducing fact – which is what we see.

This description suggests that Barnes thought of Barbara more fully than what is presented to the reader through Graham's perspective (which is necessarily biased). His first wife is indeed repeatedly portrayed as spiteful and bitter in the novel, and

---

[39] In the annotated copy of *Metroland*, Barnes wrote beneath June Ritchie in 2007: 'an early erotic icon' and in 2012, added a remark about the 1982 'TV adaptation of Stan Barstow's novel, which (then being TV reviewer for the Observer) I wrote about. He sent me a friendly letter in reply, which seemed like a closing of a long circle' (Morgan Library 16). In his review of the 1982 TV adaptation of *A Kind of Loving*, Barnes had written: 'Stan Barstow's adaptation of his own trilogy is fond, a touch stately, but enjoyably particular about the texture of long-gone, late-Fifties life.' He also referred to 'the erotic scars inflicted by the incandescent June Ritchie in the 1962 film'. Julian Barnes, 'Television. The Fatal Web', *Observer*, 25 April 1982, 40. June Ritchie also appears in *Metroland* in the list drawn by Tony of women Chris could not possibly have sex with (79).

Graham imagines her 'with her net and trident' (154). When synthetizing the main features of his characters, Barnes saw Barbara as 'short, dark hair, tight-faced cf. Mother?; practical, recriminatory'. The last adjectives aptly fit her depiction in the novel while the parallel with the writer's mother (who would be unflatteringly portrayed in *Nothing to Be Frightened Of* twenty-six years later) is here again confirmed. However, one passage in inner focalization, when Barbara is 'brooding idly about Graham' (72) a few years after their separation, qualifies the disparaging portrait. Although she hasn't forgiven her ex-husband, Barbara is still thinking about him and has softened: 'The initial contempt had died down by now, and even resentment, that normally reliable emotion, no longer invaded her' (72). In other miscellaneous notes, Barnes had included a 'Still to do'/'Add copy' section which showed one unexpected aspect of Graham's first wife: 'Barbara's reasonableness: she even let him come back & copy some of his favourite recipes out of her cookbooks.' This episode was not included in the novel as it would probably have seemed out of character and discordant with Barbara's general attitude towards her ex-husband. In the notebook where Barnes delineated the main lines of plot and characterization for *Before She Met Me*, under 'Needs: other strands', he wrote: 'Barbara: what of her?'. He tentatively thought of a 'subplot': 'Barbara is obstructive re the kids', but also put between brackets: '(reasonable amicable divorce – why, the wives even got on)' (1.1.1), thus suggesting that originally Barbara was maybe not as strident as the final portrait of her.

When it got to his characterization of Ann, Barnes was much less adamant in his response to Lee:

> Second wife. I feel more vulnerable here. I think you are probably right that we don't get inside Ann enough to understand why she goes on with the situation, though I think it's entirely plausible that she does. 'Surely she'd just go' you write. No .... It's a bit like women who stay with men who batter them – which is thought to be a working-class thing (and the woman therefore doesn't leave for economic reasons, as simple as that), but is in fact equally common in middle-class families, though it goes unreported to social workers etc because that's what the middle-classes are like. You keep up the front of marriage; you persuade yourself that things are bound to get better; you don't want to 'let down' your spouse by telling on him/her (in the reverse situation, substitute, say, the alcoholic wife for the battering husband); you don't go to a shrink, because that's not English; you maybe tell a friend (I probably should have given Ann a friend apart from Jack; but I wanted to keep the whole plot as enclosed and claustrophobic as the house it takes place in); you feel vaguely guilty about it yourself, however unguilty you know you are; you turn your face away from words like neurotic, unstable, mad, and find explanations; and you cram the lid on again and again until the whole fucking thing finally explodes. So: I think she would stay, and not tell anyone apart from Jack; but I agree I probably need to have given the reader more to go on to win him/her over the [sic] believing this.

Interestingly, some thirty-five years later in *The Only Story*, Barnes would create a fictional character, Susan Macleod, who partly corresponds to the models of the battered middle-class wife who does not leave her abusive husband and the alcoholic wife whose partner refuses to face the reality of what is taking place. In 1982, Barnes's detailed description of the middle-class attitude of keeping up appearances very closely reflects Ann's tendency to recoil from the truth. For instance, she euphemistically calls the excruciating situation 'one of those hiccups all marriages go through' (141) and decides to give a party as 'a sort of announcement to their friends that nothing was wrong' (142). When Graham starts misbehaving during the party, she significantly draws the curtains, locks the door and offers clichéd excuses: 'Overwork. Worried about the party. Too much drink' (149).

In an earlier private conversation, Ann had dared tell Graham: 'I think you're mad' (100) and 'You must be crazy' (101), but her words did not seem to be meant literally and Graham responded with 'unequivocal tenderness' (101). Later on, she worked hard at persuading herself that he was all right: 'Of course, she was sure he wasn't either of those things – an alcoholic or a potential suicide' (129). Even when their close friend Jack non-euphemistically hinted to her 'that Graham was completely off his head' (129) and suggested he might go and see a shrink – but you had to be 'less English' to do that (141) –, she ignored his comments: 'Ann knew better' (129), 'Besides, [Ann and Graham] both believed he was quite sane' (141). In one of the rare longer passages in internal focalization through Ann's mind (in the very last chapter), her refusal to use blunt words is again noticeable, as if language was performative and saying the words 'mad' or 'jealous' would make Graham that way:

> if he thinks all this is about me, he's mad, she thought; then checked herself. Graham wasn't mad. Graham was sad; upset; drunk sometimes; but he was not to be called mad. Just as he was not to be called jealous. That was a word she wouldn't use of him. Again, he was sad; upset; he couldn't handle her past; but he wasn't jealous. (181)

The shift of one letter from 'mad' to 'sad' is how Ann 'turns her face away' and 'crams the lid on', taking refuge in self-delusion. Her repetitive chiasmic construction in a halting rhythm points to her forced (but ineffective) self-persuasion: 'Graham wasn't mad. Graham was sad; ... he was not to be called mad. ... he was not to be called jealous. ... he was sad ... he wasn't jealous.' Ann's shirking away from 'words like neurotic, unstable, mad' (to quote Barnes's letter to Lee) sharply contrasts with the narrator's attitude in *Flaubert's Parrot*:

> Nowadays we aren't allowed to use the word mad. What lunacy. The few psychiatrists I respect always talk about people being mad. Use the short, simple, true words. Dead, I say, and dying, and mad, and adultery. ... Mad has the right sound to it. It's an ordinary word, a word which tells us how lunacy might come and call like a delivery van. (91)

While Geoffrey Braithwaite has no problem repeating the word 'mad', even taking delight in its sonorities, Ann's speech teems with negative forms, a reflection of her refusal to face the truth. There are few passages of inner focalization through Ann in

Before She Met Me because the book is mostly written from Graham's point of view, a narrative choice which justifies the lack of a regular direct access to her mind ('we don't get inside Ann'). In his early notebook, Barnes reflected about point of view and the necessity to enter the male protagonist's mind: 'P.O.V.: do all 4/5 from inside'; 'Not just from Graham's'; 'P.O.V. 3rd person narr. / needs: to get inside him?' (1.1.1).

Ann's relative passivity might also be part of her personality: listing her characteristic features in his notes, Barnes saw her as 'warm, sensible, practical about relationships' and wrote: 'She isn't plastic, or a tease, or remotely unfaithful' (1.1.1). However, the author's misgivings as to the credibility of her resigned and partly neglectful attitude surface not only in his letter to Lee but also in his miscellaneous notes jotted down during the process of composition: 'Ann more aware of G's malaise?'; 'why doesn't Ann say go to a shrink? or something'; 'Ann: doesn't express enough concern? – goes & asks Jack – eg- suggest shrink – talk w[ith] friend? Jack?'. For Barnes, Ann's non-sharing of her concerns with a doctor or a friend is not only due to her middle-class reticence but also due to the author's wish to make the plot 'as enclosed and claustrophobic as the house it takes place in'. And indeed, in notes to himself, Barnes described Graham's place in Clapham as a '*small*, terraced house' (my emphasis).

If the characterization of Barbara and Ann did not entirely convince Hermione Lee, her response to Sue (Jack's second wife) – whom Barnes imagined as 'sharp-charactered, pretty, unsentimental' – was positive, which partly comforted the writer: 'I'm relieved you liked Sue: otherwise I'd conclude – and still partly do – from your letter, that I can't "do" women. This is, naturally, a basic fear every male writer has, or ought to have.' In 1981, Barnes was already busy writing what was to become *Staring at the Sun* which is written from a woman's point of view, and he took it as a test as to whether he could 'do' women.

Lee's next bone of contention, what she called the 'Basic prob', had to do with the confusing mixture of genres in the novel: 'social comedy ... tragic obsession ... grand guignol'. Gently reproving his friend for being 'a bit genre-obsessed', Barnes preferred to describe the book more prosaically as 'an inevitable working-out of a given situation' which can provoke a 'bifurcated response' in the reader: 'most of the time you're meant to laugh while feeling sick in the stomach'. As a consequence, Jack's murder and Graham's suicide at the end are not necessarily tragic or Grand Guignol but can provoke an ambivalent response: 'we can merely feel a jokey frisson at it'. Barnes was deliberately aiming for the opposite of sensationalism and melodrama:

> There are deaths, it seems to me, which merely provoke a sense of the melancholy inevitability of their occurrence; there are murders which are, finally, wearyingly matter-of-fact. Oh yes, you think, yes of course, that's right, that's ... normal. Which is why, in the final chapter, one of Graham's concerns is for is [sic] all 'not to seem like the cinema'; for which, read my desire for it 'not to seem like in books'. As far as possible, given the outward events of the final chapter, I wanted it to be a rather low-key ending. There's nothing flash or over-excited in the prose, for a start; all rather plain.

Jack's murder is indeed described in a prosaic and almost gentle way: '[Graham] walked the last few feet and then, instead of stabbing, seemed merely to walk into Jack with the knife held out ahead of him.' Jack only gives a 'curious falsetto wheeze', his face comes 'slowly around' and his body rolls off 'soundlessly' on to the carpet (174). After Graham stabs his friend more ferociously and doggedly for a few minutes, he carefully rinses his hand, sits down in a chair and sips his coffee. When the time to slit his own throat comes, he makes sure Ann faces towards the garden so she will not see him: 'The main thing, he said to himself, was for it not to seem like a film .... No curtain lines; no melodrama' (182).[40] The description of the act itself is extremely calm and controlled, performed in a 'familiar' and comfortable armchair: 'He sat down again in the familiar armchair, and, with a deliberation and courage which surprised him, cut deeply into both sides of his throat' (182). The sentence is well-balanced and the suicidal gesture is enacted and reported without any sensationalism.

Closely related to the question of literary genre, Lee's suggestions when she attempted to pinpoint what Barnes was actually writing encountered more rebuttals from the author:

> No, it's not in any way a parable, covertly feminist or not. 'A cool (McEwanish) study of an extreme version of what a lot of normal people feel?' Hmmm. McEwanish – I don't <u>think</u> so; I've never thought my writing was at all like Ian's. The 'Hmmm' is mainly because I can't see my own book in that critical phrase. You don't set out to write a 'study', and you don't think of the book's situation as at all 'extreme' – not while you're writing it. You just think, well, there's this bloke, and there's Ret[rospective] Sex[ual] Jeal[ousy], and there's a catalytic event of some sort, and there's a confidant, and so on. You tell the story, and as you write it it all seems close and familiar and rather ordinary.

Here again, Barnes points out that the novel does not tap into the uncanny and the melodramatic: the adjectives 'extreme' and 'McEwanish', although softened by the term 'cool', are contested and replaced by such antithetical words as 'close', 'familiar', 'ordinary'. Barnes was not trying to create the type of unsettling defamiliarization effects his contemporaries Ian McEwan and Martin Amis were aiming for in their disturbingly violent early novels and short stories, such as McEwan's *The Cement Garden* (1978) and *The Comfort of Strangers* (1981) or Amis's *Dead Babies* (1975) and *Other People* (1981).[41] This might be the reason why Barnes discarded the opening he had originally thought of for *Before She Met Me* in his notebook and which sounded more like the incipit of a Duffy thriller (of which Barnes wrote four volumes under the pseudonym of Dan Kavanagh in the early 1980s):

---

[40] In *The Only Story*, Paul Roberts also refuses to let his last meeting with Susan on her deathbed 'seem like a film'. He therefore does not kiss her goodbye, a 'moviemaker's bromide', and she does not 'stir slightly in response ... and offer the trace of a smile' (212–13). Instead, he unmelodramatically stands up, looks at her one more time and tearlessly leaves.

[41] At the same period (1978–9), Kazuo Ishiguro started (but never completed) a novel dealing with a murder followed by a suicide. Reflecting on what he had written of the novel so far, he noted in January 1979: 'there should be much more a sense of tensions lurking beneath it all, but not quite in the way Mckewan [*sic*] uses it' (Harry Ransom Center archives, Kazuo Ishiguro Papers, 51.1).

Novel opening – retrospective sexual jealousy

'Have you ever set out to kill someone you've never met? Of course not. Why should you? Why should anyone? For a contract killing, perhaps, or for an acte gratuit, but the first is a little unlikely and the second, well, philosophically old-fashioned to say the least.' (1.1.1)

In the same way, Barnes countered Lee's comment that '[Graham]'s academic life was a bit thin' by referring to his reluctance to have his book identified with the genre of the campus novel: 'maybe I was instinctively fighting against getting near Lodge/Bradbury territory'. David Lodge's *The British Museum Is Falling Down* (1965) and *Changing Places* (1975) and Malcolm Bradbury's *Eating People Is Wrong* (1959) and *The History Man* (1975) had been successful academic novels in the previous decades. Barnes, who belongs to a younger generation (Bradbury was born in 1932 and Lodge in 1935), had clearly no intention of emulating them.[42] In *Flaubert's Parrot*, Geoffrey Braithwaite even imposes a ban on the genre: 'There is to be a twenty-year ban on novels set in Oxford or Cambridge, and a ten-year ban on other university fiction' (98). All of Barnes's remarks suggest that in *Before She Met Me*, he was looking for his own personal voice and style, unconstrained by critical categories and phrases and unwilling to follow the paths and patterns of his predecessors and contemporaries. Philip Larkin perceived the uniqueness of Barnes's tone to approach a universal theme when he chose *Before She Met Me* as his 'Book of the Year': 'Having shelved Julian Barnes's *Before She Met Me* (Cape) as improbable, I find it coming back like a personal memory. Barnes's hilarious wit is individual, but jealousy (its theme) is unfashionably universal.'[43] Larkin's initial reaction had indeed been mixed (sometimes to the point of contradiction) as in his letter of 20 April 1982 to the author, after reading the book twice, he judged it not only 'very funny, and very observant' but also 'half convincing' as according to him, 'lecturers don't meet starlets'. He concluded in the same self-contradictory vein: 'so much is credible that one wants it to be finally convincing. Only, regrettably, it isn't. But all the same it is gripping & moving'.[44]

In his letter, Larkin wrote he could not 'produce watertight reasons' to explain his response to the book, whereas Barnes's own reaction to Lee's letter offers illuminating insights into the creative process and her questions or reservations were particularly useful to initiate reflections on such essential tools of novel-writing as characterization, genre and plot. One aspect she did not comment upon was the choice of title, a choice which proved difficult and saw Barnes debating for and against a great number of options.

---

[42] In his notebook, Barnes wrote that he made Graham an academic because 'this gives him lots of spare time!' (1.1.1).
[43] Philip Larkin, 'Books of the Year', *Observer*, 5 December 1982, 25.
[44] Anthony Thwaite, ed. *Selected Letters of Philip Larkin. 1940–1985* (London: Faber & Faber, 1992), 667. At about the same period, Kingsley Amis's opinion on Barnes, in a letter of 12 May 1982 addressed to Larkin, was quite colourful: '*Julian Barnes is all right but mad. Wouldn't surprise me if he went for his missis with a hatchet any day.*' Zachary Leader, ed. *The Letters of Kingsley Amis* (London: HarperCollins, 2000), 944.

b. Finding the right title

Finding a title for a novel is often a daunting task. In the case of Barnes's production, while some titles seem to have been chosen fairly early on in the process of composition (*Metroland, Flaubert's Parrot, England, England*),[45] others took a longer time to emerge.[46] When Barnes was asked to provide a title for a non-fictional piece in the *New Yorker* in 2006, provisionally entitled 'What She Would Have Wanted' on the proofs (the final title was 'The Past Conditional'[47] and was to be the beginning of *Nothing to Be Frightened Of*), he wrote: 'I'm hopeless on titles' (3.5). For his collection of short stories *The Lemon Table* (named after the title of the last short story in the volume whose working title was *Rage in Age*), he told Hermione Lee: 'I like the idea of a title whose point you don't get until almost the last page of the book' (2.7.10).

In the case of *Before She Met Me*, Barnes still had no definitive title on the top copy with final corrections. He therefore typed a provisional mock title – *Wet Dreams about the Royal Family*[48] – which he then crossed out, writing 'title to come' (1.1.3), and on the next typescript, simply wrote 'New Novel (Untitled)' (1.1.4). Another annotated title page (on which Barnes asks his wife if she wants the dedication, to which she replies 'Si') sports 'Brains' in larger letters and boxed at the top – a title which also appears twice in Barnes's early notebook (1.1.1). One page in longhand and one typed page (with more titles added in longhand) testify to Barnes's difficulties in finding a title (1.1.4) as they include more than seventy options. At the top of the page in longhand appears the indication 'title sexy rather than safe' next to 'South from the Heart'. Although the meaning of 'safe' is unclear, one may surmise that the titles related to 'Head/Brain' and reason fall within that category, and they are the most numerous:

> A Sensible Man; A Reasonable Man; Within Reason; Without Reason; Reasoning Powers; For Reason or Reasons Unknown; Brains; Reason Enough; A Head Start; Reason Not the Need; The Season of Reason, The Dream of Reason; Dreams of Reason; Needs Must; The Soft Box;[49] Reasons for Everything; Reasons of State; Sex in the Head; Sex on the Brain; Head Over Heels; It Stands to Reason; The Brainbox; On the Brain; All in the Mind; Head First; Headlong; Mind Out; The Sleep of Reason; The Skull Beneath the Skin; Inside the Head of Graham Hendrick; Guts in the Head. (Housman)

---

[45] Barnes hesitated between *England, England* and *The Island* for the title of his eighth novel. Hermione Lee preferred the former: 'I think The I. is a little bit dull, and E, E is more intriguing' (1.4.5).
[46] See pp. 117–26 for *Staring at the Sun*, p. 133 for *A History of the World in 10½ Chapters*, pp. 192–5 for *Arthur & George* and pp. 223–5 for *The Sense of an Ending*.
[47] Julian Barnes, 'The Past Conditional', *New Yorker*, 25 December 2006/1 January 2007, 56–64.
[48] Barnes came up with another amusing mock title for the short story 'Gardeners' World', published in *Pulse* (61–78): 'What's This We Shit, Paleface?' (3.4) – a phrase his wife, Pat Kavanagh, used.
[49] The expression 'soft box' to refer to the brain appears twice in the novel: 'maybe there was only enough jealousy chemical in that soft box up there for a certain number of years' (122) and 'At some stage, obviously, the whole soft box just began to wear out; bits fell off it' (139). 'The Soft Box' was a potential title for Chapter Eight (1.1.5) and appeared as a possible title for the novel in Barnes's early notebook (1.1.1).

All these titles related to the same semantic field anticipate the first epigraph by the American neuroscientist Paul D. MacLean about man having three brains (reptilian, lower mammalian and late mammalian) – a theory prosaically relayed to Graham by his friend Jack (78–80) – so that 'when the psychiatrist bids the patient to lie on the couch, he is asking him to stretch out alongside a horse and a crocodile' (7). The title of the last chapter, 'The Horse and the Crocodile', was also considered as a title for the whole book, an allusion to the fact that 'there were two or three different layers of the brain constantly at war with one another' (169). Another option for the title of the last chapter on one draft was 'Between the Heart and the Genitals', an allusion to Graham doggedly stabbing Jack in the same area at the end of the book (174).

When Hermione Lee commented on the draft of the novel, she suggested a comparison with *Mon Oncle d'Amérique* (1980) by French director Alain Resnais, a film which relies on the theories of French physician and philosopher Henri Laborit on evolutionary psychology to describe and explain the fictional characters' behaviours and in which Laborit himself refers to Paul D. MacLean's theory of the three brains. Barnes had seen the film but found Laborit's scientific explanations 'ludicrously didactic':

> My use of MacLean's brain-theory is much more speculative; it's certainly not introduced as 'an answer'. It's just a segment of the book's second theme – namely, one's relationship with one's own brain …, and the way our patterns of cerebration can suddenly shift. I don't intend the three-tier-brain theory as an 'explanation' of how Graham behaves (I don't even know if it's scientifically approved or not), merely as a – slightly depressing – metaphor which Jack introduces him to and which, as far as it influences him, confirms him in his awful drunken determinism. (1.1.4)

The great number of potential titles in the category 'Head/Brain' is thus clearly justified by one of the main themes of the book, but they may not have been Barnes's favourites. In pencil at the top of the page in longhand appears this slightly enigmatic indication: 'K's titles make you say What? Who? Why? Where – i.e. lead you on & in – don't just state.' While 'K' stands for Kingsley Amis[50] whose novels bear such titles as *I Like It Here* and *I Want It Now*, the instruction not to 'just state' in a title may explain why Barnes discarded the most explicit (a possible meaning of 'safe'?) options. However, a few titles in that first list prove intriguing as they exude an intertextual flavour, such as 'Guts in the Head', extracted from a poem by A. E. Housman,[51] which

---

[50] Private email correspondence with the author, 7 May 2017.
[51] In this poem (XVII from *Additional Poems*), the speaker refers to the two troubles which will not let him rest – 'The brains in my head and the heart in my breast' – and pleads to be granted the ease of mind of multitudes that 'rest on their bed / With flint in the bosom and guts in the head'. In 1991, Barnes was asked to name a favourite poem to be included in *Lifelines IV* and chose an untitled poem by Housman, number XII from *Last Poems*, written in circa 1900, whose first lines are 'The laws of God, the laws of man, / He may keep that will and can; Not I'. Barnes wrote that the poem 'could have been addressed to our whole century. It is a passionate plea for individualism, for the right to be oneself, against the bullyings of religion and one's fellow men, against those who are sure they know all the answers'. Julian Barnes, 'Last Poems, XII, A. E. Housman', in *Lifelines: An Anthology of Poems Chosen by Famous People*, ed. Niall Macmonagle (London: Penguin, 1993), 150–1.

can also be related to the fact that Graham chops up giblets to send to Ann's former co-actors. As for 'The Skull Beneath the Skin', it is the second line of T. S. Eliot's 1918 poem 'Whispers of Immortality'[52] and was to be the title of one of P. D. James's detective novels, published the same year as *Before She Met Me*. Barnes also tentatively put down in pencil: 'They're Coming Through the Window' – a line from an old song ('Shut the door! They're coming through the window'), which may echo Graham impulsively 'attacking the french [*sic*] window with a garden fork' (149) and smashing the glass with the handle during a party at his own house. A bout of jealousy against Jack had made Graham take refuge in the garden with a bottle of whisky, where he got so drunk his wife decided to lock the back door, leaving him with no other option than to 'come through the window' (150).

A second category of titles relates to love, passion and jealousy: 'South from the Heart; Graham Hendrick's Meticulous Passion; A Backward Love/Passion; A Particular/Meticulous/Scrupulous/Careful/Precise/Thoroughgoing Passion; A Thoughtful Love/Passion; The Heart', but also on another page: 'The Words Man; The Fuller Life; The Sexual Life; The Jealousy Man'. The 'words man' is how Graham describes himself to Jack (125, 139), which makes it all the more surprising that his jealousy should rely so much on images, a point on which Barnes insists in his notebook: 'Make the point that it's the visual evidence which sends him tonto: the films are catalytic, whereas spoken & written evidence hasn't upset him so much'; 'the point is, G despises the cinema yet the visual evidence is what hits him hardest' (1.1.1).

The potential title 'The Fuller Life' comes from a 1919 poem by Rudyard Kipling, 'The Gods of the Copybook Headings' (1919), composed of proverbs and maxims. Two lines are quoted by Jack who is looking for a way to make Graham leave:

On the first Feminian sandstones we were promised the Fuller Life
(Which started by loving our neighbour and ended by loving his wife) (127)

While the 'Feminian sandstones' provided the title for Chapter Eight, the next (unquoted) line in Kipling's poem is 'Till our women had no more children and *the men lost reason* and faith' (my emphasis), a segment which fits Graham's downward spiral into madness.

Passion and jealousy can indeed veer on obsession and insanity, making way for a series of more ominous titles: 'A Dangerous Love; The Edge of Things; The Dangerous Edge; A Polite Obsession; Private Mania; The Possessive Case; Nature's Revenge'. Graham's neurosis leads him to send vengeful Jiffy bags of offal to actors who had played in films with his wife, thus justifying the titles related to food – 'The Tender Parts; Frivolities; The Tenderloin'. '*Frivolités*' is what a French butcher calls a bull's testicles as Graham and Ann learned in Castres (128) and it appears at the top of a page in the notebook (1.1.1), but the title was discarded for the whole novel on account of it sounding 'like short stories'.

---

[52] The first two lines are: 'Webster was much possessed by death / And saw the skull beneath the skin.' T. S. Eliot, *Collected Poems 1909–1962* (London: Faber & Faber, 1974), 56.

The last category of titles (which seem to have come later) relates to the past, thus pointing towards Graham's retrospective jealousy: 'A Previous Life; Second Time Round; Second Coming; A Backward Glance; Looking Backwards; The Day Before Yesterday; Yesterday's Love; Yesterday's Men; Recollect'. Two literary quotes evoking the past have also been considered as potential titles. The first is 'He Looked Over Her Shoulder', adapted from the first line of W. H. Auden's 1952 poem 'The Shield of Achilles' ('She looked Over His shoulder'), and an allusion to Graham's backward glance towards his wife's past. The second is 'Call Back Yesterday', taken from Shakespeare's *Richard II*, when the Earl of Salisbury tells Richard they arrived 'One day too late' so that 'all the Welshmen, hearing thou wert dead. / Are gone to Bolingbroke, dispersed and fled.' Salisbury then exclaims: 'O, call back yesterday, bid time return' (III, 2).

The title 'Before She Met Me' only appears at the very bottom of the second page of potential titles in longhand, thus suggesting that the idea came fairly late. Barnes's insistence on temporal landmarks is also perceptible in the first (then deleted) title of Chapter One – 'The Honey Time' (1.1.5) – a reference to the idyllic period at the beginning of Graham and Ann's relationship (11, 52, 153). This title appeared in Barnes's early notebook when he listed the novels he was going to write, the second one being '??The Honey Time' (1.1.1). Barnes's recurrent preoccupation with time, memory and one's relation to the past probably impelled him to choose not only *Before She Met Me* as the definitive title for his second novel but also for such more recent publications as *The Sense of an Ending* and *The Noise of Time*. The writer's painstaking efforts not only to find an adequate title but also to master his characterization of women were part of his apprenticeship as a young novelist who was gaining confidence in his own skills and would soon veer towards a more experimental type of fiction with *Flaubert's Parrot*.

3

A chronology (of sorts)

1856–7	Publication of *Madame Bovary* by Gustave Flaubert, not only 'the first modern novel, a great study of failure, a humane killer applied to the head of Romanticism' but also 'the first great shopping-and-fornicating novel, a critique of the materialist impulse'.[1]
1909	22 June. Birth of Albert Leonard Barnes, the writer's father. According to his elder son Jonathan, a man of dry wit and Air Force slang, in whom 'the art of understatement is better developed than [in] anyone else [he has] met'.[2]
1915	24 June. Birth of Kathleen Mabel Scoltock, the writer's mother. Evoking a picture of his mother in her mid-thirties, Barnes notes that she looks 'stylish', 'friendly yet determined', 'a young woman with many different possibilities of life ahead of her'. He concludes: 'I wish she hadn't turned out to be my mother – though, in a way, more for her sake than for mine.'[3]
1915	30 November. Barnes's maternal grandfather, Bert Scoltock, enlists in the 17th Battalion, Lancashire Fusiliers. He is discharged on 13 November 1917, invalided out with trench foot. Apart from a few 'available scraps', nothing much can be known about his time in the war and these silences are stimulating for the fiction writer: '[W]hat you can't find out, and where that leaves you, is one of the places where the novelist starts.'[4] In 'Tunnel', the last short story of *Cross Channel*, an elderly English writer evokes the memory of this very same grandfather, also invalided out with trench foot, also 'gone beyond memory', a man whose forgotten 'distant truths … could only be sought by a different technique, the one in which the man's grandson still specialised'.[5]

---

[1] Julian Barnes, 'Listener, They Wore It: Charles's Cap (*Madame Bovary*)', BBC Radio 3, 11 February 2013, http://www.bbc.co.uk/programmes/b01qkw6j. Accessed on 19 January 2019.
[2] William Leith, 'Too Clever by 10½', *The Tatler*, July 1989, 92.
[3] Julian Barnes, 'My Mother Before I Knew Her', *Guardian*, 5 March 2016, http://www.theguardian.com/books/2016/mar/05/writers-mothers-photographs-carol-ann-duffy. Accessed on 19 January 2019.
[4] Barnes, *Nothing to Be Frightened Of*, 238.
[5] Julian Barnes, *Cross Channel* (London: Jonathan Cape, 1996), 206.

1942–5	Barnes's father is in India in the RAF as an officer. According to his elder son Jonathan, 'it seemed clear to me that the years in India were the best years of our Father's life; and that can't have thrilled our Mother'.[6] When Albert Barnes left for India, his wife was pregnant with their first son.
1942	26 December. Birth of Jonathan Barnes, a future philosopher. In *Nothing to Be Frightened Of*, Barnes gives some basic facts about his brother so that the reader can get 'a clear enough picture' of him and finishes with: 'Oh yes, and he often wears a kind of eighteenth-century costume designed for him by his younger daughter: knee breeches, stockings, buckle shoes on the lower half; brocade waistcoat, stock, long hair tied in a bow on the upper. Perhaps I should have mentioned this before'.[7]
1946	19 January. Birth of Julian Patrick Barnes in Fielding Johnson Hospital in Leicester. The family lives in Coalville. Reflecting on the characterization of Martha Cochrane in *England, England* several decades later, he writes: 'Better if she comes from a "normal" family. /like me!?/' (1.3.3)
1946	A few weeks after Barnes's birth, the family moves to 55 Goldsmith Avenue in Acton, a western suburb of London. They occupy one half of a sturdy Edwardian red-brick villa for the next ten years. Every day to go to school, Barnes turns along Shakespeare Road, crossing Milton Road, Cowper Road, Myrtle Road and Spencer Road. He wonders: 'Did any sly literary imprinting take place?'[8] A childhood memory: 'the only moment of deep fear I can locate in my first ten years came when a boy called Kelly stepped out from behind a tree in Goldsmith Avenue, stuck something into the small of my back and snarled, "Don't move or I'll plug you." I was terrified for several elastic minutes before he let me go. As I fled I looked back and saw that he was holding in his hand a three-pin, fifteen-amp electric plug. My first introduction not just to fear, but also to wordplay. No wonder I distrust puns as cheap, sneaky things.'[9]
1951	Starts supporting Leicester City Football Club, the onset of decades spent 'poised between mild hopefulness and draining disappointment'. Remarks later: 'supporting Leicester is very good training for supporting England. You get hardened to the disappointment, so it doesn't hurt as much'.[10] See 2015 and 2016.
1953	At the age of 7, cameo (non-speaking) appearance as Third Wise Man in school production.[11] This marks the end of Barnes's acting career. The

---

[6] Email from Jonathan Barnes to Julian Barnes, 23 May 2007 (3.5).
[7] Barnes, *Nothing to Be Frightened Of*, 156.
[8] Barnes, 'Diary. Ambushed'.
[9] Ibid. The anecdote is also recorded in *Nothing to Be Frightened Of*, the detail of the plug triggering off the question: 'So why did I become a novelist rather than he?' (162).
[10] Julian Barnes, 'My Stupid Leicester City Love', *Guardian*, 6 May 2016, http://www.theguardian.com/football/2016/may/06/julian-barnes-leicester-city-premier-league-stupid-love. Accessed on 19 January 2019.
[11] Julian Barnes, *Keeping an Eye Open* (London: Jonathan Cape, 2015), 2.

epigraph to the second part of *Staring at the Sun* is: '*Three* wise men – are you serious? / *graffito, c.1984*.'

1955 Comes first in the long jump and third in the boot race.[12]

1956 The family moves to Northwood, in a northwest suburban area in Middlesex known as Metroland. For six years, travels by the Metropolitan, Bakerloo and District Lines from Northwood to Blackfriars to go to the City of London School: 'This transition from calm, green suburbia to vibrant metropolis felt in the main a simple psychological process: from family dullsville to the centre of the world.'[13]

1959 At the age of 13, first family trip to France aboard their first car, a Triumph Mayflower, voted in 2000 'one of the ten ugliest cars ever built': 'At Newhaven we watched nervously as the Mayflower was slung by crane with routine insouciance over our heads and down into the ferry's hold.'[14]

1959–60 Woken up by the *réveil mortel*, a phrase coined by the French critic Charles du Bos, friend and translator of Edith Wharton, to refer to the awareness of death. Barnes offers as a translation 'the wake-up call to mortality'.[15]

1960 Sacked as captain of his school rugby team because of his reluctance to tackle.[16]

1961 Addiction 'until shamefully late into [his] teens' to the boys' papers *The Rover, The Adventure, The Wizard* and *The Hotspur*, 'comic-land's equivalent of *Le Monde*.'[17]

1963 Wins the Arthur Tempest Pollard Prize for Modern Languages, the Sir George Carroll Prize for French[18] and the Mortimer English prize. As his award for the latter, chooses Joyce's *Ulysses*, handed over by the Lord Mayor of London with a disapproving look.[19]

1964 Wins a scholarship to Oxford. 'I got home from school and a letter was waiting for me. I opened it up and said, "I got a scholarship." My mother said, "Yes, I thought it was that." It was a classic dampening down. Let's not get too excited.'[20]

1964 Summer. First trip to Paris. 'I was lonely in the Métro, on the streets, and in the public parks where I would sit on a bench by myself reading a Sartre novel, which was probably about existential isolation.'[21]

---

[12] Barnes, *Nothing to Be Frightened Of*, 27.
[13] Julian Barnes, 'A London View', *Granta* 65 (Spring 1999): 176.
[14] Barnes, *Something to Declare*, ix. In the short story 'Tunnel', the elderly writer remembers his first 'family motoring holiday' when he was about 13: 'They anchored your car to a wooden pallet on the Newhaven quayside and swung it into the depths of the ship as if it were a piece of merchandise' (*Cross Channel* 192).
[15] Barnes, *Nothing to Be Frightened Of*, 23.
[16] Lawson, 'A Short History', 35. In the annotated copy of *Metroland*, Barnes writes that he was sacked 'probably correctly, probably for cowardice' (Morgan Library 67).
[17] Julian Barnes, 'Comic Cuts', *New Statesman*, 28 January 1977, 135.
[18] Bruce Todd, 'Endings and Beginnings: The Success of Author Julian Barnes', *The Gazette* 303 (Summer 2012): 8.
[19] Julian Barnes, 'A Life with Books' (London: Jonathan Cape, 2012), 7.
[20] Wroe, 'Literature's Mister Cool', 6.
[21] Julian Barnes, *Levels of Life* (London: Jonathan Cape, 2013), 112.

1964	Visits the Musée Gustave Moreau in Paris. First time 'consciously looking at pictures rather than being passively and obediently in their presence'.[22] In *Metroland*, the narrator visits the museum in 1968 and it becomes one of his favourite haunts. When Barnes goes back to the museum fifty years later in 2014, he finds Moreau art 'not odd enough'.[23]
1964	Sees Géricault's 'The Raft of the Medusa' for the first time in the Louvre.
1964–8	In his own words, 'remarkably inactive' at Magdalen College, Oxford.[24] Reads modern languages (French and Russian), does a year of PPP (Philosophy/Politics/Psychology) before changing back to modern languages. One of his tutors in French is the distinguished Flaubertian scholar Alan Raitt who later became a friend: 'I remember once trying to wing it rather on the French Realist novel, and being brought up chasteningly with, "Which of Champfleury's novels have you actually read?"'[25]
1964–8	Was not affected by flower power in the 1960s: 'I wore my hair long, and had a pair of purple jeans which were excruciatingly uncomfortable at the crotch; but I knew only one person who ever mentioned drugs. … I knew about LSD because I'd read my Aldous Huxley, and about opium because of Cocteau and Françoise Sagan. … I suppose I was sixties-ish in not thinking in any practical terms about the future, just blithely assuming things would turn out in some pleasant but undefined way.'[26]
1965	Goes on a six-week trip to Eastern Europe with seven other students in a dormobile, 'driving from England through Germany and Poland to Russia, up to Leningrad, down to Kiev and Odessa, into Romania, Hungary, Czechoslovakia and home'.[27]
1966–7	English *assistant* at the Collège Saint-Martin in Rennes,[28] a Catholic school: 'Most of the Fathers treated my atheism – like my nationality, my long hair, and my austerity in the face of wine – as something basically odd but tolerable.'[29]
1967	10 March, Rennes. Buys *Émaux et Camées* by Théophile Gautier and reads it for an essay on the Parnassian poets.[30] Gautier's lines on the immortality

---

[22] Barnes, *Keeping an Eye Open*, 4.
[23] Ibid., 9.
[24] Olinda Adeane, 'Barnestorming', *Harpers & Queen*, April 1982, 151.
[25] Julian Barnes, 'Alan Raitt Remembered.' The Royal Society of Literature, https://rsliterature.org/fellow/alan-raitt/. Accessed on 19 January 2019. (Barnes's speech at the memorial service for Alan Raitt at Magdalen College, Oxford, on 6 January 2007.)
[26] Julian Barnes, 'Days I'll Remember', in *Changing Times: Being Young in Britain in the '60s*, by Alison Pressley (London: Michael O'Mara, 2000), 65.
[27] Lidia Vianu, 'Giving Up Criticism Is Much Easier Than Giving Up Alcohol or Tobacco. Interview with Julian Barnes. 8 November 2000', *Desperado Essay-Interviews*. Bucharest: Editura Universitatii din Bucuresti, 2006, http://lidiavianu.scriptmania.com/julian_barnes.htm. Accessed on 19 January 2019.
[28] In 'Tunnel', the elderly writer also taught as an *assistant* in Rennes (*Cross Channel* 204).
[29] Barnes, *Something to Declare*, 21.
[30] Deleted passage from *Nothing to Be Frightened Of* (3.5).

of art are quoted in *Metroland*[31] and in *Nothing to Be Frightened Of*[32] but Barnes later doubts their validity: 'Those proud lines of Gautier's I was once so attached to – everything passes, except art in its robustness; kings die, but sovereign poetry lasts longer than bronze – now read as adolescent consolation.'[33]

1968 During a viva for his finals, 'a rather stern Pascal scholar' asks him what he wants to do. When replying he rather hopes to become an academic, the austere don counters: 'Have you thought about journalism?'[34]

1968 On coming down from Oxford, takes the Civil Service exams and fails to get into the Foreign Office (during the interview, says he does not like the idea of living abroad). Is offered a job as a tax inspector, which he turns down. Comments a few years later: 'Governor of the BBC would have suited me more at the time.'[35]

1969–72 Works in Oxford as an editorial assistant on the first volume of the *Oxford English Dictionary Supplement* (letters B to G for rude and sports words post-1880), sharing his basement office 'with an elderly lady proofreader of daunting meticulousness' whose 'bearing discouraged levity'.[36] Spends days reading through books on cricket, trying to find the earliest printed use of the word 'gully'[37] or 'leafing through fifteen books on ice-hockey in the Bodleian Library, looking for an earlier use of a term for some abstruse item of goal-tender's apparel'.[38]

Tries to get 'blow job' into the OED Supplement: '[I] presented my admittedly thin evidence – perhaps a quote from Burroughs or one from Henry Miller – to the Editor. He considered my application but declined it. "I'm afraid there isn't as much of this about as you imagine," he commented sympathetically, and so in 1972 the term was deemed not to exist.'[39]

Reads somewhere that 'carrying on at Oxford without really being a part of the university was a bit like sitting in your bathwater and feeling it getting cold'.[40]

---

[31] Barnes, *Metroland*, 55.
[32] Barnes, *Nothing to Be Frightened Of*, 18.
[33] Ibid., 205.
[34] Interview by Guppy, in *Conversations*, ed. Guignery and Roberts, 67.
[35] Peter Hill, 'A Student Dreamer Who Woke to Fame', *Oxford Journal*, 9 April 1982, 13.
[36] Julian Barnes, 'Books', *Harpers & Queen*, March 1989, 60. This lady inspired the character of the lexicographer Miss Moss in the short story 'Evermore' (collected in *Cross Channel*), except that her fiancé, instead of being killed in the First World War as in the short story, had run off to Russia to join the revolution. Annotations, 22–27 March 2018.
[37] Julian Barnes, 'Changing My Mind. Words.' BBC Radio 3, 6 December 2016, https://www.bbc.co.uk/programmes/b084fvlv. Accessed on 19 January 2019.
[38] Barnes, 'Books', 62.
[39] Ibid., 60.
[40] Nancy Robb, 'The Novel Diversions of Julian Barnes', *Quill & Quire*, June 1989, 50.

1971	Father retires from St Clement Danes school where he has taught French since 1937. As recorded by his son, 'he was engaged at a salary of £381 per annum, rising in yearly increments of £15 to a maximum of £528'. His former headmaster sends him a letter that includes the line: 'I think you could have taught French even to elephants.'[41]
1972	Moves to London to read for the bar. Shares a flat with architectural historian Andrew Saint who later becomes a professor at Cambridge and then at University College, London. Saint, the first to be thanked for 'general help and advice' in Barnes's *Literary Guide to Oxford* (1.8.6), recalls the time as one of 'drifting around in that semi-privileged post-Oxford languor'.[42]
1973	25 May. Publishes his first book review, of Donald Insall's *The Care of Old Buildings Today*, and finds the author's 'bland approval' of his own firm's preservation work on thirteen buildings 'irritating'.[43] The review takes a detour route before being published: 'A book came out on [architecture] and I thought it was terrible, so I wrote a review and sent it off to the papers. The *Spectator* and the *Times Educational Supplement* both accepted it. So I wrote a very pompous letter to the *TES* explaining that I would prefer it to be printed in the *Spectator* – and then the *Spectator* never ran it, which was rather humiliating.'[44] Has to ask the *Spectator* to send it back in order to have it published in the *Times Educational Supplement*.
1973–6	From late 1973 to January 1976, publishes forty-five reviews in the *Times Literary Supplement*, most of which are printed without a byline because of the policy at the time of publishing anonymous reviews.[45]
1975	At a literary party, meets Tom Maschler, the editorial director of Jonathan Cape which was to publish 'A Self-Possessed Woman', Barnes's first short story, in *The Times Anthology of Ghost Stories*. Introduces himself but Maschler does not recognize the name. Is asked for the title of his short story, but cannot remember it. Comments: 'Welcome to the literary life.'[46]
1976–8	Contributor to the *New Review*. Ian McEwan recalls: 'The conversation was hilarious and quick; the company irresistible. In a way it was like finding a home, a world in a set of contemporaries.'[47]
1977	Hired as deputy literary editor by Anthony Howard at the *New Statesman*, working alongside Martin Amis (the literary editor), Christopher

---

[41] 'You Ask the Questions: Julian Barnes', *Independent*, 16 January 2002, 8.
[42] Wroe, 'Literature's Mister Cool', 7.
[43] Julian Barnes, 'Scraping and Grimthorping', *Times Educational Supplement*, 25 May 1973, 24.
[44] Michele Field, 'From a Sat-Upon Son to an Honorary Frog', *Sydney Morning Herald*, 27 February 1988, 72.
[45] Roberts, *Pseudonym as Character*, 11.
[46] Julian Barnes, 'Lost for Words', in *Mortification, Writers' Stories of Their Public Shame*, ed. Robin Robertson (London: 4th Estate, 2003), 38.
[47] Caroline Daniel, 'Lunch with FT: Ian McEwan', *Financial Times*, 24 August 2012, http://www.ft.com/intl/cms/s/2/a54cd796-eba3-11e1-9356-00144feab49a.html. Accessed on 19 January 2019.

	Hitchens and James Fenton. Remembers Anthony Howard as 'a very benevolent boss': 'he was very sentimental and proud of what he called "his boys" – and they were mainly boys'.[48]
1977	23 June. Date of Uncle Arthur's death in *Metroland*. Notes in 2007: 'I see I made Arthur die on the day between my father's birthday (22) & my mother's (24). I wonder if this is significant.'[49] Almost forty years later, notes that Referendum Day for or against Brexit 'fell strangely, smack between the birthday of my Francophile father (22 June) and my Francophile mother (24 June), both long dead'.[50]
1979	1 September. Camden Registry Office. Marries Pat Kavanagh. Chooses this as his 'personal favourite moment in London'.[51] Likes to quote Ford Madox Ford: 'You marry to continue the conversation.'[52]
1979	As deputy literary editor, moves from the *New Statesman*, 'small, fraternal, left-wing' to the *Sunday Times*, 'large, internally competitive and politically centrist'.[53] Two years earlier, wrote in the *New Statesman* under the pseudonym of Edward Pygge that the *Sunday Times* had 'on the whole fewer buffoons writing for it' than the *Times* and referred to 'their normal method of acquiring talent (buying up reviewers who have proved themselves elsewhere)'.[54]
1980	29 February. Paddy Beesley (once of Barnes's pseudonyms in the *New Statesman*) sets the newspaper's Weekend Competition: 'A recent survey revealed that on average an American couple spends 27 minutes of the week actually talking to one another. This is, of course, an exaggeration: they obviously don't exchange more than, oh, 150 words. Transcribe the exchange, or exchanges, which make up this weekly tally.'[55]
1980	2 May. *Metroland* banned for its colloquial language by the board of censors in South Africa. Appears on the same list of 'publications under embargo awaiting decision' as Toni Morrison's *The Bluest Eye* (1970), Edward Lucie-Smith's *Art in the Seventies* (1980) and Melvyn Bragg's *Kingdom Come* (1980). Barnes's father found the language of *Metroland* 'a bit lower deck'.[56] His mother could not get over the 'bombardment' of filth.[57]

[48] Soumya Bhattacharya, 'Julian Barnes: "I do believe in grudge-bearing"', *New Statesman*, 12–25 April 2013, 38.
[49] Annotated copy of *Metroland* (Morgan Library 160).
[50] Julian Barnes, 'Diary', *London Review of Books* 39, no. 8 (20 April 2017): 41.
[51] John O'Connell, 'Julian Barnes: Interview', *Time Out*, 18 September 2008, https://www.timeout.com/london/things-to-do/julian-barnes-interview. Accessed on 15 October 2019.
[52] Barnes, *Through the Window*, 66; *Levels of Life*, 102.
[53] Julian Barnes, 'Union Blues', *New Yorker*, 21–28 April 2003, 145.
[54] Barnes, 'Greek Street', October 1977, 1.
[55] Julian Barnes [Paddy Beesley, pseud.], 'Weekend Competition. No 2606', *New Statesman*, 29 February 1980, 334.
[56] Annotated copy of *Metroland* (Morgan Library 177).
[57] Barnes, *Nothing to Be Frightened Of*, 161, 183.

1980	June. Under the pseudonym of Basil Seal, writes in a restaurant review about Simpson's in the Strand: 'The meat is good, but overcooked; the Yorkshire pudding relaxes beside the meat for a couple of hours without being replaced, so that late lunchers might as well chew on slices of corrugated cardboard; the cabbage has that iron, spinachy flavour you might remember from school, and it lands on your plate soggy but still faithful to the shape of the spoon that transported it.'[58]
1980	July. Appears on the front page of *Gay News* for the publication of his first detective novel *Duffy* under the pseudonym of Dan Kavanagh.[59]

Six years later, says the review which pleased him the most in his career so far was about *Duffy* and published in *Police World*.[60] In his eight-line 'review', Hugh Vectis called the novel 'about the most realistic picture of the sourdid [sic] life that is Soho you are likely to read' (1.18). |
1981	25 September. Is one of the 1,400 employees of the *Sunday Times* suspended without pay by Rupert Murdoch. Eight or nine years later, at the Edinburgh Book Festival, is asked by Murdoch's wife to sign a copy of one of his books for her husband: '"But he once *sacked* me." "Oh, I'm sure it was nothing personal," came the mollifying reply. … my pen blabbed, "To Rupert Murdoch from Julian Barnes." It is the phrase I most regret having written.'[61]
1981	29 October at 11.15 pm. Death of French singer Georges Brassens (after Boris Vian in 1959 and Jacques Brel in 1978). Moment at which Francophone song died for Barnes, 'or at least stopped being interesting'.[62]
1982	Trip to Georgia to spend the £1000 of the Somerset Maugham Award given to him for *Metroland*.[63]
1982	Summer. Stays for a week in Denston, Suffolk, with Arthur Koestler, then aged 77 and suffering from Parkinson's disease and leukaemia. 'I write in the morning, have lunch, read, play chess with Arthur, and go for a run in the early evening.'[64]
1982–6	Television critic for the *Observer* (succeeding Clive James) after having been television critic for the *New Statesman* from 1978 to 1980: 'If you're writing 50 columns a year, that's 200 columns, at 1,200 words, which is a quarter of a million words on television if you add it up …. And there are not more than 250,000 words to be said about television.'[65]

---

[58] Julian Barnes [Basil Seal, pseud.], 'Tatler Restaurants', *Tatler*, June 1980, 15.
[59] Peter Burton, 'Dan Kavanagh/Julian Barnes', *Gay News* 196 (24 July–20 August 1980): 16.
[60] Chris Lloyd, 'Chris Lloyd Talks to Julian Barnes', *Club* 1986: 52 (Barnes's papers, 1.18).
[61] Barnes, 'Union Blues', 145.
[62] Barnes, *Something to Declare*, 19.
[63] The terms of the award stipulate that the prize money be spent on travel.
[64] Julian Barnes, 'Playing Chess with Arthur Koestler', *Yale Review* 77, no. 4 (Summer 1988), 480.
[65] Elizabeth Kastor, 'Julian Barnes' Big Questions', *Washington Post Book World*, 18 May 1987, B9.

1983	Included in *Granta*'s *Best of Young British Novelists* alongside Martin Amis, Pat Barker, William Boyd, Kazuo Ishiguro, Ian McEwan, Salman Rushdie, Graham Swift and others. Rushdie is not available for the group photograph.
1984	Doubtful about the chances of success of *Flaubert's Parrot*: 'My first two novels had sold 1,000 or so copies in hardback and had just about staggered into paperback – on separate lists, each of which had collapsed shortly afterwards. I suspected that *Flaubert's Parrot* might interest a few Flaubertians, and perhaps a smaller number of psittacophiles.'[66]
1984	21 October. Refers to the television broadcast of the Booker Prize ceremony in which *Flaubert's Parrot* was shortlisted and Anita Brookner's *Hotel du Lac* won. Notes that there was no 'half-time divertissement': 'Instead we had a jolly old-fashioned interlude with swans drifting around on a lake. A *lake*? Ah-ah: clearly a tip-off that "Hotel du Lac" was going to be the winner; but by then, alas, Ladbrokes was closed.'[67]
1985	Meets Jay McInerney at the publication party of *Bright Lights, Big City*. They start a fax correspondence which is mostly devoted to wine. McInerney recalls: 'I'd been known to jump on a plane to London if my friend Julian Barnes, who has a world-class cellar and isn't afraid to uncork his treasures, invited me to dinner.'[68]
1986	29 June. Last television review for the *Observer* about football and tennis. Starts with a reference to Camus who believed that 'life was rather like football: governed by arbitrary rules, yet capable of pleasing harmony'.[69] Mentions one of the novelties in the Wimbledon tennis tournament: 'a vexingly increased volume on that service-error machine (housemen slumbering before the telly doubtless jerk awake and answer their bleepers by mistake)' (1.16.2).
1987	4 December. On a postcard to Barnes, Redmond O'Hanlon (aka Fats or Fatso) provides bibliographical references on Darwin for his novel *A History of the World in 10½ Chapters* and adds: 'write when you're ready and not before' (1.7.2).
1989	June. Publication of *A History of the World in 10½ Chapters*. 'I have a novel out this week, and am disguising anxiety by fretting about the next book instead. It's a toss-up between the Obsessive Love novel and the London novel – unless it turns out that one fits inside the other, as with those recipes where you stuff a duck into a goose and cook them together.'[70] The next book was *Talking It Over*.

[66] Julian Barnes, 'When Flaubert Took Wing', *Guardian*, 5 March 2005, 20.
[67] Julian Barnes, 'Television. The Afternoon of Vietnam', *Observer*, 21 October 1984, 26.
[68] Jay McInerney, *A Hedonist in the Cellar: Adventures in Wine* (New York: Knopf, 2006), xvi.
[69] Barnes referred to Camus's belief thirty years later in *Nothing to Be Frightened Of*: 'Life as a game of football, its rules arbitrary yet necessary.' Barnes, *Nothing to Be Frightened Of*, 184.
[70] Barnes, 'Diary. Ambushed'.

1989	The review of *A History of the World in 10½ Chapters* which pleases Barnes most appears in a British rock magazine: 'It did not say much about the book but it did firmly point out that Géricault's painting *The Raft of the Medusa* was best known as the cover for the Pogues' album *Rum, Sodomy and the Lash*.'[71]
1989	Is offered a job by the *Independent* to go around the world covering the great sporting events: The World Cup. The Kentucky Derby. The Tokyo Sumo Championship. Turns it down.[72]
1990	After visiting his friend Dodie Smith, the author of *I Capture the Castle* and *The Hundred and One Dalmatians*, then aged 94, 'incredibly frail and bedridden', writes in his diary: 'What's it like, what's it like? Even if one retains health and cheerfulness, it can't be much fun.'[73] Dodie Smith dies on 24 November.
1992	Publication of *The Porcupine*. 'When I finished *The Porcupine*, that was nearly a 20-year period when I had always been at work on a novel. I thought, why don't I step back from it for a bit and refresh my thoughts about the novel, what I can do, and what the novel can do? It didn't work. A novelist does his or her thinking about a novel when writing it.'[74]
1992	Death of his father. Writes in *Nothing to Be Frightened Of*: 'as I grow older, … my resemblance to my dead father strikes me more and more.'[75] His brother notes: 'what strikes me in your case is that you speak as he did (if I hear you on the radio, I can't tell whether it's you or our father)'.[76]
1993	September–October. Attends the Nigel Short–Gary Kasparov final at the *Times* World Chess Championship in London, not at the Savoy Theatre where the games were taking place, but across the street at Simpson's-in-the-Strand in the Grandmasters' Analysis Room with 'space to roar and burble, chunter and chatter, rage and wail'.[77] Devotes a twenty-eight-page essay to the match and mentions the limited merits of showing on television two seated players thinking in public.
1994	February. Recalls in one of his 'Letters from London' for the *New Yorker* that the month before, he took part in a 'fund-raiser for a cash-strapped Oxford college'. At short notice, Salman Rushdie replaced the other advertised novelist who 'was at the last minute unavoidably unable to make it'. Barnes clarifies: '(he had unavoidably gone skiing, but the fictioneers' freemasonry does not permit me to finger him)'. In the index to *Letters from London*, for the entry 'McEwan, Ian', the unique reference is 'unavoidably gone skiing'.[78]

---

[71] Barnes, 'Short Story/Essay', 175.
[72] Leith, 'Too Clever by 10½', 92.
[73] Valerie Grove, *Dear Dodie. The Life of Dodie Smith* (London: Pimlico, [1996] 2002), 321.
[74] Interview by the *Observer*, in *Conversations*, ed. Guignery and Roberts, 30.
[75] Barnes, *Nothing to Be Frightened Of*, 118.
[76] Email from Jonathan Barnes to Julian Barnes, 12 February 2007 (3.5).
[77] Barnes, *Letters from London*, 264.
[78] Ibid., 293, 349.

1995	19 April. Writes to Jay McInerney's wife: 'I've been reflecting on the Snore Question, how, why, when, where, and to what extent it constitutes grounds for justifiable homicide. (I think Yes is the answer and we yet live only courtesy of our wives.) Now we have established that the likelihood of snoring after white wines is less than after red wines. Port seems always to make one snore, though there is also the factor in this case that by the time you get on to port you are right pissed anyway.'[79]
1995	26 October. As visiting professor for a semester at Johns Hopkins University in Baltimore, gives a lecture entitled 'Cigarettes, Syphilis and Genius'.
1995	Had most of the ideas for *England, England* when in the United States: 'If anything the distance has given me a deeper perspective of my own country.'[80] The book 'came out of seeing the year 2000 about to arise and thinking, "This will be a time to reflect, not on the state of Britain, but on the idea of Britain, and by extension the idea of the old nation states"'.[81]
1995	2 December. Invited on the BBC Radio 3 programme 'Private Passions', chooses music by Berlioz, Georges Brassens, Noël Coward, Gounod, Mozart, Ravel, Satie and Sibelius.
1996	28 January. Invited on the BBC Radio 4 programme 'Desert Island Discs', chooses:

'Stabat Mater' by Giovanni Battista Pergolesi
'Mon Père Disait' by Jacques Brel
'Simple Gifts', Shaker song set by Aaron Copland
'Struggle Buggy' by Clinton Walker, performed by King Oliver and His Orchestra
'String Sextet No. 1, Opus 18' by Johannes Brahms
'Violin Sonata in A major' by César Franck
'Requiem in D minor – Dies Irae' by Wolfgang Amadeus Mozart (castaway's favourite)
'La Marseillaise' performed by Django Reinhardt and Stéphane Grappelli

In 1977, under the pseudonym of Edward Pygge, wrote about the programme: 'The platters chosen are often quite revealing, even if one might not exactly base serious biography on them.'[82]

Among the three books he is allowed to take (the Bible and Shakespeare being furnished), chooses Flaubert's letters and wants to trade in the Bible and take *The Joy of Cooking* instead because it has a 'wonderful recipe for

---

[79] Jay McInerney, 'Good Wine and Fax Machines Brought Jay McInerney and Julian Barnes Together', *Town & Country*, 17 August 2017, https://www.townandcountrymag.com/leisure/drinks/a10364108/argument-for-letter-writing/. Accessed on 19 January 2019.
[80] Leslie Rice, 'Giving Teaching a Go', *The Gazette. The Newspaper of the John Hopkins University*, October/December 1995, http://pages.jh.edu/gazette/octdec95/oct2395/23barnes.html. Accessed on 19 January 2019.
[81] Pablo Toledo, 'Interview with Julian Barnes, Part II: "Art tells more truth than anything else"', *Buenos Aires Herald*, 13 February 2008, 16.
[82] Barnes, 'Greek Street', October 1977, 2.

	cooking squirrel' which could be transferred to various groundhogs the writer might discover.[83] This request is refused.
1997	Death of his mother. Refers in *Nothing to Be Frightened Of* to his 'long exasperation with her'.[84] Before publishing the book, asks his brother if he thought he was being unfair to their mother. Jonathan Barnes replies: 'I think you are unkind, in places, but not unfair. She was, in her last forty years, quite intolerable, if only because she was paralysingly boring.'[85]
1997	29 August. Receives from the *New Yorker* the galleys of 'A Short History of Hairdressing' (later published in *The Lemon Table*) with editor Bill Buford's comments. Buford finds the repetitions 'a little contrived' while Barnes explains that they are deliberate and pull the whole story together. Starts his fax to Buford with: 'Well, we both knew you'd do it to me, didn't we? … obviously, we part company about what the story's doing. What you see as factual repetition I intend as the allusions and remembrances of a life' (2.7.4).
1997	December. After reading a draft of *England, England*, Hermione Lee comments: 'People will say, how extraordinary, that the writer best known for turning his English eye and tone to European history, culture, art, for making cross-channel links, had chosen to invent a totally non-European England, and to look at what that means' (1.4.5).
1998	Judge of the Prix Novembre in France, alongside Mario Vargas Llosa. By a single vote and amidst controversy, the prize is awarded to Michel Houellebecq for *The Elementary Particles*. The Maecenas get huffy and announce the suspension of the Prix Novembre: 'we decamped to a new sponsor and renamed ourselves the Prix Décembre'.[86]
1999	June. Writes to a friend: 'We've just walked from the southern Pyrenees to the Mediterranean. The hotels were weird: half the dining room would be full of dressing-gowned old ladies taking the spa waters, the other half of boastfully healthy hikers. Us halfway in between.'[87]
2001	27 October. When translating *La Doulou* by Alphonse Daudet, goes to the library of the Royal Society of Medicine to verify details about tertiary syphilis and its treatment in the nineteenth century. Writes to Jim Durham: 'I've just spent a couple of days in the library of the Royal Society of Medicine. I always used to hate libraries as a student (too hot, too full of a) bores, and b) people one suspected were cleverer than oneself), but had a really good time' (2.4.4).

---

[83] *Desert Island Discs*, BBC Radio 4, 28 January 1996. In 'Appetite', a short story collected in *The Lemon Table*, a wife reads recipes to her husband from *The Joy of Cooking* and other cookbooks to trigger off good memories of meals (161).
[84] Barnes, *Nothing to Be Frightened Of*, 11.
[85] Email from Jonathan Barnes to Julian Barnes, 23 May 2007 (3.5).
[86] Julian Barnes, 'Hate and Hedonism. The Insolent Art of Michel Houellebecq', *New Yorker*, 7 July 2003, 72.
[87] Letter to Iona Heath (Barnes's GP) of 24 June 1990 (1.9.6).

2002	The Harry Ransom Center at the University of Texas at Austin acquires Barnes's archive. Gives as a final reason for placing his papers in Austin rather than in England: 'If any horrible little journalist wants to go and look at my diaries or my working notes and find something unpleasant to write a short smirky little para about, they won't just be able to pop down to the British Library. They'll have to go all the way to Texas, so that will discourage the bastards.'[88]
2002	2 April. Meets with Croatian author and playwright Borivoj Radakovic in the Lord Palmerston public house in Tufnell Park, North London, and writes a short text for his *Posjetiteljeva Knjiga*, a publication of 7×10 cm manufactured from a single A4 sheet of paper, in which eleven other authors wrote dedications: 'We have talked of writing and publishing, of Zagreb and London, of war and peace, of the difficulties of surviving as a writer, of Boro's new play, of literary life, and of friendship across boundaries' (2.11.7).
2003	11 April. Publishes on the same day in the *Guardian* a piece criticizing the decision of Britain and the United States to bombard Iraq[89] and a cooking column about a recipe by Nigel Slater which did not work.[90] The hate mail he receives is about his attacking Nigel Slater, a 'domestic god'.[91]
2005	23 March. Emails his brother about the Rugby Six Nations Championship: 'the England team was moderate crap … France were the best team in spells but incredibly unambitious against England. … the Taffies played the most adventurous & pleasing game and deserved to win the title. The Scots were appallingly bad, Italians vaguely thuggish and vaguely expressive, and the Irish the biggest disappointment'.[92]
2006	May. Trip to Athens with his wife Pat for the promotion of *Arthur & George*: 'It was absurdly hot for May, though, and it's a city impossible to walk in. Pat noted there were absolutely no cyclists (all killed off, no doubt).'[93]
2007	8 January. Emails his brother after reading his *Coffee with Aristotle*: 'You make Aristotle sound like a really cool dude. He also sounds a bit like you, for that matter.'[94]
2007	15 September. Opens the 'Marathon Bovary' at the Lycée Corneille in Rouen to celebrate the 150th anniversary of the publication of *Madame Bovary*. A hundred and thirty people read Flaubert's novel in public over twenty hours.

---

[88] Interview by Guignery and Roberts, in *Conversations*, ed. Guignery and Roberts, 180.
[89] Julian Barnes, 'This War Was Not Worth a Child's Finger', *Guardian*, 11 April 2003, 2–4.
[90] Julian Barnes, 'The Pedant in the Kitchen. Picture Perfect', *Guardian*, 11 April 2003. Reproduced as 'The Tooth Fairy', *The Pedant in the Kitchen* (London: Atlantic Books, 2003), 56–63.
[91] Interview by Nadine O'Regan (2003), in *Conversations*, ed. Guignery and Roberts, 117.
[92] Email from Julian Barnes to Jonathan Barnes, 23 March 2005 (3.5).
[93] Email from Julian Barnes to Jonathan Barnes, 26 May 2006 (3.5).
[94] Email from Julian Barnes to Jonathan Barnes, 8 January 2007 (3.5).

2008	20 October. Death of Pat. 'The heart of my life; the life of my heart.'[95]
2009	Ian McEwan recalls a recent afternoon spent with Barnes: 'Julian was reading an article in the *Guardian* about a ship that, in 1893, got frozen in the polar ice. The explorers had set up a primitive wind turbine for electricity, and the captain's log described how they'd got it running just before the final sunset that marked the beginning of the dark Arctic winter. Julian handed the story to me. I read it and said, "That's amazing. A wind turbine in 1893!" He said, "No, no, I mean the captain's description of the final sunset. What a beautiful piece of prose."'[96]
2011	March. Awarded the David Cohen Prize for Literature. Says in his acceptance speech: 'When I was told that I'd won the David Cohen prize, I felt untrammeled pleasure. The only slight apprehension was over those two menacing words "lifetime achievement". It was as if some finely woven but heavy tweed overcoat had suddenly descended upon my shoulders. Not yet, O Lord, not yet, I almost cried. But pretty soon, I began to feel that, actually, it fitted rather well, and anyway, didn't I need a new overcoat for the rest of the journey?' (3.1).
2011	18 October. Wins the Booker Prize for *The Sense of an Ending*. Starts his speech with the following words: 'Borges, when asked – as he continually was – why he had never won the Nobel Prize, always used to reply that in Sweden there was a small cottage industry solely devoted to not giving Borges the Nobel. And at times, over the last years, in occasional moments of mild paranoia, I've wondered if there wasn't perhaps some sister organisation operating over here [about the Booker]' (3.1).[97]
2011	7 December. President of the jury for the European Book Prize in Brussels. During the ceremony, the five-piece swing quintet declines to play 'God Save the Queen' in honour of the jury's British president and plays instead 'Always Look on the Bright Side of Life', Eric Idle's comedy song which first featured in *Monty Python's Life of Brian*.
2012	September. Invited to address the Barnes-Amis Society (founded in 2001), the English Club of the City of London School which he attended in 1957–64. Comments: 'I am flattered by the order of names in its title.'[98] Amis stands for Kingsley.
2015	March. In Santiago de Compostela, hugs the bust of Saint James and requests him 'to ensure that Leicester City escape[s] relegation'. *See* May 2016.

---

[95] Barnes, *Levels of Life*, 68.
[96] Daniel Zalewski, 'The Background Hum. Ian McEwan's Art of Unease', *New Yorker*, 23 February 2009, 48.
[97] Barnes had been shortlisted for the Booker Prize three times previously, for *Flaubert's Parrot*, *England, England* and *Arthur & George*.
[98] Annotated copy of *Metroland* (Morgan Library 172).

2016	26 January. Gives a talk entitled 'Some of my Best Friends are Biographers' at Wolfson College for the Oxford Centre for Life-Writing, directed by biographer Hermione Lee.[99] Ends his talk with a final wish for his future biographer: 'that she or he include in small type, "This is not how I was – this is how I look when being biographized"'.[100]
2016	2 May. Leicester City Football Club wins the Premier League championship. Almost thirty years earlier, in the last chapter of *A History of the World in 10½ Chapters*, Leicester City 'had bloody well won the FA Cup! … Leicester City had never won anything but peanuts before and now they had secured the FA Cup for the first time in the club's history'.[101]
2017	Appears fleetingly in the background of a pub scene in the film adaptation of *The Sense of an Ending* by Ritesh Batra.
2017	10 January. Writes to the author of this book who is keeping him up to date on her discoveries in the archives: 'I do feel a bit like a Dead Author at times, the gangrene creeping up my legs.'[102]
2017	19 June. Created *officier de la Légion d'honneur*. In his acceptance speech, quotes Flaubert's line: 'Honours dishonour, titles degrade, office holding ossifies', but remarks that in 1866 Flaubert himself accepted the *Légion d'honneur*.[103]

---

[99] Barnes already had this title in mind in 2007. Interview by Guignery and Roberts, in *Conversations*, ed. Guignery and Roberts, 181.
[100] 'Julian Barnes: "Some of my Best friends are Biographers"', Oxford Centre for Life-Writing, 2 March 2016, https://oxlifewriting.wordpress.com/2016/03/02/julian-barnes-some-of-my-best-friends-are-biographers. Accessed on 19 January 2019.
[101] Barnes, *A History of the World in 10½ Chapters*, 289.
[102] Private email correspondence with the author, 10 January 2017.
[103] In 'Braithwaite's Dictionary of Accepted Ideas' in *Flaubert's Parrot*, for the entry on Flaubert, Barnes offers a different translation of the last segment: 'Honours dishonour, titles degrade, employment stupefies' (155). The translation 'office-holding ossifies' was suggested to Barnes by Alan Raitt.

4

Flaubert's Parrot from ignition to composition

In the summer of 1982, Julian Barnes spent a week with Arthur Koestler in his house in Suffolk at a time when he was writing *Flaubert's Parrot* but was reluctant to talk about it:

> Writers divide into those who happily talk about their work in progress and those who squirm in embarrassment at the prospect. I am a squirmer (of course, it's not just embarrassment; it's also caution that someone might steal the idea for your book, plus sheer vanity – however good you make it sound you probably won't be able to convey the full originality, daring, and brilliance of the project). Three or four times over the last year or so Arthur has asked me what I am working on, and each time I answer, with tight-lipped paranoia, 'A book about Flaubert.' Each time – preferring, as is his style, the challenging question to the mollifying expression of interest – he responds, 'Why not Maupassant?' I never really find an answer. I suppose I should just say, 'Flaubert's better.'[1]

In 1984, Jonathan Cape printed 3,000 copies of *Flaubert's Parrot* for the first print run. The book turned out to be Barnes's breakthrough novel and the one which has generated the most academic study. The aim of this chapter is not to add yet another layer of analysis to what already exists but to look into the genesis of Barnes's most experimental book by examining his archives and thus further the work already initiated by Ryan Roberts in his paper 'Inventing a Way to the Truth: Life and Fiction in *Flaubert's Parrot*.'[2]

The origins of *Flaubert's Parrot* and some of its passages and ideas can be found in Barnes's non-fictional essay of August 1983, 'Flaubert and Rouen,'[3] published a few days after the BBC2 series *Writers and Their Places* broadcast a television documentary on Flaubert, written and presented by Barnes and entitled 'A Complex Heart: Gustave Flaubert (1821–80).'[4] In this television documentary, the English writer retraces the

---

[1] Barnes, 'Playing Chess', 478.
[2] Ryan Roberts, 'Inventing a Way to the Truth: Life and Fiction in *Flaubert's Parrot*', in *Julian Barnes*, ed. Groes and Childs, 24–36.
[3] Julian Barnes, 'Flaubert and Rouen', *Listener*, 18 August 1983, 14–15. The essay was a version of the television script for the BBC TV documentary 'A Complex Heart: Gustave Flaubert (1821–80)'.
[4] Julian Barnes, 'A Complex Heart: Gustave Flaubert (1821–80)', BBC2 *Writers and Places*, 14 August 1983.

life of Flaubert through some of the locations in Normandy that had influenced the French novelist and in particular the composition of *Madame Bovary*. In the same week, Barnes published 'Flaubert's Parrot – A Story',[5] the first chapter of the novel of the same name. The subtitle 'A Story' is a reminder of the fact that when Barnes started work on this project he did not know whether it was 'an idea for a short story or for a novel', whereas in previous cases, he had known in advance the genre of what he was writing.[6] The sources of *Flaubert's Parrot* have also been discussed by the author in two non-fictional pieces, 'The Follies of Writer Worship' (1985) and 'When Flaubert Took Wing' (2005),[7] as well as in several interviews during which he read from his travel notebook of 1981, which is not included in the archives at the Harry Ransom Center.[8] These published documents provide useful information about the 'moment of ignition' or 'small explosion'[9] which started *Flaubert's Parrot*, namely Barnes's trip to Normandy in September 1981 when he had been commissioned to write a book on the houses of French writers. In the articles and interviews mentioned above, Barnes describes his visit to the Museum of the Hôtel Dieu and to the pavilion in Croisset, and his sighting of the two rival parrots. He refers in particular to 'four pages of notebook description' of the Croisset pavilion (where Flaubert lived with his mother) and quotes from it.[10] As shown by Ryan Roberts, a comparison between the passages in the notebook, the non-fictional essays and *Flaubert's Parrot* reveals the close connections between these texts that nevertheless draw on different genres.[11]

Although that specific travel notebook is not included in the archives, other documents (drafts, random notes, letters) provide illuminating information on the writing process of *Flaubert's Parrot*, on what the author's original plan was, what material he kept and what he discarded.

1. Flaubert Stories

An exploration of the origins of *Flaubert's Parrot* first takes the reader back to the 1970s to trace the early germ of a crucial metaphor used by the narrator Geoffrey Braithwaite in the third chapter of the novel ('Finders Keepers') to refer to the gaps and holes in a biography. At the start of the chapter, Braithwaite quotes the definition of a net by a 'jocular lexicographer' as 'a collection of holes tied together with string' (35) and compares it to the craft of biography. Barnes may have encountered this definition

---

[5] Julian Barnes, 'Flaubert's Parrot – A Story', *London Review of Books*, 5, no. 15 (18–31 August 1983): 20–1.
[6] James McCloskey, 'In Conversation: Julian Barnes with James McCloskey', *The Brooklyn Rail*, 1 September 2005, https://brooklynrail.org/2005/09/books/julian-barnes-in-conversation-with-james. Accessed on 19 January 2019.
[7] Barnes, 'The Follies of Writer Worship', 1, 16, 17; 'When Flaubert Took Wing', 20.
[8] Vanessa Guignery, 'Julian Barnes in Conversation. 9th November 2001', in *Flaubert's Parrot de Julian Barnes 'Un symbole du logos?'*, ed. Antoine Capet, Philippe Romanski, Nicole Terrien and Aïssatou Sy-Wonyu (Rouen: Publications de l'Université de Rouen, 2002), 119–33; Guignery, *Novelists in the New Millennium*, 8–26.
[9] Guignery, *Novelists in the New Millennium*, 13.
[10] Barnes, 'When Flaubert Took Wing', 20.
[11] Roberts, 'Inventing a Way to the Truth', 25–6.

in the early 1970s when he was a lexicographer for the *Oxford English Dictionary Supplement* and found it so arresting as to include it a few years later in his review of the Third Edition of the *Oxford Dictionary of Quotations*. In that piece, Barnes points out that the failings of the dictionary, produced by a team of twenty scrutineers, 'remind one that a committee is rather like a net', which can be viewed 'either as a contrivance for catching things, or as an object through which things slip', hence 'that famous cod definition of a net as "a collection of holes tied together with string".'[12] In *Flaubert's Parrot*, the narrator is aware of the omissions and gaps in his book on Flaubert and yet the first planning notes reveal that Barnes attempted to cover as much original ground as possible. In his second notebook (1.1.2), he wrote down a list of 'Flaubert Stories':

① Parrot
② Juliet Herbert Letters – &/or Flaubert in London
   E1 and E2
③ Eleanor Marx // Mme Bovary: use parallel texts, then last line say she translated MB
④ Louise Colet – in defence –
⑤ a) Mistakes – of novelists; of critics – Begins 'How carefully do we read?' physiology of reading, etc. Critics' reading v. readers' v. writers'
   b One about the unreliability of evidence: the 3 unreliable witnesses to GF's life: Ducamp, Goncourts, GF himself (also L.C.); rumours of suicide
⑥ Elisa Schlesinger – her life (its mysteries), infatuee to madwoman
~~⑦ Story on What Evidence do we have: Ducamp, Goncourts, GF~~
⑦ Ironies & Coincidences
⑧ HM Stanley, H James, Turgenev, Herbert Spencer
⑨ Something on translation – its handings-down & losses
10) & Sex
11) And the Parrot ...

This initial list gives a precise idea of what Barnes already wanted to include at a fairly early stage and some of these 'stories' were indeed included in the final version, albeit at a different place:

① → 1. Flaubert's Parrot
② → 3. Finders Keepers
④ → 11. Louise Colet's Version
⑤ → 6. Emma Bovary's Eyes
⑦ → 5. Snap!
11) → 15. And the Parrot ...

Other items became part of chapters rather than full 'stories': the Eleanor Marx/Emma Bovary parallel of ③ was presented as E1 and E2 in 'Examination Paper' (176), the Elisa Schlesinger infatuation of ⑥ is referred to in several places in the book (24,

---

[12] Julian Barnes, 'Don't Quote Me', *New Statesman*, 16 November 1979, 771.

27, 30, 60–1, 100), the anecdote of the explorer Henry Morton Stanley (named in ⑧) who took *Salammbô* on one of his trips appears in 'Snap!' (71). Other topics were dismissed, such as the last chapters on translation and on sex,[13] as well as the reference to Herbert Spencer.

It is interesting to note that Barnes uses the word 'stories' to refer to the chapters in *Flaubert's Parrot*, a word which can evoke both short stories (which could only apply to a few of the chapters) and fiction (which most chapters are not or only peripherally). The notion of 'stories' recurs in the writer's notebook when he was further along in the composition of the book and wrote an amended list of 'FLAUBERT STORIES: WRITTEN / UNDER WAY', which includes up to twenty-two potential chapters and is presented thus:

① F'S PARROT   1
② F'S PARROT   2
③ EYES OF BLUE
④ SNAP
⑤ CROSS CHANNEL
⑥ JULIET HERBERT LETTERS   ⑩ Dictionary of Acc. Ideas
    ⑦ The train-spotter's guide
    ⑧ The Flaubert Bestiary
    ⑨ Louise Colet's Version
    Chronology I
    Chronology II
What about a <u>quiz</u>: e.g. life & art   Chronology III: A Metaphorical
    Self-Portrait
    Sex Story
    = 13
    to come?   Marx/Bovary → quiz
    The F. Apocrypha
One <u>pure</u> story told by G.B.   Fl.: the Case Against/ dialogue?;
    or F & Politics
    The Trial: Censorship?
    How to become a Bourgeois
Dictionary of Acc. Ideas   ? Bouilhet
    ? Meditation on Mme Bovary C'est
Moi
    ? High Society
    ? Story in which GF is minor figure
= up to 22
+ character intro w[ith] pix

---

[13] See pp. 82–3.

A comparison of this list with the fifteen published chapters of *Flaubert's Parrot* reveals the changes in titles: '③ Eyes of Blue' became '6. Emma Bovary's Eyes'; '⑥ Juliet Herbert Letters' turned into the more enigmatic '3. Finders Keepers', the 'quiz' was called 'Examination Paper', the illuminating subtitle to the third chronology – 'A Metaphorical Self-Portrait' – which explicitly identified Flaubert as the author of the quotes, was deleted, as was another possible title: 'Simile Portrait'. In an undated letter to his editor Liz Calder, Barnes explained the rationale for some of the chapters or 'stories':

> Of the stories I'm attaching:
> the Parrot Stories stand at the beginning and end of the book: the first one in effect setting the book out on the 'search for the writer's voice'; and the second one showing the end of the quest.
> Cross Channel is the story (the longest one, probably) at the centre of the book; the one which is the hinge between the narrator and GF,/as between England and France. It's also (at the moment) the one in which the narrator steps forward for the longest period of time.
> The Bestiary and the Train-Spotter's are probably the two most eccentric stories in the book.
> Louise Colet is part of 'the case against' Flaubert – part of seeing the writer/ genius/hero from someone else's point of view for a change.
> the What-if Factor is probably the most conventional, old-fashioned story in the book. (1.5.3)

The 'What-if Factor' is a reference to 'Finders Keepers' which was also entitled 'The Low Blow', 'The Fiancée' and 'Storming the Fortress' (1.5.2) – an expression used when the narrator wonders if Flaubert stayed cosily at home with the English governess Juliet Herbert, 'staring at her over dinner and then storming her fortress' (42).[14] Barnes probably considered 'Finders Keepers' 'the most conventional, old-fashioned story' because it involves two fictional characters (the narrator and the American academic who purports to have acquired seventy-five letters between Flaubert and Juliet Herbert) and because the quest for lost letters or manuscripts has been the subject of several novels, notably Henry James's *The Aspern Papers* (in which the Aspern letters are burned just like the letters between Flaubert and Juliet Herbert in 'Finders Keepers').

When comparing the second list of stories and the published book, one may note the changes in the order of chapters and the suppression of several sections, especially the latest ones in the second part of the list, which never evolved beyond the stage of a few miscellaneous notes or else partially found their way in other chapters. The last item 'character intro w[ith] pix' is a reference to the cast of characters Barnes had thought of including at the beginning of his book, as one might find 'at the start of Russian

---

[14] The belligerent image finds its source in a letter from Flaubert to Bouilhet of 9 May 1855 (quoted one page earlier in *Flaubert's Parrot*) in which the French novelist refers to the governess: 'What a pretty comparison one could make between the slope of the breast and the glacis of a fortress. The cupids tumble about on it, as they storm the citadel' (41).

novels' as he told his editor (1.5.3). The list included Flaubert, his friends and family – Bouilhet, Du Camp, Colet, Schlesinger, Sand, Flaubert's father, mother, brother, sister and niece, 'Oncle' Parain, Juliet Herbert, Kuchuk Hanem –, his 'colleagues' (Gautier, Maupassant, Zola, Goncourt, Turgenev), 'English painters and sketchers' (Musgrave, Payne, Hockney[15]), 'English critics' (Starkie, Ricks), 'English cookery writers' (Jane Grigson, Prue Leith) and Braithwaite himself (1.5.3).

The aim of such a list, as noted by Barnes, was to make the book 'accessible to (and appreciable by) those who haven't read a word of [Flaubert]' (1.5.3). Barnes wrote two pages with all the names mentioned above, although only the first fourteen and Geoffrey Braithwaite were granted a two- to six-line description, sometimes including a quotation. Although the principle of the cast was discarded, the information offered and most quotes found their place elsewhere in the book, except for the cookery writers Jane Grigson and Prue Leith, both of whom Barnes consulted about the colour of redcurrant jam in the mid-nineteenth century[16] and who would be referred to some twenty years later in the essays on cooking collected in *The Pedant in the Kitchen*.[17] Only a few items from the entries were not retained, such as the fact that Flaubert 'complained that Du Camp sucked up to modern life: for instance, by using steel-nibbed pens for writing'[18] or the reaction of Flaubert's father when his son read to him some of his early work: 'his father fell asleep & remarked when he woke up: "If a pen had been my only instrument, the family would have starved."'[19]

On the other hand, eleven entries were moved to 'Braithwaite's Dictionary of Accepted Ideas', with the narrator adopting a sarcastic and Flaubertian tone and style while the original cast of characters was mainly factual and neutral. The original version of 'Braithwaite's Dictionary of Accepted Ideas' (1.5.4) differs from the published text as five entries were later discarded to make way for names imported from the cast of characters. The early draft therefore contained fewer proper names: 'Accepted Ideas' had been selected instead of 'Achille' in the final book; 'Bouvard et Pécuchet' – with the amusing injunction: 'Praise first, read later' – was later changed to 'Bouilhet, Louis'; 'Correspondence' had been preferred to 'Colet, Louise' (the poetess appeared under the letter L in the draft, while L is for 'Letters' in the published version); 'Monseigneur' in the draft – followed by the definition 'Gustave's nickname for Bouilhet' – was to

---

[15] The cover of the first British edition of the novel features a 1974 sketch by David Hockney, 'Félicité Sleeping, with Parrot', which was drawn to illustrate Flaubert's *A Simple Heart* and is referred to in *Flaubert's Parrot* (19).

[16] The narrator of *Flaubert's Parrot* wonders if redcurrant jam was 'the same colour in Normandy in 1853 as it is now' (92).

[17] In 2008, when asked what his favourite book was, Barnes answered: 'It varies from Shakespeare to the Oxford English Dictionary to the Michelin Guide to France to Flaubert's Letters to Jane Grigson's Vegetable Book.' Mike French, 'Mike Interviews: Julian Barnes', *View from Here*, 4 April 2008, http://www.viewfromheremagazine.com/2008/04/mike-interviews-julian-barnes-part-1-of.html. Accessed on 19 January 2019.

[18] Du Camp quotes a letter by Flaubert of 1865 in the second volume of his *Souvenirs littéraires*: 'Prends garde! tu es sur une pente! Tu as déjà abandonné les plumes d'oie pour les plumes de fer, ce qui est le fait d'une âme faible.' ('Beware! You are on the downhill path! You have already given up goose quills for dip pens, which bespeaks a feeble soul.' – my translation). Maxime Du Camp, *Souvenirs littéraires*. Tome II (Paris: Hachette, 1892), 300.

[19] Flaubert read to his father the 1845 *Éducation sentimentale*, as recounted by Du Camp. Du Camp, *Souvenirs littéraires*. Tome I, 226.

be replaced by 'Mme Flaubert' in the final book; 'Sade' in the draft – 'Be amused and frank. ... Conclude: Sade is so witty' – would be substituted with 'Sand, Georges'. In 'The Flaubert Apocrypha', Braithwaite reflects on who should be awarded an entry in his pocket guide to Flaubert: 'S for Sade, or S for Starkie?' (118). Neither of them made it to the final cut while in early drafts Barnes had also thought of Sartre, Style, *Salammbô* and Syphilis.

In his notebook, Barnes additionally refers to 'One or more Found Stories – true fables constr. out of bits of diff. biog. etc'; 'F in High Society (? Found Story)', 'Found poem/text made up of metaphors of love' (1.1.2). It is interesting to note here that Barnes mixes words which point towards fiction and invention ('stories', 'fables', 'constructed', 'made up') and words which suggest reliability and verifiability ('true', 'biog.'). A found story is a text which is put together from other people's writings and can fall into a poem if arranged in a certain way. The found story about Flaubert in 'High Society' was supposed to be 'a chapter about his salon-prancing chez the Princesse Mathilde'[20] but was never written although this period is alluded to in the first chronology for 1863 (26) and in 'Louise Colet's Version' when the poetess refers to the days when Flaubert was 'prancing by candlelight' (151). The third chronology, being entirely composed of quotations by Flaubert, is a found story, as suggested in Barnes's letter to his editor:

> The stories themselves inter-relate: the book is planned as a whole. But in manner, they run the whole spectrum between fiction and non-fiction: at one end, the old fashioned 'well-made' short story, at the other, a sort of 'found story', like a found poem, in which the information about GF appears to be flung down in front of the reader (it isn't, of course, it's chosen and shaped as much as the old-style stories; but it's done like that to throw down ideas in a seemingly brutal way). (1.5.3)

The old-fashioned short story probably referred to 'Finders Keepers' and the 'found story' was the third chronology in which quotations are offered without any explanation or contextualization as the narrator is momentarily absent or at least invisible. When he assembled that chapter, Barnes included precise date references and the page numbers in the French Pléiade edition of Flaubert's letters, invaluable information which he subsequently removed, hence what he refers to as the 'brutal' aspect of the section. On the other hand, in other sections also relying on a selection of quotations such as 'The Flaubert Bestiary' or 'The Train-Spotter's Guide to Flaubert' which he deemed 'eccentric' as well as 'Examination Paper', the narrator usually gives dates and contextualization for each quote.[21]

---

[20] Private email correspondence with the author, 1 April 2016.
[21] At draft stage, 'Examination Paper' included two topics which were then deleted: a topic on Ecology – about Flaubert and Du Camp shooting and eating animals in Egypt, and our ecological reactions to these facts – and one on Moral Philosophy/Thanatology which consisted of a comparison between the deaths of Louis Bouilhet (in 1869) and Villiers de l'Isle-Adam (in 1889), who were both attended by their respective common-law wives on their deathbeds. Upon falling ill, Bouilhet asked his companion to marry him to regularize their relationship – 'She refused, believing that if she agreed, he would know that he was dying/in articulo mortis.' – while Villiers was reluctant to get married – 'if he agreed to marry, it would mean that he was agreeing to die' – but eventually relented four days before he died, bullied by his friends. The exam question was: 'Who did right?' (1.5.1)

As for the 'Sex story' referred to in the middle of the list, at a fairly late stage of writing, it was called 'Sex and Literature' and placed in the first half of the book (as Chapter Six), before being renamed 'Dirty Story' in the table of contents of the third typescript copy and shifted to the end of the book, inserted in longhand between '13. Quiz' and '14. Pure Story' (1.5.4), two chapters whose order was then inverted. This 'dirty story' linking together creativity and sexual behaviour was completed but removed from the final book and eventually published six years later in *Soho Square III*, an anthology of texts by various writers edited by Alberto Manguel, under the title 'Dirty Story: the Making of *Madame Bovary*'.[22] In his notebook, Barnes had written the following random notes:

> Sex & Flaubert: His parallels between fucking & writing; getting bonk. Balzac – 'there goes any novel'. Did he give up sex when he started writing seriously? was it his form of becoming a bourgeois – quote his Let on that?friend who gave up?art & became a bourgeois and the symbols (briefcase?) involved. Thereafter he only came to Paris for bursts with whores. (1.1.2)

Barnes's archives include the deleted chapter composed of six pages of quotations by Flaubert which relate sex to creativity. They are arranged chronologically from 1847 to 1856 and each one is followed by the precise date (day, month, year) of the letters in which they appeared and the page number in the French Pléiade edition (1.5.1). For publication in Manguel's anthology, Barnes decided against six of them either because they did not directly relate to the composition of *Madame Bovary* or to sex, or because they were too ambiguous. One reason for not including that chapter in *Flaubert's Parrot* might be that it was too close in form to the third chronology which is also a collage of quotations by Flaubert with no intervention from the narrator (apart from their selection). Another explanation was given by Barnes in an interview with Patrick McGrath in 1987:

> I had one chapter that I dropped about sex and creativity. When Flaubert's talking about writing, there's an awful lot of sexual metaphors. 'Go fuck your inkwell!' is one of his great injunctions to a writer. And when he's writing *Madame Bovary* he says, 'I'm having a lot of trouble getting hard,' and then, 'I think I'm finally going to come!' I was trying to do a chapter on the whole of his life in terms of sexual metaphor, but it sort of didn't quite come off. I showed it to a friend who reads my books before they go to the publisher, and she said, 'Well, actually, I'm not sure if it works, but I personally find it offensive' – the idea of the Muse as a woman who has to be fucked flat before a chap can get a book out. 'That's rather disgusting,' she said.[23]

---

[22] Julian Barnes, 'Dirty Story: The Making of *Madame Bovary*', in *Soho Square II*, ed. Alberto Manguel (London: Bloomsbury, 1990), 62–5.
[23] Interview by Patrick McGrath (1987), in *Conversations*, ed. Guignery and Roberts, 14.

That friend was Hermione Lee who did indeed persuade Barnes to drop the section from the finished novel. In an interview in 2003, the writer provided yet another reason for discarding this chapter which might be seen as 'a bit crass' and therefore might be doing Flaubert 'a disservice'. Barnes noted indeed:

> When you read someone's correspondence, it goes from tremendous highs to tremendous lows, to tremendous bits of being unbuttoned to being very serious to throw-away lines to your chums. I think my doubt was that if I put all of these little throw-away lines to his chums together, it might make people fail to appreciate the intensely high and serious purpose that was behind it. So I think I was being a bit protective of Flaubert.[24]

However, the decision to discard the chapter came late as it was still included in the third typescript copy. A page entitled 'FLAUBERT COMPLETION SCHEME' in the archives reveals what Barnes still planned to do in order to complete the book by 1 December 1983 when he would hand it to Pat Kavanagh (his wife and literary agent) and Liz Calder, his editor.

In addition to finishing reading books by Flaubert, visiting places in Normandy and writing to such people as Alan Raitt, Graham Greene, Richard Ellmann (biographer of Yeats, Joyce and Wilde) or Jane Grigson, he set himself a strict schedule, crossing out each item once it was completed:

<u>Finish</u> five stories at minimum rate of 1 per week
  ~~Apocrypha~~ ~~Sun 25 Sept~~
  ~~Dirty Story~~ ~~Sun 2 Oct~~
  ~~Pure Story~~ ~~Sun 9 Oct~~
  ~~Exam Paper~~ ~~Sun 16 Oct~~
  ~~Case Against~~ ~~Sun 23 Oct (1.5.3)~~

The archives include pages of notes with the inscription at the top '<u>Inserts, Links, Additions</u>' followed by a list of items liable to be added for each chapter. Barnes also planned several last readings through to make sure the book worked as a whole:

<u>Putting together</u> Read through as a book
        Extra links/intros 1) to Dictionnaire
                2) to LC's version/status
                3) wherever else necessary
        Read through notebooks with book in front of you
for final sprucings
        Final read through & combing (1.5.3)

---

[24] Interview by Harriett Gilbert, 'Julian Barnes. *Flaubert's Parrot*', [Radio] BBC World Book Club, 31 July 2003, https://www.bbc.co.uk/programmes/p02r846w. Accessed on 19 January 2019.

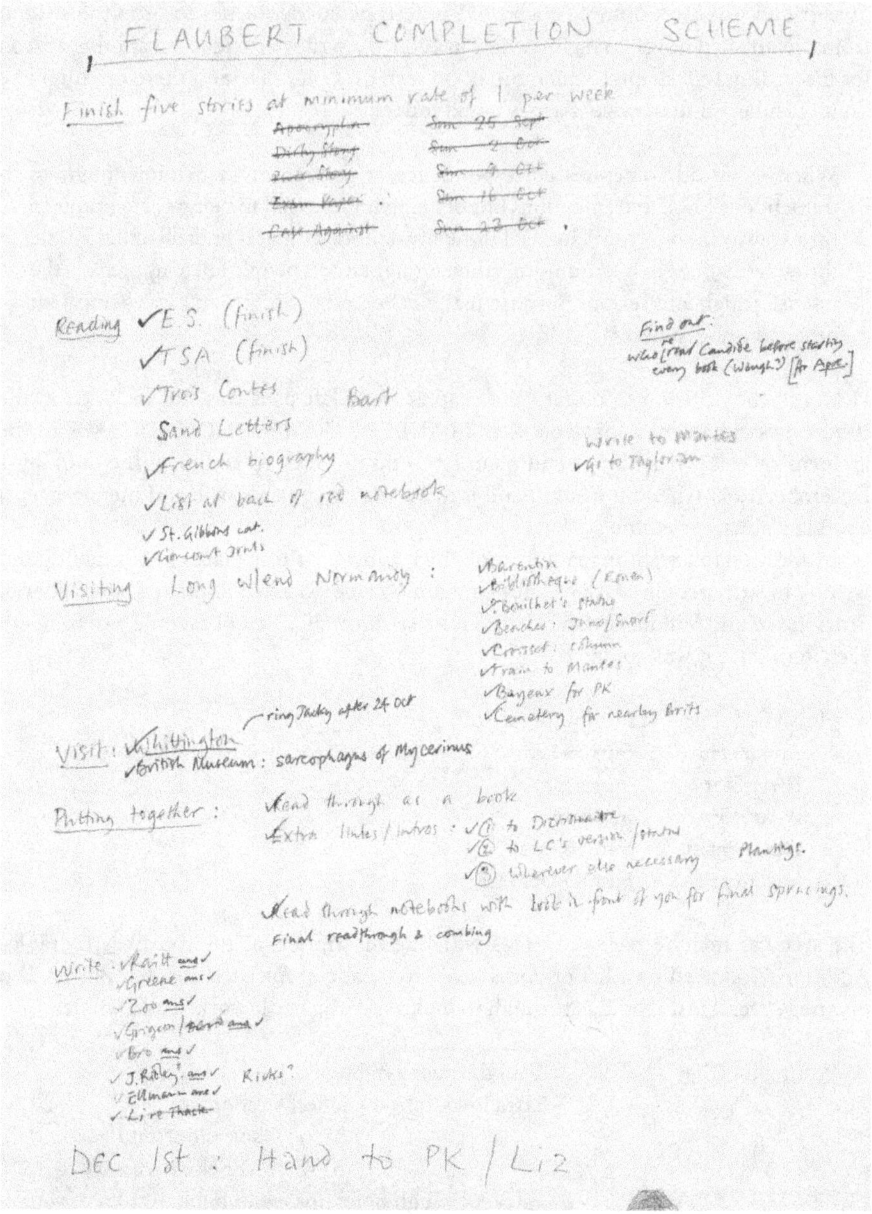

Figure 2 *Flaubert's Parrot* – 'Flaubert Completion Scheme' (1.5.3). Harry Ransom Center. The University of Texas at Austin.

The papers contain a page entitled 'Possibly useful things from Notebooks' with a list of sixty-three pieces of information about Flaubert (preceded by the page number in the notebook), but only eleven were retained as possible additions. Such lists testify to the amount of research Barnes conducted for this novel while his meticulous notes point to his Flaubertian attention to the 'combing' of his prose.

As many critics have observed, *Flaubert's Parrot* is a polygeneric book which challenges any attempt at categorization, classification and genre taxonomy: Barnes's friend James Fenton called it 'a *thing* …',[25] David Lodge drew on the ancient genre of the 'Menippean satire', with its 'wide use of inserted genres',[26] while Philip Larkin wrote to Barnes on 25 October 1984 that he had used Flaubert 'to write a – a what? Search me, O Lord, as someone says. I should hate to have to review it'.[27] The American publisher Knopf called it 'a novel in disguise' in its blurb, which led John Updike to exclaim in his review that it was 'the most strangely shaped specimen of its genre (that I have read) since Vladimir Nabokov's "Pale Fire" '.[28] The consensus is that the generic compendium *Flaubert's Parrot* offers enables the narrator to approach Flaubert through original and varied ways and to circumvent the pitfalls of each individual genre and especially those of the biography. Barnes's wariness of the certainties of the genre and his unwillingness to 'do all the boring bits' (such as the subject's family and childhood) explain why he did not want to write a biography of Flaubert and came up instead with what he describes as 'a mixture of not really approving of the biographical format and also being a novelist in any case'.[29] On 20 May 1985, the American biographer Herbert R. Lottman (who had then already published biographies of Albert Camus and Philippe Pétain) wrote an anxious letter to Barnes:

> I have begun a biography of Flaubert, and it occurred to me after reading your delightful book that I had better try to find out whether you too are doing one. I've been living in and around Flaubert's country for many years and caring about him for even longer, but at this point I don't know Flaubert as well as you do. (1.16.7)

Not only did Barnes not intend to write a biography of Flaubert but he reviewed Lottman's own biography in the *London Review of Books* on 4 May 1989,[30] acknowledging that the book has 'a certain value' but drawing attention to its 'formidable irritations' and to the 'comparative shallowness of Lottman's depth of field':

> [Lottman] arranges the known facts about Flaubert's life, and the known opinions of his contemporaries, with an efficiency that has not been seen before. As against

---

[25] James Fenton, 'A Novelist with an Experiment: Discuss', *Times*, 4 October 1984, 13.
[26] David Lodge, 'The Home Front', *New York Review of Books* 34, no. 8 (7 May 1987): 10.
[27] Thwaite, ed. *Selected Letters of Philip Larkin*, 721.
[28] Updike, 'A Pair of Parrots', 86.
[29] Interview by Vanessa Guignery (2000), in *Conversations*, ed. Guignery and Roberts, 54.
[30] Julian Barnes, 'Flaubert's Bottle', *London Review of Books* 11, no. 9 (4 May 1989): 10. Reproduced as 'Flaubert's Death-Masks; a) Biographer' in *Something to Declare*, 147–53.

this, he writes badly, translates awkwardly, has no apparent opinion on Flaubert's works, and has little feel for the nineteenth century.[31]

In his letter to Liz Calder, Barnes made it clear that in *Flaubert's Parrot*, he wanted to navigate between fiction and non-fiction, and above all avoid writing yet another biography or academic book on Flaubert or, as mentioned in a 1985 essay, applying 'another layer of papier-mâché ... to the funeral mask', adding 'another layer of holy turf ... to the tumulus'.[32] His letter to Calder employs the same metaphor:

> There doesn't seem any point in adding to the biographical or critical tumulus. I wanted to find a different way of reviving/seeing/celebrating/reseeing/reviewing Flaubert: one that can ignore traditional chronological or academic approaches, and come in from all sorts of different angles at the same time. Hence the fictional framework...
>
> So it's a book a) about Flaubert; b) about writing (not 19thc writing: writing now as well); and c) a semi-fiction in itself. I hope this doesn't make it sound an arid, theoretical book: it isn't meant to be. Nor is it meant to be a specialist book or an academic book. The idea isn't to 'add a footnore [sic] to Flaubert studies' or whatever. The idea is to tell stories (part of the fun and challenge is making stories out of awkward subject-matter) which weave in and out of a writer's life. (1.5.3)

As in previous quotes, the significant word 'stories' recurs while the adjective 'different' points to Barnes's wish to get off the beaten tracks and combine various approaches. The writer then justified the presence of a fictional homodiegetic narrator as being 'intended to do two things':

> 1) Allow more points of access, and a greater range of response, to Flaubert: the narrator, being basically quite sane but given to bursts of extremity, can go out on a limb for Flaubert, hypothesize wildly, put contradictory points of view, etc, which are impossible with a traditional lit-crit approach.
> 2) Tie the stories together. The narrator's presence runs through the book, sometimes faintly, sometimes pushily; as we read, the sub-plot of his life develops, until, in the final story, there is a tying-off of his personal history. Also, having the narrator as a character in the book, he can usefully have his life bounced off that of Flaubert, and vice versa. (1.5.3)

The book is indeed daring in its hypotheses and offers complementary as well as contradictory perspectives on Flaubert, as epitomized not only by the three chronologies and 'The Case Against' but also by the disparaging comments on Flaubert by Louise Colet, the Goncourts, Maxime Du Camp and Jean-Paul Sartre. The fictional armature also became more essential as the book developed. In a 2005 essay, Barnes

---

[31] Barnes, *Something to Declare*, 149. Barnes also judged Lottman's 1996 biography of Jules Verne 'pedestrian'. Julian Barnes, 'Back to the Future', *New York Times Book Review* 26 January 1997, 4.
[32] Barnes, 'The Follies of Writer Worship', 16.

recalls how the story of the two parrots moved from being a mere 'Curious Fact' or 'half an anecdote' to 'a freestanding short story' and finally an 'elastic and capacious' 'mix of fact and fiction' made possible by the introduction of a fictional narrator, 'someone whose life might have parallels and points of bouncing contact with Flaubert's work'.[33] The fictional story of the Braithwaites acts as the narrative which holds the threads together and Barnes was very careful about this during composition. He remarked: 'I insist upon the fictional element, the fictional infrastructure. Without it, it wouldn't be a coherent book.'[34]

2. The fictional narrator

A comparison between the various drafts of *Flaubert's Parrot* and the published novel more precisely reveals the trajectories taken by the book in regard to the fictional narrator, a retired doctor. The first chapter, whose original title was 'Flaubert's Parrot: Some Unanswered Questions', included in its sixth paragraph a thorough presentation of the narrator, which was crossed out in the first draft:

> I'm a doctor by profession, and on and off, for some twenty years now, I've been a Flaubert buff. Well, buff doesn't sound quite right: amateur is more the word; love and friendship the word implies, and that's what I feel. Perhaps I'm drawn to him too because his father and brother – the two Achilles – were doctors as well. Perhaps.
> My wife had died, that was one thing; our son, who came over for the funeral, had gone back to -------; and one's patients can only provide friendship which is spurious – or, if not, then dangerous. I wasn't *that* lonely; it wasn't *that* bad: but I needed some sort of short break. My partners agreed. (1.5.1)

In this early draft, the narrator is not yet retired and refers quite bluntly and almost casually to his wife's death, as marked by the informal phrase 'that was one thing'. In the published version, the narrator has had two children, is retired and is much more reluctant to admit to his wife's death as illustrated by the aposiopesis marked by the suspension points in the passage below:

> I thought of writing books myself once. I had the ideas; I even made notes. But I was a doctor, married with children. You can only do one thing well: Flaubert knew that. Being a doctor was what I did well. My wife ... died. My children are scattered now; they write whenever guilt impels. They have their own lives, naturally. (13)

The three-line passage about the narrator being a 'Flaubert buff' has been condensed into a brief mention of Flaubert ('Flaubert knew that'), which, placed in the middle

---

[33] Barnes, 'When Flaubert Took Wing', 20.
[34] Interview by Guignery, in *Conversations*, ed. Guignery and Roberts, 108.

of a paragraph about the narrator's personal life, already suggests the extent to which the French writer invades Braithwaite's private life and helps him sidestep traumatic issues. The references, in the draft, to his feelings of 'love and friendship' for Flaubert, his sense of intimacy related to the profession of the writer's close family as well as his personal emotions – 'lonely', 'bad', even if denied – have disappeared in the final version which is more factual and concrete with such monosyllabic or disyllabic words as 'books', 'ideas', 'notes', 'thing'. The syntax is also more rigid and less fluid, as though reflecting the partitions the narrator is intent on erecting between his inner and outer selves.

It should also be noted that the published novel refers to the narrator as having merely 'thought of writing books' while in the rewriting of the first draft, Braithwaite presents himself as a published author. Indeed, after crossing out the sixth paragraph of Chapter One reproduced above, Barnes wrote this amended version on the next page:

> I'm a bit of a writer myself. I suppose you can always call yourself that, even if you haven't published anything for nearly thirty years. Just a couple of novels, back in the Fifties; then – what? – marriage and the care of children intervened. Supervened, rather. I don't regret it, not at all, there are far too many books published anyway, and mine weren't that good – and I'm sure you should try and concentrate on doing one thing well. Flaubert would have agreed. So, family life was my thing – until last year, when my wife died. Our children, well, they're a bit scattered now. They have their own lives, naturally. (1.5.1)

While this paragraph refers to 'a couple of novels', the (then discarded) cast of characters mentioned (under erasure) a novel and a collection of short stories: 'Braithwaite, Geoffrey. b.1921. Doctor, retired. Widowed; one s[on], one d[aughter]. ~~Pub. Under the Skin (1951, novel), and These Old Bones (1956, stories)~~' (1.5.3). The two titles of Braithwaite's books are related through their use of words which point to the corporeal armature and surface (in keeping with the narrator's medical profession), possibly staying away from a deeper emotional level. They are also stereotyped expressions which suggest a clichéd relation to language on the part of Braithwaite. Incidentally, one of the discarded titles for Barnes's second novel *Before She Met Me* was *The Skull Beneath the Skin*,[35] and one of the early titles of *Arthur & George* (published some twenty years after *Flaubert's Parrot*) was *The Skin of Things*.[36] In the published text of the 1984 novel, the narrator is probably no longer a published author because it would have placed the book within a too constricting literary circle. As Barnes said in an interview, 'I very much didn't want Braithwaite to be a writer because there's nothing worse than a writer writing about writing.'[37]

In addition, the published version greatly condenses the paragraph in which the narrator presents himself, merely keeping the idea of 'doing one thing well' and of

---

[35] See p. 54.
[36] See pp. 194–5.
[37] Garth Blaine, 'Books. Mutual Admiration Society', *Queen's Counsel*, 1984, 300 (Barnes's papers 1.18).

children (rather than one son in the first version) being 'scattered' and having 'their own lives'. The revelation of the wife's death is also more hesitant than in the first draft:

My wife had died, that was one thing; (first draft)
So, family life was my thing – until last year, when my wife died. (second draft)
My wife ... died. (final version)

While the first draft disclosed the death of the narrator's wife at the beginning of a new paragraph, using the pluperfect, the second and final versions make it less obvious by placing the information in the middle of a paragraph and by using the powerful aposiopeses of dots for the final version and a dash for the second one. The second version is marked by a ternary rhythm which postpones the traumatic revelation until the end of the sentence, thus creating a similar effect to the published text in its condensed form, while the use of the preterite (rather than the pluperfect) in both cases reduces the distance between that death and the present and thus brings the narrator's sense of loss to the surface.

In the draft pages that follow, the description of Braithwaite's wanderings in Rouen and its surroundings and of his visit to the Museum of the Hôtel Dieu was less developed than in the published version, while the discovery of the two parrots themselves – 'And then I saw the parrot.'; 'And then I saw it.' – and the next descriptive paragraphs are very similar to the final text: 'Then I saw the parrot.' (16), 'Then I saw it.' (21). The interpretation of the parrot in *Un Cœur simple* was more condensed in the first draft and the narrator relied more on self-reflexive comments – 'I put that last bit rather brutally' – and on attempts to engage the reader – 'read it for yourselves', 'Look at it this way' – even if the published version also relies on imperatives, such as the anaphora of 'Imagine' (17), and regularly uses the pronouns 'you' and 'we'. In the first draft, Barnes let his narrator come up with his own original images, although self-deprecatingly: 'metaphors burst the surface of [Flaubert's] brain like schools of dolphin (he would have thought of something much more accurate than that for a start)', while in the published text, he chooses to have Flaubert's voice prevail, quoting for instance: 'I am devoured by comparisons as one is by lice' (19), from a letter to Louise Colet of 27 December 1852.

This more direct (and overwhelming) presence of Flaubert in the final version of the opening chapter can also be felt in the most personal chapter of the book, 'Pure Story'. An early draft included fewer references to Flaubert, as if the narrator allowed himself to leave the French writer aside for a while to concentrate more fully on his personal trauma. For instance, the draft did not include the reference to Bouvard et Pécuchet's advice on 'How to Forget Friends Who Have Died' (160), nor Flaubert's quotes 'Sadness is a vice' (161), 'Is it splendid, or stupid, to take life seriously' (163, 168) or 'Next to not living with those one loves, the worst torture is living with those one doesn't love' (164) – which all conclude or start paragraphs (thus leaving the first and last words to Flaubert) –, nor Alexandre Dumas *fils*'s advice to kill the adulterous woman (163), the description of Flaubert's art as 'realistic but not discreet' by the prosecutor of *Madame Bovary* (164), the quote from *L'Éducation sentimentale* about Frédéric taking Rosanette as his mistress 'out of despair, like someone committing suicide' (165), the reference to Carthaginian elephant drivers carrying a mallet and a chisel in *Salammbô* (169) or the paragraph containing maxims for life (169). The early version therefore left more room for the narrator to share his personal grief while the published text shows him as persistently hiding behind Flaubert and thus distancing his emotions further.

In the longest chapter of the book, 'Cross Channel', the narrator starts lifting the veil about his personal life and compares the three stories he has to tell, 'one about Flaubert, one about Ellen, one about myself' (85–6). In an early draft (1.5.2) and the 'third copy' (1.5.4) in the archives, this passage was absent: instead of the thirteen-line segment about the three stories – from 'Just getting braced to tell you about … what? about whom?' (85) to 'I am telling you Flaubert's story instead' (86) –, the drafts offered a condensed version of merely two lines: 'I'm just getting braced to tell you something about myself. I don't know why I should; but you seem to expect it.' (1.5.4), in which the last words echo those of the next paragraph in the published novel: 'You expect something from me too, don't you?' (86). The original drafts thus placed Braithwaite at the forefront – 'something about myself' – while leaving his wife and her story in the wings. In addition, the lack of any aposiopesis in the draft (marked by the dots and the two questions in the published text) gave the narrator an air of greater assurance.

In a later draft (1.5.1), the contending three stories were listed: Braithwaite's own story was 'the dullest' (against 'the simplest' in the final version) while his wife's story was 'the truest, the one that keeps rising up inside me and demanding to be told' (against 'more complicated, and more urgent' in the published text). This draft was also more explicit about the reason why Braithwaite was telling the reader 'Flaubert's story instead' (86) as it included an extra sentence at the end of the paragraph: 'I tell his story to stop myself thinking of hers.' Braithwaite's straightforwardness was already blatant in the second draft of the first chapter when the narrator, visiting the beaches of the 1944 Normandy landings, declares himself unmoved by the memories of his friends who died there (12) and adds: 'Was I still grieving for my wife? Yes' (1.5.2). This last fragment was probably deleted because the narrator was revealing too much too early about his trauma. The published novel thus portrays a more reticent and oblique narrator.

One should note that in *Flaubert's Parrot*, the first name of the narrator's wife, Ellen, is not revealed until the middle chapter 'Cross Channel' (84, 85–6) and then reappears in 'The Case Against' (126) and 'Pure Story' (161ff). On the other hand, in an early draft and in the 'third copy', the name did not appear in 'Cross Channel' as the pronoun 'She' was preferred to the first name in 'Ellen tapped her heel' (84) while the passage about the three stories, including 'one about Ellen' (85), was absent. The narrator's unnamed wife was thus kept even more at a distance from the reader. In a later draft, the wife's name finally appeared, but as 'Elspeth', in 'The Case Against' and 'Pure Story' (1.5.1). When asked about the change to Ellen, Barnes answered: 'Elspeth, as an English Christian name, has connotations of virtue and perhaps spinsterhood, and I needed a name which better suited the character's racier life.'[38] One may also add that the first choice made the full name 'Elspeth Braithwaite' a rather challenging name

---

[38] Private email correspondence with the author, 1 April 2016.

to pronounce with its three sibilants while the double consonant of 'Ellen' aptly mirrors the double consonant in 'Emma' (although Barnes does not think that was at issue).[39]

In 'Cross Channel', the narrator is at pains to convince the reader that he is 'aiming to tell the truth' (96) and is 'honest' and 'reliable' (97).[40] The draft made that claim more explicit thanks to an added comment between brackets: '(Though from your point of view, how can you know to believe me? I'll tell you how: check anything I've told you about Flaubert. It's all true. It's all checkable. I'm not going to bully you with footnotes, but take something at random and check it. Go on. Pick any card)' (1.5.1 and 1.5.4). This fidelity to truth is also one that Barnes insisted on in his letter to Liz Calder:

> About the fiction/fact weave: I don't intend the surface of the book to be difficult or ambiguous. That's to say, the reader must, on the whole, be able to feel his feet on the ground, to know what is true and what isn't. For instance, the narrator isn't allowed ~~(except on occasions where it is pretty obvious)~~ to make anything up about Flaubert; ~~the~~ facts ~~which the narrator dispenses about the writer are all (as far as I can make them)~~ true. (1.5.3)

Barnes asserted this again in several interviews after the publication of the book, for instance, when he declared: 'I intended the rules of the game to be as clear as I could make them. It seems to be that all the information that Geoffrey Braithwaite gives you about Flaubert is true or is as true as he and I could make it.'[41] And yet, some readers were unsure about the balance between truth and fiction, as for example Barnes's own brother, the philosopher Jonathan Barnes, who wrote to him on 13 May 1984: 'I've just read your Parrot, with great pleasure. But in my pedantic way I wonder how much is invention. In particular, <u>did</u> Daudet dislike lentils, and for that reason, or is that a product of your ingenious imagination? I think we shld be told' (1.16.7). The philosopher's question relates to the anecdote about Daudet's 'schoolboy visit to a brothel' which lasted for two or three days: 'The girls kept him concealed most of the time for fear of a police raid; they fed him on lentils and pampered him thoroughly. He emerged from this giddying ordeal, he later admitted, with a lifelong passion for the feel of a woman's skin, and with a lifelong horror of lentils' (169). The anecdote is real and related in those very terms in the Goncourts' *Journal*.[42] It was while researching *Flaubert's Parrot* that Barnes came across Alphonse Daudet's notebook on his syphilitic

---

[39] One detail about Ellen Braithwaite, 'she laughed easily, she bruised easily' (163), would find an echo some thirty-five years later in *The Only Story* in which Susan Macleod is remembered by the narrator Paul as 'laugh[ing] at life' (33) and when he notices a dark bruise on Susan's upper arm, she says carelessly: 'I bruise easily' (50). Another distant echo may be heard between Paul's remarks that 'first love cauterises the heart' (71) and 'his heart had been cauterised' (168) in *The Only Story* (Paul is 19 when he falls in love with 48-year-old Susan) and Braithwaite's reference to Flaubert's 'obsessive passion for Elisa Schlesinger' (when they meet in 1836, he is 14½ and she is 26) which 'cauterises his heart' (27).

[40] In *The Only Story*, the narrator concedes that some of the details he remembers about his past might not be accurate and that he might have invented some, but he also insists on his truth-telling: 'I'm not trying to spin you a story; I'm trying to tell you the truth' (34).

[41] Interview by Guignery, in *Conversations*, ed. Guignery and Roberts, 107.

[42] Edmond et Jules de Goncourt, *Journal des Goncourt: Mémoire de la vie littéraire. 1895–1896*. Tome XXI, ed. Robert Ricatte (Monaco: Éditions de l'imprimerie nationale de Monaco, 1956), 37.

decline, *La Doulou*, in the Taylorian Library in Oxford, and some twenty years later, he translated the notebook into English (*In the Land of Pain*, 2002).[43]

In *Flaubert's Parrot*, another interesting dimension about Braithwaite which was partially deleted in the final version concerns his literary tastes. In 'Cross Channel', instead of revealing private details about himself, the narrator presents himself, as François Mauriac did, by telling the reader about his favourite authors and the ones he disliked:

> I could play the Mauriac game, perhaps. Tell you how I brought myself up on Wells, Huxley and Shaw; how I prefer George Eliot and even Thackeray to Dickens; how I like Orwell, Hardy and Housman, and dislike the Auden-Spender-Isherwood crew (preaching socialism as a sideshoot of homosexual law reform); how I'm saving Virginia Woolf for when I'm dead. (97)

The original draft was longer, listing more writers and giving specific information about them (1.5.2). About 'Wells, Huxley and Shaw', Braithwaite revealed that he 'became disillusioned with them in the reverse order'; he presented Orwell as the 'odd example of a writer whose novels give a lot more pleasure than they have any right to'[44] and added 'some Strachey, some Kipling' to the writers he liked.[45] He was more prolific about the authors towards whom he was reticent:

> Lawrence? Well, more the sort of writer you think of as being a good thing but would pay money not to have to read. None of the dandies, from Beerbohm or Nabokov. Golding, yes, Amis when he's at his least jolly; Greene once every other book. (1.5.2)

About Woolf (who, like the fictional Ellen, committed suicide), he added: 'My wife used to read her, though I think she did so principally to annoy. Like the way she used to ask my advice about the colour of her clothes and then deliberately ignore it' (1.5.2). In 1995, when he was writing *England England*, Barnes asked Hermione Lee who was to publish her monumental biography of Woolf in 1996: 'Is V.W. the most intelligent person you know? In the top 5?' (1.3.3).

Barnes's reference to Kingsley Amis in the deleted passage above is quite ironic as the author of *Lucky Jim* never showed much interest in *Flaubert's Parrot*. Barnes recalls an evening in 1983, when he was having a drink with Amis who 'made the mistake of asking [Barnes] what [he] was working on'. Barnes 'made the mistake of telling him'

---

[43] Baron, 'Nothing to Be Frightened Of'.
[44] Barnes devoted an essay to George Orwell in 2009. Julian Barnes, 'Such, Such Was Eric Blair', *New York Review of Books* 56, no. 4 (12 March 2009): 17–19. Reproduced as 'George Orwell and the Fucking Elephant' in *Through the Window* (26–40).
[45] Barnes devoted two essays to Rudyard Kipling. Julian Barnes, 'Sentimental Journeys', *Guardian*, 11 January 2003, Review 4–6; 'Soul Brothers.' *Guardian*, 5 November 2005, https://www.theguardian.com/books/2005/nov/05/fiction.classics. Accessed on 19 January 2019. Reproduced as 'Kipling's France' and 'France's Kipling' 'in *Through the Window* (77–100). Together with Hermione Lee, Barnes took part in two radio programmes on Kipling. 'The Proper Vehicle of Passion', BBC Radio 4, 29 April 2004 and 6 May 2004; 'Kipling and France', BBC Radio 4, 10 and 17 November 2005.

and after a while 'glanced up, and was confronted with an expression poised between belligerent outrage and apoplectic boredom'.[46] This reaction is supported by a postcard Amis sent to Barnes's wife, Pat Kavanagh, on 6 January 1984: 'What a lovely party. ... Tell J. sorry I showed boredom over Flaubert's Parrot – sure it will be great in the book' (1.17.2). However, things did not improve after publication, as Barnes recalls: 'Kingsley Amis, to whom I naturally sent a copy, let it be known that he had never got beyond the third chapter; though might have considered plodding on a bit further if only one of the two chaps there had pulled out a gun and shot the other chap.'[47] Amis even rebuked his friend Philip Larkin for reading too much of Barnes in a letter of 28 November 1984:

> I don't know what you think you're playing at, all this reading Julian Barnes. I know he sends you his works, and he does admire you, and he is quite good, but he's also a bit of an R-scrawler, hoping for a puff. I stopped reading F's P as soon as it was clear that the fellow wasn't going to find in F's works concealed instructions for finding a hidden treasure in a sleepy little village in the Vosges.[48]

On the other hand, Larkin was greatly impressed by *Flaubert's Parrot*. He wrote to Barnes on 25 October 1984 that he read '2/3rds of the book one night, and the rest in bed between 5 & 6 a.m. the next day. Couldn't put it down, as they say', even if he also added: 'I am at a loss to know why it held me.' He went on:

> As I read on, I kept thinking. 'This is going to have an awfully good end', and it didn't; it didn't have any sort of end. When I read, finally, the doctor's tragedy, I thought 'But this hasn't anything to do with anything'; and it didn't, and yet it's all part of the same thing, the 'resonance of despair' (who wrote that?), the subtle echoes and repetitions, the stark misery that gets at you through this most unexpected and unlikely framework.[49]

Larkin concluded that *Flaubert's Parrot* was 'a most extraordinary and haunting book' and a few weeks later chose it as one of his 'Books of the Year' for the *Observer*:[50]

> Of *Flaubert's Parrot* all I can say is read it, and see if you can reconcile the two books it seems to hold: the explicit assemblage of marginal semi-researched ruminations on Flaubert's life and writing, and the implicit recital of agonised conclusions as the narrator's own tragedy slowly emerges. A mesmeric original.[51]

---

[46] Barnes, 'When Flaubert Took Wing', 20. Barnes also told the anecdote to Zachary Leader for his biography of Kingsley Amis: 'after about thirty seconds of fervently explaining *Flaubert's Parrot* to Kingsley, out of the corner of my eye I caught him with a look which meant "If you'd only hand me a machete I'd have this man's head off in an instant"'. Leader, *The Life of Kingsley Amis*, 776.
[47] Barnes, 'When Flaubert Took Wing', 20.
[48] Leader, *The Life of Kingsley Amis*, 986.
[49] Thwaite, ed. *Selected Letters of Philip Larkin*, 721.
[50] Martin Amis also chose *Flaubert's Parrot* as one of his 'Books of the Year' in the same newspaper. Martin Amis, 'Books of the Year', *Observer*, 2 December 1984, 19.
[51] Larkin, 'Books of the Year', 19. Many years later, Barnes agreed that Braithwaite was 'a Larkiny character' in its gloominess and Britishness. Guignery, *Novelists in the New Millennium*, 23.

Larkin thereby beautifully pointed to the richness and hybridity of the book, qualities which clearly emerge from the archives as the various drafts and notes show how meticulously Barnes conceived his 'stories' and weaved together the threads of Flaubert's life and work with those of his fictional narrator.

5

The Barnes apocrypha

1. *A Literary Guide to Oxford*: The itinerary of a book that was never published

In the early 1970s, as he was nearing the end of his job as a lexicographer for the *Oxford English Dictionary Supplement* (1969–72) and then reading for the bar (qualifying as a barrister in 1974), Barnes gathered material, anecdotes and quotes from and about writers who had lived in or near Oxford, or had read or taught at some of the colleges to write *A Literary Guide to Oxford* whose first (then discarded) main title was *Refuge of the Elect* (1.9.2), a quote from C. S. Lewis's poem 'Oxford' (1919).

In September 1971, Barnes started sending part of his manuscript to publishers (Blackwell, Oxford Illustrated Limited) who turned it down. On 31 August 1972, he was contacted by Diana Saville at A. D. Peters literary agency (for which Pat Kavanagh was working although they did not meet until March 1978). His friend Redmond O'Hanlon had given them Barnes's name, saying his 'Literary History of Oxford' was 'two-thirds finished' and Saville indicated she would 'very much like to read the manuscript' (1.17.1). On 11 October 1972, after meeting Barnes in Oxford and reading the manuscript 'with a lot of interest, and a lot of amusement', she declared that her agency would take on the book and circulate it among publishers (1.17.1). Hodders and Batsford, as well as John Murray turned it down while the publishers David and Charles objected to the construction of the book but were willing to meet the author. On 29 November 1973, Harvester Press (in Brighton) agreed to take on the book and offered a pre-publication advance of £75 but asked for substantial revisions. On 9 September 1974, Barnes sent his 304-page revised typescript to the publisher accompanied by a rather stern letter: 'Here is the final, complete, improved, expanded, perfected and unimprovable version of the Literary Guide. It's been quite a slog – lots of new material included, every page rewritten and (I hope you will tell me) more accessible and readable now' (1.17.1).

The first completed version of the guide contained 200 pages bound with a string and no introduction; it included many handwritten corrections and additions, sentences or part of paragraphs crossed out, and complementary loose sheets. In the margin, Barnes wrote such indications as 'poor', 'still poor', 'extend?', 'redo', 'expand with quotes or descriptions?', 'reorder?', '?cut some of these', '?improve', '?dull', 'no, boring' (1.8.3), which shows how relentless he was in his judgement of his own work. The final 304-page typescript is dedicated to Laurien,[1] divided into five parts, and was to include six maps (with the main streets and names of areas of Oxford mentioned in the book) and twenty-five illustrations for which Barnes had asked for reproductions and copyright permissions. The archives include the early version with corrections, the uncorrected carbon typescript, the revised typescript, Barnes's correspondence with literary critics, historians and publishers as well as some of the copious notes he took while researching the book, some of them including quotations and precise bibliographical references. One index card for 'General Quotes' includes a reference to Sir John Cecil Masterman's novel *To Teach the Senators Wisdom or an Oxford Guide-Book* (1952) about a group of dons who come together to draft a guidebook to Oxford (1.9.2). Barnes selected a quote from Masterman's novel where the don who had the original idea for the book denies the fact that his guide will 'describe every college and tell its history':

> My Oxford guide-book isn't going to be like that in the least. A guide-book of the ordinary kind, full of facts and detailed descriptions and statistics and useful information – good heavens, what could be more awful! 'Guide-books are usually *biblia abiblia*, books that are not books but assemblies of facts strung together by innocent amateurs or sweated hacks.' I read that somewhere in a review the other day. But *my* guide-book isn't like that at all. … To begin with an Irishism, the book will be full of omissions.

In the next lines of the novel, the don exclaims: 'It's not to be a book of reference; it's to be much more a work of the imagination. … all I want is the illustrative fact, not the complete list, still less the catalogue.'[2] Although Barnes did not include the selected quote in his own book, the general idea might have inspired the way he wrote *A Literary Guide to Oxford*, inducing him in particular to try and avoid the catalogue format which was the main pitfall of such a project. The table of contents shows nevertheless that the guide was organized in a fairly systematic structure:

Preface
    1. The university [pp. 1–161]
        i. Men's Colleges   [21 colleges]
        ii. Women's Colleges   [4 colleges]
        iii. Defunct Halls   [3 colleges]
        iv. The Newdigate Prize
        v. The Professorship of Poetry
    2. The city [pp. 162–232]
        i. Central Oxford
        ii. North Oxford
        iii. West Oxford

---

[1] Laurien Wade, born Beesley, to whom *Metroland* is also dedicated. See note 23, p. 139.
[2] J. C. Masterman, *To Teach the Senators Wisdom or an Oxford Guide-Book* (London: Hodder and Stoughton, 1952), 26–7.

    iv. East Oxford
    v. The River and the Canal
3. A gazetteer of parts of Oxfordshire and Berkshire within fifteen miles of the city [pp. 233–79]
4. Appendices [pp. 281–90]
    i. Burials in and around Oxford
    ii. Jane Austen and Oxford
    iii. Oxford characters in the writings of Lewis Carroll
    iv. A Key to Jude the Obscure
5. A list of novels about Oxford, with descriptive comments [pp. 291–304] (1.8.6)

The short preface (which was added on the recommendation of the publisher) states that the purpose of the book is 'to record and describe the writers who have lived in or near Oxford, or who have been educated here; to say when they were here, what they wrote and did here, why they left, if and how Oxford affected them, what they thought of it, and what it thought of them'. It goes on to explain its necessary restriction to 'the lives and works of imaginative writers' while they were in Oxford without going much further into their subsequent careers and to a fifteen-mile geographic limit for the writers living outside the city itself.

The first three subsections of the first part are arranged in alphabetical order of colleges, and in each section, Barnes briefly presents the college and then chronologically refers to the writers who studied or worked there. For each of them, he provides specific dates of when they came up to Oxford and went down, as well as results, anecdotes and quotes from or about them. For instance, drawing from Robert Graves's autobiography, he refers to T. E. Lawrence's habit (at All Souls) of ringing 'a station bell out of his window into the quadrangle, on the grounds that the college "needs waking up"', his exciting plans 'to kidnap deer from Magdalen park' and his organizing the first strike of college servants 'for better pay and better hours' (1.8.6, p. 3). He quotes Southey's harsh judgement on the University ('there is little good learnt at Oxford, and much evil', 1.8.6, p. 6) and mentions Graham Greene's heavy drinking and experimentation with Russian roulette (1.8.6, pp. 14–15), Dom Moraes's ill-fortune of mistaking his interviewers for his fellow-interviewees at Jesus College (1.8.6, p. 51) and Philip Larkin's delight at hearing Kingsley Amis do 'his motor-bike-failing-to-start noise' when they were both at St John's (1.8.6, p. 112). Barnes also dwells on Evelyn Waugh's virulent antipathy towards his history tutor Cruttwell, whose name is used several times in Waugh's novels for disreputable or pitiful characters, and mentions that Toby Cruttwell, in *Decline and Fall* and *Black Mischief*, is 'a man who is always available if a last-minute dinner-guest is required' (1.8.6, p. 49).[3] Barnes would later mistake Cruttwell for another recurring Waugh character, Basil Seal, the pseudonym

---

[3] It is actually in *Black Mischief* that Toby Cruttwell is asked to dinners at the last minute. After a party, Basil Seal's mother remarks: 'Captain Cruttwell is very silly, but it was kind of him to come at all at such short notice'; 'I had to ask poor Toby Cruttwell. Who else *was* there I could ask at the last moment.' In *Decline and Fall*, Cruttwell is a burglar who then becomes a Conservative MP. Evelyn Waugh, *Black Mischief* (Boston: Back Bay Books, [1932] 2002), 109, 111.

he took to write thirty food reviews in the *Tatler* from 1979 to 1982: 'I chose the wrong character. Basil Seal is, as you know, an Evelyn Waugh character, but I thought that he was the man who was always available for dinner. ... this was the ideal guy to have as a restaurant critic, because he always needs a meal.'[4]

The fourth section of *A Literary Guide to Oxford* is devoted to the Newdigate Prize, 'the University's most important prize for English poetry', for 'undergraduates who have not exceeded four years from matriculation' (1.9.1, p. 146), and provides information as to the requirements, prize money and well-known winners, while the next section about the Professorship of Poetry (set up in 1696) names its incumbents (among them Matthew Arnold, Cecil Day Lewis, W. H. Auden and Robert Graves) and the poets who refused to stand, like John Ruskin, Robert Browning or Sir John Betjeman.

The second part ('The city') lists specific streets and houses (meticulously including house numbers) where writers (or fictional characters) lived or places they frequented, such as the Cadena tea shop on Cornmarket Street where Robert Graves (during the First World War) and W. H. Auden (in 1956–61) would go in pyjamas and dressing gown for the former and in slippers for the latter (1.9.1, p. 175). The third part on areas of Oxfordshire and Berkshire outside the city (arranged alphabetically) allowed Barnes to focus at length on such figures as Lady Ottoline Morrell who held her 'only partially successful' literary and artistic salon in Garsington from 1912 to 1927 and received such guests as Bertrand Russell, Lytton Strachey, D. H. Lawrence, W. B. Yeats, T. S. Eliot, Virginia and Leonard Woolf, E. M. Forster, Clive Bell or Roger Fry (1.9.1, pp. 247–53). Barnes deleted several passages from the early version of this second part because the places were judged 'too far' (1.8.3, pp. 157, 180, 182). After short appendices,[5] the typescript ends with a list and brief description of eighty-seven novels about Oxford published between 1756 (*Memoirs of an Oxford Scholar*, attributed to John Cleland) and 1973 (Martin Amis's *The Rachel Papers*), ordered chronologically.

This 'final' version of the guide is one third longer than the original typescript because of the detailed remarks made by two readers from Harvester Press, which guided Barnes in his corrections and additions (1.9.2). In his four-page report, the first reader noted that he found the idea 'interesting and amusing' and remarked that the author 'handles some of his anecdotes with a neat touch'. Wondering who would buy and use the guide, he surmised that, in addition to 'Oxfordians, some faculty etc' and people 'who know "Oxford in literature"', it would be 'in the main tourists, men in crewcuts from Ohio "doing the city", and people who would like to find "cute" little houses to photograph'. He therefore recommended adding maps and organizing the text 'around "do-able" tours, rather than on a College-by-College system', thus splitting it all up 'into half a dozen walks', a suggestion Barnes did not follow up although he planned to include maps. Still thinking of '[o]ur man with all the cameras from Ohio', the reader argued that the work was obviously that of an 'insider', using some Oxford jargon that would need to be explained to the perplexed outsider: 'tell our man from

---

[4] Interview by Guigery and Roberts, in *Conversations*, ed. Guigery and Roberts, 175.
[5] The early version had more appendices announced in the table of contents ('Dickens and Oxford', 'George Eliot and Oxford', 'A Key to characters to Clough's Bothie') but these were crossed out and do not feature in the early version or any later version of the guide (1.8.3).

Ohio that a Demy was a foundation scholar of Magdalen, who had half the allowance of a Fellow'. Mentioning 'gaps', he named writers who should be added and recommended more information on living figures who are 'probably the kinds of people that intrigue users/readers'. The reader also required more anecdotes and 'yarns' to 'lighten things' and use material in a 'more vivid fashion', adding: 'desperate measures are needed to avoid any semblance or echo of a catalogue'. The second reader's report of one page merely suggested a few corrections and additions for specific writers. Barnes's marks in red pen on the two reports and his addition of a hundred pages to the typescript indicate that he took most of their suggestions into account.

If the college-by-college, street-by-street structure of the book as well as its bringing together of sometimes disparate subjects may account for a lack of dynamic drive, the guide's main achievement lies in its wealth of often amusing anecdotes and quotes, testifying to the wide amount of research such a book entailed. Literary agent Diana Saville identified the strengths and weaknesses of the guide when she wrote to Barnes on 11 October 1972:

> my concern about its format is justified, but I don't see an alternative presentation which would dispense with the guide book features. ... I do think you are to be congratulated on the fact that you have turned a massive body of research, and material which could have read like a catalogue, into something manageable and readable, despite the difficulties of the format. (1.17.1)

Barnes made the book enjoyable to read by not overwhelming the reader with ostensible marks of his research even if some sources are clearly identified, such as Stephen Spender's *World Within World* to document W. H. Auden's disconcerting attitudes towards fellow undergraduates at Christ Church (1.8.6, p. 33) or Rev. W. Tuckwell's *Reminiscences of Oxford* about Lewis Carroll (1.8.6, p. 27). Quotes from books and poems are identified by author, less frequently by title, never by page number or date of publication, and the source of anecdotes is not systematically revealed, confirming that the guide, which does not include a bibliography, was not conceived as a reference book. In the section on Evelyn Waugh at Hertford College, Barnes refers to several of his novels and added in the margin of the early version 'put in dates', but he crossed that out and added 'no' (1.8.3, p. 32). However, the copy editor who annotated the revised typescript systematically indicated 'date?' in the margin whenever a title appeared, wrote 'Source' or 'Title?' next to quotations whose source was not identified (or 'an amazing omission! what is it?' when the title of a book of sketches about Oxford by Andrew Lang is not included, 1.8.6, p. 76) and added 'f.note needed' to request an explanation for such Oxford terms as 'Schools' or 'Mods' (which are examinations). S/he also proved quite harsh in some comments, writing 'woefully inadequate', underlined twice, next to two lines listing the names of three twentieth-century undergraduates who were at Brasenose College (1.8.6, p. 20), 'crummy catalogue approach' as the section on Merton College starts with a reference to two poets (1.8.6, p. 76), 'This won't do at all' upon seeing William Morris presented as 'the great Victorian jack-of-all-trades' (1.8.6, p. 40) and 'Expand. 9 lines on Tolkien is ludicrous' (1.8.6, p. 81). S/he judged the paragraph about the poet Brian Howard ('a witty spiteful poseur who was eventually to burden the book-reviewer with a single volume of verse … limited to 150 copies') 'tedious, libellous' (1.8.5, p. 31) and singled out passages that presented a risk of libel and had to be cut.

The research cards preserved at the Harry Ransom Center show that Barnes had written down the precise bibliographical references for each quotation and that their omission in the typescript was deliberate so as not to turn the guide into an academic book. Barnes also made lists of what he still needed to do such as 'Working in 9 pages of new stuff', 'Write Preface', 'Visiting local history library re house numbering', 'Doing walk to check details', 'Typing up', 'Drive-visit?', 'Bodley', 'Maps'. The last line of this long list which also includes 'Get job at Beeb' – a reference to the BBC –, 'Get dentist's appointment', 'Deliver Ms – personally?', 'Visit home?', is – quite humorously – 'Bugger off to Florence' (1.9.2), which probably shows how gruelling the work had become. The correspondence also testifies to Barnes's thorough research as he contacted a number of people to ask for further references and anecdotal material (who are acknowledged at the end of the preface). Among them were the literary critics Dame Helen Gardner (1909–86) and F. W. Bateson (1901–87), as well as the writer Marjorie Boulton (1924–2017) who suggested several books to Barnes and wrote on 14 February 1972: 'what I saw of your book suggests it is charming. I am sure there would be a demand for it' (1.17.2). Peter Quennell (1905–93), English biographer, poet and critic, gave Barnes information about Lady Ottoline and concluded his letter of 4 August 1972 with encouragements: 'A literary history of Oxford seems a splendidly ambitious project' (1.17.2).

In 1972 Barnes contacted the poet Stephen Spender (1909–95) to check some information for his guide. Their paths would cross again in 1991 when Spender invited Barnes and twenty-five British and American writers to contribute original texts for an alphabet specially drawn by David Hockney, *Hockney's Alphabet*, published by Faber to raise money on behalf of the AIDS Crisis Trust.[6] Barnes also wrote to Kingsley Amis in August 1972 (at a time when he had not yet met his son) to ask information about a scene set in Oxford in his unfinished novel *Who Else Is Rank*, written in 1944–5 in collaboration with a fellow officer, and two years later, he contacted Philip Larkin to ask a question about the third poem of 'Livings'. Larkin features in the guide for his time at St John's and All Souls College and for his novel *Jill* (1946) set in wartime Oxford. Barnes considers this 'brilliant short memoir of Larkin's time at St John's' (p. 303) the best Oxford book since Compton Mackenzie's *Sinister Street* (1913–14). Four years later, Barnes would start sending books to Larkin to be reviewed for the *New Statesman*.

Barnes's letters to various publishers requesting copies of photographs for his illustrations suggest that he planned to have the book published by Harvester Press in the spring of 1975, at a time not only when he had already become a freelance journalist, writing reviews for the *Times Educational Supplement* (his very first review appeared in May 1973), the *Times Literary Supplement* (1973–6) and the *Oxford Mail* (1974–8), but also when he had started work on his first novel *Metroland*. On 11 June 1975, however, Barnes wrote in longhand on a letter from the new executive director of

---

[6] See p. 174, 'A Dictionary of Julian Barnes', letter U.

Harvester Press, Penny Casey: 'telephoned PC who said economic situation demanded slowing down of list: book may not appear until a year this autumn (being pessimistic), altho' possibly, with luck, next spring. Affirmed intention to publish was as unshaken as when m/s first submitted. Said, if I didn't like it, I could withdraw. I said I didn't really have any choice' (1.9.3). On 11 August 1976, Barnes lost patience and wrote what he later called 'a firm but fair letter'[7] to John Piers at Harvester Press:

> It is now 2 yrs since I sent you the Ms of my Lit Guide to Ox. Our contract, as you will recall, stipulates publication w/in 12 months; your own estimate, you may recall, was of 7 months. The Harvester Press, to judge from your catalogues, flourishes. What, precisely, has happened to my book?
>
> If you are still intending to publish it, then I shd like to hear your estimated timetable. If you are not so intending, then I shd appreciate the immediate return of my Ms & illustrations. (1.17.1)

Barnes recalled some twenty-five years later: 'Never did a manuscript come back so quickly. And, worse, it had been copy-edited up to about page 60 by someone who obviously hated it and hadn't got any further.'[8] The annotations actually stop on page 113 but it seems indeed that the copy editor was getting annoyed with the book as the comments were becoming more and more vehement as s/he went along. Barnes also remembers that the final ploy by Harvester when they were going cold on the project was to suggest he write a companion *Literary Guide to Cambridge*, but he had 'no zeal (or another five years) for that'. At that time, he was disappointed that so much work had come to nothing and resented Harvester for their behaviour, but now says he is 'philosophical/relieved'.[9]

What is remarkable is that *A Literary Guide to Oxford* is the only completed work by Barnes stored at the Harry Ransom Center which has remained unpublished (and will remain so, as Barnes insists). Other writers' archives often contain unpublished short stories or novels – usually juvenilia – but such is not the case of Barnes's papers, maybe because he did not envisage a career as a writer until he started work on his first novel in his late twenties. In addition, the novelist said in an interview that he has never 'started something and abandoned it', which is why the archives do not contain any uncompleted work.[10]

Although *A Literary Guide to Oxford* was never published, Barnes borrowed a few anecdotes from it for his later books. In the section about Christ Church, the indication that 'Inside his rooms, Auden kept the curtains closed day and night' (1.8.6, p. 33) found its way into *Talking It Over* when Oliver refers to his first meeting with Gillian at his place: 'At least she didn't ask why I kept my curtains closed in the daytime. My explanations of this foible have become increasingly baroque of late: I

---

[7] Wroe, 'Literature's Mister Cool', 7.
[8] Ibid.
[9] Annotations, 22–27 March 2018.
[10] McCloskey, 'In Conversation'.

find myself announcing everything from a rare eye disease to undying homage to the early Auden.'[11]

Barnes himself studied at Magdalen College, home of Oscar Wilde, Lord Alfred Douglas and John Addington Symonds, which gave Madgalen the 'reputation for a certain stylish unseriousness' and caused its members to be 'accused of being languid and aesthetic' (1.8.6, p. 56). In the guide, Barnes mentions an anecdote about Compton Mackenzie and the Magdalen society:

> One characteristic feature of Magdalen society at this time seems to have been the limitless number of pranks, rags, and hoaxes which were perpetrated. Some of these actually worked. Typical of those that did not was the occasion when Mackenzie and his friends smuggled a pig into college in a sack, rubbed grease all over it, and let it loose, expecting its recapture to be the occasion of many a sticky, slippery, and hilarious mischance. Alas, the pig just sat down contentedly in front of the middle of a quad and obstinately refused to be either chased or disturbed. (1.8.6, p. 68)[12]

Barnes recycled the prank (but this time with a successful outlet) in *Flaubert's Parrot* and turned it into a telling metaphor about the past:

> When I was a medical student some pranksters at an end-of-term dance released into the hall a piglet which had been smeared with grease. It squirmed between legs, evaded capture, squealed a lot. People fell over trying to grasp it, and were made to look ridiculous in the process. The past often seems to behave like that piglet. (14)

In addition, the research Barnes conducted for the book (or at least the method) may have been useful when, in 1974, he was recruited as one of the seventeen members of the research team for *The Dictionary of Biographical Quotation of British and American Subjects*, edited by Richard Kenin and Justin Wintle and published in 1978. Barnes remembers the deal was that the contributors 'got 50p for every quotation they produced which made it into the final book'. Looking at his Accounts Book, he saw that in late 1974/early 1975 he was paid £157.05 as an advance for research on the Dictionary, on 8 August 1975, £163.52 and on 9 April 1976, £417, as 'final payment for work'. He commented: 'That final payment was about a third of the money I made from writing in that year, so the work, however drudge-like, was very useful to me at the time.'[13]

The 1970s were a time when Barnes lived from hand to mouth, mainly from book reviewing, often selling copies of the books he reviewed to survive,[14] a common process at the time. Barnes remembers Gaston's bookshop, 'where review copies were

---

[11] Julian Barnes, *Talking It Over* (London: Picador, [1991] 1992), 30.
[12] The anecdote is related in the third volume of Mackenzie's autobiography. Compton Mackenzie, *My Life and Times. Octave Three (1900–1907)* (London: Chatto & Windus, 1964), 102–3.
[13] Private email correspondence with the author, 23 April 2017.
[14] Leith, 'Too Clever by 10½', 93.

sold, and where suitcase-bearing literary editors tried not to coincide visits with their own deputies carrying mere spongebagfuls of surplus literature'.[15] In *Nothing to Be Frightened Of*, Barnes describes his beginnings as 'a slow and impecunious professional start' (178). A contract had been drawn up about a new edition of Holman Hunt's *Pre-Raphaelitism and the Pre-Raphaelite Brotherhood*, to be co-edited by him and Craig Raine, but the project was soon abandoned.[16] While researching his guide to Oxford, Barnes was also writing his first novel *Metroland* and putting it aside for long periods as he felt unconfident about it. Later still, he started taking notes for future novels, some of which were eventually written while others merely exist in embryonic form and are, for that reason, all the more tantalizing.

2. The unwritten books which tantalize

Do the books that writers don't write matter? It's easy to forget them, to assume that the apocryphal bibliography must contain nothing but bad ideas, justly abandoned projects, embarrassing first thoughts. It needn't be so: first thoughts are often best, cheeringly rehabilitated by third thoughts after they've been loured at by seconds. Besides, an idea isn't always abandoned because it fails some quality-control test. The imagination doesn't crop annually like a reliable fruit tree. The writer has to gather whatever's there: sometimes too much, sometimes too little, sometimes nothing at all. And in the years of glut there is always a slatted wooden tray in some cool, dark attic, which the writer nervously visits from time to time .... (*Flaubert's Parrot*, 115)

Of utmost interest for this study is the 'slatted wooden tray' in the attic, part of whose contents are now preserved at the Harry Ransom Center while others still remain concealed from the public view in the attic of Barnes's home in London. In an interview with Hermione Lee in 2016, Barnes remarked: 'There are lots of things brooding away without them turning into novels.'[17] Although he mentioned that while writing *Metroland*, he was 'entirely lacking in ideas for future books',[18] his two notebooks of the late 1970s and 1980s testify to a process of incubation as, in addition to references to books which were eventually written and published (the Duffy thrillers written under the pseudonym of Dan Kavanagh, *Before She Met Me* and *Staring at the Sun*), the notebooks contain ideas for stories and novels that were never written. As Braithwaite remarks in *Flaubert's Parrot* when analysing Flaubert's apocrypha: 'All these unwritten books tantalise. Yet they can, to an extent, be filled out, ordered, reimagined. They can be studied in academies' (121).

---

[15] Barnes, 'The Bitter Lemon Days', 15.
[16] Barnes, 'Introduction', *Metroland*, 2. In *Arthur & George*, George Edalji is given a sepia print of *The Light of the World* (1851–3) by William Holman Hunt as a Christmas gift by his father. Julian Barnes, *Arthur & George* (London: Jonathan Cape, 2005), 67.
[17] Interview by Hermione Lee, *Guardian Live*, 16 March 2016, Islington Assembly Hall, London.
[18] Barnes, 'Introduction', *Metroland*, 1.

What is noteworthy is that the unwritten books in the early notebooks are all ideas for novels or short stories, and not for any other literary genre. Barnes mentioned indeed that he gave up writing poetry at an early age: 'I did write poetry a little, from the ages of about 16 or so to about 25. But it wasn't any good. It was always prosey, argumentative poetry.'[19] On 1 April 1980, after reading *Metroland*, the author Dodie Smith wrote to Barnes: 'you seem to me to use just the right amount of dialogue to bring the characters to life. (What about trying a play?).'[20] Although Barnes never wrote a play, he said in 1985: 'I'd like to write plays, film scripts possibly.'[21] In 1987, he was asked by Karel Reisz, film director of the 1981 adaptation of *The French Lieutenant's Woman*, to write the script of Ralph Grasser's 1986 autobiography *Growing Up in the Gorbals*, of which he completed the first eighty-page draft on 6 November 1987 (1.6.7).[22] He then collaborated with Mike Newell and in January 1989 finished the first revised ninety-nine-page draft of the screenplay of *The Private Hound* (set in Ireland in 1939) based on the 1968 book by Nicholas Blake, the pseudonym for Cecil Day-Lewis, and in June 1989 he took notes for the second draft (1.12.9). Barnes says he enjoyed writing these two scripts even if they were not turned into films, but would not adapt his own work.[23] In 1985, he confessed to having had a fantasy of Woody Allen doing a film of *Flaubert's Parrot* and even got him sent a copy of the book. The hope was that Allen would buy the book for its title but then make a completely different film, as he did with David Reuben's 1969 book *Everything You Always Wanted to Know About Sex* (*But Were Afraid to Ask)* turned into a film in 1972.[24] When nothing happened, Barnes admitted: 'I think it's a book which will always remain a book.'[25] Some of his other novels were turned into films: *Metroland* was directed by Philip Saville in 1997; *Talking It Over* was made into the French film *Love, etc* by Marion Vernoux in 1996; and *The Sense of an Ending* was directed by Ritesh Batra in 2017. The three-part television adaptation of *Arthur & George*, by Ed Whitmore, was screened on ITV in March 2015.

As for the theatre, in 2007, Barnes evoked 'the catalogue of novelists' disastrous attempts at writing plays' (among whom were Flaubert, Edmond de Goncourt, Daudet, Turgenev, Henry James and Graham Greene) and added: 'I'm not sure that I have the time to learn how to be a playwright', all the more as the ideas his mind produces come to him as novels or short stories rather than plays.[26] Other people have adapted his work for the stage, such as David Edgar with *Arthur & George* which premiered at Birmingham Repertory Theatre on 19 March 2010 before its transfer to Nottingham Playhouse in April.[27] Barnes said in an interview that *Talking It Over* resembles 'a radio

---

[19] Vianu, 'Giving Up Criticism'.
[20] 'From the archive', *Metroland*, by Julian Barnes (London: Vintage, 2016), n.p.
[21] Jason Best, 'Parroting On', *Due South*, Christmas 1985–January 1986 (Barnes's papers 1.18).
[22] In an interview, Barnes admitted to 'momentary envy of Glasser's severely deprived childhood: "Sure, you might be tempted to say, 'I wish my mum had died when I was seven, and I'd had some real suffering', or something like that, but then you think, well, come."' Ian Parker, 'Print', *Blitz* 57 (September 1987): 104.
[23] Interview by Guignery and Roberts, in *Conversations*, ed. Guignery and Roberts, 185.
[24] Annotations, 22–27 March 2018.
[25] Best, 'Parroting On'.
[26] Interview by Guignery and Roberts, in *Conversations*, ed. Guignery and Roberts, 186. See also ibid., 51.
[27] David Edgar, *Stage Adaptation of* Arthur & George *by Julian Barnes* (London: Nick Hern Books, 2010).

play one listens to on a Walkman',[28] and it was adapted several times for the stage. There have been productions in Holland, Germany, Canada (in the 1990s), in Hong Kong in June–July 1994 at the Fringe Club, in Chicago in February–March 2008 at the Lifeline Theatre and in Zürich in March 2007 at the Soger Theater which proposed a joint adaptation of *Talking It Over* and *Love, etc*. The first novel was also directed by Boris Cavazza at the Slovene National Theatre Drama Ljubljana where it opened on 23 November 2007. Barnes had been in touch with the Slovene translator Valerija Cokan as early as January 1998 when he wrote to her that he was glad the adaptation she and her friend Mojca were working on at the time was not 'a simple transposition of the novel' as that 'might as well be on the radio' and it had to have 'its own dramatic movement, which is different from a book's movement'. He concluded his letter with the following words: 'Don't be too faithful. It must be a play, not a book' (1.4.5), which is very close to the advice he gave to the film-makers of *Love, etc* and *The Sense of an Ending*, urging them to betray him.[29] Barnes was also very impressed by the three-hour stage adaptation of *A History of the World in 10½ Chapters* performed in Dutch in Antwerp in April 2007, with two hundred actors divided into four groups: 'They used about 5 and a ½ [chapters], and played it in lots of different parts of the theatre – underneath the stage, amid incredible timberwork, for the Ark; down in a hydraulic lift for The Survivor, a dance sequence for Parenthesis.'[30] After these fifteen performances in 2007, another was given in Antwerp on 12 April 2017.

For all Barnes's great interest in film and theatre, he is a novelist, short-story writer and essayist, and his early notebooks contain ideas for future novels or stories, and not for drama. In his first notebook, Barnes twice made a list of the novels he wanted to write. The first includes three items:

> Novels I want to write:
> ① sexual jealousy novel
> ② WW2 novel
> ③ Praise of younger man/older woman relationship. (1.1.1, p. 16)

The first two novels correspond to *Before She Met Me* and *Staring at the Sun* written in the early 1980s while the third remained unwritten until Barnes published *The Only Story* in 2018 (with first glimpses of 'a younger man/older woman relationship' in *The Sense of an Ending* in 2011). The second list includes six items, of which the first one, *Metroland*, had already been published:

> Novels: 1) M/land
>   2) ?? The Honey Time

---

[28] Claude Mourthé, 'Julian Barnes: un savoureux éclectisme', *Magazine Littéraire* 315 (November 1993): 101.
[29] Julian Barnes, '"Merci de m'avoir trahi"', *Nouvel Observateur*, 12 December 1996, 114; Xan Brooks, 'Julian Barnes: "I told the film-makers to throw my book against a wall"', *Guardian*, 1 April 2017, https://www.theguardian.com/film/2017/apr/01/julian-barnes-i-told-the-film-makers-to-throw-my-book-against-a-wall-. Accessed on 19 January 2019.
[30] Private email correspondence with the author, 18 April 2007.

>   3) WW2 – bravery, girl as heroine, older (doctor?) husband; airman?? lover? 'A Woman of the Century'
>   4) Future novel about Death. First line: 'Now let's get this death thing straight'
>   5) Feminist, 3-couple novel
>   ⑥ War & Peace + Anna Karenina + ££££ (1.1.1, p. 26)

'The Honey Time' was the first (then deleted) title of Chapter One of *Before She Met Me*. Next to 3) and 4), Barnes wrote 'combine' and indeed *Staring at the Sun* (one of whose working titles was 'A Woman of the Century') was to be that mixture of a book partly set in the Second World War and raising questions about death. The last two items on the list seem not to have led to any specific novels, although there is a feminist strand in *Staring at the Sun* while *Talking It Over* is based on the monologues of (mainly) three characters (rather than three couples). Interestingly *Flaubert's Parrot* does not appear in any form in these lists.

In addition to the 'Death novel' which became *Staring at the Sun*, Barnes had in mind the composition of what he called 'The American Novel'. In 1984, his friend Martin Amis had published his own American novel, *Money: A Suicide Note*, and at that time, British writers were more or less expected to show their credentials by publishing such a subgenre.

Novel

> The American novel – problem solved
>   At some congress in 18th or 19th c, a vote was taken on whether the official language of the United States shd be English or German.
>   What if the Germans had carried the vote?
>   e.g. imagine the effect on Europe 1914–86 if the Americans had been on the side of the Germans in   WW1 (everyone ganging up on plucky little Germany – invaded by Belgium)
>   WW2 (invasion of Russia) – they had a moderating effect on Hitler.
>   the East – New Axis
>   Instead of Mayflower myth – who were the first Germans to land? – their day & names will be celebrated. Also, German Founding Fathers who rewrote the rather vague English constitution.
>   • visit some German community in the sticks
>   • city names will be Germanified
>
> What about Berlin Wall – and wall somewhere else?
> But what is the personal level of the story? (1.1.2)

Alternative history novels are a common genre in literature, as in, for instance, Philip Roth's *The Plot Against America* (2004) in which Roosevelt is defeated by Charles Lindbergh in the 1940 presidential election and anti-Semitism spreads in the United

States. Barnes's ultimate question above ('what is the personal level of the story?') is one he would regularly raise when writing *England, England*, his 'English novel'. In an interview in 1987, Barnes said: 'There will be an American opus. ... I certainly want to write my American Novel in two books' time – and I've got the wonderfully original twist for it that I won't reveal because someone else will write it!'[31] Part of this American opus may have found its way in some sections of *A History of the World in 10½ Chapters* (whose first draft dates from 14 April 1986), a book which is marked by a wide scope, but the novel 'in two books' time' (which would have been *The Porcupine*), set in Eastern Europe, is not the American opus which has not yet been written. This absence might be explained by the direction in which Barnes looks, as he underlined in an interview: 'Martin Amis looked very firmly to America, and I looked very firmly to the continent – my work is as much by way of French and Russian as it is British.'[32] When referring to the split in contemporary British writers between 'those who are pulled towards North America and those who are pulled towards Europe', he places himself firmly in the European camp.[33]

Another idea to be found in Barnes's early notebooks is a book of parodies:

A Book of Parodies – interest wd be only so-so: even a Queneau-style display w[ith] the same incident done in 50 ways. But a book of parodies in which each parody advanced the story or told another side of it? e.g. a plain story like the murder (or attempted) of the Royal Family, or the Queen/ Pope? Then you have

The Times
US/French papers naming murderer
Pravda
radio bulletins, TV

You have writers attending the trial, as is normal

? Murdoch
? Greene
etc
French intellectual

You have police reports?

psychiatrist's report on the accused (e.g. killing 'Queen' = homophobia, suppressing the gay in himself)

and no basic narrative voice. (1.1.2)

---

[31] William Turnbull, 'Essential Icon. Julian Barnes', *Equator*, Fall 1987, 22.
[32] Georgie Lewis, 'Julian and Arthur and George', *Powells.com*, 13 February 2006, https://www.powells.com/post/interviews/julian-and-arthur-and-george-by-georgie/. Accessed 1 March 2014.
[33] Pablo Toledo, 'Interview with Julian Barnes, Part I: "I like the idea of chance having an effect"'. *Buenos Aires Herald*, 12 February 2008, 1.

Barnes wrote a few pages of it (which are not included in the archives) but then stopped because he could not move forward and because it seemed too similar to Raymond Queneau's *Exercices de style*.[34]

Inspired by the success of *Flaubert's Parrot* and of its narrator, Barnes thought of writing a book variously called 'The Bible: a Novel by Geoffrey Braithwaite', 'Geoffrey Braithwaite's Bible', 'The Speed-Reader's Guide to the Bible' or 'The Bible for Speed-Readers'. Barnes's notes indicate that Braithwaite has felt emboldened enough by responses to *Flaubert's Parrot* to write a new book: 'GB refers to the Parrot, talks about 2nd edition – letters he's had from people ... – the Parrot has perhaps unblocked him & allows him to talk/write more easily' (1.1.2). Reflecting about the form of this Novel-Bible-Guide, Barnes wonders: '?Do a bit like a tourist guide w[ith] lots of symbols?' (1.1.2) and he writes down the premise for the book:

> Premise: that most westerners acknowledge the Bible as a general source of their civilisation & morality, yet few read it in adulthood, & few are Christians in the way that book expects. So GB's B[ible] is a rediscovery of the book by a sceptical rationalist: it's not anti-religious, blasphemous, it's more an eyebrow-raised 'so that's what our civilisation is based on'.
>
> The Bible for Speed-Readers. Why SR? Because you mightn't have time to finish it before someone blows up the world.
> Best bits – stories reinterpreted
> Boring bits to ignore
> List of book titles (these as chapter headings?) / famous quotes from each book
> Also do Apocrypha (1.1.2)

As a note to himself, Barnes wondered if there should be 'fiction content', if it should be 'a book within a book' and reminded himself to 'Check *God Knows* to see if it's been done already', a reference to the 1984 novel by Joseph Heller narrated by the Biblical king David of Israel. Barnes even went so far as to write the first sentences of the 'novel':

> In the beginning, God created the heavens & the earth. Well, that begs a lot of questions. Who created God? What existed before the beginning began? What do we mean by the heavens, and where do they join the earth? And what do we mean by create, especially: do we mean imagine, or construct, or invent by magic? Perhaps, thought [sic] this seems the obvious place to start, it is not the best place.
> My name is Geoffrey Braithwaite and I have further stories to tell you. (1.1.2)
> You notice I use the authorised version. They keep trying to update it, of course. You might as well put picture windows into a Gothic cathedral. (1.1.2)

Geoffrey Braithwaite's sceptical and mocking tone in these lines found an echo in the cheeky voice of the woodworm in the first chapter of *A History of the World in*

---

[34] Jean-Pierre Salgas, 'Julian Barnes n'en a pas fini avec Flaubert', *Quinzaine Littéraire* 463 (16–31 May 1986): 13.

10½ Chapters, a narrator who also questions the Holy Book and refers to it as 'stories'. Barnes mentioned that discarded project when promoting his 1989 novel:

> I was going to write 'Geoffrey Braithwaite's Guide to the Bible.' Which would be the entire Bible, restructured for handy modern use, with the boring bits cut out, written by an agnostic sceptic rationalist. It's another of those things that sounds like a good idea at the time, and then you realize, 'Perhaps not.' But something of that idea obviously transmuted itself into a woodworm's account of the Ark.[35]

Braithwaite is clearly a narrator Barnes was fond of and not yet ready to let go. In 1986 and 1987, he told journalists that he had already written another chapter to *Flaubert's Parrot* and expected 'sometime in the next 10 years to publish an expanded edition'.[36] He referred in particular to a new chapter on the relationship between syphilis and genius,[37] an aspect already touched upon in *Flaubert's Parrot*'s 'Braithwaite's Dictionary of Accepted Ideas' for the entry on 'Whores': 'Necessary in the nineteenth century for the contraction of syphilis, without which no one could claim genius' (158). In October 2001, as Barnes was translating *La Doulou* (*In the Land of Pain*) by Alphonse Daudet and looking for information about syphilis (which Daudet, Baudelaire, Flaubert, Jules de Goncourt, Maupassant and many others contracted),[38] the Australian psychiatrist James Durham wrote to him:

> In the 19th century there was an idea around that syphilis brought with it enhanced creative and imaginative powers, and some people were quite proud of having it. Maupassant 1877, after starting on mercury and potassium iodide: 'My hair is beginning to grow again and the hair on my arse is sprouting. I've got the pox! At last! Not the contemptible clap … no, – no – the great pox, the one Francis I died of. The majestic pox…. And I'm proud of it, by thunder.' (2.4.3)

Although Barnes never published the intended new chapter in an expanded edition of *Flaubert's Parrot*, he referred to the 'creative and imaginative powers' supposedly enhanced by syphilis and used Maupassant's triumphant quote in 'A Note on Syphilis', an essay he wrote for his 2002 edition of *In the Land of Pain* (85). In 'The Real Thing!', his 2015 review of the exhibition 'Images de la Prostitution 1850–1910' at the Musée d'Orsay in Paris, he included the exact quotation by Maupassant who referred to the pox as 'The real thing! Not the contemptible clap'.[39]

Still very much attached to the narrator of *Flaubert's Parrot*, Barnes also thought of a story entitled 'The Dinner Mistress', which was to be narrated by Geoffrey Braithwaite:

---

[35] Alexander Stuart, 'Barnes Storm', *Time Out*, 21–28 June 1989, 27.
[36] Kastor, 'Julian Barnes' Big Questions', B9.
[37] Salgas, 'Julian Barnes n'en a pas fini avec Flaubert', 13.
[38] In his *Dictionary of Accepted Ideas*, Flaubert's entry on syphilis is: 'Everyone, more or less is affected by it.' Gustave Flaubert, *Dictionary of Accepted Ideas*, trans. Geoffrey Wall (London: Syrens, [1913] 1994), 61.
[39] Julian Barnes, 'The Real Thing!' *London Review of Books* 37, no. 24 (17 December 2015): 15.

> The Dinner Mistress – Story
> Man – wife – what he really wants is e.g. roast beef, big meat dishes, red wine – she prefers fish, salads, Alsace wine etc <u>So</u>, in the (supposed) French style of a wife approving/finding a husband's mistress, she finds a (fat) gourmande, perhaps an old schoolfriend, whither he is allowed to go once or twice a week.
> ? Open 'All married men dream of adultery, but often the dream is enough.'
> Use: sexual beliefs/laws – e.g.
>
> ① exophthalmia → high sex drive
> ② big hands → big cock
>
> psychologist says: ③ women's attitude to food/cooking → attitude to sex
> <u>Include</u>: even permitted 'adultery' fosters the habits of adultery – so husband starts sneaking off with bottles from his cellar – or buying them for a cellar he starts with his dinner mistress
> <u>End</u>: he discovers some of 'his' wine missing – dinner m. finally confesses she gave it to anô man (perhaps her husband?). He is appalled a) by the betrayal
>   b) by the fact that
> she drank it far too young – i.e. not worthy of being a true dinner mistress
> ? Narrated by G. Braithwaite – at least, by an old man able to be wise about sexual matters. (1.1.2)

Although Barnes never wrote that story, in 2010 he published 'Carcassonne', an assemblage of anecdotes and reflections on affinity and love at first sight (later collected in the volume of short stories *Pulse*),[40] in which he echoes the psychologist's saying recorded in the notes above: 'A psychiatrist friend of mine maintains that there is a direct correlation between interest in food and interest in sex. The lustful gourmand is almost a cliché' (187).[41] Barnes had also delved into the topic of the connection between food and sex in 'Appetite',[42] a 2000 short story in which a woman reads recipes from cooking books to her husband, a retired dentist who has always liked his food and is now suffering from a neurodegenerative disease which causes memory loss. The description of dishes brings back memories of meals he shared with his first or second wife but as the elderly man's health deteriorates, he starts uttering sexual insanities to his wife while she is reading the recipes.[43]

---

[40] Julian Barnes, 'Carcassonne', *The Spectator*, 18/25 December 2010, 53–7. Collected in *Pulse* (185–95).
[41] Although 'Carcassonne' was published in a collection of short stories, it consists of a series of reflections by Barnes himself, starting and ending with references to Garibaldi's first and second marriages, while the middle part is made of paragraphs separated by blanks in which the author speaks in the first person. In this piece, Barnes evokes a gay friend who once said to him: 'I had the best fucky-fuck of my life in Carcassonne', and notes: 'After he died, I put his words in a novel' (192). In *England, England* (published in 1998), Martha remembers indeed 'a gay friend of hers' to whom she sent a postcard from Carcassonne and whose letter back to her started with: 'Had the best fucky-fuck of my life in Carcassonne.' Julian Barnes, *England, England* (London: Jonathan Cape, 1998), 90.
[42] Julian Barnes, 'Appetite', *Areté* 2 (Spring/Summer 2000): 53–61. Collected in *The Lemon Table* (159–73).
[43] In *Nothing to Be Frightened Of*, Barnes remembers 'the innately courteous literary man I knew who, as senility took hold, began spouting at his wife the most extreme sexual fantasies, as if they were what he had always secretly wanted to do to her' (139).

Old age was already a topic of interest for Barnes in his early notebooks and one sentence in particular recurs twice. It stands isolated and unattributed in the first notebook: '"What are the old for," thought ---, "if not to envy the young? Isn't that the point of them?"' (1.1.1); and then as part of notes for the third part of *Staring at the Sun* in the second notebook: 'Son puzzled: 'What are the old for, if not to envy the young?' Yet his mother seemed not to envy him' (1.1.2). The aphorism was not included in Barnes's 1986 novel but reappeared thirty years later in *The Only Story* in which an elderly narrator looks back on his past and remarks: 'in case you're wondering, I don't envy the young. In my days of adolescent rage and insolence, I would ask: What are the old for, if not to envy the young? That seemed to me their principal and final purpose before extinction' (17). As an older man, he realizes that one of his human functions is indeed 'to allow the young to believe that I envy them' (18) but he fails to do so. This lack of envy is confirmed in the third part of the novel written in the third person: 'At the time he believed that the function of the old was to envy the young. So, now that his turn had come, did he envy the young? He didn't think so' (209). It took Barnes three decades to include in one of his books a maxim he had had in mind very early in his career, thus showing that what is in 'the slatted wooden tray' in the dark attic remains available for future use.

In the late 1980s he also thought of writing 'Rage in Age / Old stories', a topic which became central to his 2004 collection, *The Lemon Table*, about the process of aging.[44] One of these stories has remained unwritten:

> Murder / Suicide. Paralysed woman who hates / has been betrayed by husband tells him she wants to end it with his help. Persuades him to take out life insurance, etc, encourages him even to go out with other women. At the same time, she says they must make it clear to the world that it is her decision, so she must tell 2 other people (doctor,? brother) about her decision & do so, naturally, in private, lest there be any collusion. In fact, she tells them she fears her husband wants to kill her by suffocating her & making it look like suicide. As a final touch she calls the doctor for ½ hr after time set for her death. & last thing tells husband to sit with her body for 1 hr, then phone doctor. Doctor turns up to find husband smelling of drink perhaps, & weakly claiming 'I was going to phone you'. Husband gets an exemplary sentence.
>
> Q: How bad is the husband? Is he a shit, or just normal & she persuades herself he is worse? (1.1.2)

Until the final typescript, *The Lemon Table* featured a short story entitled 'Helping Hand' (which is not included in the archives but was apparently written in the form of a quiz or questionnaire) but Barnes removed it from the collection after Hermione Lee found it 'weaker than the others' because the tone and manner were not as deep as in the other short stories (2.7.10).

---

[44] Barnes said in an interview he absolutely planned *The Lemon Table* as a book (and not as isolated stories) and that its hidden subtitle is 'Against Serenity'. McCloskey, 'In Conversation'.

In his first notebook, Barnes also considered the death of atheists as a possible topic for a novel:

> <u>Collection</u> of descriptions of how atheists die. Called: <u>How Atheists Die</u>.
> - work on to novel – one subject of study (1.1.1)

This idea resurfaced in the second notebook when Barnes was taking notes for *Staring at the Sun* and listing what the computer (abbreviated as C.) could offer: 'C. offers lists of Last Words; lists of How Atheists Die' (1.1.2).[45] Although the second type of lists did not make its way into the novel, one question pondered by Gregory in *Staring at the Sun* is 'How do people die?', which leads him to call up on the computer 'the last words of the famous' (152). Then follows a list of the ways kings, clerics, writers, artists and American presidents died. A further equivalent may be found in *Flaubert's Parrot* where the narrator lists the deaths of nineteenth-century French writers (167) and in *Nothing to Be Frightened Of* in which Barnes refers to the deaths of many people, be they atheists or not, famous or not. In this non-fictional book, Barnes quotes Montaigne who wrote: 'If I were a scribbler … I would produce a compendium of the various ways in which men have died' (169), and then offers his own condensed version of this unpublished book – 'The short version of Montaigne's scribblerish anthology would be a collection of famous last words' (169) – by quoting the last words of Hegel, Emily Dickinson, the grammarian Père Bouhours and Mozart.

Although there are no other notebooks with discarded ideas for novels or stories at the Harry Ransom Center, a folder about *England, England* includes two ideas which are unrelated to the 1998 book. The first imagined fictional work is compared to Albert Camus's unfinished autobiographical novel, *Le Premier Homme* (*The First Man*)[46]: 'The novel as unfinished (or finished) first draft, with editor's footnotes, etc, i.e. Le Premier Homme but deliberately planned as such' (1.3.3). The second idea concerns the opening of a novel:

> Opening para of novel completely conventional 3rd-person story-telling, with 'normal' characterisation, etc. Then a para-break (double space) and start again: 'No, you can't tell stories like that any more …' (1.3.3)

---

[45] In his first notebook, Barnes also thought of a 'story title: "What Do Atheists Shout When They Come?"' (1.1.1).

[46] Camus could not finish the book (which was to be the first part of a trilogy) as he was killed in a car accident in 1960. The manuscript was published in 1994 by Gallimard. In a piece of non-fiction, Barnes refers to the evolution of Camus's writing who 'began by creating in Meursault [in *The Stranger*] one of the most disaffected characters in postwar fiction' and 'ended by writing "The First Man," in which ordinary lives are depicted with the richest observation and sympathy.' Barnes, 'Hate and Hedonism', 75.

In a list of recommended books with a French bias entitled 'Good Book Guide', Barnes includes *The First Man* and calls it 'an account of growing up dirt-poor in French Algeria', as well as 'Camus's act of memory on behalf of others, a lustrous, generous and scrupulous act' (2.5.1). The published version of this piece has not been found.

The next handwritten page might be related to that metafictional opening as Barnes singles out three items traditionally featuring in conventional novels: (1) The Weather; (2) When; (3) Where. In relation to the weather, the prospective narrator notes: 'I'm going to need y[ou]r help w[ith] this' and adds: 'Denunciation of w[eather]/theory – Wordsworth / Does it really make a difference?'. Barnes's disapproval of weather references goes back to the rules he had laid down for himself when he started writing fiction, which included 'no weather'. The working title of his very first novel *Metroland* was 'No Weather' which, he explained in the annotated copy of the novel, was 'because I was going to put absolutely no references to the weather into it, having long held a readerly prejudice about "significant" weather (storms, bright spells, rainbows) in fiction. But the novel took so long to write that I tired of this title – which also came to seem a little coy.' (Morgan Library, title page)[47] Barnes was thereby echoing Mark Twain's declaration in the opening pages of his 1892 novel *The American Claimant*: 'No weather will be found in this book.'[48] Some forty years after laying down that rule for himself, Barnes had the narrator of *The Only Story* warn the reader from the onset of his story: 'don't ask me about the weather. I don't much remember what the weather has been like during my life. ... nothing significant in my life ever happened during, let alone because of, weather. So if you don't mind, meteorology will play no part in my story' (5). The narrator also imagines other questions raised by an imagined reader: 'The time, the place, the social milieu? I'm not sure how important they are in stories of love' (4), questions which recall the two other items listed for the (as-yet-unwritten) metafictional novel mentioned above: (2) When; (3) Where.

As regards 'When' in this unwritten novel, the narrator indicates: 'When I was born. Show certificate?', but asks: 'Again, what details significant?', thereby echoing Braithwaite's questions in the middle chapter of *Flaubert's Parrot* after he mentions that the reader can see the colour of his eyes – 'But do they help you?' (95) – or gives details of his height, hair and health: 'what matters about me?' (96) It also recalls Barnes's own question in *Nothing to Be Frightened Of* after he provides biographical facts about his brother: 'Does any of this help?' (156). For 'Where', the narrator of the unwritten novel notes: 'My Country', which is easily identified through the reference to the British patriotic song 'Land of Hope and Glory', but a sarcastic tone emerges from the estimation of the percentage of 'hope' and 'glory': 'on a 10pt system Land of Hope (4.5pts) x Glory (2.4 pts)'. The first-person speaker also gives information about his

---

[47] Barnes wrote this annotation in 2012; a very similar version of that sentence appears in *Nothing to Be Frightened Of*, published in 2008 (148). In a draft of *Nothing to Be Frightened Of*, Barnes offered another possible reason for discarding the title *No Weather*: 'The fact that the poet Paul Muldoon had by this time published a collection called New Weather perhaps had something to do with it as well' (3.5). Muldoon's collection of poems was published in 1973.
[48] The American author was jokingly complaining about the author 'having to stop every few pages to fuss-up the weather' and the reader suffering 'delays on account of the weather'. While Twain conceded that weather was 'necessary to a narrative of human experience', he added that 'it ought to be put where it will not be in the way; where it will not interrupt the flow of the narrative'. He therefore placed seven quotes about the weather 'by qualified and recognized experts' in an appendix entitled 'weather for use in this book'. Mark Twain, *The American Claimant* (New York: Oxford University Press, [1892] 1996), ix.

status: 'at one time, started as schoolmaster', adding 'You'll have to forgive me my little ways'.[49] Finally, he provides a humorous list of the contents of his book:
Promise of what I'm going to tell you:

(1) murders
(2) suicides
(3) …. (that was just a joke)
(4) Insights into the very heart and soul of this country (1.3.3)

The page stops here and this idea for a novel seems to have remained at this embryonic state.

More recently, in the notebook which includes the handwritten draft for *The Sense of an Ending*, Barnes wrote down a list of possible books:

- → A Question of Height
- …
- → TIO 3
- → Post-Myth novel
- → 50year novel
- → Internet suicide pact
- → halfwritten Upside Down Life story: expand /interweave
- → Euridice (3.3)

None of the ideas mentioned above have turned into novels or stories so far (not even 'TIO 3' to form a trilogy with *Talking It Over* and *Love, etc*), except for the first and last which became *Levels of Life* (2013), in which the first narrative is entitled 'The Sin of Height' and the third one about Barnes's grief and mourning after his wife's death includes a reference to Gluck's opera *Orfeo ed Euridice* (92–4). On the same page and next to the first lines, Barnes took the following notes:

	Equilibrium	
	Flat	
The Sin of Height	On the Level	~~The Delusion of Depth~~
	Surface	The Loss of Depth (3.3)

The three narratives of *Levels of Life* are entitled 'The Sin of Height' (on ballooning), 'On the Level' (in which 'lovers try to work out if the beloved is "on the level"' [3.3]) and 'The Loss of Depth' (about the descent into death and despair). Barnes's notes show that the middle narrative (dealing with the relationship between English colonel Fred Burnaby and French actress Sarah Bernhardt), which was meant to be 'not fictional – same mode as 1 & 3' and is referred to as the 'earthly story', was to connect the first and third sections: 'gradually linking pts 1 & 3?' (3.3). The insistence on its non-fictional

---

[49] In this unwritten novel, the narrator's voice partly echoes those of Geoffrey Braithwaite in *Flaubert's Parrot* and Tony Webster in *The Sense of an Ending*.

status in the preliminary notes is surprising as it is the one narrative in the book which reads like a story. It led Hermione Lee to raise the question many readers must have asked themselves: 'Did you invent their affair? It's wonderfully unclear whether the actual event of the affair is fiction or fact' (3.2). Barnes invented the affair but there is no way of knowing he did just by reading the piece.

In an interview, Barnes referred to the three sections as respectively a biographical essay, a short story and a memoir,[50] which are meant to be related through the themes of love and loss. In his notes, he defined love as 'truthfulness + magic' and associated this equation with 'photography + ballooning' (3.3),[51] two essential activities of the first narrative centred on Nadar, which are viewed with circumspection in the third: 'nowadays – having lost height, precision, focus – we are no longer sure we trust photography as we once did' (110). Barnes had been thinking about Nadar as a possible subject for a book many years before: 'It was an idea looking for a form, which it finally found.'[52] As for the meditation on grief and mourning in the third section of the book, it is only one manifestation of the writer's obsession with death, one which frequently appeared in his early notebooks and in random notes, and found its way in his novels, culminating in his non-fictional book *Nothing to Be Frightened Of*.

In *Flaubert's Parrot*, Geoffrey Braithwaite 'thought of writing books', 'had the ideas', 'even made notes' (13), but unlike his creator, he never went beyond these ideas and notes. The unwritten books are not 'a cause for resentment' (13) for Braithwaite who refers to Frédéric and Deslauriers's favourite memory of their aborted visit to the brothel at the end of Flaubert's *L'Éducation sentimentale* and remarks: 'Isn't the most reliable form of pleasure, Flaubert implies, the pleasure of anticipation?' (14). In Barnes's notebooks and random notes, the ideas for novels or stories that were never written and the sentences that have not (or not yet) been included in books may trigger off in the reader the pleasure of anticipation as the writer may still get back to them several years or decades later.

---

[50] In Lawson, 'Front Row'. In her email to Barnes of 2 September 2012, Hermione Lee writes that *Levels of Life* is 'a book with no definable genre, it's self-invented' (3.2).
[51] He writes in the second part: 'love is the meeting point of truth and magic. Truth, as in photography; magic, as in ballooning' (37).
[52] Annotations, 22–27 March 2018.

6

Staring at the Sun: A novel of forking roots and paths

Julian Barnes already had *Staring at the Sun* in mind when he was writing his second novel *Before She Met Me* and by 1983 he had completed one third of it. According to an early notebook, it was to be 'Vol. 3' of Barnes's books (1.1.1) but *Flaubert's Parrot* elbowed itself in between. Referring to his visit to Arthur Koestler in the summer of 1982, he remarked: 'I seem to be writing two novels at the same time, one of which is about Flaubert.'[1] Soon afterwards, he decided to concentrate on *Flaubert's Parrot* and *Staring at the Sun* had to be set aside for eighteen months.[2] The examination of the archives reveals Barnes's difficulties in finding a title for this book, his hesitations over epigraphs, the prologue and the beginning of the third part, and his decision to strip literary references to a bare minimum.

1. Multiple roots and titles

In an interview, Barnes gives more information about the origins of the novel:

> *Staring at the Sun* had four separate roots. I wanted to write something set in the past, partly because I was born in '46 and the time just before you were born has a peculiar sort of glow, the time which you couldn't know but which people talked about while you were growing up. Then I had wanted to write a book which had courage as a theme. Also I wanted to write a book from a woman's point of view. Also I wanted to write a book which covered 100 years.[3]

In his early notebooks, the novel appears as the 'Death novel', the 'Future novel about Death', 'Novel re death – set in future – fear of death is the one instinct they haven't been able to eradicate by drugs or social engineering', as well as the '2nd WW novel' (1.1.1/2). However, the book was not meant as a war novel, as suggested by another

---

[1] Barnes, 'Playing Chess', 480.
[2] D. J. R. Bruckner. 'Planned Parenthood and the Novel', *New York Times*, 12 April 1987, section 7, 3.
[3] Kastor, 'Julian Barnes' Big Questions', B9.

note: '2nd WW novel: no air battle descr.[iption]: just use some pilot who comes to see the heroine (perh.[aps] in love with her) & tells her what it's like (so if it's not 100% accurate, he'll be not telling her quite right)' (1.1.1). In the first part of the book, Thomas Prosser is a sergeant-pilot in the Royal Air Force during the Second World War but he has been grounded and billeted with the Serjeants in 1941 and therefore can only tell the heroine Jean about his past missions.

Because the book includes a large number of references to planes and flight manoeuvres, Barnes asked Chris Peachment, then film critic at *Time Out* and former RAF pilot, to check his typescript for any inconsistencies (1.13.5). Peachment mainly approved of Barnes's descriptions: 'Details all seem fine, re. flying', 'The tactics seem right', 'Good description of altitude flying', 'The details of the Vampire are just right'. He also gave some technical advice, for instance, 'you don't "put the stick back" and beat it', but 'open the throttle and beat it' – Barnes deleted the whole sentence which does not appear in the published version (25) – or 'Once in the descent, you don't need to keep pushing on the stick' – the ambiguous sentence Peachment was referring to was suppressed: 'I had to push hard on the stick to keep it in its dive' (1.13.4; 45). Interestingly, Barnes did not always follow the former pilot's advice on the types of planes mentioned in the book. Thus, for instance, he kept the reference to a 'Skua' (27), described by Peachment as 'a naval, carrier-based dive bomber' with a hood, even if a 'Tiger Moth' would have suited the scene better, and he retained the 'Catalinas' (31, 184), 'American amphibians which were used by the British later in the war', instead of substituting a 'Sunderland', which, according to Peachment, would have been 'safer, if less romantic'. Barnes may have elected not to follow the former pilot's suggestions precisely because he was more interested in the connotations of the plane names than in historical accuracy.

Barnes's second notebook starts with a list of the essentials of the book, which was then called 'A Woman of the Century': it was to be in three parts (1940, 1980, 2020),[4] written in the third person from a 'woman's eye' and the thematic structure was to display: 'part I physical courage; part II social courage; part III moral courage', with the following progression: 'JS becomes more brave & more intelligent as she gets older' (1.1.2). The book tallies some thirty-five occurrences of the noun 'courage', thus confirming the centrality of the theme. On a loose page of notes, Barnes wrote that Jean Serjeant's social courage was shown by her leaving her husband to bring up her child by herself and having an affair with a woman, and then added: 'or you could say that is the only form of courage we tend to experience' (1.13.4). He also wondered if he should delete Part II and merge it into Part III but decided against it as it would 'burst the 3 types of courage structure' (1.13.4). The stability of the three-part structure seems appealing to Barnes and also characterizes *Metroland*, *England, England*, *The Noise of Time* and *The Only Story*, as well as the partly non-fictional *Levels of Life*. In four of these books (the notable exceptions being *Staring at the Sun* and *The Only Story*), the three parts are given short and striking titles which form a temporal, geographical or

---

[4] In a letter to Dan Franklin, his publisher at Jonathan Cape, Barnes also gave a time scale to present *England, England*: 'c1980/c2010/c2040' (1.4.5).

thematic sequence.⁵ *Metroland, Staring at the Sun, England, England* and *The Noise of Time* are all characterized by a chronological progression and portray the main characters at specific periods of their lives, which can generally be dated precisely, thus adopting one of the structural specificities of the Bildungsroman.⁶

The original roots for *Staring at the Sun* can be guessed from the many titles Barnes conceived before and during composition. In his first notebook, when the novel was still at embryonic stage and referred to as the 'Future (+ Death) novel', a potential title was 'The Day they Put the Clocks Back', which is thus explained: 'Title from: they put clocks back 12 hours; theory: so am becomes pm & vice versa: thus people think it's morning by the sun & wake accordingly; have lunch, & find it's am. So they go on working as hard' (1.1.1). Neither the title nor the idea of putting the clocks back by twelve hours to make people work more (which may have evoked a dystopian world such as that of Orwell's *Nineteen Eighty-Four*) were retained. Later on, when Barnes had started writing the novel (and maybe even finished a draft), he wrote at the top of a loose sheet: 'Titles, in order of thinking them up', followed by:

The Only Life of Jean Serjeant
Christ/God and the Aviator
The Chinaman's Ear
The Echo Wall
A Woman of the Century
The Sky's the Limit
Question & Answer
But what is the Question?
Lindbergh's Sandwiches
~~Beneath~~ a Bomber's Moon
Questions in the Life of Jean Serjeant
The Lives of J.S.
Ordinary Miracles (1.13.5)⁷

A slip of paper also included 'The Real Question' (an allusion to the General Purposes Computer's [GPC] frustrating reaction to some of Gregory's queries: 'NOT REAL QUESTION'), 'Incidents in the Life of Jean Serjeant' ('Incident' is the word Jean euphemistically uses to refer to important events in her life, their significance to her

---

⁵ *Metroland* includes I. Metroland (1963); II. Paris (1968); III. Metroland (1977). *England, England* comprises I. England; II. England, England; III. Anglia. *Levels of Life* contains I. The Sin of Height; II. On the Level; III. The Loss of Depth. *The Noise of Time* includes I. On the Landing; II. On the Plane; III. In the Car.

⁶ In *Metroland*, Christopher is depicted as a teenager in 1963, in his early twenties in 1968 and aged 30 in 1977; *Staring at the Sun* follows Jean from childhood during the Second World War in Part I, as a mother from her forties to her early sixties in Part II and as a near-centenarian in 2021 in Part III; *England, England* shows Martha Cochrane in her childhood until she is just over 25 in the first part, in her early forties in the second part and in old age in the third part; *The Noise of Time* focuses on three important leap years in Shostakovich's life (1936, 1948, 1960).

⁷ When reading this list of titles in 2018, Barnes wrote in the margin: 'terrible titles, all of them'. Annotations, 22–27 March 2018.

being signalled by the capital letter), 'Flying' and 'Up in the Air'. In both lists, the titles relating to flying (and metaphorically to a form of transcendence) subtly connect the various parts, time periods and characters as the anecdotes behind them are repeated within the novel, thus binding the book together. For instance, the meaningful and polysemic phrase 'The Sky's the Limit' is first told by Uncle Leslie to Jean (20), and then by Jean to her son Gregory (193), and encourages characters to challenge human limitations. The anecdote of 'Lindbergh's Sandwiches' – the aviator took five sandwiches with him when he flew the Atlantic but only ate one and a half – makes Jean wonder what happened to the ones he did not eat and is a story which is transmitted from one generation to the next as Uncle Leslie first tells it jokingly to Jean (12), who takes it seriously and tries it on Prosser (23) and her husband Michael (33), before sharing it with Gregory in her old age (151). The 'ordinary miracle' of Prosser seeing the sun rise twice (2) is remembered by Jean when she is trying to relax while inserting a diaphragm (52), and the phrase is applied to Gregory when he is born and Jean is now staring at her son: 'He was an ordinary miracle' (79). As for bombers, they are regularly referred to by Prosser during the war,[8] but are transposed to a domestic scene during Jean's honeymoon when she notices that the night was cloudless and 'a full summer moon hung in the sky like a pathfinder's flare; a bombers' moon, they called it' (57). Such a bright moon illuminates the earth almost like daylight and during the Second World War, pilots used the light of a bomber's moon to zero in on their targets. In her old age, Jean uses the same image to calmly assert and accept the non-existence of God: 'We live beneath a bombers' moon, with just enough light to see that nobody else is there' (191).

As Barnes said in an interview, these, among others, are 'images, and incidents, and stories, which, as the story continues, take on more depth and significance. At first, they're just odd stories, but by the end they become metaphors'.[9] In his early notebook, he had written down a few notes about these recurrent images, which justified the tripartite structure and created a special bond between the first and third parts: 'Photos / Pictures / built into structure: e.g. Pt I ones return in Pt 3; pt3 echo things seen in book before' (1.1.2). In addition to the examples above, this binding process applies not only to the leitmotif of the mink which puzzles the young Jean for its characteristic of being 'excessively tenacious of life' (14, 15, 25, 35, 148, 149, 150, 185) but also to the vision of a 'man riding across the top of the waves on a motorbike' which appeared to a Catalina pilot off the west coast of Ireland, first related to Jean by Prosser (31) and then by Jean to Gregory (184) who transforms it into an image of God as a motorcyclist (187) or 'trick-cyclist' (188). This echoing strategy testifies to Barnes's careful attention to structure and also characterizes his later books in which words, phrases and images recur and gather meaning through accretion. As he said in an interview about *The Noise of Time*, '[t]his is often how I do write, with recurring motifs

---

[8] As evidenced by an early notebook (1.1.2), Barnes read and took notes from Rainer Minns's book about how women coped during the Second World War, entitled *Bombers and Mash: The Domestic Front 1939–45* (London: Virago, 1980). The reference to 'All Clear sandwiches' in *Staring at the Sun* (22–3, 37, 105) is borrowed from Minns's book (132).

[9] Patrick McGrath, 'Julian Barnes', *Bomb* 21 (Fall 1987): 23.

and phrases. And that's a way of building up the structure'.[10] In another interview, he referred to 'the internal skeleton' of the book, which is 'more like gristle – something between bone and muscle': 'In the course of the writing, a different skeleton develops. The first images are separate but then they become cartilage. There's also a link through language, through repetition.'[11]

The other titles imagined by Barnes for *Staring at the Sun* highlight either the central role of the heroine (by naming her right from the very first paratext) or the significance of questions. There are 112 occurrences of the noun 'question' in the novel and 83 occurrences of 'answer' as noun or verb, which shows how central these notions are. 'What is the question?' were Gertrude Stein's last words to her partner Alice B. Toklas on her deathbed, uttered after there had been no reply to 'What is the answer?' This reaction is reported in *Staring at the Sun* but Stein is only identified as an 'American writer' (153), which Hermione Lee thought 'a bit coy' as, according to her, 'the <u>one</u> thing everyone knows about Gertrude Stein is this' (1.13.5). However, Barnes deliberately kept the number of literary allusions low in this book which he wanted to be less intertextual than the highly literary *Metroland* and *Flaubert's Parrot*. As he mentioned in an interview: 'I wanted to write a book in which no one reads books.'[12] Therefore, a number of quotes in *Staring at the Sun* are offered without their authors being identified (even if their names appeared in the first draft) or were deleted.

For instance, when Gregory wonders how people die – an anticipation of a similar discussion in *Nothing to Be Frightened Of* – and considers the case of writers, dying 'with writerly things on their lips' (152), an early draft offered two names and quotes: 'Oscar Wilde had said "I am dying, as I have lived, beyond my means," and Emily Dickinson had said, "I must go in, the fog is rising"' (1.13.4). Later drafts and the published version only retain the second quote and conceal the identity of its author: 'There had been an American poet, a woman, whose final words had been, "I must go in, the fog is rising"' (152). The same process of erasure was applied to other figures (whose last words were recorded) who were named in an early draft of *Staring at the Sun* but only identified through their nationality in later drafts and in the published text: 'the French painter' (Jean-Baptiste Camille Corot), '[a]n Italian painter' (Pietro Perugino) (152), 'the French grammarian' (Père Bouhours) (153). Twenty years later, in *Nothing to Be Frightened Of*, Barnes repeated the final words of Emily Dickinson (*Nothing* 169), of the Swiss physiologist Albrecht von Haller – 'My friend, the artery ceases to beat' (*Staring* 152; *Nothing* 111) and of the grammarian Père Bouhours – 'Je vas, ou je vais, mourir: l'un ou l'autre se dit' (*Staring* 153; *Nothing* 169), but in this non-fictional book, the authors of the quotes were quite logically identified by name.

In a late draft of *Staring at the Sun*, three additional quotes and authors were cut: 'Rabelais died with a pun – on the word <u>domino</u>.[13] The naturalist Lacépède said,

---

[10] Freeman, 'How the Writer Edits'.
[11] Interview by Lee, 'An Evening with Julian Barnes'.
[12] Kastor, 'Julian Barnes' Big Questions', B9.
[13] According to the legend, the dying Rabelais wrapped himself in his domino (a hooded cloak) because of the Latin formula: '*Beati qui in domino moriuntur*' (Blessed are they who die in the Lord/in a domino). In *Nothing to Be Frightened Of*, Barnes writes that Rabelais's 'supposed deathbed utterance' was 'I am going to seek a Great Perhaps' (208). *The Oxford Book of Death* cites four different sentences as Rabelais's possible last words, including the two above (the other two are: after

"I go to rejoin Buffon." Lagny the mathematician, was unable to recognize his friends at the end, but when one of them asked him the square of twelve, he replied at once, "144"' (1.13.4). These references and the precise names were probably deleted because the form of the passage (a selection of memorable quotations) felt closer to *Flaubert's Parrot* or to a non-fictional book (like the future *Nothing to Be Frightened Of*) than to *Staring at the Sun*, and maybe Gregory sounded in those lines a bit too much like Geoffrey Braithwaite (or even like the author himself). Barnes is always very alert to his characters' specific speech type and cautious not to let them sound like him. On an early draft of the last chapter of *A History of the World in 10½ Chapters*, 'The Dream', narrated in the first person, he thus wrote: 'Cut out JB prose – he's an ordinary bloke' (1.6.9).

In *Staring at the Sun*, the omission of names for the quotations that remained may have been an incentive for the reader to try and guess who said or wrote them, possibly creating frustration and establishing a difference between the erudite readers and the less well-read. This separation would find an echo in Barnes's next book, *A History of the World in 10½ Chapters*, in the chapter entitled 'Shipwreck' when two eyes offer their interpretations of Géricault's painting 'The Raft of Medusa': the ignorant eye mirrors the uninitiated reader while the informed eye reflects the ideal reader. In an early draft of *Staring at the Sun*, Gregory wonders if death is final or the prelude to life everlasting and the narrator writes: 'He thought of Pascal at the roulette wheel' (1.13.4). In later drafts, the name was deleted and replaced by 'One of those old philosophers had once described belief as being a wager. ... Gregory imagined a moustachioed Frenchman with a feather in his hat, canted over the roulette wheel' (1.13.6; 177–8). The reader is thus expected to identify Pascal and Chris Peachment certainly did when he commented on the draft: 'This is getting like Mastermind' (1.13.5).[14]

The names of authors often remain concealed when the quotes originate from the GPC or its new function TAT (The Absolute Truth). For example, Gregory remembers: '*Immortality is no learned question*: TAT had quoted this to him at some point' (186). This sentence did not appear in the first draft which did not include the quote as an epigraph to Part III either (1.13.4), but the epigraph was added in a later draft, followed by the name of the Danish philosopher Kierkegaard (137). The reader can thus rely on their memory to identify the author when the quotation recurs fifty pages later. Another instance of an unidentified source is Gregory's remark to his mother: 'GPC came up with a good line when I was asking something else. About how it was impossible to look at either the sun or death without blinking' (155). In an early draft, the author (the French seventeenth-century aphorist La Rochefoucauld)

---

receiving extreme unction, 'I am greasing my boots for the last journey' and 'Ring down the curtain; the farce is over!'). D. J. Enright, ed. *The Oxford Book of Death* (Oxford: Oxford University Press, 1983), 330.

[14] Other examples based on pastiche or echo rely even more on the reader's erudition, as, for instance, the narrator's reference to a morning 'when the grey sky sat low and flat on the city like a saucepan lid' (168), a comic pastiche of the first line of the poem 'Spleen' by Charles Baudelaire: 'When low and heavy sky weighs like a lid.' Charles Baudelaire, *The Flowers of Evil*, trans. James McGowan (Oxford: Oxford University Press, [1857] 1993), 149.

was also unnamed but identified as belonging to a 'large category of people who are both wise and dead. I think this one was French' (1.13.4).[15]

Before coming to the final choice of *Staring at the Sun*, other possible titles were still considered. In his first notebook, Barnes described the novel as 'set in the future, with a state committee admitting (privately) that bureaucratic materialism hasn't got on top of death, explained it to the people's satisfaction (unlike religion) & that a New Answer must be found. Title: The New Answer?' (1.1.1) 'Question & Answer' was the title which remained for the longest time: it appears typed on the title page of the final draft copies (1.13.6/7), with 'The Only Life of Jean Serjeant' handwritten at the top right corner of the page on the second final draft copy (1.14.1), while Hermione Lee's notes about the book refer to 'Q&A' (1.13.5). On 29 January 1986, a reader at Jonathan Cape's delivered their report on the book which was still entitled *Question and Answer*, while two months later, on 26 March, Alison Mansbridge from Cape wrote to say she finished 're-reading Staring at the Sun' and would have proofs ready by the end of April (1.13.5), thus confirming that the final title was decided on fairly late.

Other potential titles (The Chinaman's Ear, The Echo Wall) sound more enigmatic and only become clear upon reading the book: in the Temple of Heaven in Beijing – a spiritual and larger scale version of the mundane golf course or 'Old Green Heaven' of Uncle Leslie in the first part (7) –, Jean and her fellow travellers are shown a circular 'Echo Wall' which allows people who stand at opposite points to hear one another; a young English couple, noticing an elderly Chinese man leaning his ear against the wall, believes he can hear what they say to each other (88–90). Barnes and his wife visited that Temple and saw the Echo Wall during the two-week trip to China they took in April 1981 after Barnes won the 'Restaurant Critic of the Year Competition' (Corning Prize) as Basil Seal for the *Tatler*. The writer even took a photograph of an elderly Chinese man listening to the wall. When Jean, in her old age, remembers the scene at the Temple of Heaven, she imagines what the Asian man might have made of these Western voices: 'Perhaps the words sounded beautiful to him, the voices transcendental', when they were actually very prosaic, saying 'something rude about a dead Chinese leader, then some amatory prattle' (157). This episode is significant for what it suggests about the ambiguities of language, the multiplicity of interpretations (and possibilities of misinterpretation) and the obstacles to human communication (or the suggestion for original forms of communication).

On the typescript in 1.13.4, the title for the whole book was 'The Chinaman's Ear' and the three parts each bore a title (or several to choose from) although none appears in the published text: 'Sun-Up Prosser' was chosen for Part I; 'In Asian Times' (the only typed title), 'The Chinaman's Ear', 'Cadman the Aviator' and 'The Chinese Marriage' for Part II; and 'Not a real question', 'The Real Question' and 'Question & Answer' for Part

---

[15] The quotation had already appeared in the first drafts of *Metroland* (see pp. 23–4). Martin Amis borrowed the quote for *Night Train* when referring to the female protagonist: 'she quoted some aphorism. Some French guy. Some duke. Went something like: "No man can stare at the sun or at death with a, with an unshielded eye."' Martin Amis, *Night Train* (London: Vintage, [1997] 1998), 95.

III. The intriguing titles for Part II gather meaning within the different sections: 'In Asian times' is how tour guides often start their sentences when actually meaning 'In ancient times' (90), thus confusing time and place, while the Chinese marriage is a reference to Jean's own marriage based on 'practising family planning' rather than having sex, and thus complying with Article 12 of a Chinese Marriage Act, which read: 'Husband and wife are in duty bound to practise family planning' (119). As for (Robert) Cadman the Aviator, he tried to fly from the top of the church of Shrewsbury in 1739 but crashed to death – maybe an anticipation of the fate of some characters in the book –, and Gregory mostly remembers that he was praised for his courage, a central theme in the book (111).

It is interesting to note that Jean's trip to China was considered so meaningful as to deserve to be incorporated in a title in one form or another. When she commented on the draft, Hermione Lee remarked that she was uncertain about the lengthy development on China in the second part but that it fell into place in the third part: 'There's been so little detail about her English life ("village", "market towns"), now there's all this detail about China – I wondered whether at this point you didn't know what to do with her next. Then by the time I got to part 3 I began to see why she went to China & what all that was for' (1.13.5). Jean's transformation after her trip to China is probably what allows her to reconcile herself with the uncertainties of life and to approach death with serenity. For instance, when, in her mid-fifties, she reads about the controversial anti-Buddhist essay by the Chinese philosopher Fan Zhen called 'The Destructibility of the Soul' (87), she finds it paradoxical as she surmises that the soul is an absolute which either exists or does not exist and therefore cannot be destroyed. Later in life, however, she calmly accepts the notion of a destructible soul and the absence of an afterlife: 'Of course we each had a soul, a miraculous core of individuality; it was just that putting "immortal" in front of the word made no sense. It was not a real answer. We had a mortal soul, a destructible soul, and that was perfectly all right' (191). The novel shows that Jean might be capable of visionary experiences but she remains a convinced and relaxed atheist, while Gregory follows a more traditional route and finds comfort in belief and faith, even if he is not interested in God as 'the master magician, the great prestidigitator' (188).

In the published book, the epigraph for Part II is '*Three* wise men – are you serious? *graffito, c. 1984*' (65), which is also one of Rachel's sarcastic remarks about men (123). However, the original (later deleted) epigraph was an extract in French from Jacques Brel's song 'Fernand':

Et puis, si j'étais le bon Dieu
Je crois que je serais pas fier
Je sais on fait ce qu'on peut
Mais y a la manière.
   Jacques Brel, Fernand (1.13.4)[16]

---

[16] 'And if I were God / I don't think I'd be too proud / I know, you can only do what you can / But it's the way you do it that counts.'

Barnes would later quote this passage in his 1989 non-fictional piece on Jacques Brel,[17] after mentioning the Belgian singer's 'understanding of the complication and weak starting-point of most human dealings' and adding: 'Logically, the source of all this imperfection must be imperfect Himself.'[18] By replacing Brel's censure of God (couched in popular language and irregular grammar) by a facetious mockery of men, Barnes shifted the perspective in a way which better suited the content of Part II, in which Jean becomes disillusioned with her husband and the feminist Rachel steadily denounces the deficiencies of men, while Part III is more centred on God and religion, and addresses spiritual and metaphysical questions. However, as Barnes noted in an early notebook, Rachel was not supposed to turn into a stereotype and therefore, next to her description as 'crude, aggressive', he wrote 'no – not a parody feminist'. Her other characteristics were: 'kneejerk, but right on the whole; contrasts with JS's reticence & assumptions of moribundity re sex' (1.1.2).

In the same notebook, when *Staring at the Sun* was in embryonic stages, Barnes had imagined epigraphs for Part III and written: ' "The Ruffian on the Stair"; Wittgenstein; Culture & Value; Why not believe? Go on; Camus – suicide only real philosophical question' (1.1.2). Camus's opening sentence in the first essay of *The Myth of Sisyphus*, 'An Absurd Reasoning' (whose first section is entitled 'Absurdity and Suicide'), is 'There is but one truly serious philosophical question, and that is suicide,'[19] a statement which, in *The Sense of an Ending*, is uttered by Adrian who was to commit suicide several years later: 'Camus said that suicide was the only true philosophical question' (13, 141). Although the quotation was not chosen as an epigraph for Part III in *Staring at the Sun*, a variation of it may be found in Gregory's reflections when he declares at the end of the novel: 'Suicide was not the only real philosophical dilemma of our age; it was an alluring irrelevance' (187). *Culture & Value* is a selection of thoughts from Ludwig Wittgenstein's personal notes compiled after his death and published in 1977 in German and in 1980 in English. Some of these reflections are concerned with death and could have offered Barnes a suitable epigraph although he did not select a specific one. Wittgenstein is a regular figure in *Nothing to Be Frightened Of* and is read by the teenage characters in *Metroland* and *The Sense of an Ending*. As for 'The Ruffian on the Stair', it comes from an 1877 poem by William Ernest Henley (who, in 1888, published a collection of poems entitled *England, My England*) about life and death in which the first stanza reads:

> Madam Life's a piece in bloom,
> Death goes dogging everywhere:
> She's the tenant of the room,
> He's the ruffian on the stair.[20]

---

[17] Julian Barnes, 'My Hero: Julian Barnes on Jacques Brel', *Independent Magazine*, 10 June 1989, 46. Reproduced in *Something to Declare*, 17–33.
[18] Barnes, *Something to Declare*, 26.
[19] Albert Camus, *The Myth of Sisyphus and Other Essays*, trans. Justin O'Brien (New York: Vintage Books, [1955] 1960), 3.
[20] Joe Orton wrote a play entitled *The Ruffian on the Stair* (broadcast on BBC Radio in 1964) and in 1990, Rosemary Dinnage published a compilation of interviews with a variety of people on the subject of death entitled *A Ruffian on the Stair. Reflections on Death* (London: Viking, 1990). On 25

The personification of Life as a temporary tenant (and prostitute) and of Death lurking in the stairs was also implicit in the title Barnes had written down for Part III in his notebook: 'Perhaps each part has a title. E.g. Pt 3 "The Rented World" (Aubade < Larkin)' (1.1.2). This quote had already appeared in the first notebook (1.1.1) and comes from the last stanza of Philip Larkin's poem 'Aubade' (1977) which is a meditation on the fear of death and death's inevitability. Larkin's poem ends with daybreak and the return to everyday life, but the tone remains sombre:

> Meanwhile telephones crouch, getting ready to ring
> In locked-up offices, and all the uncaring
> Intricate rented world begins to rouse.[21]

If the world awakens, it is one which is ours only temporarily (a 'rented world'), thus reminding us of our mortality. While Larkin's poem suitably resonates with the main themes of *Staring at the Sun* in the third part, the title 'The Rented World' was not transferred to the typescript as it does not appear on any draft and none of the three parts bears a title in the published text.

On the final draft copy (1.13.7), the title page of the typescript includes seven titles which had already been thought up earlier: Question & Answer (the only typed title), The Only Life of Jean Serjeant, The Sky's the Limit, Questions in the Life of Jean Serjeant, A Woman of the Century (all handwritten in pencil), Beneath a Bomber's Moon (in red pen) and the last one, written in red and circled, is 'Staring at the Sun'. This is the first occurrence of the title in the archives, although the phrase had been used within the drafts to refer to Prosser's and Jean's experiences of staring at the sun and at death while flying (29, 104, 155, 194).[22] This final choice proved particularly adequate as a point of entry into the novel as it hinted at the notions of bravery, courage and defiance which are so central to the book, while retaining a poetic and enigmatic dimension.

2. Early starts

Apart from the title, the two passages in *Staring at the Sun* which went through the greatest transformations are the prologue and the beginning of Part II. The novel

---

February 2006, when doing research for *Nothing to Be Frightened Of*, Barnes wrote to his friend the philosopher Galen Strawson (the first interviewee of Dinnage's book under the name of 'Thomas'), telling him he was reading *A Ruffian on the Stair* and had recognized him as 'Thomas' (3.5). Neither Dinnage nor her book are explicitly named in *Nothing to Be Frightened Of*, but Barnes writes: 'About twenty years ago I was asked if I would be interviewed for a book about death. I declined on writerly grounds: I didn't want to talk away stuff which I might later need myself' (124).

[21] Philip Larkin, *Collected Poems*, ed. Anthony Thwaite (London: Faber & Faber, 1988), 209.

[22] In 1988, the British jazz/funk band Level 42 released an album called *Staring at the Sun* (the title of the seventh track on the album). It was also the title of the second single on the 1997 album *Pop* by the Irish rock band U2. In 2008, the psychiatrist Irvin Yalom published *Staring at the Sun: Overcoming the Terror of Death* (San Francisco: Jossey-Bass, 2008).

originally started with a (then discarded) prologue which showed the heroine (aged almost a hundred) smoking a cigarette:

> As she took the fourth puff of her cigarette, ---- ----- felt entirely happy. This would have surprised people, because you weren't meant to feel entirely happy when you were almost a hundred. You also weren't meant to surprise people; so she didn't mention her feelings. She merely smiled to herself, and let them think, as they predictably did, Oh, there she goes again, looking back over it all, remembering some tangy incident from the foolish age before we were all born. But she wasn't. She was thinking, as far as she was thinking about anything, about the future. (1.13.5)

In a second draft, the heroine was named 'Ann Serjeant' and Barnes added 'Jean' in red pen above the first name.[23] Although Jean insists that she is thinking about the future (the second draft included an additional ominous three-word sentence at the end of the paragraph: 'The short future'), the words 'looking back' and 'remembering', combined with the knowledge that the heroine is soon to be centenarian, suggested that this would be a retrospective novel. The concern with memory here anticipates the incipits of later novels such as *Talking It Over*, *England, England* or *The Sense of an Ending*, which all start with a reference to what a character remembers,[24] while *Metroland*, *Flaubert's Parrot* and *The Noise of Time* all include reflections on the vagaries of memory.[25] In the first draft of *Staring at the Sun*, the next three paragraphs of the prologue describe the way Jean smokes her cigarettes, counting the puffs and listing the emotions she feels with each series of puffs – the first inflating her with 'sudden pleasure', the second being 'less active' and 'merely supportive', the last containing 'a streak of panic' –, a passage which was moved to Part III in later drafts and in the published novel (140). On the other hand, the last paragraph of the original prologue was deleted:

---

[23] Barnes asked writer and political activist Jean Sargeant if he might use her name for the main character of *Staring at the Sun*. Sargeant, who worked at the *Sunday Times* when Barnes was deputy literary editor there, accepted but requested a change of spelling (1.18). As Barnes recalled, although he had told Sargeant his fictional character had nothing to do with her, 'after the book came out she wrote an article saying how she had read this book and how she was very irritated that this woman wasn't very intelligent' (Interview by Xesús Fraga (2006), in *Conversations*, ed. Guignery and Roberts, 139). In Sargeant's article entitled 'Would His Woman Fit My Name?', her reservation was about the early chapters covering Jean's childhood, in which she appears as 'a naïve, even dim child, given to asking seemingly silly questions of her male mentors'; Sargeant 'resented finding Jean when young much less interesting than the clever schoolboys in Metroland', but as she read on she found that Barnes 'had imperceptibly created a strong and credible female character who breaks out from her conventional, lower middle class background to acquire a convincing identity of her own' (1.18).

[24] In *Talking It Over*, the monologues by Stuart, Oliver and Gillian start with: 'My name is Stuart, and I remember everything' (1, 7), 'I'm Oliver, and I remember all the *important* things' (9), 'What I remember is my business' (8). *England, England* opens with: ' "What's your first memory?" someone would ask. / And she would reply, "I don't remember" ' (3). *The Sense of an Ending* begins with: 'I remember' (1), with the proviso: 'but what you end up remembering isn't always the same as what you have witnessed' (3).

[25] The epigraph to *The Noise of Time* (whose source is identified as 'traditional') is 'One to hear / One to remember / And one to drink' (n.p.).

> Once, about five years ago, she had explained this cycle of emotion to Ladak, the cleverest of her grandchildren, who had smiled sadly, then come over and kissed her. No, she wanted to say, as the sympathetic kiss struck home, you've got it wrong. Because you're clever you think you understand metaphors, you think they mean things. They don't. My life – that's what you were supposing, isn't it? – hasn't been like that at all. It hasn't been like that at all … (1.13.5)

This reticence towards metaphoric interpretations (seeing Jean's life as having followed the same sequence of sudden pleasure, lesser activity and panic) recalls Freud's famous phrase 'Sometimes a cigar … is only a cigar', quoted by Jack in *Before She Met Me* while smoking a cigar (138). It also partly echoes the epigraph to the first part of *Staring at the Sun* about the meaning of life, taken from a letter by Chekhov: 'You ask me what life is? It is like asking what a carrot is. A carrot is a carrot, and nothing more is known' (3). In the published novel, Jean has no grandchildren and the metaphor of the cigarette puffs is not explicitly related to Jean's life, so that the image is more subtly conveyed and relies on the reader's active participation for its interpretation. The dots at the end of the deleted prologue appear as the typographical signal for the retrospective narrative to begin. While the structure of the book and its progression were clearly delineated on Barnes's three-column planning sheet for the novel (1.13.4), he was still hesitant about the opening as he wrote at the top of the first column for Part One:

> smoking intro: transfer to ③; or just cut?
> Or have Sun-up intro?? i.e. have a full description here, & then a Prosserish one later?
> Or start w[ith] looking back – & straight into childhood (1.13.4)

Barnes decided indeed to transfer part of the introduction to Part III (at the top of the third column for Part Three, he wrote: 'Smoking intro here, perhaps'). The suppression of the narrative device of 'looking back' and the replacement of the first prologue by a focus on Prosser 'poaching over Northern France' in 1941 and seeing the sun rise twice (1–2) make the retrospective process less blatant, with the author replacing the description of a prosaic activity (smoking) by the poetic and lyrical narration of an 'ordinary miracle' (2). Referring to this opening, Barnes told D. J. R. Bruckner: 'I had been writing for a long time before that came to me and I tried it here and there. Once I put it at the start, I couldn't see how it could have been otherwise.'[26]

Part II also started differently in the first drafts. In the published novel, Part II opens with Jean's disillusionment with her marriage to Michael: 'After the guilty disappointment of the honeymoon came the longer, slower dismay of living together' (67). The typescript in 1.13.4 started with a paragraph which was then deleted and offered a very apt metaphor of the fragility of the couple:

> Prop two playing cards up against each other and you would think they could stay like that for ever, each depending on the other for support. Yet leave them there,

---

[26] Bruckner, 'Planned Parenthood', 3.

in a room where no draught blows, and they will collapse without any outside interference. Some inner loss of energy, perhaps; after standing together so long the only thing left to do is not stand against one another. (1.13.4)

In another draft, the cards metaphor was used in a more explicit and extended way as it was directly applied to Jean and Michael:

> She saw herself and Michael as two playing cards, standing up and leaning against one another, supported only by the other's presence. You could do that quite easily – anyone could do it, just stand the two cards up on their ends – and it seemed that they might stay like that forever. But if you went away and left them, standing on the floor in a room where no draught blew, they would collapse without any outside interference. Some inner loss of energy must be the cause, she decided; they had stood leaning against one another for so long that the only thing left to do was not lean against one another any longer. That was the only was [*sic*] in which they could change, and so, sooner or later, that was what they did. (1.13.4)

While it is not possible to decide from the archives which version came first, as Barnes's tendency when revising his drafts is towards condensation, one may surmise that the longest and more developed version came first. However, both versions were deleted and instead of this fairly explicit image, Barnes opted for a more ambiguous opening paragraph focusing on the way Michael would 'hammer steel corners into the heels of each new pair of shoes he bought' so that when he walked, one could 'hear the sliding scrape of a carving knife on a back step, and fire would be struck from the pavement' (67). This image is more enigmatic than the original one and maybe unexpected as the starting point for a new part. However, it clearly conveys a sense of virility – all the more as Michael 'would walk ahead of her, a little too quickly, so that every few strides she would have to break into a clumsy half-run' – as opposed to Jean's 'picture-book' dream of their nestling against each other as 'a pair of spoons' (67). As she grows out of such romantic ideas, Jean pragmatically concludes: 'A spoon couldn't nestle with a knife, that was all' (68), and years after her divorce, she placidly reflects: 'She and Michael had been like a spoon and a knife' (126).

One of Barnes's challenges in *Staring at the Sun* was to tell the story in the third person mainly through the perspective of an ordinary woman and adapt the tone and style accordingly. He was therefore committed not to turn her into a literary person and not to make her sound like himself. Barnes was aware of this difficulty when revising a passage which dealt with the characteristics of dying on a plane: 'Ignorance, Certainty, Enclosure, Company. These were the four aspects of the engineers' modern form of death' (1.13.4). The three words 'Certainty, Enclosure, Company' were crossed out and Barnes wrote in the margin: 'too much like me – not enough like her?' The three nouns were deleted,[27] but the use of the female pronoun in Barnes's note ('like her') might

---

[27] The published text reads: 'Ignorance, that was the first aspect of the engineers' modern form of death. It was well known that if anything went wrong with an aeroplane, the passengers were told no more than they needed to know' (94).

seem surprising as this particular passage was focalized through Gregory who, in his fear of death and reflections about God and religion, may be said to resemble the author of *Nothing to Be Frightened Of*. Hermione Lee, when commenting upon the draft, referred to one of Jean's thoughts in Part I: ' "Perhaps courage comes from hatred, or at least is sustained by it." – it's important we're told this now, but it doesn't sound at all like her – too measured, philosophical and articulate' (1.13.5). The sentence comes up when 17-year-old Jean asks Prosser about his hatred of the Germans and the published version is only slightly different from the original but maybe less literary: 'Perhaps courage comes from hatred, or at least is kept going by it' (50–51).

Mainly, however, Lee resented the set phrases and clichés characteristic of Jean's thoughts in her early life. She remarked: 'Couldn't she, even when she's naïve & ordinary, be a bit less conventional & woman's magazines than that?' When Jean reflects 'it must be right to love Michael' (36), Lee commented: 'Why is she so gormless like this? She seems so sharp and sensitive otherwise', and later on: 'I can see she has to be naïve & sentimental so as to grow out of it, but do her marital illusions have to be quite so picture-book soppy?'; 'I resented the fact that her ideals about being a parent were written in such conventional terms. Do ordinary illusions have to be soppy clichés, is the Q[uestion] I suppose' (1.13.5). Barnes was clearly looking for the right tone as his meticulous pages of handwritten notes on items to improve on the typescript include such remarks as: 'is this too naïve?', 'last line soppy?' (1.13.5). Jean's characterization as a clueless and 'soppy' ordinary woman in the first part may feel frustrating to some readers but is necessary to make way for her evolution in the second and third parts towards a more intelligent and incisive person. She herself remarks that at 18, she was 'foolish' and 'at twenty-three, with Michael, … felt less confident and therefore less intelligent' (71); it is only after she becomes an independent woman and starts opening her horizons that she becomes bolder and wiser, and that enchantment can emerge from her ordinary life.

The examination of the genesis of the novel has shown the various ways in which the author sought to address important questions related to courage, fear, death, suicide, God and religion, which would resurface in later books. The rewritings and omissions of passages or names, as well as the hesitations over titles, also suggest that Barnes relied on the reader's ability to connect and decode images and sometimes fill in the gaps. Carlos Fuentes perceived the necessity of an active participation of the reader when he wrote in his laudatory review of *Staring at the Sun* that in this novel Barnes 'stares not only at the sun but at the reader's intelligence'.[28]

---

[28] Carlos Fuentes, 'The Enchanting Blue Yonder', *New York Times Book Review*, 12 April 1987, 43.

7

Fragments of stories: *A History of the World in 10½ Chapters*

Published three years after *Staring at the Sun*, *A History of the World in 10½ Chapters* marks a stark change of direction from the former novel in terms of form and structure, returning to the inventivity of *Flaubert's Parrot*. Barnes's fifth novel relies on a form of narrative which is neither continuous nor stable, but diverging, and at times disorderly. Despite the many echoes, connections and links between the different chapters, the book as a whole favours fragmentation and multiplicity. The archive likewise contains a profusion of disparate papers and documents and it seemed appropriate to echo this heterogeneity and fragmentariness in our own reading of the archive rather than attempt to convey a misleading sense of order and exhaustiveness. This section will therefore offer a selection of separate snapshots which will cast some light on the genesis of the book and on the changes that affected the titles and order of chapters, before focusing on a few specific chapters (especially the first of 'Three Simple Stories' and 'Parenthesis').

1. Planning, naming and arranging chapters

A History of the World in 10½ Chapters was the result of a combination of several separate projects Barnes had in mind. As mentioned earlier in this book,[1] one of the writer's ideas was to write 'Geoffrey Braithwaite's Guide to the Bible' (1.1.2), a project that was abandoned but transmuted itself into the first chapter of *A History of the World in 10½ Chapters*, 'The Stowaway'. The first draft of the book was started on 14 April 1986 (1.6.9) and the book was then entitled *The Raft*, a reminder of another of Barnes's projects: 'At one time I had planned a whole book about the Gericault painting, about the seemingly mysterious way in which "catastrophe becomes art." This idea was then slimmed down and integrated into my novel to form a central, hinge chapter', the one entitled 'Shipwreck' about Géricault's painting 'The Raft of the Medusa'.[2] Barnes's great interest in painting led him to publish a number of art essays over the years, notably

---

[1] See pp. 108–9.
[2] Barnes, 'Short Story/Essay', 174–5.

in *Modern Painters* and in the *London Review of Books*, most of which were collected in *Keeping an Eye Open. Essays on Art* in 2015, with the chapter 'Shipwreck' as its opening piece.

'Shipwreck' is divided into two parts, the first of which relates the catastrophe of the shipwreck of the *Medusa* in 1816 while the second examines the genesis of Géricault's painting and the result. However, this chapter was not originally shaped as it now stands, as Barnes recalls: 'As I first saw it, the chapter would be in three sections: the two that survive, plus a third which brought the story up to date (and returned art to life) by describing the rediscovery of the frigate's wreckage off the Mauretanian coast in 1981.'[3] His second notebook preserved at the Harry Ransom Center confirms this original tripartite structure:

> The Raft [of the Medusa]
> 1) The Event (doctor's account; anthropophagy; pushing injured overboard; riot & mutiny)
> 2) The Painting: visits to carpenter, building of models, to doctor locked in studio, cutting off hair so can't go out
> its reception / vilification
> [3) The Diaspora → alive!]
> 3) The Recovery
> Scrapbook vol 25 – page 8 – the wreck of the Medusa found 1981 (1.1.2)

The reference to a 'scrapbook' suggests that Barnes pasted a newspaper cutting about the recovery of the wreck of the Medusa on page 8 of volume 25 of his scrapbooks, a practice which is also that of the narrator in a deleted chapter of *Metroland*.[4] Next to the third section about the recovery, Barnes wrote:

> What is the plot?
> e.g. the discoverer finds that some of the corpses have been murdered (by the survivor)
> → 2 survivors perhaps, one of whom is mysteriously murdered some time afterwards (had been blackmailing first survivor)
> but the survivors become national heroes, so the murder investigation isn't proceeded with. (1.1.2)

However, this plot was abandoned and the third section never written, as noted by Barnes: 'This third part never took off; instead, it atrophied into a couple of lines in a later chapter of the novel.'[5] A brief sentence about the recovery of the wreck appears indeed in the half chapter entitled 'Parenthesis' amidst a development about how history is 'good at finding things', even the ones people try to cover up: 'They found the wreck of the *Medusa* not long ago, off the coast of Mauretania' (243). These changes

---

[3] Ibid., 175.
[4] See p. 29.
[5] Barnes, 'Short Story/Essay', 175.

in the shape of the overall book and in the structure of the individual chapter seem to offer a very apt example of the pliability of artistic intention and the flexibility of the creative process, which the narrator of 'Shipwreck' is intent on demonstrating about Géricault's painting.

On a page of notes for this novel, Barnes wrote: 'Title? It says all or nothing' (1.7.1) and it is difficult to decide whether the final title does one or the other, or both. In the first draft, the title *The Raft* was crossed out and replaced by *A History of the World in 9½ Chapters*. Random notes in an early notebook also point to Barnes's ambition to write a History of the World in a still uncertain number of chapters:

> Call it: A History of the World in 12½ Chapters (8½? 13½?)
> final chapter is the ½, as it breaks off; also it's not clear whether this is the diary of a nuke survivor, or of a lunatic who has produced the symptoms of a nuke survivor. Very fragmented – full of mad warnings which might or might not relate to events that have taken place already. (1.1.2)

In the published version, the half chapter ('Parenthesis') is placed between Chapters Eight and Nine (therefore not at the end) and is a complete piece in itself, with a neat ending echoing its beginning as both show the narrator in bed with his wife, waiting for sleep (225, 246). The last chapter ('The Dream') is also a complete story which ends in a circular way by repeating its opening sentence ('I dreamt that I woke up. It's the oldest dream of all, and I've just had it', 283, 309). On the other hand, the apocryphal sixteenth-century manuscript of a legal case in Chapter Three, 'The Wars of Religion', breaks off '*without giving details of the annual penance or remembrance imposed by the court*' as noted by the person who passes as the editor of the manuscript, because the parchment '*has been attacked, perhaps on more than one occasion, by some species of termite*' (80).[6]

The half chapter referred to in the early notebook, which was supposed to come last, was moved to the penultimate position in early drafts before becoming Chapter Four in the published text, entitled 'The Survivor'. In this chapter, the main character believes she survived a nuclear war, a subject matter which Barnes related to 'Atwood' in one of his notes (1.7.1) – maybe a reference to Margaret Atwood's *The Handmaid's Tale* (1986), which is set in the future after the United States has undergone a nuclear war. In an early draft, this chapter was entirely written in the first person in fragments separated

---

[6] As mentioned in the Author's Note, 'The Wars of Religion' is 'based on legal procedures and actual cases described in *The Criminal Prosecution and Capital Punishment of Animals* by E.P. Evans (1906)' (311). However, the case of the inhabitants of Mamirolle against the '*bestioles*' as recorded in the chapter is invented as is the reference to the '*Archives Municipales de Besançon (section CG, boîte 377a)*' (61). And yet, Professor Thomas A. Fudge treats this case as authentic in *Medieval Religion and Its Anxieties: History and Mystery in the Other Middle Ages* (2016). Fudge never names Barnes in his book and writes in an endnote about the case: 'Besançon, Archives Municipales CG 377a contains the relevant documents and forms the basis for the summary.' In November 2018, scholar Andrzej Ksiezopolski went to Besançon and Mamirolle and ascertained that such documents did not exist in the Archives Municipales. The local historian in Mamirolle also confirmed that the case had been invented. I would like to thank Andrzej Ksiezopolski for sharing this information with me. Thomas A. Fudge, *Medieval Religion and Its Anxieties: History and Mystery in the Other Middle Ages* (New York: Palgrave Macmillan, 2016), 17, 40.

by asterisks, bringing to mind the genre of the diary (but without the mention of any dates) or the form of an interior monologue. However, on a loose page of notes, Barnes wrote: '?3rd person'; '3rd & 1st person mixed?' (1.7.1), and the published version shifts between third-person and first-person narration (also with asterisks between sections), an (irregular) alternation which adequately blurs the genre of the piece.[7] As noted by Hermione Lee in a letter dated 1 August 1988 after she had read a second draft of the chapter: 'the change does make the reader more nervous and uncertain from early on, which is good' (1.7.1). In that intermediary draft, Barnes introduced the sections which started with a change of pronoun with the capitalized conjunction 'OR' (1.7.1), thus explicitly pointing to the coexistence of diverging interpretations. Lee wrote: 'I even wonder whether you do need ORs?' and Barnes removed them from the final draft, thereby probably increasing the reader's uncertainty as to the status of the various narrations. Barnes's first notes on this chapter (where the main character had first been conceived as male) insisted on its ambivalence:

> End is 100% ambiguous – he has?fantasies that men in white coats keep telling him his symptoms are neurotic & that he has imagined the explosions to justify his situation. He tells them they are dreams; they reply that they are reality. We don't know who to believe. / last line: what do you think? (1.7.2)

The survivor became female as soon as Barnes started writing the chapter and although the intended question for the last line does not appear in any draft, the ambiguity prevailed and was furthered by the change in pronouns.

In the published version, the main character of 'The Survivor' is named Kathleen Ferris (107) while she was called 'Mary Thorburn' in an early draft (1.6.8) – after the snooker player Cliff Thorburn. In a private correspondence, Barnes gave an insight into his process of naming characters: 'I have a vague default position to name characters after sportspeople … and then subsequently change them. Characters' names usually aren't central for me when creating them.'[8] In the second chapter entitled 'The Visitors', an early draft had the main character (an Irish television presenter and lecturer on a Mediterranean cruise) named 'Langston Hughes' (1.6.9) – a homonym of the American poet of the Harlem Renaissance although Barnes had not thought of him – but it was later changed to Franklin Hughes (other possibilities were Brian Hughes, Wilson Hughes and Hugh Langston).[9]

---

[7] The alternation is irregular because several sections in third person are followed by several sections in first person, before it changes again.

[8] Private email correspondence with the author, 10 January 2017. In *Talking It Over*, the dog in the village in the south of France is called Poulidor after the French bicycle racer Raymond Poulidor. In *The Sense of an Ending*, Adrian Finn is named after the British cricketer Steve Finn. See p. 227.

[9] Hughes is Stuart's family name in *Talking It Over* and *Love, etc*. It was chosen to echo not a writer's name (Ted Hughes or Langston Hughes) but that of a lexicographer Barnes knew on the *Oxford English Dictionary*, Alan Hughes (Annotations, 22–27 March 2018). The two other main characters bear the names of writers: Gillian Wyatt may evoke the poet Sir Thomas Wyatt and Oliver Russell the philosopher Bertrand Russell. When the highly literary Oliver goes to the emergency room in *Talking It Over*, he says his surname is 'Russell' and his first names 'Oliver Davenport de Quincey' (175).

As suggested by Barnes's notes in his notebook, the order and original titles of chapters in the first drafts differ from the final version. The table below draws from the order of chapters in the draft that was read by Hermione Lee and takes up the titles that appear on several drafts and loose pages (with differences marked in bold character):

Chapters	Early drafts	Published version
1	The Stowaway**s**/**A Floating Cafeteria**	The Stowaway
2	The Visitors	The Visitors
3	**The Trial**/The Wars of Religion	The Wars of Religion
4	Shipwreck/**The Raft**/**The Artist**	The Survivor
5	**Forwards & Backwards** (= The Mountain)	Shipwreck
6	Three Simple Stories	The Mountain
7	Upstream!	Three Simple Stories
½ --- 8	Parenthesis/**Intermission**	Upstream!
8 --- ½	Ararat/The Ararat Project/**The Astronaut**	Parenthesis
9	The Survivor	Project Ararat
10	The Dream	The Dream

The final choice of titles points to a greater ambivalence despite the deceiving straightforwardness of mostly nominal titles. For the first chapter, the metaphorical 'A Floating Cafeteria' was added in longhand on the typescript and the expression appears within the text (14) but the original 'Stowaway' remained, though in the singular. 'The Trial' (also called 'The woodworm's trial') and 'The Astronaut' were more explicit in identifying the topic of the chapters than 'The Wars of Religion' and 'Project Ararat', respectively, two titles which highlight their religious dimension. For the Géricault chapter, the title 'The Artist' would have echoed similar titles ('The Stowaway', 'The Visitors', 'The Survivor') but 'Shipwreck' was probably preferred for its reference to the original title of Géricault's painting in the Salon catalogue in 1819, 'Scene of Shipwreck', rather than the more political and well-known title 'The Raft of the Medusa' (129). 'Intermission' evoked the performance of a play or the screening of a film, whereas 'Parenthesis' connotes a written form. The most important change was the deletion of 'Forwards & Backwards', a title which might have created a slight lexical imbalance in the book since, apart from the adverbial 'Upstream!', all titles contain simple nouns, with or without a definite article, thus offering a linguistic continuity within an otherwise deliberately non-linear book. Other potential titles for that chapter were 'The Holy Mountain', 'The Vineyard', 'Water & Vine', 'The Halo of Cloud' and 'He Planted the Vine', but Barnes finally opted for the simplest title: 'The Mountain'.

In terms of order, the main change pertains to the shift of 'The Survivor' from ninth to fourth chapter, possibly as a consequence of Lee's comments. Her detailed ten-page letter on the novel was full of enthusiasm and her only reticence related to the position of the last two chapters ('The Survivor' and 'The Dream'):

> My only slight pulling back from the shape of the whole is that (a little as in SATS[10]) the last two chapters become more conceptual, more to do with last questions & answers, where you push things as far as they can possibly go & (I suppose) make two versions of survival, one as ultimate nightmare & one as inadequate consolation – one female one male – both are kinds of 'fabulation': what you <u>make up</u> depends on who you are. But they are both, in their very different ways, abstracted (I don't mean they're not intensely <u>physical</u>, but they're not grounded in actuality the way the Gericault or the woodworm or the Arab terrorists are) & difficult to connect. But I think this is necessary because of what you are doing – I don't think it's anything <u>wrong</u>, I think it just gets <u>harder</u> towards the end.
>
> ...
>
> The last 2 chapters are the most difficult: because they make you very depressed, partly, because they're the hardest to do & the most 'invented' & extreme. (1.7.1)

It made sense to end a book which started with the biblical Flood with a chapter on a nuclear cataclysm emblematic of the end of the world, followed by a chapter on a 'dream' of life after death. 'The Survivor' was written at a time when the danger of nuclear apocalypse was, according to Martin Amis, 'the highest subject' and 'the lowest subject',[11] as manifested in such novels as Graham Swift's *Waterland* (1983) and Maggie Gee's *The Burning Book* (1983). However, a book like *A History of the World in 10½ Chapters* precisely eschews linearity and teleology, which might explain Barnes's decision to move 'The Survivor' to the first half of the book. Such a shift also suggests that for all its apparently chaotic dimension and generic plurality, *A History of the World in 10½ Chapters* is carefully structured and the distribution of chapters (as in *Flaubert's Parrot*) is far from random.

2. Not so simple stories

From the very beginning, Barnes was well aware of the generic hybridity of his book as he wrote in his notes: 'Hist World uses – fiction / non-fiction / myth / straight history / art history / bits of autobiography / essay' and he imagined the 'extreme reviews' the book might receive: 'a triumphant mixing of the genres', 'a complete mess' (1.6.9). On the title page of the typed draft of the seventh chapter, 'Three Simple Stories', he added in longhand: 'called 3 simple stories & that's what they are – the first 2 have a moral, the 3rd speaks for itself / also prose becomes simpler between first story & third'. He noted

---

[10] *Staring at the Sun.*
[11] Amis, *Einstein's Monsters*, 9.

that the tone was 'lighthearted at first, bit more serious, then sombre' and identified the different genres and modes of the three stories:

1) autobiography
2) myth & art history
3) 'straight' non-fiction (1.6.9)

The generic heterogeneity of this chapter is emblematic of the mixture of genres in the whole book and may also be related to the generic malleability of *Flaubert's Parrot* and *Levels of Life*. In the seventh chapter of *A History of the World in 10½ Chapters*, the second story reflects on the biblical parable of Jonah swallowed by a whale, which is paralleled with the (supposedly) authentic case of a sailor named James Bartley who was swallowed by a sperm whale in 1891.[12] The third story relates the historical plight of the 937 passengers (most of them Jews) on board the German transatlantic liner *St Louis* in May and June 1939, who were fleeing the Third Reich but were not allowed to disembark in Cuba and had to sail back to Europe. The prose is more straightforward and factual than in the two previous stories (it includes precise historical dates and figures), as any rhetorical flourish would have seemed inappropriate to record such a tragedy. In the author's note, Barnes indicates that this third part takes its facts from *The Voyage of the Damned* (1974) by Gordon Thomas and Max Morgan-Witts and the archives reveal that the writer also read *Times* newspaper reports from June 1939 as well as extracts from historical studies on the Jewish refugees of the *St Louis* (1.7.2).[13] The historical documents present in the archive (not only for this part but also for several other chapters) give an idea of the amount of research Barnes (or his research assistant Rebecca John) conducted for this specific book.[14] However, the novelist was also well aware of the shortcomings of excessive research when writing a work of fiction:

> 'Research,' I find, is a very double-edged matter: on the one hand it gives you confidence that you are getting things right; on the other, it is constricting, temporarily anesthetising. If you remember an original text too well, your own writing cannot flow, and it becomes impossible to put a new shape on an old

---

[12] The archives show that Barnes drew inspiration from an article by David Gunston entitled 'The Man Who Lived in a Whale. And His Name Was Not Jonah', *The Compass. A Magazine of the Sea* 42, no. 2 (Spring 1972): 9–11 (1.7.2). In his novel, Barnes dates the incident from 25 August 1891 (179), although other sources (including Gunston's article) date it from February 1891. An American academic, Edward B. Davis, who contacted Barnes about the story on 23 July 1990 (1.7.6) published a paper a year later in which he argued that the incident had been invented and was just a 'story', a 'tale', a 'yarn'. Edward B. Davis, 'A Whale of a Tale: Fundamentalist Fish Stories.' *Perspectives on Science and Christian Faith* 43 (1991): 224–37.

[13] The archives include four reports which appeared in the Imperial and Foreign News pages of the *Times* in June 1939, as well as two pages from Judith Laikin Elkin's article, 'The Reception of the Muses in the Circum-Caribbean', in *The Muses Flee Hitler: Cultural Transfer and Adaptation 1930–1945*, ed. Jarrell C. Jackman and Carla M. Borden (Washington, DC: Smithsonian Institution Press, 1983) and one page from Michael R. Marrus's *The Unwanted: European Refugees in the Twentieth Century* (Oxford: Oxford University Press, 1985).

[14] In addition to Rebecca John's notes and photocopies from a variety of books, the archives include a magazine article on Steven Callahan's survival on a raft for seventy-six days on the Atlantic Ocean after his sloop capsized, which he recounted in his 1986 book *Adrift: 76 Days Lost at Sea* (1.7.2).

narrative. *Research* often reminds me of building a compost heap: if you try to use what you've piled up too soon, all you get is a forkful of cabbage stumps, purulent apples, and unreconstructed teabags. You have to let it all settle and decompose in the mind first.[15]

Barnes would again be confronted by that precarious balance when writing *Arthur & George* which draws from a great quantity of historical documents.

The first of 'Three Simple Stories' deals with the first-person unnamed narrator's encounter with the octogenarian Lawrence Beesley, an authentic survivor from the *Titanic* who supposedly escaped the sinking of the ship by dressing in women's clothes and later founded a crammer where the narrator taught for a term at the age of 18. In an interview in 2000, Barnes confirmed that he was this young narrator and worked in Beesley's school: 'That simple story is completely true, that's about me.'[16] If we follow that premise, the first sentence of the story gives interesting (although maybe not totally accurate) information about Barnes in 1964: 'I was a normal eighteen-year-old: shuttered, self-conscious, untravelled and sneering; violently educated, socially crass, emotionally blurting' (171). The narrator's 'adolescent anger against life' and 'mixture of deference, fear and cheek' towards the elderly man (172) recall a similar disposition in Christopher in the first part of (the partly autobiographical) *Metroland*. Although Barnes described Beesley in an interview as 'some rogue',[17] he used his name as a pseudonym for twelve reviews published in the local newspaper the *Oxford Mail* in the mid-1970s and acknowledged him for providing 'important points of detail' in his *Literary Guide to Oxford* (1.8.6). As noted by Ryan Roberts, Barnes 'typically employed a pseudonym in order to publish two reviews simultaneously, one as Julian Barnes and the other as Lawrence Beesley'.[18] While this publishing habit is common to avoid having two pieces in the same issue under the same name, it might seem surprising to choose as a pseudonym the name of a man one 'didn't like', but Barnes suggested it was perhaps a way 'to be retrospectively cheeky'.[19]

Barnes also used Beesley as the family name of the 25-year-old female medium Ellen and her husband William in his first published short story, 'A Self-Possessed Woman' (1975), which deals with a woman whose mind is possessed by the spirits of dead writers who communicate through her. He finally invented the pseudonym Paddy Beesley to sign two literary reviews in the *New Statesman* in 1977,[20] as well as some of the newspaper's Weekend Competitions. Barnes admitted there was 'something liberating' about using a pseudonym as 'you could be nasty about someone without them knowing it was you'.[21] This might have been the case for Barnes/Paddy Beesley's acerbic review of Angela Carter's *The Passion of New Eve* in 1977 which is

---

[15] Barnes, 'Short Story/Essay', 175.
[16] Interview by Guignery, in *Conversations*, ed. Guignery and Roberts, 56.
[17] Interview by Guignery and Roberts, in *Conversations*, ed. Guignery and Roberts, 176.
[18] Roberts, *Pseudonym as Character*, 12.
[19] Interview by Guignery and Roberts, in *Conversations*, ed. Guignery and Roberts, 176.
[20] Julian Barnes [Paddy Beesley, pseud.], 'Just Like Us', *New Statesman* 4 February 1977: 163; 'Be Bad', *New Statesman*, 25 March 1977: 407.
[21] Interview by Guignery and Roberts, in *Conversations*, ed. Guignery and Roberts, 176.

judged 'jagged and cluttered' and inspired the following comment by the unsparing pseudonymous reviewer: 'Miss Carter leaves all plot on the escapes-and-captures level, shuns dialogue, and despite snatches of sharp phrasing, is prone to court silliness: what is offered as a harsh contemporary imagination comes across too often as exuberant zaniness.'[22] Although Barnes in his early thirties was sometimes ruthless in his own reviews, he might have felt less constrained as Paddy Beesley to deliver such a severe judgment on the work of an already well-established writer.

In the first 'Simple Story' of *A History of the World in 10½ Chapters*, Barnes directed his sarcasm towards the real Lawrence Beesley who is presented not only as a decrepit old man with 'historically stained clothes' (172) but also as a forger and 'transvestite imposter' (174) who crossed the Atlantic in 1912 'according to subsequent family legend at least – in half-hearted pursuit of an American heiress' (173). In addition to the 'speculation that their ancestor had escaped from the *Titanic* in women's clothing' (a version which differs from Beesley's own account in his 1912 book *The Loss of the S.S. Titanic*), the 'more sceptical members of his family' maintained that the embroidered blanket Beesley supposedly received on the rescuing ship the *Carpathia* 'acquired its lettering' much later than 1912 (173). Forty years later, as 'based upon the account' Beesley's daughter gave to the narrator, Beesley 'counterfeited the pass required to let him board the facsimile *Titanic*' for the film *A Night to Remember* (174–5).[23] In the quotations above, the narrator repeatedly insists on the fact that he received these pieces of information directly from the family, even if some of it is only 'speculation' or mere 'theory' (173). However, after the publication of the novel, Barnes received a letter from Beesley's nephew in Ontario, P. M. Beesley, who said he enjoyed the book, found parts of it 'excellent' and congratulated the writer on his 'erudition and originality'. Nevertheless, he strongly contested the 'allegation' that his uncle dressed in woman's clothing to escape the *Titanic* and objected to Barnes's 'device of attributing the story to his family' (1.16.4).

P. M. Beesley's letter confirms the book's general theme of the irretrievability of the past and of the existence of diverging interpretations of any event instead of 'some God-eyed version of what "really" happened' as stated in 'Parenthesis' (245). One may point out that the narrator of the first simple 'story' took precautions by using such words as 'legend', 'speculation' or 'theory', and by phrasing the family's arguments as questions rather than assertions (173). An earlier draft also included the (later deleted) sentence: 'I joined in such *suppositions* enthusiastically' (1.6.9, my emphasis). In addition, although Barnes later said in interviews that the piece was autobiographical,

---

[22] Barnes [Paddy Beesley, pseud.], 'Be Bad', 407.
[23] Beesley's daughter was Laurien (to whom *A Literary Guide to Oxford* and *Metroland* were dedicated) and her half-brother was Alec Beesley, Dodie Smith's husband. It is through Laurien that Barnes met Dodie Smith in 1968 when the young man was 22 and the writer of *I Capture the Castle* and *The Hundred and One Dalmatians* 72. They became good friends and Smith named Barnes her literary executor in 1987, three years before her death. He wrote about his work as literary executor in an essay dated 19 May 1996, entitled 'Literary Executions' and reproduced in *The Writing Life: Writers on How They Think and Work*, ed. Marie Arana (New York: Public Affairs, 2003), 382–6. As literary executor, he asked Valerie Grove to write the biography of Dodie Smith which appeared in 1996. It was republished in 2002 with a foreword by Barnes. Julian Barnes, 'Foreword', *Dear Dodie. The Life of Dodie Smith*, by Valerie Grove (London: Pimlico, [1996] 2002), vii–viii.

the reader is given no explicit indication of that in the text itself and therefore could probably assume the narrator to be fictional, all the more as the simple 'story' (and not history) is inserted within a novel, although one which recurrently blurs the lines between fiction and non-fiction.

In the same letter, P. M. Beesley noted that Barnes's 'little story' was penned by someone who, 'by his own admission', was 'a person without compassion for the decline and frailties of old age'. By doing so, he was confusing the author who was in his forties when he wrote the novel and the character who was 'a violently-educated eighteen-year-old' when he met Lawrence Beesley (175), and whom the older narrator-author looks back on with a pinch of irony and humour. Indeed, the older self is able to deconstruct the mechanism of his younger self's feeling of contempt for the elderly man: 'His decrepitude … set off in me a general adolescent anger against life and its inevitable valedictory condition; a feeling which smoothly translated itself into hatred of the person undergoing that condition' (172–3). The teenager thus transmuted his resentment against the finitude of life and the indignities of ageing into a violent rejection of an individual suffering from these limitations. In an earlier draft, Barnes pointed to the flaw in his younger self's reasoning in an interpolated clause: 'This translated itself – quite unfairly, I realized a decade or so later – into hatred of the person undergoing that condition' (1.6.9). The removal of the clause made it more difficult (though not impossible) to perceive the distinction between the perspectives of the younger and older selves. Several decades later, Barnes wrote short stories (collected in *The Lemon Table*) about ageing and the 'frailties of old age', and a memoir about death (*Nothing to Be Frightened Of*), which demonstrate his great subtlety in approaching these topics and his commiseration for ageing people.

While there might be some ambiguity as to the identity of the narrator in the first 'Simple Story', a similar ambivalence is deliberately exploited in the half-chapter of the book, 'Parenthesis'.

3. 'Parenthesis'

Nearly all the early titles of *A History of the World in 10½ Chapters* included the fraction which pointed to the half-chapter first called 'Intermission' and then 'Parenthesis'. When referring in his notes to the 'didactic bit' about the writer's status in this half-chapter, Barnes wrote: 'The novelist's job isn't to speak himself but to make others speak. But occasionally he wants to shout "Listen to me, listen to me"' (1.6.8). This is a faithful description of what is presented in this first-person narrative in which the name Julian Barnes appears in full – 'when I say "I" you will want to know within a paragraph or two whether I mean Julian Barnes or someone invented' (227) – and about which the author wrote in his notes: 'only chapter of authorial voice' (1.7.2) and 'Must end personally – & more such bits interspersed' (1.6.8). The half-chapter does end personally with an image of the husband and wife in bed – 'I sense the map of her body beside me in the dark' (246) –, thus coming full circle with the beginning – 'She's lying on her side, turned away from me' (225) – and includes a few autobiographical details. However, the final version of 'Parenthesis' turned out to be less personal than the original draft in which Barnes had been more precise about a few specific elements.

In the published version, the narrator notes: 'I've loved twice in my life (which seems quite a lot to me), once happily, once unhappily. ... Dates and details – fill them in as you like' (231), and some ten pages later, he insists that he is not recommending one form of love over another: 'I don't know if prudent or reckless love is the better' (240). In an early draft, these two separate indications were synthesized in one sentence: 'I have loved twice, once recklessly, once prudently (I refer to the manner in which the feelings grew as well as to the person involved), and I don't know which way is better' (1.6.8). Although the sentence was not giving away any specific date or name, the adverbs 'recklessly' and 'prudently' and the indication between brackets were slightly more specific than the vaguer 'happily'/'unhappily'. Later in the published book, the narrator writes: 'We must be precise about love. Ah, you want descriptions, perhaps. What are her legs like, her breasts, her lips, what colour is that hair? (Well, sorry.)' (244). An earlier draft did not include the brief and unambiguous '(Well, sorry.)', but a choice of two longer clauses: '(If you want such things, you will have to look elsewhere in my fiction – and even there you will not know what you have found.)' and in longhand '(The answer is that they are all good because I love them)' (1.6.8). The second option was probably too personal and therefore dismissed, while the first one and in particular the reference to 'my fiction' disambiguated the identity of the narrator, which Barnes had kept partly ambivalent.

In addition to these minor changes, one personal passage relating to the use of language was removed (apart from the first sentence). It appeared after a paragraph in which the narrator refers to the 'mocking heard-it-all-before echo' when the words 'I love you' uttered on the phone automatically lead to the metallic response 'I love you' (230).[24]

> We must be precise with love, its language and its gestures. Have you heard brutes in suits condescending to their wives, calling them 'Dearest Angel heart' or whatever in the middle of a sneer about the female inability to understand some mechanical process? That will not do. How can the suited brute use 'Dearest Angel heart' the next time, in the middle of some dulcet night, without his wife hearing it as a mocking telephone echo? I do not know. He will use it again, of course, and he may mean what he says, but what will his wife remember?
>
> We must be precise with love. A phrase comes back to me from a poem of domestic love: <u>the sootfall of her clothes</u>. Do you hear that gentle noise on the soft bedroom carpet? I envy the perfection of the phrase; though I do not want

---

[24] In 'Parenthesis', the narrator remarks: 'Love and truth, that's the vital connection, love and truth. ... Love makes us see the truth, makes it our duty to tell the truth' (240). Thirty years later in *The Only Story*, the narrator writes: 'Truth and love, that was my credo. I love her, and I see the truth. It must be that simple' (74).

to steal it. First, because she normally hangs her clothes up before coming to bed; and secondly, because if she were diverted from the tidy process by some sweat of hurry, she would probably drop her clothes on a chair. You cannot have <u>sootfall</u> onto a chair. <u>Sootfall</u> must happen at floor level. We must be precise, as the poet says.

When she comes to bed, this is what she does. She takes off her bra, and with her fingernails she scratches lightly at her ribs where the skin has been caught into a soft compression. It is not an itch, it is a moment of smoothing-out. And she does not scratch, really – that is a little misleading, because, you see, she uses the flat of her fingernails and she rubs downwards with them. Her arms make triangles with her torso, and she half-flicks, half-smooths the flesh over her ribs. I have seen her do this in silhouette on soft afternoons. I have heard her doing it when all is dark and I am half-asleep. A soft, flicking flutter of the fingernails … She is coming to bed. (1.6.8)

The rhyming 'brutes in suits', the comments on the 'sootfall' quote and the sensual intimate anecdote of his wife coming to bed were all deleted, despite the relevance of this development to the discussion in 'Parenthesis'. Barnes dropped the first paragraph in case one of his friends recognized himself in the description and the last one because it was too personal.[25] As for the erotic connotation of 'sootfall', it had evidently marked Barnes as it appears twice in his notes. The quote is taken from the last stanza of Seamus Heaney's poem entitled 'The Skunk' – published in *Field Work* (1979) –, composed when the poet was separated from his wife in 1970–1. At the time, Heaney was a lecturer at the University of California at Berkeley, a situation similar to that of the narrator writing the half-chapter while in Michigan (*History* 232). As the poet laments the absence of his wife and thinks of her, the last quatrain starts with the sentence: 'It all came back to me last night, stirred / By the sootfall of your things at bedtime.'[26] Barnes remembers: 'I'd always thought "sootfall" of underclothes was a great, great find (or hearing) by Heaney, and wanted to work it in', but his removal of the third paragraph (judged too personal) would have left the second 'rather hanging by itself'.[27] It might also be because Barnes did 'not want to steal' the phrase (as mentioned in the middle of the second paragraph) that he cut the reference altogether. The novelist's insistence on the precision of language in this deleted passage and other passages in the half-chapter might also explain why he cut the sentence 'Let me come into your dreams', which appears twice among loose notes as well as in an early draft, underlined and isolated (1.6.8). The phrase probably sounded too much like the type of romantic clichés used by lovers, which the narrator resents for their staleness.

---

[25] Private email correspondence with the author, 10 January 2017.
[26] Seamus Heaney, *Opened Ground: Selected Poems, 1966–1996* (New York: Farrar, Straus and Giroux, 1998), 168.
[27] Private email correspondence with the author, 10 January 2017. In a second draft, only the first and second paragraphs were retained while the third was deleted (1.7.1). In the final draft, all three paragraphs were cut.

4. With a little help from my friends

Barnes not only conducted a vast amount of research for *A History of the World in 10½ Chapters*; he also appealed to friends and writers for help on very specific points, thus confirming his minute attention to precise details. Thus, the American writer Russell Banks provided information about the replica ark in Kitty Hawk on the Outer Banks of North Carolina in a letter dated 8 February 1988: 'I can tell you that the bow faces east, the ark itself is located on the west side of the road, and the ark is quite large, the size of a barn, appropriately. It's painted brown, to look like rough-hewn cedar' (1.7.2), which is echoed at the very beginning of 'Project Ararat' (249). Barnes's long-time friend Jay McInerney (who is acknowledged in the Author's Note) suggested a few Americanisms for the same chapter although he praised the faithful imitation: 'It reads very well, and practically all-American. ... no one would guess you're a limey' (1.7.6). Barnes followed McInerney's advice by changing 'clouts round the ear' into 'whack upside the head' (253) and 'augured in' (for dying) into 'bought the farm' (254), but he kept the recurrent expression 'minus some buttons' (260, 261, 263, 266), even if McInerney wrote 'Don't sound kosher to this Yank' and suggested 'minus some marbles' (1.7.6). When reading the proofs of the book, Martin Amis suggested changing the spelling of 'fellers' to 'fellas', which Barnes did (1.7.5).

In a letter of 28 September 1988, Kingsley Amis gave Barnes permission to quote him for saying that the film *Jaws* is 'about being bloody frightened of being eaten by a bloody great shark' (1.7.6), a sentence which is reproduced in 'Three Simple Stories' and attributed to the English novelist (178). On the other hand, an unacknowledged quote by Amis appears in 'The Survivor' when the main character remembers an anecdote about her husband whose insensitivity towards animals is frequently referred to: 'Once I told him they were turning all the whales into soap. He laughed and said that was a bloody good way of using them up' (88). This was Kingsley Amis's reaction as reported by his son Martin in the introductory essay to *Einstein's Monsters* (1987), a piece about nuclear arms: 'Once, having been informed by a friend of mine that an endangered breed of whales was being systematically turned into soap, he replied, "It sounds like quite a good way of *using up* whales."'[28] Julian Barnes and Martin Amis were well aware of the details of each other's works, and sometimes playfully borrowed from each other, or deliberately refrained from doing so.[29]

---

[28] Martin Amis, *Einstein's Monsters* (London: Penguin, [1987] 1988), 17.
[29] For echoes between *Metroland* and *The Rachel Papers* in early drafts of Barnes's novel, see p. 22. In *Talking It Over*, Stuart, who is depressed and drunk because he has just learned that Oliver and his wife Gillian are having an affair, keeps listening to Patsy Cline's song 'Walking After Midnight' (165). When annotating the proofs of the book, Martin Amis wrote in the margin: 'aha – another plagiarism – from London Fields' (1.15.1). In Amis's 1989 novel, a female character named Nicola is shown drinking brandy and singing Patsy Cline's song. Martin Amis, *London Fields* (London: Jonathan Cape, 1989), 347.

A few years later, Amis retaliated by borrowing one of Oliver's graphic expressions in *Talking It Over* when the latter alludes to the sexual fiasco of the night before – 'Like trying to ease an oyster into a parking meter' (85). In *Information*, Amis uses the same image to refer to the relationship between Casaubon and Dorothea in *Middlemarch*: 'it must have been like trying to get a raw oyster into a parking meter.' Martin Amis, *Information* (London: Flamingo, [1995] 1996), 168.

Barnes's friend Redmond O'Hanlon (nicknamed Fatso in their correspondence and acknowledged in the Author's Note) not only sent several cards with bibliographical references about Darwin (1.7.2), as well as insects and beetles (1.7.6), but also provided information for the eighth chapter 'Upstream!' which takes place in the Amazonian jungle. In an undated letter (1.7.6), Barnes asked O'Hanlon to send him 'typically Indian words' for a number of things ('river, junghole, tree, big bird like stork, canoe made out of treetrunk, monkey, fat explorer'). O'Hanlon had made several journeys to remote jungles in Borneo, related in *Into the Heart of Borneo* (1984), and in the Amazon basin, the subject of *In Trouble Again: A Journey between the Orinoco and the Amazon* (1988), and was therefore able to help his friend. However, Barnes's letter to O'Hanlon starts with a taunt about his friend's previous reply:

> Thank you for sending me 2,000,000 names for tribes in the junghole. This is fantastically useful as one of the things I've put into my story is that this particular tribe is distinguished by not having a name, not even for itself. (1.7.6)

While indeed the tribe in 'Upstream!' has no name for themselves (200), O'Hanlon jokingly noted in the margin of Barnes's letter: 'They're Sotomak right, they're just not telling you.' He also suggested several words for what Barnes asked but the novelist ended up using none of them, perhaps in response to what his friend jokingly wrote at the top of the letter: 'You silly Bigbum Macaw O'Berk, / You'll have to coin new words, that's why it's called a novel' (1.7.6). In the book, the actor Charlie writes only one word in the vernacular language in a letter to his girlfriend: 'There's a big white stork sort of bird called a *thkarni*' (201) even if O'Hanlon had suggested 'watuba' for that word – but we learn later that the girl who taught Charlie the language played a trick on him as '*thkarni* is the Indians' name … for you-know-what' (209). In an early draft, Barnes included two other words in the local language (another opportunity for the Indian girl to make fun of the conceited white man by teaching him the wrong words) but he later deleted the whole paragraph:

> One of the girls is trying to teach me the language. I didn't ask, she just decided to do it. We point at things and I repeat what she says. <u>Mwenda</u>, that's the river, though I'm not sure if it's this particular river or a river generally. <u>Ngkara</u>, that's a tree, but a bit of the same problem. Writing it down makes it look African, but it's much more nasal and sing-songy. When I repeat my words, the girl sometimes bursts out laughing. Well, I never was much good at languages though I pride myself I've got a pretty good ear. Maybe it's the first time they've had a real white man trying to say things to them. Still, I got my own back by telling her to say Charlie. After about 20 goes she finally comes out with something like Pwelly or Hwelly, which makes me sound all Welsh so I laughed back. (1.7.1)

O'Hanlon had suggested two other words for the river ('mahekoto kē u') and the tree ('yoawë kē sihi'), but Barnes logically invented others, before cutting the passage altogether. Incidentally, 'Upstream!' is the chapter in which Barnes deleted the greatest number of passages, maybe because Charlie's gross misunderstandings, coarse jokes and what Hermione Lee called his 'raw struggling slaphappy language' (1.7.1) did not need more emphasis. On a loose page of notes, Barnes wrote about that chapter: 'too long – letter 4/5 – too much Indian setting up?' (1.7.1) – and he indeed slimmed down the original draft.

Barnes's appeal to friends or historical sources for specific details of history, geography or linguistics testifies to his concern with accuracy in *A History of the World in 10½ Chapters*, but the book also vindicates the novelist's freedom to invent, one he would need to defend when writing and publishing *The Porcupine* three years later.

8

The Porcupine in the making: Writer and translator

In October 1992,[1] three years after the fall of the Berlin Wall and in the midst of the collapse of the East European Communist countries and their stumble into capitalism, Barnes published *The Porcupine*. The novella follows the trial of a deposed Communist party leader, Stoyo Petkanov, and deals with his confrontation with Prosecutor General Peter Solinsky who, after much exertion, eventually manages to have Petkanov convicted even though his own life is shattered. The unnamed fictional country resembles Bulgaria and the invented dictator often uses the words of Bulgaria's former head of state, Todor Zhivkov (1911–98), who was sentenced to seven years' imprisonment after an eighteen-month trial in August 1992. Barnes is used to such an intertwining of fiction and historical or real facts, and explains it thus:

> I like having information in books. It's a nice thing to do to a reader. Otherwise it's like inviting someone into your living room and providing no furniture and nothing to look at. I prefer a room with musical boxes, and books on shelves. They might clutter things up – but if they're arranged round the walls in an interesting way, that seems fine to me.[2]

Never, however, had Barnes written so simultaneously with events as in *The Porcupine*. In a letter to his Bulgarian translator and publisher of 28 November 1991, he wrote: 'I've just started writing something which may be a short novel or a long short story, I'm not sure. It just started in the middle of one night.'[3] In the first drafts, the date of the fictional events appeared as January and February 1991, but the year

---

[1] A version of this chapter was published in 'Untangling the Intertwined Threads of Fiction and Reality in *The Porcupine* (1992) by Julian Barnes', in *Pre- and Post-Publication Itineraries of the Contemporary Novel in English*, ed. Vanessa Guignery and François Gallix (Paris: Éditions Publibook Université, 2007), 49–71. I would like to thank Dimitrina Kondeva for giving me permission to quote from her letters and for very kindly sharing extra information on the composition of the book and patiently answering her queries.
[2] John Walsh, 'Faction, Fiction and Flaubert', *Books and Bookmen*, October 1984, 20.
[3] This letter to Dimitrina Kondeva is reproduced in the introduction to the Bulgarian edition of *The Porcupine* and in Kondeva's 2011 paper but is absent from the archives at the Harry Ransom Center. Dimitrina Kondeva, 'The Story of Julian Barnes's *The Porcupine*: an Epistolary ½ Chapter', in *Julian Barnes*, ed. Groes and Childs, 83.

was then deleted because, as noted by Barnes, 'two things referred to – the coup against Gorbachev and the death of Husak – happened afterwards'.[4]

The historical and geographical concordance proved challenging and meant that Barnes partly relied on Bulgarian sources which, to a certain extent, influenced the course of his book. The aim of this chapter is to examine the genesis of the book so as to unravel the intricate interweaving of fact and fiction at the level of composition and analyse the reaction of a few people who read the draft of the novel before it was published and sometimes perceived the risks of blurring the frontiers between the ontological realms of fiction and reality. Special consideration will be given to the ending of the novel and in particular to the differing ways in which the author and his Bulgarian publisher interpreted it.

1. An outsider's view

The first paratext of *The Porcupine* which is bound to draw the attention of readers who are familiar with Barnes's production is its dedication. While most of his novels are dedicated to Pat Kavanagh (Barnes's wife),[5] *The Porcupine* is dedicated to 'Dimitrina', that is, Dimitrina Kondeva, the author's Bulgarian translator and publisher, who had already translated *Flaubert's Parrot* in 1990, and with whom Barnes developed a correspondence during the composition of *The Porcupine*. The book was first published in Bulgarian in September 1992, under the title *Bodlivo Svinche*, six weeks before the English edition in the United Kingdom. This was partly due to the fact that Barnes sent Kondeva the second draft of the novel on 2 April 1992, asking for her comments on its plausibility, and she started translating it barely ten days later. As Barnes recalls, 'her comments were, "I finished the translation; we'll publish in June"'.[6] The folders relating to the novel in the archives contain twelve faxes, four letters and three postcards by Kondeva to Barnes from 20 February 1991 to 23 March 1993, and nine letters by the

---

[4] Letter from Barnes to Kondeva, 21 July 1992 (1.11.11). The August Putsch against Gorbachev took place on 19–21 August 1991; the Secretary General of the Communist Party of Czechoslovakia Gustáv Husák died on 18 November 1991.

[5] Together with *The Porcupine*, the notable exceptions among his fictional works are Barnes's first novel, *Metroland* (1980), dedicated to Laurien (Laurien Beesley, the daughter of Lawrence Beesley evoked in the first 'Simple Story' of *A History of the World in 10½ Chapters*, whom Barnes met in 1964), the First Vintage International edition of *Staring at the Sun* (of October 1993), dedicated to the memory of American publisher Frances Lindley (1911–87) who was a good friend of Pat Kavanagh's – all other editions of *Staring at the Sun* (previously and later) are dedicated to Pat – and *The Only Story*, dedicated to Hermione (Lee). Apart from that latest novel, Barnes changed the dedication of the books published after his wife's death from 'To Pat' to 'For Pat'. It is mainly Barnes's non-fictional or pseudonymous books which have a different dedicatee. His first collection of essays, *Letters from London 1990-1995*, is dedicated to the American writer Jay McInerney and his third wife Helen, while his essays on France, *Something to Declare*, are published in memory of his parents and *The Man in the Red Coat* (2019) is dedicated to Rachel (Cugnoni). The thrillers Barnes wrote under the pseudonym of Dan Kavanagh are, respectively, dedicated to Pat Kavanagh for *Duffy* (1980), the British poet Craig Raine and his wife Li for *Fiddle City* (1981), Martin Amis and his then wife Antonia for *Putting the Boot In* (1985) and Ruth Rendell and her husband Don for *Going to the Dogs* (1987). Rendell lent her cottage to Barnes so he could write some of his thrillers there.

[6] Interview by Michael March (1997), in *Conversations*, ed. Guignery and Roberts, 26.

author to his translator from January 1992 to 9 September 1992. Some correspondence between the two is missing, but the file is nevertheless fairly complete as, from January 1992, Barnes and Kondeva sent their letters by fax. Thus the author retained his original letters, which was almost never the case for postal mail, and this is what makes *The Porcupine*'s archives so valuable. If Barnes's part of the correspondence mostly focused on factual information he needed for his novel (he faxed his letters during composition because he wanted fast answers), Kondeva's letters frequently mixed the personal and the factual. While answering the author's queries about political, social or legal aspects in Bulgaria, she also kept him posted about her everyday life in an ex-Communist country opening up to liberalism and shared her expectations and despair with him, swaying as she was 'between utter hopelessness and great enthusiasm'.[7] Her hopes for the future of her country as well as her incredulity towards the 'new' government and reformers seem to be reflected in some of the exchanges of the students in *The Porcupine*. Thus, both her factual answers and some of her unprompted personal remarks may have found their way into the fictional material.

Kondeva and Barnes first met in November 1990 when the author and his wife spent nine days in Bulgaria to promote the Bulgarian translation of *Flaubert's Parrot*. Kondeva accompanied Barnes to promotional events in Sofia and for his day out of the capital when he visited the Rila monastery, Plovdiv (the second largest city) and a small old town. Struck by the disastrous political and economic situation of the country in the wake of the fall of Communism and at the dawn of the introduction of a free market economy, Barnes jotted down many notes in his red notebook. On 22 November 1990, he published a long essay in the *London Review of Books*, 'Candles for the Living', in which he described the state of the suffering nation, drawing attention to food shortages, ration coupons, electricity cuts, queues, pollution, the lack of petrol and the upsurge of pornography and erotica.[8] One reaction to that article included in Barnes's archives testifies to the difficulty of reporting about a foreign country both from the perspective of an outsider and from that of a fiction writer, even though Barnes's piece is non-fictional. Julia Stefanova, who had met Barnes and his wife in Sofia a few weeks before, admired the piece but shared her mixed feelings with Pat Kavanagh in a letter dated 12 December 1990: 'Most of it is accurate even to the point of unfeelingness which makes it painful to read at times.' As an 'insider', knowing the reality from within, she remarked: 'I have this strange feeling that right now it is too raw, too turbulent, too disturbed and vulnerable to be generalized upon and to be denied the chance of choosing its own path of development by becoming fictional material to be impressed upon by the writer's doubts and apprehensions.'[9] Julia Stefanova thus seems to resent the simultaneity of the report with the present situation in Bulgaria and to suggest that one should write with the benefit of hindsight, from a temporal distance, once it is less 'painful', 'raw' and 'turbulent'. In addition, she sets up a contrast between her position as a suffering insider and that of Barnes, the foreign writer who

---

[7] Letter from Kondeva to Pat Kavanagh and Barnes, 20 February 1991 (1.12.1).
[8] Julian Barnes, 'Candles for the Living', *London Review of Books* 12, no. 22 (22 November 1990): 6–7.
[9] Letter from Julia Stefanova to Pat Kavanagh, 12 December 1990 (1.12.1).

can only describe the situation of her country from outside and therefore may have no legitimacy to write about present-day Bulgaria.

In a letter relating to *The Porcupine*, Hermione Lee imagines how a hostile critic could react to the novel:

> He goes to Eastern Europe a few times, takes some notes, watches the telly, reads the newspapers, thinks he can tell us what it's really like – who does he think he is, Milan Kundera? ... He's one of the tourists who feels guilty about only eating half his breakfast, & then turns that guilt into an Englishman's gnawed, ironical observations, making it up from the outside.[10]

The insider/outsider dichotomy was well-known to Barnes who, in 1982, published a short story, 'One of a Kind', in which an Englishman asks an exiled Romanian writer whether there are any dissidents in his country. The Romanian author is irked by the question and answers with irony and 'a sort of funny pride', as if the Englishman 'didn't have the right to an opinion – or even a question – on the subject of his homeland'.[11] Some critics reviewing *The Porcupine* precisely castigated Barnes's status as an outsider. This was the case of Michael Scammell, professor of Russian literature at Cornell University, who compared Barnes's novella to Arthur Koestler's *Darkness at Noon* (1941) and noted that Koestler 'had the benefit of having himself been a Communist and been intimate with the Communist mentality' and could therefore identify with his subject, a process which 'is probably beyond someone who has never endured similar experiences'.[12] Salman Rushdie powerfully broaches that topic in the first pages of *Shame* (1983) when the Indian-born, England-based, migrant narrator writes about a fictional country resembling Pakistan and imagines people rejecting his authority and calling him an outsider, trespasser and poacher: '*We know you, with your foreign language wrapped around you like a flag; speaking about us in your forked tongue, what can you tell but lies?*' Then, however, the Rushdian narrator raises an important question which may also be addressed to Barnes's Bulgarian reader: 'is history to be considered the property of the participants solely?'[13]

Julia Stefanova had remarked in her letter about Barnes's non-fiction piece that he had used Bulgarian reality as 'fictional material'. Months before he started writing *The Porcupine*, Barnes could thus gauge the fragility of the demarcation line between fiction and reality, and foresee the problems he would be confronted with and would have to overcome. When, some sixteen months later, he sent Kondeva the draft of *The Porcupine*, he still remembered Stefanova's reaction to his article and wondered 'how much more might such a person object to the "fictional reality" of a piece of fiction like this'. He feared his Bulgarian publisher and translator might take offence at the book both because of his status as a foreign writer and because of his fictionalization of reality: 'Who am I, a nine-day visitor who's never lived under Communism (despite

---

[10] Letter from Hermione Lee to Barnes, 4 April 1992 (1.12.4).
[11] Julian Barnes, 'One of a Kind', *London Review of Books* 4, no. 3 (18 February 1982–3 March 1982): 23.
[12] Michael Scammell, 'Trial and Error', *New Republic*, 4–11 January 1993, 38.
[13] Salman Rushdie, *Shame* (London: Picador, [1983] 1984), 28.

travelling under it fairly widely), to steal your story like this? ... How dare he steal our story – and then mess it up, I hear you say.'[14] If Kondeva attempted to assuage Barnes's doubts in her next letter, this apprehension was still very much alive when he travelled back to Bulgaria in September 1992 for the promotion of the book. In the article he wrote in December 1992, 'How Much is that in Porcupines?', he remembered his anxiety when he was about to meet his Bulgarian readers: 'would they think I had imaginatively transformed their recent history, or merely pillaged and perverted it?'.[15] The frontier between what is perceived as fictionalization and falsification of history is uncomfortably thin, and readers might have taken offence at a book that drew so much from their own recent past.

2. Is and is not

The main reason for Barnes's apprehensions is that his unnamed Balkan country turned out to look very much like Bulgaria. Even though he first envisioned the book 'being set in a kind of Nowhere ex-Communist country – not identifiably Bulgaria, certainly with bits of Romania & other C/ist countries I'd visited',[16] the sources of his documentation (in particular a new weekly Bulgarian magazine with articles in English, *The Insider*), his correspondence with Kondeva, the information she gave him and her reactions to the draft inevitably moulded the fictional country into a pseudo-Bulgaria. In his letter of 28 November 1991, he wrote to Kondeva: 'Now it's not set in Bulgaria, but obviously the trial of Zhivkov is very useful to me as none of the Other Communist leaders has come up for trial.'[17] Therefore, the former dictator Stoyo Petkanov resembles Todor Zhivkov[18] even if Barnes insisted on making his fictional protagonist robust and unrepentant while the original was sick and fragile. There are also common points with the East German leader Eric Honecker (1912–94) and Romania's head of state Nicolae Ceausescu (1918–89), but Zhivkov is the main model. As he was just starting work on the novel, Barnes asked Kondeva if she could send 'any English-language accounts, comments, background material on his trial', as well as 'of the life in your country' as he was 'interested in the texture of life in the period from the fall of Zhivkov until now'. He also sent a series of precise questions about Zhivkov, the trial, the prosecutor and the demonstrations.[19]

Thus Barnes deliberately blurs the frontier between reality and fiction when he faithfully reproduces in his novel Zhivkov's open letter to the National Assembly in its entirety (24–5), merely deleting from the original 'the Bulgarian people' and 'Bulgaria' (replaced by 'our own people' and 'my country'), substituting the original date ('29 July

---

[14] Letter from Barnes to Kondeva, 2 April 1992 (1.11.11).
[15] Julian Barnes, 'How Much Is That in Porcupines?' *Times*, 24 October 1992, 5.
[16] Private email correspondence with the author, 16 March 2006.
[17] In Kondeva, 'The Story', 83–4.
[18] For a selective list of common points between Zhivkov and Petkanov, see Guignery, *The Fiction of Julian Barnes*, 87.
[19] Letter from Barnes to Kondeva, 28 November 1991, in Kondeva, 'The Story', 83–4.

1990') for a vaguer one ('3rd January') and changing the name of the dictator.[20] He also has Petkanov criticize his successor for running up 'the nation's foreign debt … so that it now represents two years' salary for every man, woman and child in the country' (61) – a sentence directly borrowed from a newspaper clipping about the authentic Zhelyu Zhelev after his re-election as president of Bulgaria in 1992, which features in Barnes's archives (1.11.11). While the novelist invented fictional identities for his protagonists, he mostly retained the authentic names of places, for example, using the list of real complexes in Sofia provided by Kondeva[21] to refer to the places the women demonstrators of the incipit had come from: 'Youth', 'Hope', 'Friendship', 'Red Star', 'Gagarin', 'Lenin' (3).

When Barnes sent Kondeva the second draft of his novel on 2 April 1992, he asked her to point out whatever struck her 'as impossible, implausible, wrong or bad' and to tell him if the names were 'OK' (1.11.11), a recurrent concern as in December 1991, he had already asked her to provide 'a list of common Bulgarian Christian names and surnames', which she had sent.[22] Kondeva's comments on the second draft mainly focus on that aspect as she drew attention to Barnes's use of non-existent Russian or Hungarian names. She objected to Russian names because '[t]his unnamed country is perceived as different from, even opposed to Russia'. In his final draft, the author willingly replaced the invented or foreign names with Bulgarian ones. Thus, one of the students lost his Hungarian name, 'Tamas', to a Bulgarian one, 'Atanas'; the Head of the Patriotic Security Forces moved from the Russian 'Galatin' to the Bulgarian 'Ganin'; the 'non-existent' name of the decadent poet, 'Milanescu', was replaced by the Bulgarian-sounding 'Devinsky'; the Russian town of 'Sverdlov' became the Bulgarian 'Sliven'.[23] This shift of names made the novel's Bulgarian setting and background more explicit and more identifiable, although it was not what Barnes had originally intended and he somewhat regretted it, even as he made the changes.[24] In her 2011 article on the genesis of the book, Kondeva remarks: 'I knew that Julian's initial idea to have a mix of pan-Communist names in order to make the country a nowhere-place would be an unnecessary distraction for the Slavic countries readership'; 'a Balkan-Russian-Polish-Czech mix of characters would have been more confusing for all the East Europeans' even if it 'would have been almost unnoticeable for a Western reader'. This justified her efforts to persuade him to make the names 'more locally applicable'.[25] In addition, in the final draft, Barnes changed the Bulgarian name of the prosecutor Peter Sarotov to Peter Solinski as he wanted to distinguish him clearly from Petkanov: 'I think a Western reader might want the names to be as different from one another as the characters are

---

[20] In his first draft, Barnes had pasted a copy of the original letter onto the page where it was meant to appear and made the emendations in longhand (1.12.1).
[21] Letter from Kondeva to Barnes, no date, answering Barnes's letter of 16 December 1991 (1.12.1).
[22] For his short story 'The Story of Mats Israelson' (2000), collected in *The Lemon Table* (23–48), Barnes asked his Swedish friend Kersti French for some 'typical Christian (male & female) names & surnames for the professional provincial middle-class' in Sweden in 1890–1900 (2.7.4), and for 'Marriage Lines' (2007), collected in *Pulse* (120–7), he asked Sally Beauman for typical Christian names for inhabitants of the Outer Hebrides (3.4).
[23] Typescript draft, pp. 15, 33, 33, 33 (1.12.3); *The Porcupine*, pp. 19, 44, 45, 45.
[24] Annotations, 22–27 March 2018.
[25] Kondeva, 'The Story', 90.

different from one another, and so one of them should have a name that doesn't end in -ov.'²⁶ As for Stoyo Petkanov, he was called Andrei Ilyenov in the first draft (1.12.1) but Petkanov in the second (1.12.3).

A few instances show Kondeva uneasy when Barnes modified authentic facts for the sake of fiction. For instance, three times in the novel, the author refers to the statue of the Russian Soldier, Alyosha – 'the Statue of Eternal Gratitude to the Liberating Red Army' (8) – which some think should be taken away (43–4 and 128). Barnes had seen that Red Army monument in Plovdiv during his visit to Bulgaria in 1990,²⁷ and he decided to transpose it to the capital city in his 'unnamed Balkan country', 'changing the posture of the soldier'.²⁸ Kondeva (who told Barnes the statue was called Alyosha) found the shift of places 'challenging', compared it to moving 'Nelson's Column to a town which resembles Oxford', and at first suggested a change of name to Seryozha, at least in her translation, before apparently accepting the original choice: 'I myself like it, but … OK, Alyosha!'²⁹ However, in his letter of 1 June 1992 which accompanied the final draft, Barnes interestingly agreed to the change of names in the Bulgarian translation: 'We've agreed to change Alyosha to Serozha (Seryozha?). I give you carte blanche to do similar things if they would grate on Bulgarian ears.'³⁰

A further example of Kondeva's attachment to authentic facts concerns the accusations against the former dictator. In *The Porcupine*, one of the students following the trial on television hopes the Prosecutor General will ask Petkanov: 'What is the number of your Swiss bank account?' (23), a question which has been kept as such even if Kondeva wrote in the margin of the second draft: 'it <u>has been established</u> that he has none!' and suggested at first replacing it with 'your grandchildren's bank accounts'.³¹ The third-person pronoun in Kondeva's comment ('he has none') clearly refers to Zhivkov as though Petkanov was an exact duplication of the real dictator. But the translator herself then pointed to the distinction between the fictional protagonist and the authentic person: 'The problem is that your character has no grandchildren, while Zhivkov has 3, so let the dollars be his!'³² When tempted to question an invented element, Kondeva would typically put down a question mark and add 'Ok, this is fiction after all!', or 'O, this is <u>your</u> character'.³³ When reflecting on her correspondence with Barnes some twenty years later, Kondeva gracefully acknowledged the novelist's right to imaginatively transform reality: 'Whatever facts and comments I sent, Julian skilfully transformed them so they acquired metaphoric meaning.'³⁴

In his letters of the early 1990s, Barnes repeatedly insisted that *The Porcupine* was a work of fiction and resisted any temptation to see in his book a reflection of reality. On 28 November 1991, as he was just starting the book, he wrote to Kondeva: 'since it's not B/ia in the book (it's nowhere named) I can invent things', a passage which is

---

²⁶ Letter from Barnes to Kondeva, 2 April 1992 (1.11.11).
²⁷ Barnes, 'Candles for the Living', 7.
²⁸ Letter from Barnes to Kondeva, 20 January 1992 (1.12.1).
²⁹ Typescript draft, p. 7 (1.12.3).
³⁰ In Kondeva, 'The Story', 89.
³¹ Later on in *The Porcupine*, Petkanov asserts that he has no bank account in Switzerland (60, 84).
³² Typescript draft, p. 17 (1.12.3).
³³ Typescript draft, pp. 24 and 29 (1.12.3).
³⁴ Kondeva, 'The Story', 86.

reproduced in the foreword to the Bulgarian edition to the novel, as though issuing a warning to the reader.³⁵ This foreword entitled 'Unplanned introduction' was added by Kondeva herself with the author's permission and is composed of passages from three letters by Barnes in which he insists that his novel is fictional and of a description by Kondeva of the author's first visit to Bulgaria. When Barnes sent her the draft of the book in April 1992, one of his first remarks (also reproduced in the introduction to *Bodlivo Svinche*) explicitly pointed to the distinction between fiction and reality: 'You will see that the country is not Bulgaria, though much of it resembles Bulgaria, that Petkanov is not Zhivkov, though he often speaks his lines (there is an additive of Ceausescu, of course), and that the trial, though it parallels Zhivkov's trial, is not his.'³⁶ When, later on, Kondeva asked him to clarify some factual details, such as his use of the terms 'Prosecutor General' or 'monarchy', he remarked: 'I think you may be worrying too much about tieing in Bulgarian reality to my reality. ... This may not have much basis in reality (yours).'³⁷ When she wondered if Barnes wanted to write a couple of words to the Bulgarian reader, he only suggested 'Don't forget this is a novel', a quote which appears in the foreword to the Bulgarian edition.³⁸

The interaction between fact and fiction in *The Porcupine*, which suggests that the unnamed country is and is not Bulgaria and that Petkanov is and is not Zhivkov, reminds one of the ancient Arab storytellers' formula – 'is and is not' – so favoured by Salman Rushdie. In *Shame*, the unnamed country imagined by the novelist is and is not Pakistan: 'There are two countries, real and fictional, occupying the same space, or almost the same space. My story, my fictional country exist, like myself, at a slight angle to reality. I have found this off-centring to be necessary.'³⁹ This off-centring, echoing Magritte's *This Is Not a Pipe*, introduces an ambiguity which dissociates the original country and its representation, while confusing them at the same time and therefore heightening the satirical charge against Pakistan. While this analysis can partly be applied to *The Porcupine*, the absence of any metafictional remarks similar to those of *Shame* in Barnes's book makes the political satire more universal, directed towards such metanarratives as Communism or liberalism rather than against one specific country. In both cases, however, the fictional country is the product of a fantasist's imagination and, as such, an impure combination.

3. The ending of the novel

During the composition of *The Porcupine*, the correspondence between author and translator/publisher worked both ways (as opposed to the common situation of the translator asking questions to the author after the book has been published in English) and Barnes's manuscript partly evolved thanks to the comments and information

---

³⁵ Dimitrina Kondeva, 'Непредвиден Предговор [Unplanned Introduction]', *Bodlivo Svinche*, by Julian Barnes, trans. Dimitrina Kondeva (Sofia: Obsidian Press, 1992), 7.
³⁶ Letter from Barnes to Kondeva, 2 April 1992 (1.11.11).
³⁷ Letter from Barnes to Kondeva, 7 July 1992 (1.11.11).
³⁸ In Kondeva, 'Unplanned Introduction', 8.
³⁹ Rushdie, *Shame*, 29.

offered by Kondeva. The publisher always showed herself extremely respectful and scrupulous in her remarks, suggestions and translation, but in her fax of 8 September 1992, sent just before the manuscript was taken to the Bulgarian printer and a few weeks before Barnes's visit to Bulgaria to promote the novel, she communicated to Barnes her concern about the ending which might make some Bulgarian readers uncomfortable. After sharing her enthusiasm over the major coverage of *The Porcupine* in the Bulgarian media and suggesting a couple of spelling corrections for proper names, she wrote:

> Julian, you were off when I decided to cut the last paragraph: 'In front of the vacant Mausoleum …' because of the reaction of everybody who had read the book, and mine too. The last impression is of the steadfastness of the communists, which is correct of course, but here might be, actually is interpreted as a tribute to their cause. Believe me, it's better without it in the translation.[40]

Barnes had been away for three weeks and Kondeva waited another ten days after he had returned to London before announcing her 'decision' to cut the last paragraph, at a time that was so close to publication date as to make it impossible to back-pedal. The timing of this momentous message was also surprising given that Kondeva had known about the ending since June 1992. As *The Porcupine* was to be the first book to be released by Kondeva's own newly funded publishing house, Obsidian, it might have been that she feared the potentially negative effects on her business of a novel whose ending some might misinterpret as a tribute to the Communist cause.

The contentious conclusion of the novel was actually not the original one and ten different scripts of the ending exist in Barnes's archives. Five of them are variations on the original conclusion which Kondeva read in the second draft in April 1992 and which appears on the last but two pages of *The Porcupine* (134). This ending takes place a day before the former leader's sentence is made public and consists of the final highly tense private confrontation between Peter Solinski and Stoyo Petkanov, the two main protagonists whose initials are the same though reversed, which may suggest that they are alter egos of one another (although that was not intentional on Barnes's part). Even though the former dictator will be convicted, he demonstrates his ascendancy over the Prosecutor General by telling him he will haunt his thoughts and Solinski will never be able to get rid of him or of the old regime. As the Prosecutor General shouts '"To hell with you. Curse you"' and prepares to leave, Petkanov grips his upper arm, brings their faces closer and hisses: '"You are wrong. I curse you. I sentence you." The unvanquished stare, the whiff of hard-boiled egg, the old fingers clamped bruisingly around the upper arm. "I sentence *you*"' (134). These last words are certainly more powerful than the very first version which was more explicit and therefore more restrictive in the scope of the curse: '"I sentence you," said Ilyenov. The unvanquished stare, the whiff of hard-boiled egg, the old fingers clamped on the upper arm. "I sentence you to remember me"' (1.12.1). In all five versions, however, the play on the first- and second-person pronouns, intensified by the repetition of the sentence and the use of italics or

---

[40] Letter from Kondeva to Barnes, 8 September 1992 (1.11.11).

underlining, echoes Coriolanus's famous 'I banish you' speech, excoriating the Roman rabble (III, 3, 121) – but it was not a conscious reference by Barnes at the time of writing.[41] Petkanov talks to his exhausted interlocutor in a 'sarcastic and ingratiating' voice and feels 'strangely cheerful' (135), while the Prosecutor General, whose father is dead, whose wife wants a divorce and whose daughter is refusing to speak to him, looks 'defeated' and 'pathetic' (135). The original ending thus focused on the reversal of power between the two protagonists: even if the Prosecutor General has managed to have the erstwhile dictator sentenced to prison, Petkanov turns the tables, reminds Solinski of the corrupt means inherited from the old regime which he has resorted to in order to condemn the deposed leader, so that in the end Solinski is the one who seems to have been condemned.

However, Barnes was dissatisfied with this ending and Kondeva mentions in her letter of 17 May 1992 that he 'intended to add something' (1.12.3). This is confirmed in Barnes's letter of 1 June 1992 which accompanies the final draft, in which he refers to 'some new sections at the end'.[42] Barnes added two pages: on the last but one page, Solinski is shown in church, lighting candles and reappropriating his Orthodox faith (137); the last page is composed of three paragraphs that follow a camera-eye movement leading from the empty pedestal of the statue of Alyosha to the marshalling yard containing the discarded statues of former Communist leaders, to the Mausoleum of the First Leader in front of which the grandmother of one of the students, a devout Leninist, is standing:

> Evening and rain fell softly together. On a low hill to the north of the city stood a concrete pedestal, sullen and aimless. The bronze panels round its sides gleamed dully in the damp. Without Alyosha to lead them into the future, the machine-gunners now found themselves fighting a different battle: irrelevant, local, silent.
>
> On the piece of waste ground beside the marshalling yard, rain gave a gentle sweat to Lenin and Stalin, to Brezhnev, to the First Leader, and to Stoyo Petkanov. Spring was coming, and the first tendrils would soon try once again to take a hold on the skiddy bronze of military boots. In the dark, locomotives lurched on wet points and dragged at overhead cables, flashing brief light on to sculpted faces. But argument had ceased in this posthumous Politburo; the stiff giants had fallen silent.
>
> In front of the vacant Mausoleum of the First Leader an old woman stood alone. She wore a woollen scarf wrapped round a woollen hat, and both were soaked. In outstretched fists she held a small framed print of V.I. Lenin. Rain bubbled the image, but his indelible face pursued each passer-by. Occasionally, a committed drunk or some chattering thrush of a student would shout across at the old woman, at the thin light veering off the wet glass. But whatever the words, she stood her ground, and she remained silent. (138)

---

[41] Annotations, 22–27 March 2018.
[42] Kondeva, 'The Story', 89.

Five versions of this last page exist in the archives, and the first is the only one which does not play on the mesmerizing epiphora of the adjective 'silent'.[43] The very last paragraph is the one Kondeva decided to cut in her translation. Barnes's answer to her fax came on the next day – 9 September 1992 – in the form of a two-page letter starting with 'If I were not very fond of you, I would be very cross with you. No, I am very fond of you and very cross with you.' He added: 'in all our dealings up to now you have always shown yourself completely scrupulous towards what I write and the way I write it', so that he was 'quite simply flabbergasted' by her decision, all the more as she had never mentioned any misgivings about the new ending before.[44]

Barnes then turns into a critic and analyst of his own work – an activity he would normally balk at – and gives six instructive arguments in favour of the last paragraph: 'So let me explain to you about the final paragraph.' The first one is structural: '1. The last section is in triadic form, the most powerful rhythmic form in prose. It makes as much sense if you lop off the last section as a three-legged cow.' The ternary rhythm is conveyed not only by the epiphora of 'silent' but also by the repeated insistence on rain and feeble light. The lexical field of dampness impregnates the three paragraphs and contributes to the bleakness of the scene ('rain', 'damp' in the first paragraph; 'rain', 'wet' in the second; 'soaked', 'Rain', 'wet' in the third). Darkness is also emphasized and accompanied with references to feeble light ('Evening', 'gleamed dully' in the first paragraph; 'dark', 'flashing brief light' in the second; 'the thin light' in the third) which might refer to the dying off of the Communist era and aura. The Communist heroes are all reduced to lifeless solid forms ('a concrete pedestal', 'bronze panels' in the first paragraph; 'bronze', 'sculpted faces' in the second; 'a small framed print' in the third) and set in a desolate and deserted environment: the statue of Alyosha has been carted away and its pedestal is 'sullen and aimless'; the discarded statues have been moved to a 'piece of waste ground'; the Mausoleum of the First Leader is 'vacant' as his embalmed corpse has been taken away (43). However, while the first two paragraphs clearly suggest the demise of Communism, the last one is more ambivalent as the old woman silently symbolizes the resilience of that ideology. Barnes points to the necessity of this ambivalence in his fifth argument:

> 5. So instead of a three-part closing section which goes 'Alyosha has departed, the Soviet giants have fallen silent, the old woman stands outside the mausoleum', we have 'Alyosha has departed, the Soviet giants have fallen silent'. Oh, so that's all right then, they've all gone away, and it's a happy ending. It's not my job to give a happy ending, it's my job to give something a bit more difficult than that. See my other books.

The ambiguous ending is indeed a characteristic of Barnes's novels: he typically avoids providing a definitive and reassuring conclusion, preferring instead to end with a scene

---

[43] In the first version, the second paragraph ends with 'light flashed on the faces of the silent giants' (1.12.3).
[44] Letter from Barnes to Kondeva, 9 September 1992. All the following quotes by Barnes are taken from this letter (1.11.11).

that opens onto a plurality of interpretations and makes the reader both free and active. The concluding word of *The Porcupine* – 'silent' – is therefore appropriately unsettling because of the indeterminacy and unreadable vacuum it opens onto, faintly echoing Hamlet's last words before he dies: 'The rest is silence' (V, 2, 372).

The second structural argument which Barnes proposes relates to the symmetry of the ending with the beginning: '2. The last paragraph deliberately picks up on the opening section of the book; but now, in place of thousands of candlelit women, there is a single protester.' The narrative circularity is actually provided both by the echo between the vision of the steadfast Communist ex-leader, Petkanov, in the first sentence of the novel – 'The old man stood' (1) – and that of Stefan's defiant grandmother – 'an old woman stood' (138) – and by the reminder of the wordless demonstration of women taking place in the evening. Instead of shouting slogans against the food shortages, the women produce a non-verbal cacophony by clattering kitchen implements. This remarkable and eloquent scene was inspired by genuine demonstrations of that type in Bulgaria, which a Bulgarian friend of Barnes's commented upon during a phone call: 'She said that a group of women were outside her window demonstrating by banging their kitchen utensils and it was the most terrifying sound she had ever heard.'[45] Other Bulgarian friends referred to similar scenes: 'There were heartbreaking demonstrations in Sofia of the empty saucepans. The clatter all over the city centre was sinister.'[46] The noisy and yet wordless poise of the candlelit protesters in the incipit mirrors the silent dignity of Stefan's grandmother in the conclusion. However, the emphasis on light with its attached symbolism is different in the two scenes, as Barnes remarks: 'Note – and this is important – that instead of carrying a candle as they do, that [sic] she has no light; she, and Lenin, are only seen because of a street light's thin glow. In other words, she and her icon now give off no light of their own.'

Even though they give off no light of their own for the time being, the very presence of Stefan's grandmother testifies to a form of resilience of Communism. The last paragraph echoes another symmetrical passage which also highlighted the persistence of the Communist ideology, when the old woman 'had wrapped a woollen scarf over her woollen hat, taken the picture off the wall' and gone to a Communist rally with a few hundred other loyalists (54). The symmetry is here reinforced by the repetition of the same sartorial details. The old woman's narrative function is therefore emblematic of the belief in the circularity of history as Barnes suggests in his third point: '3. What is she doing there? She is there for her own steadfastness; she is there to echo Petkanov's horrible predictions of the return of his system; she is there to give a last echo of Solinsky's fear.' Throughout the book, Petkanov indeed shows that he still firmly believes in the Communist ideology. He argues that Communism has only had one chance so far and, quoting a morsel of priestly wisdom – 'You don't get to Heaven at the first jump' (105, 114) – he foretells that 'inevitably, the spirit of Socialism will shake itself again' (114). Solinski for his part fears the advent of revisionism, imagining the publication of a book such as '*Stoyo Petkanov: the Rehabilitation of a Helmsman*'

---

[45] In Matthew Pateman, 'The Trials of Barnes', *Leeds Student Independent Newspaper*, 29 October 1993, 16.
[46] Letter from Peter and Rada Sharlanjieva to Barnes and Pat Kavanagh, 22 December 1990 (1.12.1).

(103). Stefan's grandmother silently sticks to Communism and is patiently waiting for its inevitable return: 'she also saw, beyond that, the moment when men and women would rise and shake themselves, recovering their rightful dignity and starting again the whole glorious cycle of revolution' (55). The term 'revolution', which Bulgarians are reluctant to use, preferring a euphemism such as 'the Changes' (42), etymologically suggests both a categorical transformation and the idea of return, of restoration, just like the turning of a wheel. The old woman's resolute gravity at the end and the 'indelible face' of Lenin which 'pursued each passer-by' therefore hint at the cyclical nature of history and the steadfastness of the master narrative that is Communism.

It is precisely this 'steadfastness' of the Communists which Kondeva resented because, although correct, it 'might be, actually <u>is</u> interpreted as a tribute to their cause', an awkward position at a time – the early 1990s – when most Bulgarian people were enthusiastic about the political changes in their country and had no nostalgia for the past. Barnes's last two arguments centre around the question of interpretation and the status of the reader:

> 4. ... I find this extraordinary. What I write is correct, but you delete it because it might be misinterpreted. If someone reads <u>The Porcupine</u>, reads the story of Petkanov, reads my account of his political thought and political operation, and then concludes that the book ends with 'a tribute' to communism, then they are simply a very dim reader. ... I have come across this category of reader before, who looks at the ending of a novel and decides that it consists of the novelist's final beliefs in a disguised form. Nothing of the sort. A novel ends how it has to end, according to its own internal motions and forces ...
>
> 6. So suddenly we're afraid of an old woman, a silent one, a fictional one? What's going on? We're afraid of being 'misinterpreted'? <u>That's what they used to do in the old days</u>. Readers will always misinterpret books, but when the book is right and the reader wrong, then the publisher should stand by the author. I am dismayed to discover that you have not stood by me.

Instead of postulating an ideal or model reader capable of actively participating in the actualization of the book, Barnes's publisher has, to a certain extent, imagined a rather passive reader who would be guided in their interpretation of the conclusion. Two opposite conceptions of the figure of the reader and of the status of the text are thus brought face to face. On the one hand, Kondeva, as an insider, is concerned about how Bulgarian readers might react and wishes she could protect both them and Barnes against any misinterpretation. On the other hand, Barnes's position echoes that of Umberto Eco who values open works of art which authorize a plurality of interpretations – 'a creative text is always an Open Work' – and refers to the 'necessity to leave the conclusion to float around, to blur the prejudices of the author through the ambiguity of language and the impalpability of a final sense'.[47] To that extent, *The Porcupine* is an open work of art because of its ambiguous ending which makes the

---

[47] Umberto Eco, Richard Rorty, Jonathan Culler and Christine Brooke-Rose, *Interpretation and Overinterpretation*, ed. Stefan Collini (Cambridge: Cambridge University Press, 1992), 140–1.

reader active and, possibly, uncomfortable. Deleting the last paragraph because some might misinterpret it thus drastically reduces the play of 'unlimited semiosis'[48] and curbs the reader's participation.

Barnes's letter ends not only with his insistence on having the last paragraph restored in the 'next' edition (thus suggesting that there was not enough time to restore it for the first edition) but also with a surprising offer of a postmodern way out:

> Dimitrina, I must insist that the final paragraph be restored to the book in the next and any subsequent editions. You can do it silently, if you prefer, or you can do it in a post-modern afterword, using portions of this letter. But you must do it, and you must fax me back that you will do it.
>
> I cannot attend to anything else in your fax until this is cleared up. Nor can I feel any of the happiness you do over publication. And of course, if anyone congratulates me in Bulgaria on the ending of the novel, I shall have to say, 'But that is not what I wrote'.

Barnes's commanding tone and his six arguments in favour of the ending proved convincing and when Kondeva received his explanatory letter, she immediately wrote back to say she would restore the final paragraph for the first edition. Several British and American reviewers of *The Porcupine* referred to the final powerful image of the old woman and its touching ambivalence but none concluded that it was a tribute to the cause of Communism or that Barnes was an apologist for the old order. Robert Harris, for example, was well aware of the desired ambiguity: 'Is this an icon being kept alive for the future, or the pathetic madness of a bag lady?'[49] If Michael Scammell suggested that 'emotionally and subliminally', Barnes weighed the scales in favour of Petkanov as he is given some of the most memorable lines, he nevertheless added that ideologically, it would be impossible 'to conclude that Barnes is rooting for the old woman and Leninism'.[50] The only dissonant voice was that of the Czech-Canadian novelist Josef Skvorecky[51] who, from his perspective as an insider who had witnessed the hypocrisies of Communism and struggled for forty years against ideology, was irritated by the final ambivalence and could not be convinced that the poor old woman, 'the traditional figure of sympathy', projected 'the image of a faithful believer in something good, which has been betrayed by renegade communists'.[52] In Bulgaria, as far as Kondeva remembers, reviewers did not comment on the ending, nor did they suggest that Barnes was extolling Communism.[53]

If Barnes seems not to have been confronted with any misinterpretation of the last paragraph, he did have to face the uneasiness of a specific category of readers

---

[48] Umberto Eco, *The Role of the Reader. Explorations in the Semiotics of Texts* (Bloomington: Indiana University Press, 1979), 40.
[49] Robert Harris, 'Full of Prickles', *Literary Review*, November 1992, 26.
[50] Scammell, 'Trial and Error', 36–7.
[51] In 1976, Barnes reviewed Josef Skvorecky's third novel *Miss Silver's Past*, first published and banned by the Communist authorities in 1969, a book belonging to 'the older tradition of bureaucratic satire'. Julian Barnes, 'Ductile', *New Statesman*, 12 March 1976, 334.
[52] Josef Skvorecky, 'In the Court of Memory', *Washington Post Book World*, 15 November 1996, 6.
[53] Private phone conversation with the author, 6 May 2006.

before the book was published in Great Britain – the solicitors and underwriters who were concerned with the libel risks – which confirmed, yet again, the fragility of the demarcation line between fact and fiction.

4. The libel risks

On 6 August 1992, solicitor Bernard N. Nyman wrote a letter to the managing director of Jonathan Cape, explaining that there were real people named in *The Porcupine* who 'present various different levels of libel risks'.[54] Nyman proceeds with a list of thirteen items and argues in particular that Frank Sinatra, Nancy Reagan and the Queen of England are defamed by the sexual references to them. Nancy Reagan is said to have gone 'down on her knees to' Sinatra, and the latter to have 'fucked Nancy Reagan in the White House' (18–19), an information which, as Nyman indicates, is based on the allegations in Kitty Kelley's *Nancy Reagan: The Unauthorized Biography* (1991), about which Nancy Reagan did not sue. As for the Queen, Nyman esteems that she is defamed by the accusation 'that she willingly participated in sexual intercourse with the President of a fictional eastern bloc republic' according to the statements of the students watching the trial on television, such as '*He fucked the Queen of England*' (118), '*she made him do it in the bath*' (119); '*It was all those collars and girdles he was wearing. She couldn't see who was underneath*' (120). According to Nyman, such allegations suggest not only 'active complicity on her part' but also 'that she is prepared to do this with anyone'. Finally, Nyman refers to the world leaders whose praise in favour of Petkanov the dictator quotes before the court (122–5), which leads the students to comment: '"*He fucked them all. He really fucked them all.*" / "*Takes two to fuck.*"' (125), which again implies active complicity. Nyman argues that the latter statements could open up the risk of a libel complaint by any of the world leaders mentioned and therefore proposes deleting them. In the three latter cases, Nyman admits that the libel risk is low, given the fictional context in which they appear, 'but not non-existent'. The highest libel risk, according to Nyman, concerns Mikhaïl Gorbachev, described in the book as 'that weak fool in the Kremlin who looked as if a bird had shat on his head' (79), 'a hypocrite, such a betrayer of socialism' (87), 'that self-important fool' compared to 'a dimwit *babushka*' (88) and a 'Judas' (115). Nyman argues that such qualifications hold Gorbachev up to ridicule, are defamatory and therefore could make him sue for libel.

What is striking in this libel report is that the solicitor never situates the context in which the quotes appear nor pays attention to focalization. The derogatory references to Sinatra, Reagan and Gorbachev are all focalized through Petkanov, the Communist ex-leader, who considers Americans as 'bandits' (18) and despises Gorbachev for having implemented reforms that led to the demise of socialism. The defamatory accusations therefore stem from an unapologetically intransigent dictator whose

---

[54] Letter from Bernard N. Nyman, of Rubinstein Callingham Polden & Gall (solicitors), to Jenny Cottom, managing director of Jonathan Cape, 6 August 1992. All subsequent comments by Nyman are taken from this letter (1.11.11).

contemptuous views of America and of Gorbachev necessarily derive from his own ideological bias. Moreover, the narrative technique of interior monologue justifies the obscene and foul-mouthed vocabulary which pertains to Petkanov's idiolect. The ribald speculations concerning the Queen and the world leaders, which should be understood metaphorically rather than literally, are uttered by disillusioned and sarcastic students who have taken part in the anti-Communist demonstrations but also have misgivings about the role of Western countries and the advent of liberalism. The libel report keeps acknowledging that the context is that of a work of fiction[55] but fails to perceive the subtleties of voice and perspective, of satire and humour, and of the rhetorical devices exploited by the author.

As a consequence of Nyman's report, Lloyds' Underwriters decided to withdraw libel cover for *The Porcupine*. On 14 September 1992, Simon Master from Random House, the transatlantic corporate company of which Jonathan Cape is part, wrote to John Mottram from Lloyds' Underwriters, giving three main arguments to explain why they had decided to publish *The Porcupine* unaltered.[56] He first argues that *The Porcupine* being a work of 'heavy political satire', 'evident exaggeration, non-literal figures of speech (even hyperbole) are devices used in arguments to make political, social and moral points'. He then draws attention to voice and perspective: 'Views, opinion and received gossip are expressed through the recollections of clearly prejudiced and cynical characters whose statements or assertions are clearly not to be taken seriously or literally in many instances.' Finally, he indicates that the scope of the satire is not to be overstated: 'This is a witty, ironic and at times sarcastic treatment of its subject and characters – but not a calculatedly malicious new attack on anyone. I'm certain far worse things have been said and written about Gorbachev.' In spite of these arguments, on 17 September 1992, underwriter A. Loucaidas wrote back to say Lloyds would not provide insurance cover because there was no research to back up the 'stories' Barnes included about prominent public figures, and he added: 'Although this is a work of fiction, real life characters are portrayed with no apparent attempt made to disguise their identities.'[57] Loucaidas here implicitly alludes to the ontological clash which occurs when real-world figures are inserted in a work of fiction, thus violating the ontological boundary between the real and the fictional. Thus, there is not only a moral but also an 'ontological scandal'[58] when a real-world figure such as the Queen of England is said to have had sexual intercourse with a fictional protagonist such as Petkanov, if one follows Bernard N. Nyman's literal interpretation of the students' statements.

However, the underwriters were not so much concerned about the interaction between real and fictional characters as about the critical comments and disparaging remarks about Gorbachev, portrayed as a betrayer of socialism. In order to be able to provide defence to a libel action should Gorbachev sue, Simon Master from Random House asked Barnes on 22 September 1992 to offer 'some background to the way he is

---

[55] 'given the context of this fictional book', 'given the context of the allegations, in a work of fiction', 'considering the context in which this appears, namely a work of fiction'.

[56] Letter from Simon Master (Random House) to John Mottram (Lloyds' Underwriters), 14 September 1992 (1.11.11).

[57] Fax by A. Loucaidas, underwriter, 17 September 1992 (1.11.11).

[58] Brian McHale, *Postmodernist Fiction* (New York: Methuen, 1987), 85.

characterized in the book', that is, 'published articles or record of speeches that might have bearing on the public or private perception of Gorbachev' as Barnes portrays him in *The Porcupine*.[59] Barnes's answer[60] focuses on point of view, underlining the fact that the forceful attacks on Gorbachev in the book all come from Petkanov, 'a hardline Communist', 'responsible for destroying the country economically, presiding over a deeply corrupt system, setting up concentration camps and permitting the assassination of oppositionists'. Therefore, it is most unlikely that 'anyone reading Petkanov's denunciations of Gorbachev' would 'lower their opinion of Gorbachev as a result', and 'a reader would have to seriously misunderstand it [the book] to imagine that Petkanov's opinions were those of the author, or those towards which the author wished to persuade the reader'. This remark reminds one of Barnes's arguments, in his letter to Kondeva, relating to readers' misinterpretation of the last paragraph of the novel as a tribute to Communism and a reflection of the novelist's beliefs. This discussion on libel risks reveals how a specific category of readers – solicitors and underwriters – has been tempted to ignore some of the narrative devices emblematic of the writing of fiction and to read fiction as a factual report, confusing a fictional protagonist's opinions with those of the author.

The analysis of the genesis of *The Porcupine* has revealed how Barnes's Bulgarian translator and publisher played an important role in drawing the unnamed fictional country closer to Bulgaria. The reactions of several readers before the publication of the book – Kondeva on the one hand and Lloyds' solicitors and underwriters on the other hand – show in very different ways how the intertwining of fiction and reality can sometimes prove disturbing. After the book's publication, as Barnes reports in his article 'How Much is that in Porcupines?', some Bulgarian readers were tempted to consider the novel as history à clef, that is, as a reflection of Zhivkov's trial rather than a fictional creation. They told the author either 'You have told the truth' or 'You have falsified history', thus momentarily forgetting the demarcation line between fiction and fact.[61] As a Bulgarian reviewer rightly suggested, the Bulgarian reader was bound to be 'seriously embarrassed' by *The Porcupine*: 'A participant in those events he unwittingly compares his experience with/to the book. It is impossible for a Bulgarian to be impartial and detached because a year or two is no historical distance at all.'[62] What is more surprising is that Michael Scammell, in his review of *The Porcupine*, should have drawn a list of 'crucial and suggestive' disparities between Zhivkov and Barnes's fictional Petkanov, seemingly regretting that what is 'so recognizably present in the real live Zhivkov' should be 'lost in Barnes's version of a dictator at bay'. However, in an extraordinary example of retraction, Scammell adds cautiously: 'Barnes, of course, cannot be held to account for not portraying the historical Zhivkov', as though warding off the accusation of confusing fiction with factual report.[63]

---

[59] Letter from Master to Barnes, 22 September 1992 (1.11.11).
[60] Barnes, '*The Porcupine* and Gorbachev', no date, no addressee (1.11.11).
[61] Barnes, 'How Much Is That in Porcupines?', 5. For other examples of such confusions by readers once the book was published, see Guignery, *The Fiction of Barnes*, 87–9.
[62] Poliana Atanasova, 'Englishman Writes a Novel about Zhivkov's Darned Socks', *Democracy* (Sofia), 18 September 1992 (1.18).
[63] Scammell, 'Trial and Error', 37–8.

This ontological confusion may be tempting as many facts, details and events are borrowed from Bulgaria's history in the early 1990s so that the informed reader may sometimes feel a fictive deficit. In *The Porcupine*, the fictional dimension emerges not so much from the constituents of the plot proper or the historical and geographical background, as from the narrative drive of the story which is provided by the constant shift of perspectives and focalizations – from the dictator to the Prosecutor General, from the students to the prosecutor's wife and Stefan's grandmother. Fiction also derives from the creation of scenes and images which are not necessarily invented – the women's demonstration in the incipit or the gathering of young men in the Square of St Vassily the Martyr, organizing their own visa queue for the American embassy (51–3, 64–5), a scene which had struck Barnes during his 1990 visit[64] – but their force and intensity derive from the narrative pulse and the richness of inventive details and minute descriptions. Creation is also linguistic in the way Barnes both borrowed set phrases and invented a specific idiolect for his dictator, full of Marxist-Leninist jargon, bits of peasant wisdom and scurrilous obscenities – one that would find echoes twenty-four years later in *The Noise of Time*.

Despite the factual inspiration for *The Porcupine*, the book should therefore be approached as a work of fiction, and not as a journalistic pamphlet. In his extrapolation of Bulgaria's recent history, Barnes has addressed political and moral issues that extend beyond the historical and geographical specificities of one particular country to embrace the broader issue of twentieth-century Eastern European politics, questioning, in a fictional environment, the legitimacy of such master narratives as Communism and Capitalism.

[64] Barnes, 'Candles for the Living', 6–7.

9

A dictionary of Julian Barnes

Academics: 1980: 'what the fuck good are they – they're only reviewers delivering their copy a hundred years late.'[1]
2001: 'This is no longer the case: nowadays they're jostling the freelancers out of the weekly literary pages.'[2]
2001: 'academe and Grub Street need one another: like teeth, they work best when in nutritious opposition.'[3]

Amis, Kingsley: On 31 July 1985, Richard Ellmann, biographer of Yeats, Joyce and Wilde, wrote to Barnes: 'You are probably the only person alive who could do a biography of Amis alive – and I look forward to AMIS AND THE SPARROWHAWK.'[4] In a letter of 27 September 1985, Philip Larkin asked: 'How far have you got with Kingsley? "Berkhamsted: The Realms of Gold"?'[5]

In the late 1980s, idea for a 'Rage In Age / Old stor[y]': 'Something based on Kingsley. Knowing no-one else is any good, pissing on everyone, best-is-gone, etc, sentimental, valedictory, misanthropic' (1.1.2).

Brookner, Anita: Met in 1984 when they had both been shortlisted for the Booker Prize. Barnes's conversation changed when sitting opposite her: 'Vocabulary and grammar were self-scrutinised in the microsecond before they emerged from my mouth; I even found myself punctuating my own conversation – putting in semicolons, for God's sake.'[6]

A source of inspiration for the character of Mme Wyatt in *Talking It Over*: 'I slightly had Anita Brookner in mind when writing Mme Wyatt – not physically or linguistically – but in the attitude to life.'[7]

---

[1] Barnes, *Metroland*, 146.
[2] Julian Barnes, 'Introduction', *Reliable Essays: The Best of Clive James* (London: Picador, 2001), xvi.
[3] Ibid.
[4] Letter from Richard Ellmann to Julian Barnes, 31 July 1985 (1.16.7).
[5] Thwaite, ed., *Selected Letters of Philip Larkin*, 751. In his biography of Kingsley Amis, Zachary Leader writes: 'Barnes admired Amis and for a time seriously contemplated writing his biography.' Leader, *The Life of Kingsley Amis*, 756.
[6] Julian Barnes, 'Julian Barnes Remembers His Friend Anita Brookner: "There was no one remotely like her"', *Guardian*, 18 March 2016, http://www.theguardian.com/books/2016/mar/18/julian-barnes-remembers-anita-brookner. Accessed on 19 January 2019.
[7] Annotations, 22–27 March 2018.

Brothers: Jonathan Barnes about their father, in an email to his brother on 12 February 2007: 'Father took us to Wembley one year to see that final of the London Schools Football Cup. During half-time a man of about his age came up and chatted with him for ten minutes. When he had gone our Father said "That's my brother – haven't seen him for ten years". And he never saw him again.' Jonathan Barnes commented: 'I think it shows a surprisingly rational attitude to family connections' (3.5).

Cicadas: In 1976, made a sculpture out of cicada cases picked up in Washington, entitled 'London Literary Life': it seemed like a 'circular slow ramp making a progression towards the top and when you got to the top, it was like Masada, and the only thing to do was either throw yourself off or be sort of crushed to death by the others'.[8] Pointing to a few beetles which had fallen with their legs in the air, Barnes commented: 'They don't get reviewed any more'.[9]

Cookbooks: In 2003, the Pedant in the Kitchen had about a hundred of them. 'Is this

(a) Modest?
(b) Just right
(c) Obscenely large?'[10]

Doctor Barnes: 22 July 1984. This was how Francis Steegmuller, translator of Flaubert, addressed Barnes in his first letter to him. He wrote: 'Should you happen ever to see Geoffrey Braithwaite, will you please tell him that I find his translations impeccable?' (3.1).

1 September 1984. Francis Steegmuller in his second letter: 'Dear Mr. Barnes: / Please forgive the "Doctor." I wonder why I was taken in by that feature of the delightful performance' (3.1).

20 February 1986. In response to the letter of a reader of *Flaubert's Parrot*, Cynthia Pettiward, who addressed him as 'Dr. Barnes': 'I'm no Dr, just plain Mr, BA (Oxon) being the limit of my qualifications' (2.6.10). The correspondence between Barnes and Cynthia Pettiward in the late 1980s was the source of inspiration for the epistolary short story 'Knowing French' in 2003,[11] in which the character is renamed Sylvia Winstanley. In her second (fictional) letter, Sylvia gently chastises the writer: 'Now why did you say you were a doctor in your sixties when you obviously can't be more than forty? Come now!'[12]

---

[8] Clive James, 'Clive James and Julian Barnes Talking in the Library', 2001, https://www.youtube.com/watch?v=XZfIBIBD6No. Accessed on 19 January 2019.
[9] Parker, 'Print', *Blitz* 57 (September 1987): 106.
[10] Barnes, *The Pedant in the Kitchen*, 26.
[11] The story was originally published in *Granta* 84 (Winter 2003): 237–53, and later collected in *The Lemon Table* (137–58).
[12] Barnes, 'Knowing French', *The Lemon Table*, 142. The archives do not include Cynthia Pettiward's letters but only Barnes's two-page letter to her of 20 February 1986. His remark 'I am glad you are bilingual and pronounce a treat' (2.6.10) is echoed in Sylvia's first fictional letter (139). The anecdote

Europe:	3 February 2012. Adds an extra scene to *England, England*, in which Angela Merkel is the 93-year-old European President-for-Life, and European countries lead 'a swift campaign to evict England'. That was four years before the Brexit won in the referendum of 23 June 2016.[13]
	In 2014, defines himself as 'English first, European second and British third'.[14]
Fireworks:	Every November, invites chef Simon Hopkinson and some friends to his house for dinner and fireworks. Hopkinson comments: 'Julian is more of a rocket man and I'm more of a big bang man.'[15]
	Flaubert, Gustave: 'A genius.'[16]
Football:	18 June 1986. Watches the football game between England and Paraguay during the FIFA World Cup. Writes in his television review for the *Observer*: 'As England went in 1-0 up at half-time, [the football commentator] John Motson chummily told us, "You should be able to enjoy your cup of tea." "Cup of tea?" me and the lads bellowed back at him in awed incredulity. ... When the third goal went in, me and the lads had several large "cups of tea" to celebrate' (1.16.2).
Forfeited Pledges:	Early 1980s. Works in his study in a Victorian house in St George's Avenue, Tufnell Park, which has a big railway station sign proclaiming BARNES and another saying FORFEITED PLEDGES.
Gin and Bitter Lemon:	His choice of liquor in the late 1970s when working at the *New Review*. The editor Ian Hamilton, cringing at this 'unbutch choice', would buy the drinks at the pub The Pillars of Hercules but would not pronounce the words 'bitter lemon'.[17]

about Sylvia meeting the 'furious' owner of a parrot which looked miserable (140–1) also comes from that correspondence with the 'extra high-grade coincidence' pointed out by Barnes in his letter that the woman Cynthia Pettiward met was none other than the mother-in-law of Barnes's brother, whom Barnes met only once and indeed had a parrot (1.6.10). In the first draft of the story, Sylvia/Cynthia was called Felicity, a homage to the servant in Flaubert's *Un Cœur simple* which Sylvia says she knows by heart.

[13] Julian Barnes, 'The Defence of the Book', *Guardian*, 3 February 2012. Reproduced in *The Library Book*, ed. Rebecca Gray (London: Profile Books, 2012), 9–13.
[14] In Lawson, 'Mark Lawson'.
[15] Kate Mikhail, 'Life Support', *Observer*, 24 February 2002, https://www.theguardian.com/theobserver/2002/feb/24/julianbarnes. Accessed on 19 January 2019.
[16] Julian Barnes, 'Preface'. *Dictionary of Accepted Ideas*, by Gustave Flaubert, trans. Geoffrey Wall (London: Syrens, 1994), vi.
[17] Barnes, 'The Bitter Lemon Days', 18.

Hamilton, Ian:	'I remember the funeral, one cold December afternoon, of one of my first literary encouragers, the poet Ian Hamilton. … For the first time at a funeral I noticed that the coffin is carried into the church with the thinner end pointing forwards, and that, after the service, it is turned so that it exits in the same fashion: you really are carried out feet first. I turned to my friend Russell Davies, and said: "Why do the pallbearers always look like minor criminals?" "Because they are," he cheerfully replied.'[18]
Hiking:	Ian McEwan likes to place his friends along a divide: 'those who enjoy hiking (Barnes, Michael Frayn) and those who consider it a fatuous premodern practice (Amis, Christopher Hitchens)'.[19]
Ishiguro, Kazuo:	'I ate kangaroo at a literary dinner in Australia with Kazuo Ishiguro, who ordered it with the words, "I always like to eat the national emblem." ("What does he eat in England?" a nearby poet growled at me, "Lion?")'[20]
James, Clive:	First met in the Bung Hole, a London wine bar in the 1970s. Clive James and Martin Amis were 'roaring away about Keats while consuming several glasses of wine. [Barnes] was spectacularly silent'.[21]
Koestler, Arthur:	Committed suicide with his wife Cynthia on 1 March 1983. Barnes owns 'an unopened packet of Disque Bleu' that was found at the writer's elbow after his suicide.[22]
Language:	Bridles 'when the word "decimate" is used to mean "massacre" as it routinely is, whereas in fact it comes from the old Roman legionnaires' punishment which is to kill one out of ten'. However, refuses to be cast as a 'linguistic pedant'[23] since 'the English language has always been in a state of tumultuous motion' and should be celebrated for its 'endless malleability'.[24]
Larkin, Philip:	Considered 'the best English poet of the second half of the twentieth century'. They never met but corresponded and once had a telephone conversation

---

[18] Passage deleted from *Nothing to Be Frightened Of* (3.5). A close version of the dialogue with Russell Davies appears in Julian Barnes, 'I Remember', *Areté* 23 (Summer/Autumn 2007): 57.
[19] Zalewski, 'The Background Hum', 49.
[20] Barnes, *The Pedant in the Kitchen*, 81.
[21] Caroline Daniel, 'Interview: Clive James', *Financial Times*, 27 August 2015, http://www.ft.com/intl/cms/s/0/a6393156-4c33-11e5-9b5d-89a026fda5c9.html. Accessed on 19 January 2019.
[22] Barnes, 'The Follies of Writer Worship', 17.
[23] In Lawson, 'Mark Lawson'.
[24] Barnes, 'Changing My Mind. Words'.

	in which they discussed 'the delights of watching sport on television'.[25]
Letters:	In an interview in 1988, says he loves receiving letters from his readers: 'My wife says, three-quarters seriously, that she thinks I became a novelist so that I'd get letters. ... It is always my first question when we come back from holiday: "Do you think there will be a lot of letters?" '[26] In an interview in 1999, refers to 'that dreadful part of the writer's life', which includes 'answering letters'.[27]
Mackenzie, Lucy:	Painter. Barnes's wife started collecting her work in the 1970s. One of her first presents to him was 'a coloured-pencil study of tulips in a vase sitting on a stripped tablecloth'. For her fiftieth birthday, the novelist commissioned from Mackenzie a picture of a woman reading, which is now in his sitting room.[28]
Marathon:	In the summer of 1982, training for the London Marathon which is 'a safe nine months away': 'All kinds of mental stratagems have to be employed (dreaming up dinners, playing through sexual fantasies) to keep my legs moving, to rebuff the tempting voice which says, "What are you doing this for, you don't need this running shit, nobody can see you, come on, give up ...." But I just about don't give up in my low-level quest for a certain healthiness.' Then, 'the winter snow interfered with my training schedule – and besides, in the end my application was rejected, probably because I put "journalist" on the form and they decided they had far too many journalists running already and didn't need any more coverage'.[29]
Nabokov, Vladimir:	'Creation of character is, like much of fiction writing, a mixture of subjective feel and objective control. Nabokov boasted that he whipped his characters like galley slaves; popular novelists sometimes boast (as if it proved them artists) that such-and-such a character

---

[25] Julian Barnes, 'Acceptance Speech for the Shakespeare Prize', Stiftung F.V.S zu Hamburg, 12 June 1993, 21, reproduced in *Shakespeare Prize 1937–2006*, ed. Jürgen Schlaeger (Trier: Wissenschaftlicher Verlag Trier, 2013), 208.
[26] Field, 'From a Sat-Upon Son', 72. There are three thick folders of fan mail relating to *Flaubert's Parrot* at the Harry Ransom Center (1.16.5–7).
[27] Interview by Freiburg, *Conversations*, ed. Guignery and Roberts, 31.
[28] Julian Barnes, 'Lucy Mackenzie: Showing the World in a Particular Light', *Lucy Mackenzie: Quiet* (New York: Nancy Hoffman Gallery, 2015–), n.p.
[29] Barnes, 'Playing Chess', 480, 488.

	"ran away with them" or "took on a life of his/her own." I'm of neither school: I keep my characters on a loose rein, but a rein nonetheless.'[30]
Onions:	Peeling out an onion without blubbing: 'if, as I once did, you try wearing a pair of strimmer's goggles, the plastic lens will quickly steam up and there will be much blood on the chopping board'.[31]
Partick Thistle Football Club:	A Glaswegian football team. 'I supported them since I was three because I thought they were *Patrick* Thistle and my middle name's Patrick.'[32] Stopped supporting them around the age of 40, for no particular reason.
Politics:	Defines himself as 'Europhile but Bureausceptic, internationalist but culturally protectionist, liberal-left, green'.[33] Over five decades, has voted in local, parliamentary and European elections for Labour (or New Labour with Tony Blair in 1997), Conservative (Edward Heath in 1974), Liberal, Liberal-Democrat, Green and Women's Equality parties.[34]
Quijote, Don:	In 2008, donates his copy of the translation of *Don Quijote de la Mancha* by Thomas Shelton (1675) to the Biblioteca Popular de Azul in Buenos Aires to form part of the Cervantes collection.
Raine, Craig:	12 November 1987. Diary. *London Review of Books*. In a piece on the Booker Prize, Barnes refers to the habit in the United States of giving 'cosy Christian names' to hurricanes and imagines one named Craig.[35]
	10 December 1987. Letter. *London Review of Books*. Craig Raine is flattered that his friend Julian Barnes put forward his name 'for a natural phenomenon as subtle as a hurricane' and offers a quote from Primo Levi's *If This Is a Man* in which the name Jules is used to a refer to a lavatory bucket.[36]
	7 January 1988. Letter. *London Review of Books*. 'I name a hurricane after him; he calls me a pisspot. If this is "my friend" Craig Raine's grasp of proportionate

---

[30] Interview by Guppy, in *Conversations*, ed. Guignery and Roberts, 73.
[31] Barnes, *The Pedant in the Kitchen*, 21.
[32] Jonathan Meades, 'Parrot Fashion', *Time Out*, 27 September/3 October 1984, 27.
[33] Barnes, *Something to Declare*, xvii.
[34] Julian Barnes, 'Changing My Mind. Politics', BBC Radio 3, 7 December 2016, https://www.bbc.co.uk/programmes/b084fvlx. Accessed on 19 January 2019.
[35] Julian Barnes, 'Diary', *London Review of Books* 9, no. 20 (12 November 1987): 21.
[36] Craig Raine, 'Letters', *London Review of Books* 9, no. 22 (10 December 1987): 4.

	response, then we should all be glad he hasn't yet acquired a driving licence.'[37]
Renard, Jules:	French writer. Turning his back to the great descriptive and expansive fiction of his predecessors, Renard concluded the only way forward 'was through compression, annotation, pointillism'.[38]
School food:	'Do you remember your school food? And if so, you'll probably remember too the passing slang schoolchildren generate to ward off the horror of reality. There were those livid, surgical cross-sections of Spam, which we used to call Matron's Ankle; the three wizened prunes on a mockingly large plate, known as Bushmen's Balls (there were always three: ethno-sexual fears start early); the mounds of piped, hard-crusted mash which we passed off on younger boys with the explanation that they were meringue (not always a joke that worked: the meringue wasn't that different); and the seething trayloads of macaroni cheese which we termed Albino Rabbit's Bowels.'[39]
Sense of Place:	'I'm sorry, I don't have a sense of place.' Despite having lived nearly a half century in the same area of northwest London, lacks 'any sense of having roots here'.[40]
Smacked and wheedled:	In 1980, discovers that John Coleman, the *New Statesman*'s film reviewer, scraped a living in Paris in the 1950s by writing pornographic novels for the Olympia Press in Paris and gets hold of a copy of one of them, *The Enormous Bed*: 'The erotic parts were banal, but there was a brilliant description of a cricket match, in which a batsman "smacked and wheedled" the ball round the field. Subsequently, when Coleman – who was a somewhat erratic contributor – failed to deliver sufficient copy, I would put into the contributor's box "John Coleman is the author of *The Enormous Bed* (Olympia Press, Paris)." If the offence was more serious, I would insert into Coleman's review, at some plausible moment, the phrase "smacked and wheedled".'[41]

---

[37] Julian Barnes, 'Letters', *London Review of Books* 10, no. 1 (7 January 1988): 5.
[38] Barnes, *Nothing to Be Frightened Of*, 48.
[39] Julian Barnes [Basil Seal, pseud.], 'Tatler Restaurants: Basil Seal Goes Back to School', *Tatler*, September 1980, 15.
[40] Julian Barnes, 'Out of Place', *Architectural Digest* 54, no. 5 (April 1997): 36.
[41] Annotations, 22–27 March 2018.

	In his notes for *Talking It Over*, makes a list of the words he should use and includes 'smack & wheedle', adding '(or have you used it previously?)' (1.14.5). The two verbs do not appear together in the novel, although Oliver phones Stuart 'attempting to wheedle him back towards normality'.[42]
	In *Arthur & George*, during the cricket season, Arthur 'smacks and wheedles the ball around the field'.[43]
	In *Nothing to Be Frightened Of*, human beings are compared to Emperor penguins: 'We are just as good as they are at passing for God-created while being smacked and wheedled by implacable evolutionary urges.'[44]
	In *The Only Story*, the narrator sees two ways of looking at life. According to the second, 'a human life was no more than a bump on a log which was itself being propelled down the mighty Mississippi, tugged and bullied, smacked and wheedled, by currents and eddies and hazards over which no control was possible'.[45]
Speed Six:	The book Barnes has read most often is not *Madame Bovary* but the children's book *Speed Six* (1953) by Bruce Carter about Le Mans 24 Hour Race, with a pre-war Bentley, liveried in British racing green, competing and winning against post-war French, German and Italian cars. Comments in 1989: '[Carter]'s story supplied a gust of retro-chic, an endorsement of chauvinism …, and a taste for British racing green – a colour which many years later I painted my study.'[46]
Swahili:	'An irate early reader of [*Metroland*] wrote to me to complain about the profusion of French phrases in the novel. He filled his letter satirically with lots of Swahili phrases & words, so that I would feel what he felt when reading M/land. I doubt he is still one of my readers.'[47]

[42] Barnes, *Talking It Over*, 214.
[43] Barnes, *Arthur & George*, 173.
[44] Barnes, *Nothing to Be Frightened Of*, 93.
[45] Barnes, *The Only Story*, 173.
[46] This piece about influential books dating from 1989 is included in the archives (2.5.3). The published version has not been found. Barnes named *Speed Six* as his favourite childhood book in Louise Rimmer, 'Shelf Life: Julian Barnes', *Scotland on Sunday*, 13 January 2002, http://news.scotsman.com/index.cfm?id=44002002. Accessed on 19 January 2002.
[47] Annotated copy of *Metroland* (Morgan Library 89).

Translations:	a) Note for *Flaubert's Parrot* in 1984: 'The translations in this book are by Geoffrey Braithwaite; though he would have been lost without the impeccable example of Francis Steegmuller.'[48]
	b) After the publication of *Flaubert's Parrot*, is asked if he might be interested in translating *Madame Bovary* for Penguin, and some years later for the new Vintage Classics list. Turns down both offers. In 2010, devotes an essay to translations of *Madame Bovary*.[49]
	c) In three weeks, translates the German cartoons *The Truth About Dogs*, by Volker Kriegel, published in 1986.[50]
	d) In a letter of 5 May 2002, praised by John Updike for his translation of Alphonse Daudet's *La Doulou* (*In the Land of Pain*): 'I envy you being able to put your name to a translation – a translation of the hitherto untranslated, better yet.'
	e) In 2002, is invited by Michael Attenborough to translate *Athalie* by Racine for the Almeida theatre in London. Agrees to do it in prose (not in verse) and translates the second act of the play (3.3). The Almeida finally decides they want it in verse. The project is abandoned.
	f) On 16 June 2008, is asked by Liz Foley if he might want to translate Voltaire's *Candide* for Vintage Classics. Turns it down (3.1).[51]
	g) Is urged by the Belgian Australian writer Pierre Ryckmans (whose pen name was Simon Leys) to translate Prosper Merimee's tribute to Stendhal, *H.B.*, and feels guilty for not doing it, until Leys translates it himself in 2010.[52]
Travel:	'What you need in a travelling companion is someone who makes up for your social deficiencies …; someone who speaks the languages you don't; an

---

[48] Barnes, *Flaubert's Parrot*, 8.
[49] Julian Barnes, 'Writer's Writer and Writer's Writer's Writer', *London Review of Books* 32, no. 22 (18 November 2010): 7–11, reproduced as 'Translating *Madame Bovary*', in Barnes, *Through the Window*, 146–63.
[50] Julian Barnes, trans., *The Truth about Dogs*, by Volker Kriegel (London: Bloomsbury, [1986] 1988).
[51] In 2011, he paid tribute to *Candide* in an essay. Julian Barnes, 'A Candid View of *Candide*', *Guardian*, 1 July 2011, https://www.theguardian.com/books/2011/jul/01/candide-voltaire-rereading-julian-barnes. Accessed on 19 January 2019.
[52] Julian Barnes, 'Foreword', in *Simon Leys: Navigator Between Worlds*, by Philippe Paquet (Carlton, Australia: La Trobe University Press, 2017), xi.

	expert on art and architecture; a canny organiser; a natural historian; and – perhaps most important of all – someone who knows how to shut up for hours on end if necessary. In other words, a combination of Wilde, Peter Ustinov, Ruskin, Jeeves, Redmond O'Hanlon and the elderly Ezra Pound' (2.5.3).[53]
Triumvirate:	Phrase used by Tom Maschler, publisher at Jonathan Cape, to refer to Ian McEwan, Martin Amis and Julian Barnes who were 'much the same age when they joined Cape' and 'happened to be the best of friends'.[54]
Unless:	Chosen as 'the most sinister word in the English language' for *Hockney's Alphabet*: 'It's the oiled hinge of a sentence, a slick chunk of the points. Remember it from frightening stories in childhood: *Unless this isn't the door we came in by* … Imagine it in bankruptcy: *Unless I've misread the figures*. Fear it close to home: *Unless, of course, I don't love you any more*. It remains menacing even in clichés: *Unless I'm very much mistaken*.'[55]
Vallotton, Felix:	While teaching at Johns Hopkins University in 1995, visits the Baltimore Museum of Art between classes. Is entrapped by a small intense oil by Vallotton, *The Lie*, in which a man and a woman are entwined on a sofa, the woman whispering in the man's ear. For Barnes, 'Clearly, the woman is the liar.' For one of his female students, it is 'obvious that the man is the liar'.[56]
Vuillard, Édouard:	*Woman Sweeping* instantly enters Barnes's top ten when he sees the painting in the Phillips Collection in Washington, DC. Adds: '(In fact, I saw several others that did the same – a Courbet, a Degas and a Bonnard – but then I've never counted up my top ten, which runs to well over a hundred by now.)'[57]
Washington, DC:	Place of first trip to the United States. First American museum visited is the Hirshhorn Museum.

---

[53] This two-paragraph piece on travelling was written for the *New York Times*. The published version has not been found.
[54] Tom Maschler, *Publisher* (London: Picador, 2005), 79.
[55] Julian Barnes, 'U', *Hockney's Alphabet*, ed. Stephen Spender with drawings by David Hockney (London: Faber & Faber, 1991), n.p.
[56] Barnes, 'Vallotton: The Foreign Nabi', *Keeping an Eye Open*, 175.
[57] Barnes, 'Vuillard: You Can Call Him Édouard', *Keeping an Eye Open*, 155.

Wharton, Edith:	Among preliminary notes on *England, England*, comments upon a quote by Edith Wharton:[58] 'Starting a novel was like a spring morning [*Yes, it's the most unreliable season*], being in the middle was in the Gobi desert [*one hopes for better scenery*], and finishing it was a lovers' meeting [*Well, perhaps a lover's meeting where one says to the other "I never want to see you again for the rest of my life."*]' (1.4.5).[59]
Wine:	Becomes interested in wine in his thirties thanks to a series of nudgings: 'One such came from the chance of living in a flat above that of Clive Coates MW.' This Master of Wine came up one evening 'with half a dozen near-full bottles under his arm. "Cooking wine," he announced jovially'. Among the bottles were some 1978 or 1979 Bordeaux including a bottle of Petrus. The Barneses did not cook with any of them.[60]
Xylophone:	Entry for X in 'Braithwaite's Dictionary of Accepted Ideas' in *Flaubert's Parrot*: 'There is no record of Flaubert ever having heard the xylophone.'[61]
Yorkshire:	In his preparatory notes for *England, England*, plans for Martha's father to leave with the piece for Yorkshire from Martha's Counties of England jigsaw puzzle (2.3.2). In the book, it is Nottinghamshire which goes missing.
Zola, Emile:	In his early twenties, while working on the *Oxford English Dictionary* in Oxford, applies for a job at a crammer school: 'I had gone for the job interview, ready to confess that you could get a degree in French, as I recently had, without reading a word of Zola …. Indeed, all I had read of him was *Germinal*, and that some years previously. But the crammer's principal, a figure from early Evelyn Waugh, didn't want to become mired in the matter of my qualifications, let alone scruples. He looked up from my tentative letter of application and extended his hand. "Good to have a Zola expert on board." '[62]

[58] Barnes's handwritten comments on the typed quote have been added in italics between square brackets.
[59] The quote comes from a diary entry of 10 December 1934, when Edith Wharton, aged 72, had reached page 166 of her unfinished novel *The Buccaneers*. The original quote is slightly different from the version quoted by Barnes: 'What is writing a novel like? / 1. The beginning: A ride through a spring wood. / 2. The middle: The Gobi desert. / 3. The end: A night with a lover. / I am now in the Gobi desert.' Hermione Lee, *Edith Wharton* (New York: Knopf, 2007), 712.
[60] Julian Barnes, 'Bin End: A Highly Personal View of the World of Wines and Spirits', *Decanter*, November 1989, 144.
[61] Barnes, *Flaubert's Parrot*, 158.
[62] Julian Barnes, 'Blood and Nerves', *Guardian*, 25 November 2006, https://www.theguardian.com/stage/2006/nov/25/theatre.stage. Accessed on 19 January 2019.

10

Arthur & George: Beginnings and endings

1. First and final steps

When Hermione Lee read a draft of *England, England* in 1997, she made the following comment about the replica of England created on the Isle of Wight: 'One thing that's been missing from all this, I now realise, is any mention of race. … You deal with government, economics, class, media, nature and sex, but you never deal with race' (1.4.5). Barnes put a question mark in the margin but did not add any mention of race in later drafts of the 1998 novel. However, his interest in the issue of race in Britain partly led to his writing of *Arthur & George*, published in 2005, a novel concentrating on a miscarriage of justice and involving George Edalji, a solicitor of Parsee origin wrongly accused of horse mutilations in Shropshire in 1903 and sentenced to seven years of penal servitude. Three years later, Edalji was released without being told why and without being pardoned, and he appealed to the creator of Sherlock Holmes, Arthur Conan Doyle, who led his own investigation in order to prove the solicitor's innocence. Barnes had read about the case in the introduction to Douglas Johnson's 1966 book about the Dreyfus Affair in France,[1] but he explained in an interview that there was an earlier origin to the novel:

> When I was writing *Arthur & George*, I could – and would – say that it had its origin in reading about the Edalji case in a book about the Dreyfus affair. What I had forgotten, and didn't remember until I had nearly finished the novel, was that it actually – or also – came out of an earlier interest. … I planned – hoped – to write something fictional about the forgotten and hidden black population of Britain in the eighteenth and nineteenth centuries. I got some books and I read up a bit, and then nothing happened: nothing was sparked.[2]

---

[1] Douglas Johnson compares the Dreyfus case to the Edalji Affair in the introduction to his book *France and the Dreyfus Affair* (London: Blanford Press, 1966), 5–7. Barnes refers to Johnson's 'wise and cogent' book in his review of Pierre Birnbaum's *The Anti-Semitic Moment: A Tour of France in 1898*. Julian Barnes, 'Holy Hysteria', *New York Review of Books*, 10 April 2003, 32.
[2] Interview by Guignery and Roberts, *Conversations*, ed. Guignery and Roberts, 163.

If nothing came out of reading these books, a contemporary case involving a British Afro-Caribbean man caught Barnes's attention in 1999, the year when Sir William Macpherson's report on the 1993 murder of black British teenager Stephen Lawrence and on what has been called 'institutional police racism' was published. Barnes recalls being haunted by the case of Errol McGowan, the victim of racist threats in Telford, Shropshire, which culminated in him being found hanged from a doorknob on 2 July 1999. The police concluded there was no evidence that McGowan was murdered and that he had therefore committed suicide, even if the man had repeatedly reported having received death threats peppered with racist abuse. Six months later, McGowan's nephew, Jason, who had been investigating his uncle's death, was found hanging from railings and a reinvestigation into both deaths opened but the same conclusion of suicide was reached. Barnes remembers being shocked by this dismissal of the case:

> I was staggered by this, and appalled. I couldn't get it out of my head, and imagined writing something either about the case itself, or a fictional version of it. Then the idea for A&G came to me. So I thought I could play off one story against the other. But this idea evidently didn't last very long. Because – and I remember this – I realized fairly quickly that I didn't need a modern analogue for George's story, because merely by laying out the facts, every reader would recognize that exactly the same things could happen again nowadays with only the tiniest changes. It wasn't an 'old' story, it was a contemporary one.[3]

The writer abandoned the idea of a double-time structure when the novel was still in pre-planning stage, which explains why the archives contain no trace of that original beginning. Instead, Barnes concentrated on the Edalji case and very carefully planned his novel as shown by several documents in the archives.[4] In the third part of *Arthur & George*, as Arthur starts investigating the Edalji case, he reflects that the work he is engaging in bears similarities with the first stages of planning a novel. The passage in internal focalization could be read as a fairly close metafictional description of the way Barnes himself conceived *Arthur & George* (as well as some of his other novels):

> It was like starting a book: you had the story but not all of it, most of the characters but not all of them, some but not all of the causal links. You had your beginning, and you had your ending. There would be a great number of topics to be kept in the head at the same time. Some would be in motion, some static; some racing away, others resisting all the mental energy you could throw at them. Well, he was

---

[3] Private email correspondence with the author, 18 February 2017. In an interview, Barnes also emphasized the contemporary significance of George Edalji's story: 'the strength of the original story was such that you don't have to put a parallel story today into the book in order for people to realise that it's about today as well as it is about a hundred years ago'. Interview by Fraga, *Conversations*, ed. Guignery and Roberts, 135.

[4] In addition to the archives at the Harry Ransom Center, a notebook which Barnes has retained contains seventy-five pages of notes relating to *Arthur & George*. Barnes has kindly let the author consult this document on 22 June 2017. It will be referred to as 'AG notebook' in these pages.

used to that. And so, as with a novel, he tabulated the key matters and annotated them briefly. (237)

Barnes might not have had his beginning and his ending from the start but like Conan Doyle, he tabulated key matters and annotated them for his novel. In addition to lists of notes as to what to include, he made planning sheets for each part with a column for George and another for Arthur, listing the main subjects and indicating the age of the characters for each major stage as well as the rough number of words written (2.1.6). Barnes started the book on Christmas day in 2003, contacted Conan Doyle's biographer, Daniel Stashower, in January 2004 to ask questions about some incidents in the writer's life and sent requests to a friend about how to approach horses in February 2004. He said in an interview: 'It's the novel I wrote most intensely in terms of hours per day,'[5] and indeed the dates and word count at the bottom of the planning sheet for 2004 confirm that extraordinary intensity:

1st April: 87,000
19 April: 111,000
2 May: 141,000
13 May: 160,000 (2.1.6)

After writing this first draft within a very short time, Barnes took five months to revise it between July and November 2004 – as shown by a document entitled 'Progress' (2.2.6) –, with 90 pages revised in July (for Part One and 35 pages of Part Two), 65 in August and 50 in September (for the rest of Part Two), 132 in October (for the beginning of Part Three) and 94 in November (for Arthur's wedding and Part Four). The programme for September was also to 'incorporate all notes & research so far into all drafts' while November included 'final research' and December was devoted to 'read[ing] through' (2.2.8). The final typescript (and book) ends with the date 'January 2005', with last revisions taking place in February and March of that year.

Interestingly, *Arthur & George* is the only one of Barnes's novels which Hermione Lee read in parts between July 2004 and January 2005, and she therefore sent her comments as the novelist was still in the process of revising the book.[6] Research also took place simultaneously with writing and revising as the email exchanges between Barnes and his research assistant show that she conducted research between April and December 2004. Barnes himself went to Great Wyrley and Stafford on 24 August 2004 and was assisted by the archivist of the Staffordshire Constabulary, Sgt. Alan Walker: he visited Green Hall, where Chief Constable Captain Anson used to live, as well as the Staffordshire Police Headquarters, and was shown photographs of Captain Anson.[7]

---

[5] Jasper Rees, 'The Inscrutable Mr Barnes', *The Telegraph*, 23 September 2006, http://www.telegraph.co.uk/culture/books/3655483/The-inscrutable-Mr-Barnes.html. Accessed on 19 January 2019.
[6] Lee also read the essay/memoir *Nothing to Be Frightened Of* in parts over a period of three-and-a-half months.
[7] In his essay on the genesis of *Arthur & George*, Barnes explains that the first scene he drafted was 'a violent exchange that occurs towards the end of the novel between Conan Doyle and the Chief Constable of Staffordshire, Captain Anson'. He wrote some twenty pages of the scene but then realized he needed to know what Anson looked like: 'I couldn't properly animate a scene in which

The whole process of planning, researching, writing and revising therefore took a little more than a year, an impressive achievement for a book which came up to 451 pages in the final typescript (360 pages in the hardback edition) and which, of all Barnes's novels, is probably the one which required the most extensive research.

2. The blind spots of research

At the end of *Arthur & George,* Barnes included an 'Author's Note' which provides information about what happened to the main historical figures referred to in the book until their deaths. It is followed by a paragraph in italics which starts with the following sentence: '*Apart from Jean's letter to Arthur, all letters quoted, whether signed or anonymous, are authentic; as are quotations from newspapers, government reports, proceedings in Parliament, and the writings of Sir Arthur Conan Doyle*' (360). In a note to his wife, Barnes wondered if this last paragraph 'would be better left off' and remarked: 'it obviously changes the feel you have at the end whether this para is there or not' (2.2.5). The fact that he left it shows that the novelist felt it important to vouch for the historical accuracy of the documents quoted in the novel, thereby probably answering interrogations readers may have had about them such as the ones Hermione Lee put forward after reading a first draft of Part Two: 'These letters: have you made them up? To what extent, I mean, have you made them up?' (2.2.6). She also wondered if the sentence quoted above in the author's note should be kept: 'Am trying to imagine the book without the last para of the author's note. I am divided. It is in a way a hostage to fortune. But it is also honest – as honest as Sir A would have been' (2.2.6). In the final typescript, the paragraph appeared without italics (and without the three lines of thanks to people who had helped Barnes for research), and before the signature and date 'J.B. January 2005', but Barnes drew an arrow on the page to have the paragraph moved after the signature and date (2.3.2), which is how it appears on the type specimen (2.3.7). On that page, Barnes added the acknowledgements in longhand and asked the copy editor at Jonathan Cape: 'do you think this last para should be set differently? Smaller typeface? Italics? The book "ends" just before it, at "Leckie" & "JB"' (2.3.7). This comment is interesting as it tends to blur the status of the 'Author's Note', a paratext placed after the end of the novel, in which the voice is identified as that of the 'Author' whose initials appear before the date. Barnes's remark to his copy editor that the book 'ends' after 'JB' distinguishes the 'Author's Note' from the last paragraph in an enigmatic way, pointing to a duality in the figure of the author between one who focuses on the future trajectories of the historical figures in the story and another who provides information on the making of the text itself. Barnes's meticulous concern as to the placement of the paragraph and its setting apart from the rest of the author's note testifies to its singular status as a paratext meant to guarantee the authenticity of historical documents inserted within a work of fiction.

I knew precisely what one participant looked like but had no idea about the other.' Barnes, 'The Case of Inspector Campbell', 292.

What is also interesting about the paragraph is that it does not provide the title of any of the books Barnes drew information from, as was the case in the author's note for *A History of the World in 10½ Chapters* and would be the case in *The Noise of Time*. Nonetheless, the research for this novel was extensive and the archives offer insight into its multiple forms.[8] Barnes read and took notes on Conan Doyle's 1921 *The Wanderings of a Spiritualist* (an account of his voyage to Australia and New Zealand) and his 1924 autobiography, *Memories and Adventures*, as well as John Dickson Carr's *The Life of Sir Arthur Conan Doyle* (1949), Pierre Nordon's *Conan Doyle* (1966), Daniel Stashower's *Teller of Tales. The Life of Arthur Conan Doyle* (1999) and the 2004 biography by Georgina Doyle, the widow of one of the writer's nephews, *Out of the Shadows: The Untold Story of Arthur Conan Doyle's First Family*. Barnes's copy of *The Story of Mr. George Edalji by Sir Arthur Conan Doyle* (1985), edited and with an introduction by Richard and Molly Whittington-Egan, is heavily underlined and annotated.[9] The novelist also employed a research assistant, Sumaya Partner, who gathered information for him, and he visited several libraries himself.[10] The archives therefore include articles,[11] letters, reports and proceedings on the case, as well as obituaries of the main characters, Edalji's death certificate, information on Conan Doyle's and his mother's private lives (including a printed report of the cricket game in which the writer played in August 1900) and on his memorial service at the Royal Albert Hall on 30 July 1930, a copy of Edalji's book *Railway Law for the 'Man in the Train'* (whose front cover page is reproduced in the novel, 67), extracts from law books, guides to the main places where Conan Doyle and Edalji lived or which they visited and books on the Royal Albert Hall.

Barnes's notes and Sumaya Partner's emails reveal that the writer asked for such broad information as 'structure of police force (provincial) c1900', 'structure of education in Staffordshire c1900', 'Parsees in England c1900' or 'Conditions of someone sentenced to hard labour between 1903 and 1906' (2.1.2). He also required very precise details as, for instance, the correct etiquette at Lord's for lady guests of cricketers or members (they would have sat in 'A' enclosure, as mentioned in the novel, 173), the price of bowler hats at the beginning of the twentieth century – Barnes

---

[8] In 1979, Raymonde Debray Genette coined the notions of exogenesis and endogenesis to differentiate the writing processes devoted to research and therefore relying on external source material (exogenesis) and the elaboration of a text without recourse to outside documents (endogenesis). For a definition of these terms, see de Biasi, 43–4.

[9] This book is in Barnes's library in London. It includes Doyle's investigation of the case of George Edalji published in the *Daily Telegraph* on 11 and 12 January 1907, as well as further material published by Doyle in the same newspaper on 23, 24 and 27 May 1907 ('Facsimile Documents'; 'Who Wrote the Letters' and '"The Martin Molton" Letters'), and Doyle's 'Statement of the Case Against Royden Sharp', which he presented to the Home Office in 1907.

[10] For example, Barnes saw the originals of the anonymous letters sent to Edalji as well as the local newspapers covering the case at the Birmingham Central Library, and he went to Colindale library in London on 6 May 2004 to read Edalji's 1906 version of the case in *The Umpire* as the volume was too fragile to copy from (2.1.1). Private email correspondence with the author, 6 March 2017.

[11] The archives contain photocopies of an article about the case published in the *Umpire* in September 1903, articles and letters published in *Truth* in 1905 and 1906, in the *Daily Telegraph* in 1907 and a 1934 *Daily Express* article about the arrest of the culprit of the poison pen letters. The archives also include several articles on Conan Doyle's memorial service in 1930 at the Royal Albert Hall (2.2.1–3). The 'AG notebook' contains notes about articles, several of them published in the Birmingham *Daily Gazette*.

entitled his email: 'this may be tricky/impossible' (2.1.1) –, the exact address where Conan Doyle's sister Connie and her husband Willie Hornung lived in 1900 ('Nine, Pitt Street', 174), the type of uniforms worn in prison in the early 1900s (the archives include pictures of Portland convicts and of uniforms with 'clumsily printed arrows' as indicated in the novel, 149) or the train timetables from Wyrley & Churchbridge to Birmingham in 1903 (referring to the 7.39 am train which Edalji would take every morning, Barnes asked his research assistant: 'Where would it stop, and when?', and the different stops and times are punctiliously included in the book, 73, 75).[12] Such requests show how meticulous Barnes was in his quest for historical accuracy. When asking a correspondent what the cricket ground at Lord's looked like in 1900, Barnes wrote: 'I don't want to say "They were walking arm in arm behind the Tavern Stand" if the TS didn't exist then, or women wouldn't have been allowed to walk behind it' (2.1.2).

Although Barnes worked hard to get his historical and biographical facts right, he also noted, in an email to biographer Daniel Stashower, 'how difficult it is to integrate biographical facts into a novel without them reading like a biography' (2.1.1) – a problem he had already encountered when writing *Flaubert's Parrot* and would be confronted to again with *The Noise of Time*. Barnes devoted an essay to the genesis of *Arthur & George* and especially focused on the intricate mixture of fact and fiction in this novel. He explained for instance that the extensive knowledge he had of the 'world-famous, inspected, biographed, autobiographed' Doyle of whom there are images 'from cradle to grave'[13] proved an inhibiting impediment while the fact that Edalji 'left few traces' was liberating, allowing him to extrapolate, imagine and invent:

> At first it seems that the more you know, the easier it must be. If this person had this mind and this temperament, and this is how he/she behaved in a known situation, then this is how he/she would behave in a fictional situation. But such knowledge swiftly becomes a hindrance: established fact and character box you in as a novelist, give you less room for manoeuvre.[14]

Barnes therefore needed to look into the dark spots of Conan Doyle's biography to find room to invent. This was the case in his rendering of the incident at Lord's cricket ground in August 1900 when the writer and Jean Leckie encountered Conan Doyle's sister Connie and her husband Willie Hornung who were unaware of his relationship with Jean and later showed their disapproval. The encounter and its consequences on that day and the next occupy a single page in the biographies of John Dickson Carr (102–3), Daniel Stashower (225–6) and Andrew Lycett (276–7) against five pages in Barnes's novel (173–8). The novelist gives the reader access to Arthur's mind through

---

[12] Conan Doyle's biographer John Dickson Carr was not as accurate as the novelist about George's train schedule as he wrote: 'Each morning he took the seven-twenty train to his office.' The 1903 official working timetables that were sent to Barnes's research assistant and are included in the archives show there was no train leaving Wyrley & Churchbridge station at 7.20 am, but one at 7.39 am. John Dickson Carr, *The Life of Arthur Conan Doyle* (New York: Harper & Brothers, 1949), 179.

[13] Barnes, 'The Case of Inspector Campbell', 294, 290.

[14] Ibid., 294.

free indirect speech as he reflects on the incident while the biographers concentrate on facts and actions. He quotes the three lines which appear in direct speech in Carr's biography and were borrowed from a letter Conan Doyle sent his mother soon after the incident,[15] but expands the scene further by inventing a whole conversation between Arthur and Hornung (while the biographers adopt the narrative mode and do not venture beyond what Conan Doyle's letter to his mother reveals). This difference of treatment clearly highlights the generic differences between a biography and a novel.

While biographers may resent the dark shadows which surround some episodes in their subject's life, novelists find them enticing and stimulating. Barnes was therefore – and not paradoxically – pleased when Stashower was unable to provide definite information about Bryan Waller, the first lodger of Conan Doyle's mother who later lived on her estate under what the biographer called in an email an 'unorthodox arrangement'. Stashower's words – 'we know almost nothing about him'; 'The letters I'm editing do nothing to clear up the mystery' – were the best the fiction writer could hope for, as shown by Barnes's reply: 'Nothing a novelist likes more than a confirmation that Little is Known. Hooray – I can do with him more or less what suits my purpose.'[16] Barnes also remarked that he did not find it frustrating that Charles Foley, Conan Doyle's great nephew, would not give him access to documents related to the writer: 'I don't mind Foley not letting me see the papers – it's often a problem using factual elements in a novel – & they might pull me where I don't want to go' (2.1.1).

In May 2004, when Barnes was writing his first draft of *Arthur & George*, a collection of Conan Doyle's personal letters, notes and drafts for books was put up for auction at Christie's. It included the Edalji dossier with letters from Conan Doyle's informants and investigators on the case as well as original anonymous letters of denunciation of Edalji, some of which the writer had reproduced in the *Daily Telegraph* in May 1907 and are quoted in *Arthur & George* (Barnes rightly wondered how these letters ended up in Conan Doyle's hands). The novelist went to the first viewing of these papers on 14 May 2004 and took notes from the sale catalogue.[17] He told Stashower in an email: 'were I writing a non-fiction book they would be essential', but as he was writing a novel, he was less dependent on these authentic documents (even if the

---

[15] Hornung's sentences reported by Conan Doyle in the letter to his mother (in Lellenberg et al.), by Carr in his biography and by Barnes in *Arthur & George* are the following: 'I'm prepared to back your dealings with any woman at sight and without question' (Jon Lellenberg, Daniel Stashower and Charles Foley, eds. *Arthur Conan Doyle. A Life in Letters* (New York: Penguin Press, 2007), 454; Carr 102; Barnes 175), 'It seems to me … you attach too much importance to whether these relations are platonic or not. I can't see that it makes much difference. What *is* the difference?' (Lellenberg et al. 454; Carr 103; Barnes 178); Conan Doyle's own response to Hornung is: 'When have I ever failed in loyalty to any member of my family? And when before have I appealed to them?' (Lellenberg et al. 454; Carr 103; Barnes 177).

[16] In his analysis of *Arthur & George*, D. Michael Risinger resents Barnes's fictional liberties and offers a series of arguments against the novelist's suggestion that Doyle's sister Dodo may have been fathered by Bryan Waller. D. Michael Risinger, 'Boxes in Boxes: Julian Barnes, Conan Doyle, Sherlock Holmes and the Edalji Case', *International Commentary on Evidence* 4, no. 2 (published online 27 February 2007), https://law.shu.edu/faculty/fulltime_faculty/risingmi/articles/ICE.pdf. Accessed on 15 October 2019.

[17] *The Conan Doyle Collection. Wednesday 19 May 2004* (London: Christie's International Media Division, 2004).

archives show that he relied on a large number of them related to the Edalji case).[18] It is mostly in his rendering of Arthur's private life that the novelist could enjoy more imaginative freedom, especially in regard to his relationship with Jean Leckie, of which little is known.[19] In an early notebook, Barnes wondered if he should offer Jean's perspective: 'Do we need, say, Jean's diary? letters? view of?' (AG notebook), but he decided against it in order to concentrate on Arthur's view of the relationship.

As noted by Barnes, '[i]n his autobiography [Conan Doyle] completely lies about Jean, and early biographers completely cover it up'.[20] Indeed, in *Memories and Adventures*, Conan Doyle does not mention Jean until his marriage to her in 1907, although they met and fell in love ten years earlier, at a time when the writer was married to his ailing first wife. As Stashower remarks in his biography, Conan Doyle 'gracefully sidestep[s] any closer examination of the issue'[21] by declaring in his autobiography: 'There are some things which one feels too intimately to be able to express.'[22] In *Conan Doyle. His Life and Art* (1943), Hesketh Pearson refers in passing to Doyle's marriage to Jean Leckie 'whose family he had known for some time'.[23] Although John Dickson Carr entitles the ninth chapter of his 1949 biography 'Romance: Jean Leckie', barely more than three pages are devoted to the relationship in that chapter.[24] In *Sir Arthur Conan Doyle. L'homme et l'œuvre* (1964), Pierre Nordon refers in a single paragraph to the 'attachement, mais jamais liaison' ('An attachment, but never a liaison') which brought Jean and Arthur together from 1897 to 1907.[25] On one of Stashower's printed emails, Barnes underlined in red the fact that Conan Doyle destroyed his second wife's letters and that 'we can only assume that she did the same with his' (2.1.1).[26] He wrote in his

---

[18] At another auction in March 2015, some ten years after the publication of *Arthur & George*, a collection of thirty autograph letters by Conan Doyle (dating from 1907 to 1911) were put up for sale, twenty-four of which were addressed to Captain Anson, the chief constable of Staffordshire police. The sale, apparently originating from Anson's descendants, also included a printed report in whose appendix Anson revealed that he attempted to discredit Conan Doyle by fabricating a letter signed 'A Nark, London' (partly quoted in *Arthur & George* 245) which he sent to the writer who was investigating the case. Anson also admitted to setting up various informers to make the writer believe the letter had been sent by Royden Sharp, the man Conan Doyle thought was responsible for the horse maiming. This fabrication of evidence was meant to show what an amateur sleuth Conan Doyle was as he originally failed to detect the hoax. When Barnes was told about this revelation, he told journalist Alison Flood he had 'no plans to revisit *Arthur and George* in the wake of the new evidence, but he may include the revelation in an afterword for the next edition'. An afterword has not yet been included. Alice Flood, 'Arthur Conan Doyle was the Victim of a Police Conspiracy', *Guardian*, 18 March 2015, https://www.theguardian.com/books/2015/mar/18/arthur-conan-doyle-set-up-by-police-fabricated-letters. Accessed on 19 January 2019.
[19] He wrote: 'it was a moment of relief and breakthrough when I found a vital area … which had never been described in any detail or properly accounted for'. Barnes, 'The Case of Inspector Campbell', 294.
[20] Rees, 'The Inscrutable Mr Barnes'.
[21] Daniel Stashower, *Teller of Tales. The Life of Arthur Conan Doyle* (New York: Henry Holt, 1999), 205.
[22] Arthur Conan Doyle, *Memories & Adventures* (Ware, Hertfordshire: Wordsworth Editions, [1924] 2007), 215.
[23] Hesketh Pearson, *Conan Doyle: His Life and Art* (London: Methuen, 1943), 158.
[24] Carr, *The Life of Arthur Conan Doyle*, 101–3.
[25] Pierre Nordon, *Sir Arthur Conan Doyle. L'homme et l'œuvre* (Paris: Marcel Didier, 1964), 48; *Conan Doyle*, trans. Frances Partridge (London: Murray, 1966), 44.
[26] Stashower was probably referring to their letters when the relation was illegitimate as in his biography, Carr writes: '[Conan Doyle's] letters to [Jean Leckie], in his seventy-first year, read like those of a man who has been married for about a month' (101). Family papers had been unavailable

essay on the genesis of the novel: 'The novelist in me was delighted to discover that all their love letters had been destroyed, and the secret relationship (before marriage and respectability struck) airbrushed from family history: at last the imagination was free.'²⁷ What is surely a source of lamentation for biographers – Stashower deplores in his email the fact that 'there's precious little in the way of evidence, and almost nothing has ever come to light about their relationship in the limbo year' (2.1.1) – is precisely what allowed the novelist to include an invented letter from Jean to Arthur in his novel (235) and to feel less constrained in his fictional rendering of their relationship.

3. The art of beginning

Another example of the freedom granted to the novelist can be found as early as the very beginning of the novel (the first section entitled 'Arthur', 3–4) where Barnes devotes a full page to an incident which occupies a single sentence in Conan Doyle's 1924 autobiography. Early in *Memories and Adventures*, Conan Doyle refers to his maternal grandfather and notes: 'He had married Katherine Pack, whose death-bed – or rather the white waxen thing which lay upon that bed – is the very earliest recollection of my life.'²⁸ The boy was 3 years old and the grandmother 52. From this first visual memory, Barnes imagines a scene in which a child is eager to see. The brief opening paragraph of the novel is: 'A child wants to see. It always begins like this, and it began like this then. A child wanted to see.' In the second short paragraph, the boy walks to a bedroom door, opens it, goes inside, looks (the reader does not know yet what he sees), turns back and walks away. In the third paragraph (opening with the mysterious 'What he saw there became his first memory' and ending with a reference to 'what was on the bed: a "white, waxen thing"'), the narrator reflects on the way the former boy would describe what he saw sixty years later, and in the fourth, he gives information on the context of the scene (a Catholic household in Edinburgh), identifies the corpse ('the body [was] that of Arthur's grandmother, one Katherine Pack') and wonders about the implications of the child's first encounter with death, ending the paragraph with

---

until 2004 because of a family lawsuit so that, according to Jean Conan Doyle (Jean and Arthur's daughter), only three biographers had been able to see the papers before that date: Hesketh Pearson who was given access to Doyle's private papers by his sons, Denis and Adrian; John Dickson Carr whom Adrian authorized to see the papers in the mid-1940s and who briefly lists the contents of the eleven boxes in an appendix to his biography (a black metal box contains envelopes, labeled by Jean, with letters from Arthur to her, 350) and French scholar Pierre Nordon whom Adrian authorized to see the papers in the late 1950s. Dame Jean Conan Doyle. 'Foreword', *The Quest for Sir Arthur Conan Doyle: Thirteen Biographers in Search of a Life*, ed. Jon L. Lellenberg (Carbondale: Southern Illinois University Press, 1987), xiv. See also *The Conan Doyle Collection*, 8.

Biographer Andrew Lycett, author of *The Man Who Created Sherlock Holmes* (2007), says for his part that the couple's love letters 'were solemnly burnt by their son Adrian after [Jean] died in 1940'. Andrew Lycett. 'Adultery, my dear Watson', *Guardian*, 15 September 2007, https://www.theguardian.com/books/2007/sep/15/history.biography. Accessed on 19 January 2019.

²⁷ Barnes, 'The Case of Inspector Campbell', 294.
²⁸ Doyle, *Memories & Adventures*, 5. When Barnes took notes on Conan Doyle's autobiography, he wrote down the quote and put an asterisk next to it (2.2.5). The only other case of an asterisk in his notes concerns the reference to Conan Doyle meeting his 'first wife through the <u>death</u> of her brother' (2.2.5).

'The boy wants to see? Then let the boy see.' The last paragraph reflects further on this encounter between 'A small boy and a corpse' and the possible meanings of that 'thing' the boy stared at.

The archives comprise seven different drafts of this incipit,[29] and the corrections, additions and deletions point to an evolution of the general tone of this section from a narrator's tentative voice as he makes hypotheses about a scene he cannot have witnessed to a more assured mode indicative of the novelist's affirmation of his creative licence. As seen above, in the published book, the striking image of the 'white waxen thing' only appears at the end of the third paragraph, isolated between inverted commas after a colon. It is revealed after the camera-eye movement has gradually zoomed in on it, the narrator stealthily moving from one monosyllabic item to another: 'The door, the room, the light, the bed, and what was on the bed: a "white waxen thing." '[30] This 'thing' is only identified in the fourth paragraph, so that the suspense as to the mysterious nature of 'What he saw there' has been maintained for half a page. On the other hand, the first draft (which bore the title 'Chapter 1: George and Arthur', which was then crossed out) disclosed this precious information in an explicit first paragraph which closely echoed Conan Doyle's words in his autobiography: 'Arthur's first memory was of "a white waxen thing" which lay upon a bed. It was his mother's mother, one Katherine Pack, and, as the routine adjectives imply, she was dead' (2.2.5A).

While the published book retained the expression 'first memory' at the beginning of the third paragraph – 'What he saw there became his first memory' –, Barnes had crossed it out on the first draft and replaced it by hand with 'The very earliest recollection in Arthur's life' (bringing his own words even closer to Conan Doyle's), and then with 'In later life, Arthur would cite his very earliest recollection'. This third formulation on the first draft draws attention to the perspective of an adult identified by his first name, who is taking a retrospective glance at the past, whereas the first sentence in the published book delivers a general truth about children in the present tense – 'A child wants to see' –, thus offering a different temporal viewpoint at the onset of the novel.

---

[29] The different versions are stored in three different folders. The order in which the versions seem to have been written is the following:

(1) 2.2.5A: typed with corrections by hand
(2) 2.2.5B: clean computer copy which has included hand corrections from (1)
(3) 2.2.5C: typed with corrections by hand
(4) 2.2.1: longhand version
(5) 2.2.5D: typed with corrections by hand
(6) 2.2.2A: typed with corrections by hand
(7) 2.2.2B: typed with corrections by hand

[30] The expression 'white waxen thing' appears three more times in the novel: two pages later, the narrator refers to the man 'who had led Pack's Brigade at Waterloo, and was the uncle of the white, waxen thing he never forgot' (5); then, after Arthur qualifies as a doctor, he agrees to take Jack Hawkins (his future wife's brother) into his house as a resident patient, where the young man dies: 'Arthur looked more carefully at this corpse than he had done at the white, waxen thing of his infancy' (37); finally, when Arthur's wife dies, he 'knows that this abandoned husk, laid out on the bed, is not all there remains of Touie. This white and waxen thing is just something she has left behind' (199). In all occurrences, the expression deprives the person of their humanity and puts them at a distance.

Part I Beginning(s)
Chapter 1: George and Arthur

Arthur In later life, Arthur would cite his very earliest recollection. It
The very earliest recollection in Arthur's life
Arthur's first memory was of "a white waxen thing" which lay upon a bed.
The thing
It was his mother's mother, one Katherine Pack, and, as the [routine] adjectives
imply, she was dead.
                    n't admit
We should not be surprised at the thought of a small boy being presented to
a corpse. This was the early 1860s: Specific religion, generalised piety, or the
desire to impress upon an innocent child the final realities of life might have
caused the gesture. Or it could merely have been the consequence of cramped
                      we are in a A small flat in Edinburgh,
domestic circumstances. One room out of action, solemn visitors, hushed voices –
of course
the boy wants to know. Then let the boy see.
                                            turned into his
More surprising is that this moment proved-to-be-his first official recollection.
Does this mean that he has no memory of his grandmother being alive? This is
                                                    Might she have been
perhaps strange, since she lived with the family. Was she constantly ailing –
                                                  from the onset of his consciousness
who knows, perhaps infectious? – and thus separated from him? This seems unlikely.
      plausible   theory   what
More likely is the notion that the shock of seeing her dead drove out the slight
                                                                        might
memories he had of seeing her alive. That would explain it.

On the other hand, he does not tell us that the "white, waxen thing" produced
                             at the time
the effect of a shock upon him. Are children shocked by death? Can you be shocked
                                      cannot fully
by something whose significance you do not understand? Further, if you haven't
                                                        One way of calibrating adulthood
seen any alive, can you be shocked by the sight of them dead? Perhaps only
maturity is to say that it begins when you are capable of being shocked, not by the sight or fact or alarming
   adults are shocked by death.   details of death, but by the understanding of what it means
                                                                an item
He saw a "thing". Which we could take one of two ways: he saw something which
falling   specify, to which task was
fell into a category which his infant mind was unable to locate, and thus given
                                        recognised an item   formally
the general notation of 'thing'. Or, he saw something which had once been
                              but
characterised by life, and from which life had been withdrawn.

            There is also the question of whether the word "thing" was
                                            later reflection
applied by him at the time, or applied later after further/thought on what he
                                            amounted to
had seen as a small boy. Quite what a "thing" was – or, to put it more
                              This tremendous   only
accurately, quite what happened when a change took place, leaving a "thing"
           ? subsequently
behind – was later to become of great importance to Arthur.

Figure 3 *Arthur & George* – early draft of the first page (2.2.5A). Harry Ransom Center. The University of Texas at Austin.

The first draft included none of the first three paragraphs of the published version, and after the identification of Arthur's first memory, moved directly on to a second paragraph in which the narrator remarked that such encounters between a boy and a corpse were not rare in Edinburgh at the time, followed by hypotheses as to why this encounter may have taken place – which corresponds to the main content of the fourth paragraph in the published version. This second paragraph in the first two drafts concluded with 'of course the boy wants to know. Then let the boy see', which was deleted in the third draft and then reappeared under a different form in the fifth draft and in the published book: 'The boy wants to see? Then let the boy see' (3). The new formulation is not only more efficient in terms of rhythm and sonorities, but the shift from 'know' to 'see' is better suited to the difference between a boy (who wants to see) and an older man (who wants to know). On the fourth draft, Barnes wrote at the bottom of the page:

? repeat trope –
        A young man wants to ~~see~~/believe
        An old man wants to ~~see~~/know (2.2.1)

On another page, Barnes identified the key words of the novel as 'think/believe/know' (2.2.5). These words are borrowed from a sentence Doyle uttered in a short film of 1928 recorded by William Fox, which Barnes himself saw and from which he copied a sentence in his unarchived notebook: 'CD film, re spiritualism': 'When I talk on this subject, I'm not talking about what I believe, I'm not talking about what I think, I'm talking about what I know' (AG notebook).[31] Barnes offers a pastiche of this sentence in the third part of the novel after George asks Arthur if he thinks he is innocent at the end of their first meeting at the Grand Hotel and Arthur replies: 'No, I do not think you are innocent. No, I do not believe you are innocent. I *know* you are innocent' (219, italics in the original). George would remember these words when sitting in the Royal Albert Hall in 1930, as recorded in the last part of the novel: 'His champion's words: I do not think, I do not believe, I *know*' (355, italics in the original).[32] The keywords thus direct the reader towards what Barnes identified as the 'central theme' of the novel: 'belief (of various sorts) & how we come to believe what we do believe, & why we stick to it despite all discouraging evidence – how we make the evidence fit our beliefs' (AG notebook). In his notes, the novelist wrote that George and his father

---

[31] The film entitled *Sir Arthur Conan Doyle* was recorded by William Fox in the garden of Doyle's house at Windlesham, Crowborough, Sussex, in October 1928, https://www.arthur-conan-doyle.com/index.php?title=Sir_Arthur_Conan_Doyle_(movie_1928). Accessed on 19 January 2019.

[32] When writing about his stage adaptation of the novel (performed at the Birmingham Repertory Theatre in March–April 2010), David Edgar drew attention to these key words in the book: 'As he worked on the novel, Julian realized that the connecting membrane between the legal, romantic and religious strands in his story was the distinction between thinking something, believing it, knowing it and proving it. This distinction – expressed in the use of those four words in all the different sections of the story – unlocks the novel.' However, Edgar knew that this linguistic distinction was too delicate 'as the spine of the play' and therefore focused instead on another conceptual link in the novel which could be more efficiently shown onstage: 'the idea of seeing (a process of which thinking, believing, knowing and proving are subsidiaries)'. David Edgar, 'Ways of Seeing', *Guardian*, 13 March 2010, 17.

believe in British justice[33] and perhaps the Church of England while Arthur believes in 'scientific detection & various forms of spiritualism', Anson in 'structure, procedure, hierarchy' and Jean 'must believe in CD's love while Touie lives, then after T's death, she will know' (AG notebook). The shift from belief to knowledge is indeed at the core of the novel. However, on the first page of the book, Arthur is a 'small boy' (the age indication of 3 years old appears only in the sixth draft, added by hand, but was not retained) and the lexical field which prevails is that of seeing (with verbs such as 'see', 'look', 'observe' and 'stare'), as the child is probably still too young to want to believe or to know: he wants to see and the question of clarity or impairment of vision is central to the novel, down to its very last words.[34]

Later drafts and the published book start indeed with a focus on children's curiosity: 'A child wants to see. It always begins like this, and it began like this then. A child wanted to see' (3). This incipit is characterized by a shift from the general (marked by the present tense, the indefinite pronoun and the adverb 'always') to the specific (marked by the past tense and the adverb 'then') through a symmetrical construction in the form of a chiasmus. This paragraph first appeared on the fourth draft with definite pronouns ('The child wants to see. ... The child wanted to see', 2.2.1), but the first word was crossed out and replaced by the indefinite pronoun 'A', thus shifting the meaning from the specific to the general. On the other hand, the definite pronoun in the last sentence ('The child') remained in all drafts and was only changed to 'A child' in the final typescript, thus making the stylistic parallel with the first sentence more blatant.

On the fourth and fifth drafts, the opening paragraph of the published book was followed in the next paragraph by 'He was able to walk, and reach up to a door handle' and then by suppositions as to what the boy 'may have done': 'He may have done this' (instead of 'He did this' in the published version); 'He might have pushed the door' (instead of 'A door was there to be pushed'); 'There might not have been anyone' (instead of 'There was nobody'); 'he might have turned round and walked away' (instead of 'he turned and walked away'). In the published book, the succession of precise actions without epistemic modality, expressed as assertions – 'he walked in, stopped, looked'; 'he turned and walked away' –, makes it possible for the reader to visualize the scene stage by stage without doubting at any moment that it happened that way. The novelist assumes his role as a creator and invents the scene as though he were seeing it. On the contrary, earlier drafts exhibit the cautiousness which would characterize a prudent narrator, a biographer or a historian, constrained to imagining what could have taken place because of the lack of corroborating sources.

---

[33] During their first meeting, George tells Arthur: 'the process of the law will, in the end, deliver justice. That is what I believed, and what I still believe' (213). In his notes, Barnes wrote: 'George – he's the key – he starts off believing in what others believe in (law, justice, British values) / – then has these 2nd hand beliefs destroyed / – so q. is, does he find a substitute or does he end up beliefless' (AG notebook).

[34] The last words of the novel, as George is pressing binoculars to his spectacles in the Royal Albert Hall, are: 'What does he see? What did he see? What will he see?' (357).

In several drafts, this guarded narratorial figure also wonders why the boy happened to enter that room in the first place and the text is based on a series of suppositions, as in the following fourth draft:

> More likely, perhaps, is that there was someone in the room already, who turned at the sudden intrusion, lifted the boy from his feet, deposited him outside & firmly closed the door again. Or perhaps someone was passing and noticed the open door, went in and recuperated the child.
> Or the child's attention might have been drawn by the fact that the door was unexpectedly/inhabitually closed in the first place; that there were adult glances in its direction, and a different kind of whispering to what he had previously known.
> Or again, might the child have actually asked, by gesture or by word?
> Or again, might it have been decided from above that it would be instructive for him to see? Perhaps he did not want anything. (2.2.1)

The extensive use of the modal 'might' and of the adverb 'perhaps', as well as the anaphora of the conjunction 'Or' to juxtapose several options emphasize the narrator's inability to know what actually took place and his frustrated reliance on conjectures (which may recall Braithwaite's own frustration with his inability to know 'trivial, crucial details' in *Flaubert's Parrot* [101]). The third draft did not include any of the opening paragraphs mentioned above but directly started with suppositions:

> It could have happened in one of several ways.
> It could have been no more than a small boy's natural curiosity, the instinct to push at any closed door and see what lay behind. It could have been a little more than this, a boy's awareness that something was going on, something hidden from him, something to do with the adult world; he might have become aware that one room in the small flat was out of bounds, he might have asked, insisted, been pressing with curiosity; they might have thought, the boy wants to know, then let the boy see. Or it could have been something more specifically intended, part of his education, his induction into one of the realities of life. (2.2.5C)

The anaphora of 'it could have been', the use of the modal 'might' and the repetition of the vague 'something' point to the uncertainty that prevails about how the scene took place, just as in the fourth draft. However, the fact that this passage above constituted the incipit of the novel (instead of the firm statement 'A child wants to see' followed by the description of the boy's actions) makes this version more enigmatic, all the more as the opening pronoun 'it' is deprived of any antecedent and therefore remains mysterious. The published version reduces all these conjectures to only two in the fourth paragraph – 'Perhaps the door had been deliberately kept ajar. There might have been a desire to impress upon the child the horror of death' (3) – thus toning down the indecisive mode.

In four of the drafts, the speculations as to why the boy found himself in this room are accompanied by more questioning as to the reliability of this being Arthur's first recollection (a passage which exists in four different versions but was later cut):

> More surprising is that this turned out to be Arthur's first official recollection. If so, it would mean that he had no memory of his grandmother being alive – despite the fact that she had lived with the family. Might she have been constantly ailing, perhaps infectious, and thus quarantined from him since the onset of his consciousness? This seems unlikely. More plausible would be the theory that the shock of seeing her dead drove out his frail memories of having seen her alive. (2.2.5B)

In these early drafts, the narrator reflects not only on the biographical details of Arthur's infanthood but also on the way memory works (thus echoing the incipits of *Talking it Over*, *Love, etc* and *England, England*). Such conjectures (marked by the modal 'might', the question, the supposition introduced by 'if', the use of the conditional and the adjectives 'likely' and 'plausible') were probably deleted not only because of the way they highlighted uncertainty, whereas the final text is more assertive, but also because they entailed a greater focus on memory while the incipit of the published book seems more interested in the boy's encounter with death. The final version nevertheless retained a question which pointed to the lapse of sixty years between the time Arthur saw the corpse and the time he wrote about it 'publicly' in *Memories and Adventures*, and therefore to the effect of the passage of time on the transcription of the experience through language (maybe more so than on memory): 'How many internal retellings had smoothed and adjusted the plain words he finally used?' (3).

In three early drafts, questions also related to the boy's reaction to that vision:

> On the other hand, when recalling the event in later life, he did not mention any effect that the 'white waxen thing' produced. Are children barely past the brink of memory shocked by something whose significance they cannot fully comprehend? If you can't remember Grandma Pack alive, can you be shocked by the sight of her dead? One way of calibrating adulthood might be to say that it begins when you are capable of being shocked, not by the sight or the alarming details of death, but by a grasp of what it means. (2.2.5B)

Here again, the paragraph gives the narrator room for reflection and might anticipate some of the questions raised a few years later in *Nothing to Be Frightened Of* or recall some of the deleted passages on death in *Metroland*. These developments might have been cut because they were taking the reader away from the specific case at hand and making the incipit more philosophical and meditative, and less directly arresting.

In the last paragraph of the incipit in the published book, the vague noun 'thing' which had been chosen by Conan Doyle in his autobiography to refer to his grandmother is repeated three times, two of which are between inverted commas to emphasize the enigmatic dimension of the term.[35] Several drafts included a penultimate paragraph

---

[35] 'A grandchild who ... had just stopped being a thing, and a grandmother who ... had returned to that state. ... Quite what a "thing" amounted to – or, to put it more exactly, quite what happened when the tremendous change took place, leaving only a "thing" behind – was to become of central importance to Arthur' (3).

which commented on the use and meaning of the word 'thing'. The paragraph exists in several versions and was retained until the last draft in which it was crossed out and therefore disappeared from the final typescript:

> It is important to be precise. Arthur saw a 'thing' – though it is unclear whether the word 'thing' was applied by the small boy himself or, after decades of reflection, by the mature adult. We may, however, take the noun in one of two ways. Either, he saw an item falling into a category which his infant mind was unable to specify, and to which he therefore gave the general notation of 'thing'. Or, he recognised an item which had formerly contained life, but from which life had now been withdrawn. (2.2.5C)

In the version quoted above, the first sentence (which does not appear in any other draft) may remind the reader of similar formulations in 'Parenthesis' of *History of the World in 10½ Chapters*, a section in which the author appears to be speaking in his own name: 'We must be precise with love' (230, 244), 'We must be precise' (233). The sentence was probably deleted in the later drafts of *Arthur & George* because it echoed the more reflexive and at times playfully didactic tone of 'Parenthesis', which was not adapted to a novel in which the narrator deliberately abstains from any didacticism. Indeed, the omniscient narrator gives access to the characters' minds through the use of free indirect style but refrains from offering his own perspective or interpretation on events. The second fairly pedagogic sentence 'We may, however, take the noun in one of two ways' was crossed out in the draft and replaced by a question – 'And what did either of them mean by the noun?' – which opened a discussion on semantics which was later deleted, maybe to give more density to the first section. The interrogation as to what the 'thing' amounted to was, however, retained and had been present from the start in the first draft.

The final version of the incipit therefore appears to be much more condensed and compact than the earlier drafts: it consists of 356 words while the longest draft (2.2.5C) was twice as long despite not including the first two paragraphs of the published book. The tentative tone of the narrator making hypotheses as to what might have happened and wondering about the workings of memory, the effect of death on a child and the meaning of the word 'thing' was replaced by a more assured voice delivering statements with only minimal traces of hesitations. One might suggest that the final version of the incipit makes the book more novelistic and striking from the start, drawing on suspense and stimulating the reader's curiosity, as in the opening pages of the best detective fiction.

4. Finding a JB title

The first draft of the incipit bore the title 'Chapter 1: George and Arthur' but this was crossed out and replaced by 'Part I Beginning(s)' (2.2.5A). The published novel is divided into four parts ('Beginnings', 'Beginning with an Ending', 'Ending with a Beginning', 'Endings') and in sections that bear the names of the characters (Arthur, George, Campbell, Anson) but not in chapters. The titles of the parts seem to have been decided upon at an early stage as those of Parts I, II and IV appear on the first planning sheet of May 2004; the original second part was then divided into two on the second planning sheet (2.1.6).[36] On the other hand, the title of the whole book was chosen much later because *Arthur & George* is one of those novels for which Barnes was at pains to find an adequate title, even after he had finished writing it. When Anne Collins, editor at Random House Canada, sent her editorial queries on the book in early February 2005, she referred to 'the big (still untitled?) novel' (2.2.5). The archives include the various titles Barnes had thought of:

THE TITLE

These are titles which have come to mind so far:

George & Arthur
Arthur & George
The Next Valley
Distant Lands
News from Distant Lands
The Skin of Things
The Right Sort
The Wrong Sort
The Great Wyrley Outrages
Beginning, Ending
Beginnings, Endings
Conviction
Sentences

I don't want a cod-ACD title – The Casebook of … Besides, Mark Haddon has already had The Curious Incident …
It must be a JB title. And suggestive rather than descriptive.

…

HL thinks Law shd be in the title somehow[37]
I don't want to give away GE or ACD's identities in the title
Outrage now has a gay implication (2.2.5)

In this list, the necessity for a 'suggestive' title which would not reveal the identity of the two historical figures is stressed upon and complied with in all titles, except maybe for 'The Great Wyrley Outrages' which was how the horse mutilations were referred to in the press in 1903. In other notes, Barnes also insisted on this need to keep the protagonists' names unknown: 'Withhold CD's identity as long as possible /

---

[36] In his notes, Barnes wrote: 'Two Parts, first ending "And then George decided to write to Sherlock Holmes / Arthur C.D."' (AG notebook). This sentence does not appear in the book although the second part ends with a scene of Arthur looking at his tray of letters and one in particular signed by 'a name that means absolutely nothing to him: George Edalji' (206).

[37] In a letter of 5 August 2004, after she had read one fifth of the book (until the description of the horse mutilation, 73), Hermione Lee wrote: 'I am beginning strongly to feel the title should have the word LAW in it somewhere, as in The Law of the Land – or some oblique reference to the law' (2.2.6).

Withhold Edalji's surname & colour as long as possible' (AG notebook).[38] Barnes did not want a title which would evoke Conan Doyle's own work like Mark Haddon's *The Curious Incident of the Dog in the Night-Time* which was published by Jonathan Cape (Barnes's own publisher) in 2003 and whose title is borrowed from Conan Doyle's 1892 short story 'Silver Blaze' in which Sherlock Holmes investigates the disappearance of a race horse and the murder of his trainer. Barnes also dismissed the title 'Conviction' because it was too similar to *Atonement*, Ian McEwan's 2001 novel also published by Cape, but he remembers he 'was very close to calling it this'.[39] The notion of a 'JB title' is intriguing and recurs in a note to Barnes's wife when he asked for her opinion on the title:

> title????????? Anything jump out at you? the only two still in the frame from my pt of view are News from Distant Lands and The Next Valley. But neither is a typical JB title. Endings & Beginnings? (2.2.5)

'Endings & Beginnings' or variations thereof would probably have been too close to the titles of the four parts. Another page showed the prevalence of a few titles from the longer list:

> Titles
>   (The Right Sort)
>   News from Distant Lands
>   Beneath the Surface
>   The Skin of Life / Things
>   The Next Valley (2.2.6)

The common point between all these titles is that they appear at significant moments in the novel. For instance, it is with the sentence 'You're not a right sort' that George is greeted by one of his schoolfellows in the novel (9, 12), and the sentence is used in one of the authentic letters George received at the time of the horse mutilations in 1903 – 'they do not think you are a right sort' (83) – as well as in another sent to Arthur in 1907 (revealed in 2015 to have been fabricated by Captain Anson): 'he is not a right sort' (245). As for the third and fourth titles above, Barnes explained in an interview: 'One of the early titles of the book was *The Skin of Things*, because it was about the surface of the world and what was immediately underneath it and the skin of George and the skin of Arthur.'[40] This title might have been considered a 'JB title' because it has the same structure as the titles of his later novels, *The Sense of an Ending* and *The Noise of Time*, with a head noun followed by an *of* prepositional complement. The phrase 'the skin of things' appears in the novel when Arthur evokes 'the world of Spiritism' and the progress of science and notes: 'The invisible and the

---

[38] As recommended in that notebook, Edalji's name is only revealed during the first police interrogation (26).
[39] Annotations, 22–27 March 2018.
[40] Interview by Guignery and Roberts, in *Conversations*, ed. Guignery and Roberts, 140.

impalpable, which lie just below the surface of the real, just beneath the skin of things, are increasingly being made visible and palpable' (199). As for 'The Next Valley', it is used by Arthur during his first meeting with George who has just told him about his father, born in Bombay but converted by Scottish missionaries. This inspires Arthur to refer to the existence of two valleys – 'The truths of one's race and the truths of one's religion do not always lie in the same valley' – and to insist on the necessity of crossing the bridge between the two: 'Down there, you indicate, down there is the truth, down there in the next valley' (218).

'News from Distant Lands' had certainly been the most likely title as it appears on the title page of a typescript, but was then crossed out and replaced by 'Arthur & George' in longhand (2.2.5). 'Distant Lands (News from)' (2.2.6) also features on an index card, together with a few handwritten notes on the passage from the novel in Part Two when Arthur, unable to understand Jean's 'bouts of low spirits' compares women to distant lands: 'I have come to think that women – other women – are like distant lands. Except that when I have been to distant lands – out on the veldt in Africa – I have always been able to find my bearings' (189). The expression appears twice in Part One to refer to the stories Arthur would compose as a budding writer – 'He set his adventures in distant lands' (24) – and to his conception of a 'true courtly knight' who would be 'departing to a distant land on a long and preferably perilous quest' (33). It recurs in Part Three when Arthur defines himself as a man 'constantly in motion' and not the sort of man who stays at home and longs to 'wait for the paper boy to bring him news from distant lands' (222). It also appears in the last part when George refers to people's reaction to him and his sister – whose father came from 'distant Bombay' (57) – after they moved to London: 'there were even some people who, on learning that you came from Birmingham, expressed disappointment, because they had been hoping for news from distant lands which you were quite unable to supply' (337).

The last occurrence takes place during Arthur's memorial at the Royal Albert Hall, when the medium Mrs. Roberts enters into communication with the dead writer and George begins to be shaken in his rationalist beliefs: 'What if the theatrical Mrs. Roberts, despite herself, was truly bringing news from distant lands?' (354). A reader at Jonathan Cape pointed to the repetition of the phrase in the last part, but Barnes wrote in the margin: 'Yes, I want to press on this phrase & the different contexts it applies to. (It used to be part of the title)' (2.2.6). The various quotations from the novel point to the polysemy of the phrase and suggest that Barnes might have thought of this title from early on as it regularly appears in the book. However, he eventually dismissed it because it sounded 'too much like a Jonathan Raban travel book'.[41] Whether the ultimate choice of *Arthur & George* is a 'JB title' or not remains open to interpretation, but Barnes admits it has been a choice by default: 'In the end, I went with the working title, which other people seemed to like but I hadn't'.[42]

---

[41] Interview by Jeffries, in *Conversations*, ed. Guignery and Roberts, 131.
[42] Ibid.

5. Working out tenses

The archives have shown that Barnes had to go through several drafts before coming to the final version of the incipit and that he gave much thought to the title of his novel. Even before coming to these crucial aspects, however, the novelist asked himself a key narratological question about the form the novel would take: 'omniscient narr.? / diary? Diaries? [tho' how much wd ACD reveal, if autobio is anything to go by] how do you do his guilt/grief/suppressions?' (AG notebook). Barnes put aside the idea of the diary form and opted for third-person omniscient narration, alternating between Arthur and George, and giving access to their thoughts and feelings through internal focalization. This alternation required that an utmost attention be paid to the use of tenses. In notes to himself, Barnes wrote: 'tenses: work out' (2.2.6) and this question is one that keeps recurring throughout composition. This is probably not surprising for a novel which starts with a shift from the present to the past tense in its very first sentence – 'A child wants to see. It always begins like this, and it began like this then. A child wanted to see' (3) –, and which ends with three questions in the present, past and future: 'What does he see? / What did he see? / What will he see?' (357). In Part One of the published book, the sections devoted to Arthur are written in the past tense, and those devoted to George in the present tense. When Barnes sent Hermione Lee one-eighth of the novel in July 2004, he asked: 'Did you notice/have any trouble with the past/present tense split?'. After confirming that she had noticed it and 'rather liked it', she offered an interpretation for the alternation: 'I presumed it was because Arthur is historical, known about, has had his story told, whereas George (though also historical) is unknown to us, is being recreated for the first time' (2.2.6). The ingenious distribution of tenses not only in Part One but also in later parts was the result of much rewriting as an analysis of several drafts reveals.

In an early typescript draft of George's very first section, the first sentence marks Barnes's hesitation: 'George does/did not have a first memory' (2.2.5), and the rest of the section is written in the past, but Barnes wrote at the top 'present tense?' and then corrected the past to the present in longhand. In another draft of Part One (2.2.1), Barnes numbered in pencil (presumably only for himself) the sections devoted to George from 1 to 16 (several sections were later conflated since Part One in its final version only has twelve unnumbered sections for each character).[43] While sections 1 and 2 (corresponding to the first two sections in the published book, 3–7), as well as sections 6 and following (from page 12 onward in the book) were written in the present tense, sections 3, 4 and 5 (pages 8 to 12 in the book, about George being sent to the village school) appeared in the past tense on the typescript but were corrected in longhand to the present. It is not clear why these pages were singled out to be written in the past tense in the early draft as Barnes seems to have decided on the alternation of past and present for Arthur's and George's sections in Part One quite early on.

On the other hand, Barnes clearly wondered which tense he would use for George's sections in Part Two as 'Beginning with an Ending' starts in a draft with

---

[43] The sections devoted to Arthur in Part One were numbered from 1 to 12 in one typescript draft (2.2.1). All sections devoted to Arthur were written in the past tense from early drafts.

the indication: 'George (part 2, past tense)' – and is indeed written in the past on the typescript – but next to this, Barnes wrote in longhand: 'why?', crossed out 'past tense' and corrected the typescript to the present tense. For a later section about George in that second part, Barnes still hesitated between the past and the present tense – 'Each morning George took/takes the 7.39 train to Birmingham' – but wrote at the top of the page in longhand: 'present until he's arrested' (2.1.8). This indication is precious as it reveals the logic behind the distribution of tenses at the beginning of the novel and the first section for George in the past tense is indeed the one when he is arrested: 'At Newton Street they took away his money' (100) – whereas the previous section for George had concluded with an ominous sentence in the present tense: 'He does not realize that these are the last normal twenty-four hours of his life' (93). The shift to the past tense once he is in jail not only signals his imprisonment in a frozen past with no immediate hope of a present or future but also indicates that he has become a 'public figure', like Arthur (if in a minor way).

This decision to confine George to the past from that time on explains why, although the typescript entitled 'George (main trial)' was originally written in the present tense, Barnes wrote at the top of the page 'tense – PAST' (2.1.7) and indeed the passage in the book is in the past tense (116). The same tense change applied to the development entitled 'Prison' (2.2.4), which refers to the time after George was sentenced to seven years of penal servitude, brought back to Stafford gaol and then sent to Lewes and Portland before being freed. This section was originally written in the present tense but was then corrected to the past (147–62), which emphasizes further the contrast between the isolated sentence 'He was free' at the end of George's section and the separate opening line 'And then he meets Jean' (162)[44] at the beginning of Arthur's section, which marks the first use of the present tense for Arthur as all previous sections had been written in the past. It is very meaningful that the development devoted to Arthur and Jean's intimate relationship should be written in the present, a tense which reduces the distance between readers and characters. This secret relationship is also the one place where Arthur is not a public figure.

As for Part Three, 'Ending with a Beginning', in which Arthur and George meet for the first time at the Grand Hotel in London, the first pages were originally written in the past tense (except for the paragraph when Arthur 'enters the foyer' [210]), but Barnes wrote at the top of the first page 'tense? present surely' and changed the past tenses to the present in longhand (2.1.8), therefore making the scene more vivid for the reader. The next section, in which Arthur starts his investigation, is written in the past tense in the draft and in the published book (219–20) even if Barnes wrote at the top of the page: 'continue present, as w[ith] Jean, or past?', but he then decided on a significant distribution of tenses: 'past for action / present for Jean' (2.2.4). This also

---

[44] One of the stylistic devices of the novel consists in starting a paragraph with a startling 'And then', as in 'And then Touie dies' (199) or 'And then there was Waller' (248) – not only an echo of the stories Arthur's mother used to tell her son when he was a child – 'And then the knight'; 'And then the black-hearted villain'; 'And then the maiden' (5) – but also of the typical question raised by fictions based on suspense and by interrogators in a trial: 'And then what happened?' (124). The recurrence of this phrase seems fitting for a book which relies so much on suspense and keeps stimulating the reader's curiosity.

ties in with what Barnes wrote in his notes: 'Tenses: ACD → present for inner life sequence' (AG notebook). And indeed, once Arthur visits Jean in her flat and reflects on his relationship with her, the narrative moves to the present (221). This balance of tenses along public and private lines explains why Barnes changed the present tense for Arthur's visit to Wyrley on the draft (2.2.3) to the past tense in the published book – 'Arthur sat on the Birmingham train' (222) – as this scene relates to the Edalji case and what qualifies as 'action'.

As for the second meeting between George and Arthur at the Grand Hotel in Part Three (which was invented by Barnes),[45] it was originally written in the present tense (2.2.3) – like the first meeting in the book – but Barnes changed the beginning to the past (297–99) and then shifted to the present when the two men start talking to each other (299–302), making the dialogue more vivid – with Barnes writing in the margin on a draft 'present', 'present continues' (2.2.3) – and back to the past after they part (302). In the next section, Arthur's commenting upon the Report of the Gladstone Committee in a private conversation with Jean is in the present tense (305–11) – thus sticking to the choice he had made earlier of using the 'present for Jean' – while the official reactions that follow are in the past tense (311–15). Barnes had originally rendered these reactions in the present tense but then wrote in the margin 'tenses from here?' and corrected them to the past (2.2.3). Only when the section returns to the conversation between Arthur and Jean does the present tense logically reappear (315). The beginning of the next section (and last one of Part Three) about George's life after the verdict was written in the present tense on a draft – 'As the summer weeks begin to pass' –, but Barnes wrote in the margin 'past here, then present for wedding?' (2.2.3). In the published book, the first pages of that section are indeed in the past (315–8), until the present tense reappears for the wedding (318–21), probably because it pertains to Arthur's intimate life – with Barnes writing on the draft 'change here to present?' (2.2.3) – before moving back to the past for the last paragraphs of Part Three which focus on George returning to his life and the Doyles to theirs (321–2). The draft for these closing paragraphs was in the present – 'The next morning he [George] buys the Times' – but Barnes wrote 'past' in the margin (2.2.3) and the published book ends that third part in the past – 'The next morning he bought the Times' (321) – an indication of the distance which is reinstalled between Arthur and George as 'their paths had crossed' but the wedding 'had marked the end of that crossing point' (322).

Finally, an early draft (consisting of two pages) of the beginning of Part Four had the first two paragraphs (on Arthur's death) written in the past tense and the next ones (focusing on George reading the paper and reactions to the news) in the present tense. At the top of the page, however, Barnes wrote in longhand '? or poss past tense until → A. Hall, then present' (2.2.2), and in later drafts, he either used the past tense or corrected the present tense to the past, typing at the top of a page: 'PAST T!!' (2.2.3). On a draft, when George enters the Royal Albert Hall, Barnes wrote: 'THE MOMENT

---

[45] When David Edgar commented on his adaptation of the novel for the stage, he wrote: 'In life, the two men only met once during the course of Conan Doyle's work on the case. In terms of Julian's take on the story, his invented second meeting is what the French call a *scène à faire* and we call an obligatory scene.' Edgar, 'Ways of Seeing', 16.

WHEN PAST → PRESENT' (2.2.3) and in the published book indeed, the past tense is used until George settles in the Royal Albert Hall, from which time the narration is in the present, thus reducing the reader's distance from the scene (341).

These numerous tense changes on successive drafts and Barnes's notes to himself in the margin about this essential technical aspect reveal how meticulous he was about the distribution of tenses, which was meant to be particularly meaningful and followed a specific logic in each different part. Thus, the more intimate passages (scenes with Jean but also fictional conversations between Arthur and George) are written in the present while those related to Arthur's childhood and the historical case and investigation are in the past. The intricate alternation of tenses is constantly modifying the distance the reader feels towards the characters and the scenes taking place. The present makes the events more vivid, in keeping with the novelistic mode of the book, while the past sheds light on the historical basis of the case and on the well-known figure of Arthur Conan Doyle.

Arthur & George constitutes an interesting case in Barnes's archives of a novel which required extensive research and yet was written in a relatively limited amount of time. Like *Flaubert's Parrot* and *The Noise of Time*, it is a novel which presented a generic challenge because of the considerable biographical information available on Arthur Conan Doyle and the historical basis of the story, elements which could have impeded the novelist's imagination. However, the archives reveal that Barnes took advantage of the gaps and absences in biographical and historical documents to very nearly create the character of George (relatively little was known about this man who, in Barnes's book, admits to feeling like 'a character in a novel' when reading Arthur's articles about him [297]) and to invent or flesh out scenes in the life of Arthur relating to his infancy (as shown by the incipit) and to his relationship with Jean. The numerous corrections pertaining to tenses and the long hesitation as to the title to be given to the novel confirm Barnes's great attentiveness to narratological tools and paratexts, as much as plot, language and characterization.

11

Nothing to Be Frightened Of as an echo chamber

In an interview with Julian Barnes, Mark Lawson recalls that around 2003 the writer said that for reasons of privacy, he 'couldn't ever imagine writing a memoir'.[1] Like Gustave Flaubert, Barnes believes in 'the insignificance of the writer's personality' (*Flaubert's Parrot* 2–3) and has no desire to be confessional. And yet, in an interview in 2007, he admitted to being 'an unsatisfactory or defective Flaubertian' because in *A History of the World in 10½ Chapters*, he included a half-chapter, 'Parenthesis', which he described as 'autobiographical, openly so'.[2] In addition, in 2008, he published *Nothing to Be Frightened Of* which starts as a family memoir, followed in 2013, five years after the death of his wife, by *Levels of Life*, in which the third section focuses on his mourning and grief. In these more recent instances when Barnes ventured into autobiography, he mainly approached the genre through the question of death (or decline). He justified his use of autobiographical experience by the fact that he was 'willing to use [his] own life as an example of something'. Thus, he explained that in the case of *Nothing to Be Frightened Of*, he was approaching the general (death, religion) through the particular (his family and himself): 'The reason I am starting in memoir mode in my new book is because I think that's the easiest way to lead the reader in to longer sections about death and God which they might otherwise not want to get into.'[3]

Nothing to Be Frightened Of can be considered as a landmark in Barnes's œuvre not only for the way it recapitulates and interrogates his thoughts on death, which have accompanied him since his adolescence, but also because it acts as an echo chamber of his former and future work. The book indirectly draws light on the writer's trajectory as he looks backwards at his early diaries and first novel, and seemingly projects forwards by evoking subjects that would find a fictional development in later books, particularly in *Levels of Life* and *The Only Story*. Threads can thus be woven between the early notebooks which contain specific sentences and ideas that remained unexploited for several decades, the fiction in which a few autobiographical elements are transformed through imagination and the non-fiction which casts light on the origin of some quotes and episodes. This chapter proposes to focus on these networks of resonances,

---

[1] In Lawson, 'Front Row'.
[2] Interview by Guignery and Roberts, in *Conversations*, ed. Guignery and Roberts, 165.
[3] Ibid.

with a special interest in the themes of decay, death and mourning, and to ponder over the overlappings between life and fiction, memory and invention.

1. The obsession with death: From the early notebooks to *Nothing to Be Frightened Of*

Barnes defines himself as 'a slow-burn writer' and remarks: 'Things tend to have to compost down and I store things up without knowing that that's what I'm doing.'[4] The writer's early notebooks and diaries thus often include ideas or phrases relating to death which later found their way into books. This is the case of the expression 'Nothing to be frightened of' which appeared in Barnes's private papers several decades before he published the book of the same name:

I find this in my diary, written twenty and more years ago:

> People say of death, 'There's nothing to be frightened of.' They say it quickly, casually. Now let's say it again, slowly, with re-emphasis. 'There's NOTHING to be frightened of.' (*Nothing* 99)

Another example of this slow-burning process is the sentence 'Let's get this death thing straight' which appears several times in the notebooks of the 1970s and 1980s and was intended to be the first line in what Barnes referred to as the 'Death novel' (1.1.1). This novel was to become *Staring at the Sun* but the sentence was not used in that book and only appeared some thirty years later in *Nothing to Be Frightened Of* in the course of a discussion about the last book Barnes intended to write (which did not turn out to be his last): 'Although I didn't know if it was going to be fiction or nonfiction, I had the first line planned and noted many years ago: "Let's get this death thing straight"' (100). Later on in the book, Barnes uses the third person to refer to himself as a man who 'writes a book about death' and to the long period between 'the time he thinks of his opening line – "Let's get this death thing straight" – and the time he types his actual and different opening line' (186). The powerful beginning to the book is 'I don't believe in God but I miss him' (3), a sentence Barnes had pronounced in an interview with Rudolf Freiburg as early as 1999[5] and written in one of his private diaries in the same year.[6]

In the first notebook preserved at the Harry Ransom Center which dates from the late 1970s and early 1980s, Barnes wrote the following for a novel opening:

> Novel Opening
> Let's get this death thing straight. I plan to die as raucously, as protestingly, as impolitely as possible. Not for effect, or as a pose of naturalism, but because that is

---

[4] O'Connell, 'Julian Barnes: Interview'.
[5] Interview by Freiburg, *Conversations*, ed. Guignery and Roberts, 41. Barnes also used that phrase in an interview with Nadine O'Regan in 2003. Ibid., 116.
[6] Annotations, 22–27 March 2018.

how I know I shall feel. I shall be encouraged to be polite, to be dignified, to set an example, but I know that I shall be irritated by the unsuitable collection of people who come to see me, and petrified by the certainty of my coming non-existence. Therefore I have decided to behave badly. (1.1.1)

A shorter version of this opening in the second notebook of the 1980s was: 'Let's get this death thing straight. It's been hanging around far too long' (1.1.2). Looking back on this arresting first sentence in 2014, Barnes judged it was not 'a very good first line' because of 'that terrible /th/ together "death thing" which you can barely say or read' but he acknowledged: 'the fact that there would be a death book was in my mind for a number of years'.[7] In a folder called 'used notes' for *Nothing to Be Frightened Of*, Barnes wrote: 'end – have I "got this death thing straight"? I don't know. Perhaps I've just run my brain out of thoughts on the matter, an exhaustion which might pass for – what? – a conclusion? Wisdom? hardly' (3.5). The final version in the book is denser: 'I must try to verify a number of things. ... Whether I have got this death thing straight – or even a little straighter' (249). The recurrence of the phrase several decades after it was first written down points to the long process of maturation of some ideas and sentences, as well as to their free circulation from one text (published or unpublished, fictional or non-fictional) to another across the years.

Another thread can be woven between the narrator's meditations on his fear of death in the first part of *Metroland* and Barnes's own musings in *Nothing to Be Frightened Of*. In *Metroland*, Chris's fear of death comes to him at night, while lying powerless in bed: 'A sudden, rising terror which takes you unawares; a surging need to scream, which the house rules forbid (they always do), so that you lie there with your mouth open in a trembling panic' (54). In the margin of the annotated copy of *Metroland*, Barnes wrote: 'A theme worth returning to, in, say, 2008...' (Morgan Library 54), and indeed the description of Chris's 'nocturnal terrors' (54) is echoed in *Nothing to Be Frightened Of* by Barnes's 'nocturnal attacks' (24), which were also recorded in the (partly autobiographical) 'Parenthesis' of *A History of the World in 10½ Chapters* when the narrator refers to his troubled nights: 'Every so often I find myself catapulted out of bed with fear of time and death, panic at the approaching void' (223). In addition, Chris's short paragraph about 'the fear of dying' versus 'the fear of being dead' in *Metroland* (54) gave way to a longer development in *Nothing to Be Frightened Of* in which Barnes quotes Arthur Koestler's *Dialogue with Death* (1937) when the Hungarian writer tells the ace fighter pilot at the controls of their plane: 'I have never been afraid of death ... but only of dying', to which the pilot shouts back: 'With me, it's exactly the opposite' (138). This induces Barnes to ask, using one of the several unanswerable would-you-rather constructions which pepper the book: 'Fear of death or fear of dying, would you rather?' (139).[8] Both Barnes and his fictional alter ego Chris

---

[7] In Lawson, 'Mark Lawson'.
[8] There are eleven would-you-rather constructions relating to death in *Nothing to Be Frightened Of*. In his review of Joyce Carol Oates's and Joan Didion's diaries of widowhood, Barnes wonders what would be the less 'crappy age' to be widowed and concludes: 'there is no correct answer in that game of would-you-rather' (*Through the Window*, 217). *The Only Story* starts with a similar formula: 'Would you rather love the more, and suffer the more; or love the less, and suffer the less?' (3).

would rather opt for the former, with Chris's 'I wouldn't mind Dying at all, I thought, as long as I didn't end up Dead at the end of it' in *Metroland* (54) being quoted by Barnes thirty years later in *Nothing to Be Frightened Of* (149)[9] and applied to himself (*Nothing* 139).

In *Metroland*, 16-year-old Chris asks his older brother Nigel 'if he were ever frightened of death' and is given a 'practical, logical' answer emblematic of Nigel's personality: 'Bit early, isn't it?' The narrator's insistence – 'But don't you ever worry about it? Try and work out what it's all about?' – only yields further evidence of his brother's 'firmer, less anguished grasp of the termination of his own existence': 'It's quite obvious what it's all about, isn't it? Kaput, finito, curtains' (56). In his annotated copy of the book, Barnes wrote: 'My own brother, a philosopher, was naturally quite unlike this' (Morgan Library 56) and he remarked in 2018: 'I'm sure that as a boy, I never asked Jonathan about death. Indeed, I (seem to) remember making the exchange up when I wrote *Metroland*.'[10] Although Jonathan Barnes was quite unlike fictional Nigel as a teenager, he came to share the same attitude towards the termination of life as an adult. Indeed, in *Nothing to Be Frightened Of*, Barnes's elder brother, then in his early sixties, appears quite as pragmatic about death as his young fictional predecessor, stating that although he does not 'exactly welcome' death, it 'doesn't worry [him] either' (62). In an email of 30 March 2005, he wrote to his younger brother: 'Do I fear my personal extinction? No. I don't want to be extinguished this morning (I've got some things to finish off); but I don't fear extinction' (3.5). Jonathan Barnes's 'detachment in death's face' at the age of 63 (*Nothing*, 62) might well match the casualness of Nigel Lloyd whose younger brother's fear of death in *Metroland* seems as visceral as Julian Barnes's.

One should nevertheless remain cautious when suggesting such parallels and not forcibly apply an autobiographical reading onto fiction. Although Barnes presented *Nothing to Be Frightened Of* as being partly a family memoir, he also insisted that it was not his autobiography.

2. This is not an autobiography

In notes written down before a public reading of an extract from *Nothing to Be Frightened Of*, Barnes drew attention to the generic malleability of the book: 'genre moves back & forth between particularity of the memoir & the generality of the essay' (3.5). In the blurb he wrote for the book (which is very close to the published blurb), he described it as not only 'a family memoir, an exchange with his philosopher brother, a meditation on mortality, a celebration of art, an argument with God, and a homage to the French writer Jules Renard' but also 'a wise, funny and unsettling book which defies category and classification – except as Barnesian' (3.5).

---

[9] After quoting the sentence, Barnes offers an example of self-criticism between brackets: '(Rereading that sentence, I wonder if I should be embarrassed by the repetition of *end*. Though if challenged, I would probably argue that it was a deliberate stressing of finality. Whether it was or not, I can't remember.)' (*Nothing*, 149).

[10] Annotations, 22–27 March 2018.

In a deleted passage from *Nothing to Be Frightened Of*, Barnes remembers the blunt categorization his collection of short stories *The Lemon Table* was submitted to by librarians, which led him to meditate on the fate of *Nothing to Be Frightened Of*:

> When I wrote a book of short stories concerned with the later stages of life, with deliquescence and dissolution, with what happens when the heart, the mind and the body age – as they invariably do – at different speeds, the Library of Congress, in one of those brutally pithy summaries to which it reduces books on the reverse of their title page, cast it into two categories: 1. Aging – Fiction. 2. Aged – Fiction. I recently saw a book categorized as: Self-Help – Grief. How do you think they categorize the Bible? Self-Help – Bright Side. Or perhaps: Self-Help – Fiction. A tricky one. And how will they – and how would you? – categorize the present work? Self-Help – Self-Pity? I wonder. You may well judge the matter of a man considering his own death to be self-indulgent. Though as I said, this isn't an autobiography, and I offer my own case, at this particular time and in this particular society, only as an example. Nor am I asking for your sympathy (though I certainly wouldn't turn it away). And in any case, I'm not just considering my own death; I trust I'm considering yours too. (3.5)

The sheer inanity of labels is clearly expounded here. If Barnes willingly presents *Nothing to Be Frightened Of* as a family memoir, he also insists early in the book that 'This is not, by the way, "my autobiography."' (34), the inverted commas drawing further attention to the author's reluctance towards the genre. When she read a first draft of the beginning of the book, Hermione Lee admitted that the 'self-exposure … frightened [her] at first' (3.5). A deleted passage provided more argumentation against the autobiographical mode:

> I said this was not an autobiography, even if it occasionally veers in that direction. I have never intended to write one, for two reasons. First, a writer's life (compared to most autobiographed lives) is generally quite dull, and mine is no exception. By dull, I do not mean to me, I mean to you: it's like the wife-leaver's plea. It doesn't feel dull to me, but I know it would be to you. And the second, more important reason: I am a private person, and my private life is private. And third – yes, I know I said two – thirdly, it goes against my aesthetic: I am not an autobiographical writer – though here and there I have used bits of my life, though always in an illustrative rather than confessional manner. (3.5)[11]

One of the specificities of the genesis of *Nothing to Be Frightened Of* which made it more autobiographical than the writer had originally planned is that it evolved from being a meditation and silent monologue to a form of dialogue between Barnes and his

---

[11] In an interview in 2002, Barnes was asked what his autobiography would be called if he were to write one and he jokingly answered: 'It's got such a good title that I can't tell you because one of your readers would nick it and I'm going to need it in 20 years' time. I've always liked the title of Eric Ambler's autobiography, *Here Lies*.' Rimmer, 'Shelf Life'. In 2018, Barnes remarked that he 'obviously' did not have a title. Annotations, 22–27 March 2018.

brother. On 22 March 2005, Barnes started asking his brother questions about family memories by email and wrote 'I'd rather not tell you why I would like to know, as it might prejudice your answers' (3.5). Jonathan Barnes replied 'NO' to the first three questions his brother asked in that very first email:

> 1) Do you remember coming second in the wheelbarrow race with Dion Shirer (if so, who was the barrow?)
> NO. [I do remember DS, and I can well imagine that we barrowed together at Derwentwater County Primary. But I'm glad to say that I've not the slightest memory of it.]
> 2) Do you remember a disappointing ham sandwich on a train journey to Switzerland?
> NO. [I don't recall any train journey to Switzerland taken before my Mature Years, when I was quite old enough not to risk a ham sandwich.]¹²
> 3) Do you remember Grandpa conducting the Messiah on the radio (presumably with the Huddersfield Festival Chorus)?
> NO. (3.5)

This repeated and forceful admission of non-remembering marked the start of a correspondence which lasted about two years and inspired many passages of the part-memoir, part-essay, not only about death but also about the unreliability of memories which can sometimes be generated by imagination, a topic Barnes had already tackled in the short story 'Tunnel' collected in *Cross Channel* as well as other novels and to which he returned in more detail in *The Sense of an Ending*. In his reply to Jonathan Barnes's email, the writer gave more information about his project: 'I am writing something which is going to begin with childhood memories and end (probably) in the neurophysiology of religious belief. How it will get from A to Z I'm not at present sure' (3.5). What he did not know yet was that he was going to include his brother's replies in his book. Two years later, on 21 May 2007, Barnes wrote to his brother:

> I didn't think or intend when I started asking you questions by e-mail that I would incorporate your replies in the way that I did. I thought I was just verifying info. But your replies were v[ery] pungent, and so it became a more immediate (as well as truthfully contradicting/misremembering) way to write part of the thing. (3.5)

The book (which refers to Jonathan Barnes as early as its third sentence: 'I asked my brother', 1) evolved as the writer incorporated comments by his brother (as well as his nieces and friends), insisting in particular on the discrepancies between their memories of family stories. In a deleted passage of the book, Barnes refers to his brother's own project of writing a memoir about their maternal grandparents: 'He told me that

---

[12] Barnes quoted this exchange in *Nothing to Be Frightened Of*: 'My brother doesn't remember that more than half a century ago he came second in a wheelbarrow race with Dion Shirer, and is therefore unable to confirm which of them was the barrow and which the trundler. Nor does he remember the unacceptable ham sandwiches on the journey to Switzerland' (37).

he had once intended to write some short passages of memoir about them, but had abandoned the project because he could no longer distinguish between memory and imagination' (3.5). This echoes Barnes's own misgivings about using autobiographical elements in fiction, which he voiced in another discarded passage from *Nothing to Be Frightened Of*: 'the danger in writing fiction when it is close to your own life is that the fictionalising obliterates the true memory' (3.5).

Barnes was well aware of his fictionalizing of his parents' life when he wrote the short story 'The Fruit Cage', first published in the *New Yorker* in 2002[13] and then collected in *The Lemon Table* in 2004 (175–99).[14] In this story, the fictional narrator (called Chris as in the partly autobiographical *Metroland*) asks his father: 'What would Mum do without you?', to which the father answers: 'Paddle her own canoe' (188), and later on, Chris's mother muses: 'I wish I'd paddled my own canoe' (189). Six years later in *Nothing to Be Frightened Of*, Barnes remembers a remark of his own mother: 'when I was an adolescent, she said, "If I had my time again, I'd paddle my own canoe"' (166). This echo is not fortuitous as in an earlier passage from *Nothing to Be Frightened Of*, Barnes confessed to his deliberate mixture of real facts and invention in 'The Fruit Cage':

> During my mother's widowhood, I wrote a short story set in the recognizable ground plan of my parents' bungalow (a 'superior chalet' in estate agents' terminology, I later discovered). I also used the basic ground plan of my parents' characters and modes of interaction. The elderly father (quiet, ironic) is having an affair with a doctor's widow in a neighbouring village; when the mother (sharp-tongued, irritating) finds out, she responds – or so we are invited to believe, though we may not be quite certain – by assaulting him with heavy French saucepans. The action – the suffering – is seen from their son's point of view. Though I based the story on a septuagenarian dégringolade I heard about elsewhere, which I then grafted on to my parents' home life, I didn't deceive myself about what I was up to. I was retrospectively – posthumously – giving my father a bit of fun, of extra life, of air, while exaggerating my mother into a demented criminality. And no, I don't think my father would have thanked me for this fictional gift. (162–3)

Barnes already had this story in mind in the late 1980s when his parents were still alive (his father died in 1992 and his mother in 1997) and he was thinking of a 'Passion in Old Age story/novel'. He wrote in his second notebook two pages of notes and an eleven-line opening which is a denser version of the third paragraph of twenty-eight lines of 'The Fruit Cage' (175–6), starting with 'I have known my parents all my life' (1.1.2).[15] The ending Barnes thought of in the late 1980s is also very close to the one in the 2002 short story:

---

[13] Julian Barnes, 'The Fruit Cage', *New Yorker*, 13 May 2002, 78–85.
[14] The page references are from *The Lemon Table*. The title of the short story in the first draft was 'Viable Options' and Barnes also thought of 'A Game of Billiards' (2.6.8).
[15] The opening in the notebook is the following: 'I have known my parents all my life. That may seem to be a statement of the obvious but it isn't. Known them, you see. Lived with them normally, as a child; left home without trauma; kept in touch; given them grandchildren; had responsible adult conversation with them about the realities of ageing; looked at sheltered-housing projects with

<u>End</u>: father is in hospital, brain-damaged, visited alternately by wife & mistress, each of whom he identifies to the nurses afterwards (or he says to narrator, You must go now, my wife's coming) as being his wife, & goes into the same spiel about their long years of happy marriage. (1.1.2)

In 'The Fruit Cage', the half-paralysed father is visited alternately by his wife and his mistress, and when each of them leaves, he says 'very clearly, to anyone who will listen, "My wife, you know. Many happy years"' (198–9). One may venture further and suggest echoes between the quiet father and irritating mother portrayed in 'The Fruit Cage' and *Nothing to Be Frightened Of*, and Paul's parents in *The Only Story*, the mother policing him, 'never stuck for a phrase' (10), the father 'milder, and less given to judgement' (11).

In an early draft of *Nothing to Be Frightened Of*, Barnes referred not only to his parents but also to a question raised by his wife relating to the structure of the book:

My wife asked me yesterday if my book had chapters. I was taken aback, as she rarely asks about my work in progress (she knows my retentive nature). 'No,' I replied, and as I did so I wonder if what she had really meant was, 'Does your book have an argument?' I hope it's more than rhythmical grumbling.[16] As with life, I can see a short way ahead but not a long way ahead. As with life, the book finds its own pace and seeming purpose, which may or may not be a good thing.[17] I always knew where it would start and how it would finish. Or at least, I always knew the last two words of the book. I'm sure you can guess them. (3.5)

In the first drafts, the book had indeed no divisions or gaps and in her comments on an early version, Hermione Lee recalls a conversation when Barnes was 'absolutely definite about having no breathing spaces at all'. Lee wrote that because the book was 'relentless and painful in some ways', she would welcome 'a few breath-drawing places' and the writer did include some blank spaces and dividing lines in the final text.[18]

It is maybe significant that Barnes should have deleted the passage above which included a reference to his wife as she rarely features in the book while the writer gives a number of autobiographical details about his family and offers quotes from his friends about death and religion. Except for a few passing references to 'my wife' (99,

---

them; even discussed their wills, and what they wanted doing with their ashes after cremation. <u>Known</u> them, you understand. And now this' (1.1.2).

[16] A decade after he wrote *The Waste Land*, T. S. Eliot dismissed it as 'just a piece of rhythmical grumbling.' T. S. Eliot, *The Waste Land. A Facsimile and Transcript of the Original Drafts Including the Annotations of Ezra Pound*, ed. Valerie Eliot (San Diego: A Harvest Book, Harcourt, 1971), epigraph.

[17] Barnes adopted a similar structure for his 2019 non-fiction book, *The Man in the Red Coat*. He remarked: 'the structure developed out of that of NTBFO – a kind of controlled wandering'. Private email correspondence with the author, 29 August 2019.

[18] In the e-book published by Borzoi Books for Knopf, chapter divisions have been introduced instead of less conspicuous separating lines and blanks: each chapter is numbered (amounting to a total of sixty-eight) and starts on a new page, which modifies the rhythm of the original, giving longer breathing spaces to the reader and the sense of a more systematic, rather than fluid, structure.

148, 167), one to 'P.' (103) – 'P.' is also the dedicatee of the book whereas she is fully named as 'Pat' in the dedication of Barnes's novels –, and a mention of her 'laconic approach to dream-narration' (147), Barnes's wife remains mainly in the shadows. Lee commented on this 'noticeable omission' on 14 January 2007:

> In all this I catch myself wondering, what about the fear of the death of the person you love? No connection or parallel? Is it never an equally strong obsession – what it will be like for them to die, what it will be like for you when they die, how much you fear this also? Only that it never seems to come up as a subject. Given that 'your wife' fleetingly enters into this autobiographical book (being wonderfully noncommittal on her dreams), it does repeatedly occur to me that you don't say anything about fearing HER death, or HER fear of death – seems odd that you cite yr friends so often, and talk about yr family so much, but don't cite the person closest to you. (3.5)

This omission was probably deliberate on the writer's part not only because Pat Kavanagh was 'a very private person' and 'hated seeing her name in print' (which is why Barnes does not use her name in *Levels of Life* either)[19] but also because her death before his seemed inconceivable to him. Her death was very sudden, a mere eight months after the publication of *Nothing to Be Frightened Of*, and as mentioned in *Levels of Life*, with only 'thirty-seven days from diagnosis to death' on 20 October 2008 (68). The third section of this later book, entitled 'The Loss of Depth', which Barnes signs off with the date of 20 October 2012, addresses some of the questions raised by Lee, focusing on the widower's grief, mourning, loneliness (or rather 'her-lessness', 113), anger and thoughts on suicide.

Here again, echoes between fiction and non-fiction across several decades can be perceived as nearly thirty years before, Barnes had already written about the grief of widowhood in *Flaubert's Parrot*, in which the narrator (like Barnes in 2008) is in his sixties when his wife dies. In *Levels of Life*, Barnes reproduced a passage from the chapter entitled 'Pure Story' in *Flaubert's Parrot*, which he read at his wife's funeral in October 2008 and which eerily anticipated his own feelings of grief (*Levels*, 114). Barnes commented: 'perhaps, rather than inventing the correct grief for my fictional character, I had merely been predicting my own probable feelings' (*Levels*, 115). He also wrote a short story about widowhood in the summer of 2007, 'Marriage Lines',[20] then collected in *Pulse* (120–7), in which the widowed narrator briefly sums up the manner of his wife's death: 'The sudden tiredness, the dizzy spells, the blood tests, the scans, hospital, more hospital, the hospice. The speed of it all, the process, the merciless tramp of events' (121). Referring to that short story, Barnes explained in an interview that the choice to write about a man who was suddenly widowed had been 'a purely technical decision':

---

[19] In Lawson, 'Mark Lawson'.
[20] The short story first appeared in *Granta* 100 (Winter 2007): 317–23.

I had a couple in mind and a Scottish island in mind[21] and I wanted to write about a separation and then almost casually I remember saying to myself: 'no, no, they don't get divorced. I think she dies.' And so I was writing imaginatively about grief.[22]

When *Pulse* came out in 2011, three years after the death of Barnes's wife, reviewers interpreted 'Marriage Lines' as 'a sort of elegy' even if the story had been written before her death. Barnes referred to this as 'a strange way of fiction becoming pseudo-true.'[23]

In 2010, the *New York Review of Books* asked Barnes to review two diaries of a first year of widowhood, Joyce Carol Oates's *A Widow's Story: A Memoir* and Joan Didion's *The Year of Magical Thinking*. The author said in an interview that he was 'very apprehensive about writing that review' and was not thinking of writing his own memoir at the time.[24] However, this piece, later collected in *Through the Window*,[25] allowed him to reflect on grief and mourning, without yet referring to his own bereavement, and several meditative passages and quotations in the review would later be included in the third section of *Levels of Life*. While writing this review and before starting on the grief section of *Levels of Life*, Barnes also kept a diary of his wife's last weeks and of his first years as a widower. He mentioned in an interview:

> There is a parallel to the grief section of *Levels of Life* which is an enormous diary that I kept throughout my wife's illness and in the months and immediate years thereafter, which is hundreds of thousands of words. And that was written in part for therapeutic reasons, I suppose, in part to get it down ... exactly as it happened in case I forgot. ... I wrote everything down and I didn't consult it at all when I wrote the grief section of *Levels of Life* because I wanted that to be the movement and process and unshiftingness of grief viewed from four years on.[26]

Barnes's perspective ('viewed from four years on') in the last section of *Levels of Life* (which is not a day-to-day diary) therefore greatly differs from that of Oates and Didion who published diaries which they started very soon after the death of their respective husbands. Didion's opening lines were jotted down a day or two after her husband died and, as noted by Barnes, 'she waited eight months before beginning to write' (*Through the Window*, 218), while Oates's diary is mainly from the earlier part of her widowhood: 'in a 415-page book, we find that by page 125 we have covered just a week of her widowhood, and by page 325 are still only at week eight' (218).

The question of the right distance from which to consider events (and the risk of losing perspective if you stand too close to the present) is at the heart of *Levels of Life*

---

[21] The unnamed Scottish island in the story is the island of Barra in the Outer Hebrides where Barnes and his wife went on vacation, visiting Sally Beauman and Alan Howard. Barnes sent emails to Beauman in July and August 2007 with queries about male and female Christian names on the island, details of clothing and the tradition of 'marriage by declaration' (3.4).
[22] In Lawson, 'Front Row'.
[23] Ibid.
[24] In Lawson, 'Front Row'.
[25] Barnes, 'For Sorrow', 10–14, reproduced in *Through the Window* as 'Regulating Sorrow' (215–27).
[26] In Lawson, 'Mark Lawson'.

whose three sections bear the titles 'The Sin of Height', 'On the Level' and 'The Loss of Depth', but it is also central to other books by Barnes. In *Nothing to Be Frightened Of*, the writer refers to the difficulty of seeing the people that are the closest to you – 'They may be so close as to be out of focus' (157) –, whereas in *Flaubert's Parrot*, Braithwaite has doubts about the benefits of looking at the past from too great a distance: 'As it [the past] recedes, does it come into focus? … I wonder' (100). In *The Sense of an Ending* and *The Only Story*, the elderly narrators reconsider events from their youth more than fifty years after they took place, and in *Levels of Life*, the narrator of the first section reflects on American astronauts' view of the Earth from 240,000 miles away in 1968 and comments: 'To look at ourselves from afar, to make the subjective suddenly objective: this gives us a psychic shock' (27). It would appear that the lapse of four years after the death of his wife was the right amount of time for Barnes to find the correct focal distance at which to consider his grief in *Levels of Life*.

Barnes's memoir differs not only in genre and temporal distance from those of Oates and Didion but also in content:

> Didion is essayistic and concise, seeking external points of comparison, trying to set her case in some wider context. Oates is novelistic and expansive, switching between first and third persons, seeking (not with unfailing success) to objectify herself as 'the widow' and though she occasionally reaches for the handholds of Pascal, Nietzsche, Emily Dickinson, Crashaw and William Carlos Williams, she is mainly focused on the dark interiors, the psycho-chaos of grief. (*Through the Window*, 218)

Unlike these two books, the concise grief section of *Levels of Life* is a meditation which examines different modalities of grief and mourning, gives examples of friends who have also been widowed, refers to Barnes's own evolution over the years (and in particular his new interest in opera) and mentions the more or less adequate reactions of friends. The book respects the privacy of Barnes's wife as no intimate detail about her or anecdote about their life together is given. Barnes noted in an interview: 'I don't go back into "This was how our life was together and then this dreadful thing happened." I start at the point at which grief starts, really, with tiny little bits of backtracking.'[27] In addition, her name is never used in the book, except on the blurb which features her photograph together with a short biographical presentation. This presentation ('Pat Kavanagh was born in South Africa and moved to London in 1964. She worked in advertising and then, for forty years, as a literary agent. She married Julian Barnes in 1970, and died in 2008.') may echo Braithwaite's own concise biography of his wife in *Flaubert's Parrot*: 'She was born in 1920, married in 1940, gave birth in 1942 and 1946, died in 1975' (162), an inadequate summing up of her life, which leads the narrator to begin a new paragraph with: 'I'll start again' (162). Barnes's awareness of the inadequacy of such informal presentations might have led him to favour a meditation on grief over a more personal and autobiographical recollection of moments shared with his wife.

---

[27] In Lawson, 'Mark Lawson'.

The privacy of Barnes's wife was thus preserved both in *Nothing to Be Frightened Of* and in *Levels of Life*, as was the identity of living friends in the former memoir since they were not named but only referred to through their initials[28] or such vague formulas as 'a friend' or the 'man I knew'. However, two passing references to an unnamed and un-initialed female friend in *Nothing to Be Frightened Of* (who might be two different persons or the same one) deserve special attention as the woman reappeared in fictional form ten years later in *The Only Story*.

3. Fictionalizing memory in *The Only Story*

In *Levels of Life*, Barnes wrote: 'Every love story is a potential grief story' (36–7, 67), a sentence which perfectly encapsulates his thirteenth novel *The Only Story*. Upon its publication, Barnes remarked: 'When you're writing about the emotional life, you're using what you've observed, what you've experienced, and what you've imagined, and you try to make them into the same paste.'[29] Such a subtle mixture is indeed to be found in *The Only Story* whose main plot was foreshadowed not only by the idea for a novel about a 'younger man/older woman relationship' in the early 1980s in the writer's first notebook (1.1.1) and by the relationship between Adrian and Veronica's mother in *The Sense of an Ending*[30] but also by the writer's memory of a friend of his. In *Nothing to Be Frightened Of*, Barnes writes: 'I once spent many years failing to save a friend from a long alcoholic decline. I watched her, from close at hand, lose her short-term memory, and then her long-term, and with them most of everything in between' (140–1). Just as Paul in *The Only Story* powerlessly observes his lover Susan Mcleod's memory getting poorer due to the effects of alcohol (142), persuading itself 'towards coherence only by fabulation' (143), Barnes painfully witnessed what he called after Durrell 'the mind's fall from grace', 'the loss of specific and general memories being patched over by absurd feats of fabulation' and the accompanying fall of 'those who knew and loved her' (*Nothing*, 141):

> We were trying to hold on to our memories of her – and thus, quite simply, to her – telling ourselves that 'she' was still there, clouded over but occasionally visible in sudden moments of truth and clarity. Protestingly, I would repeat, in an attempt to convince myself as much as those I was addressing, 'She's just the same underneath.'

---

[28] Barnes wrote in his notes: 'rule here is, the dead have earned their names, & involving those names keeps them as alive as they are ever going to be now. The living have not yet earned their names' (3.5).

[29] Hermione Lee, 'Julian Barnes in Conversation with Hermione Lee', 21 February 2018, Royal Institute, London.

[30] Barnes said in an interview about *The Only Story*: 'In part, this novel came out of *The Sense of an Ending*, in which there is a central relationship between a young man and a middle-aged woman, about which we are told nothing. We just have to intuit what it must have been like from the scantiest of evidence. Here [in *The Only Story*], we are told all, though this couple is different from that couple.' Cooke, 'Julian Barnes'. Another common point between the two books is the mysterious five hundred pounds Veronica's mother bequeaths the narrator (now in his sixties) in *The Sense of an Ending* – 'five hundred pounds seemed a very specific sum. Bigger than nothing, not as big as something' (63) – and the 'cheque for £500' Susan gives the youthful narrator in *The Only Story*: 'The sum seemed both very large and also meaningless' (48).

Later I realized that I had always been fooling myself, and the 'underneath' was being – had been – destroyed at the same rate as the visible surface. (*Nothing*, 141)

Ten years later, the fictional narrator of *The Only Story* addresses others in the same way when they see Susan drunk and is then faced with a similar realization:

when they saw her drunk, you'd say, 'But she's till the same underneath. She's still the same underneath.' How many times did you tell this to others, when the person you were actually addressing was yourself?

And then comes the day when you no longer believe such words. You no longer believe that she is still the same underneath. You believe that being 'not herself' is her new self. (144)[31]

One may wonder why, ten years after referring to someone he knew in *Nothing to Be Frightened Of*, Barnes felt impelled to transform her into a fictional character. One possible reason may be found in *Flaubert's Parrot* when the bereaved narrator (whose adulterous wife committed suicide) remarks: 'Books say: She did this because. Life says: She did this. Books are where things are explained to you; life is where things aren't' (168). In real life, Barnes felt powerless in front of his friend's decline; in the novel, the fictional character is just as confounded but the creation of a specific context for the story and the main character's reflections on the situation reported in first-person, second-person and third-person narration in different parts of the novel might be seen as tentative ways to complete the sentence 'She did this because'.

The shift from real life to fiction, from memoir to novel, can also induce a change of tone. When hospitalized, fictional Susan Mcleod echoes remarks that were uttered by an 'elderly and demented friend' of Barnes's when he visited her in hospital:

Then a nurse might walk past, and her mood change swiftly. 'Of course,' she would assure me, 'the maids here are frightfully good.' Sometimes I would let such remarks pass (for her sake, for my sake), sometimes (for her sake, for my sake) correct them. 'Actually, they're nurses.' My friend would give a cunning look expressing surprise at my naivety. 'Some of them are,' she conceded. 'But *most* of them are maids.' (*Nothing* 101)

… A nurse walks by.

'The maids here are frightfully good,' she says, giving a wave to the passing figure.

You think: What's the right tactic? Go along with it? Challenge it? You decided that you mustn't indulge her dream world.

---

[31] In a short non-fictional piece published in 2015, Barnes argued that such diseases as dementia or Alzheimer's are forms of '[a] death of the self which precedes the death of the body' and added: 'We sometimes tell one another, hopefully, consolingly, of someone close to us whose self is disappearing, "He's still there underneath." Mostly, this is wishful thinking: the self may be six feet under before the body is.' Julian Barnes, 'The Big Question: What's the Best Sense? Julian Barnes: A Sense of Self', *Intelligent Life*, July/August 2015, http://www.intelligentlifemagazine.com/intelligence/the-big-question/whats-the-best-sense. Accessed on 19 January 2019.

'They're not maids, Susan, they're nurses.' ...
'Some of them are,' she agrees. Then, disappointed with your lack of perspicacity, adds, 'But most of them are maids.' (*The Only Story*, 146–7)[32]

While these remarks may make the reader temporarily smile in *Nothing to Be Frightened Of*, a book which, for all its concern with death, is to some extent light-hearted and interspersed with humour, the tone greatly differs in *The Only Story* in which Susan's inexorable decline is raw and painful to read. The echoes between fiction and non-fiction as well as the differences in treatment thus point to the various trajectories an image, an idea or a piece of dialogue can take depending on the generic context in which it is placed.

Nothing to Be Frightened Of includes other seemingly anecdotal elements or subjects that later, consciously or unconsciously, found their way into future books. References to Shostakovich's approach to death in *Nothing to Be Frightened Of* may have been among the sparks which encouraged Barnes to write a biographical fiction about the Russian composer in *The Noise of Time*,[33] while the writer's interest in Jules Renard revealed in the memoir prompted him to write a review of Renard's *Nature Stories* in 2011[34] and to accept Riverrun's proposal to publish an English edition of a selection of the French writer's journals (expected in 2020).[35] As for the passing recollection, in *Nothing to Be Frightened Of*, of a schoolfriend named Alex Brilliant who committed suicide in his twenties, it went on to inspire in him a longer fictional development for his eleventh novel *The Sense of an Ending*.

---

[32] Real friend and fictional character also, respectively, tell Barnes and Paul: 'I do think you will be remembered as one of the worst criminals in history' (*Nothing*, 101); 'I do think ... you will be remembered as one of the greatest criminals in the history of the world' (*The Only Story*, 148), with 'the history of the world' maybe subconsciously echoing the title of Barnes's 1989 novel, thereby blurring further the lines between fiction and autobiography.

[33] Among other sparks were Barnes's own interest in Shostakovich since the mid-1960s and his reading of the controversial *Testimony: The Memoirs of Shostakovich* by Solomon Volkov, which the author alleged was based on conversations he had with the composer, a claim which was challenged by critics and historians. In a television review of Tony Palmer's biographical film *Stravinsky: Once at a Border* in 1982, Barnes referred to Shostakovich being forced to make a disparaging remark on Stravinsky and his genuine opinion that Stravinsky was 'the greatest composer of our century' – facts Barnes would include thirty-five years later in *The Noise of Time*. Julian Barnes, 'Television. Devilish Cunning', *Observer*, 18 April 1982, 40.

[34] Julian Barnes, 'Badger Claws', *London Review of Books* 33, no. 13 (30 June 2011): 23–4.

[35] In December 2007, Barnes referred to Renard's journal which he kept from 1887 to his death in 1910 and wrote: 'An excellent, if much shortened, edition came out in the US in 1964 (Braziller), so another publisher might think of making the book available in the UK in time for the anniversary of 2010.' This was not done. Julian Barnes, 'Christmas Books. Past, Present and Future', *Guardian Weekly*, 21 December 2007, 50.

12

The Sense of an Ending: Time in reverse

Julian Barnes's eleventh novel *The Sense of an Ending*, which won the Man Booker Prize in 2011, is the work of a mature and confident writer: the archives reveal that Barnes had a fairly precise idea of where he was heading from an early stage and that the novel required fewer revisions than earlier books (apart from the crucial severance of links with his first novel *Metroland*). He explained in an interview that he had a clear sense of the structure of the book from the start:

> I thought in advance that the set-up would take one third of the book and the pay-off two thirds, and that the whole would be about a hundred and thirty pages. The set-up ended up being longer than planned. The set-up is done with the pace, or rather the anti-pace of memory, and the pay-off is done in real time. The weight of each part is an intellectual decision you take from the beginning.[1]

Barnes wrote down in a green notebook five pages of detailed notes and questions to himself about the plot and its developments, which touch upon all the main elements of the novel (3.4).[2] He then wrote the first draft by hand, in pencil and in single spacing in a blue notebook, on which he added corrections in black pen (3.3). The forty-eight handwritten pages of the novel on the right-hand side of the notebook (the equivalent of 120 typed pages) were complemented by additions and corrections on the left-hand side. Barnes then produced a first typescript which he revised with corrections by hand. The examination of the genesis of this novel reveals that it found its origin in the recollection of two boys Barnes knew at school and started with echoes of *Metroland*, published some thirty years earlier.

---

[1] Interview by Lee, 'An Evening with Julian Barnes'.
[2] This green notebook (3.4) mainly contains notes about the short stories which would be included in *Pulse* (published in the same year as *The Sense of an Ending*) as well as notes on books Barnes read. Only five pages concern *The Sense of an Ending*.

1. Prequels in real life

In *The Sense of an Ending*, the fictional character of Adrian Finn whom his friends at school hold in high esteem was inspired by two boys Barnes knew at the City of London School, which he attended in 1957–64 from New 2A to the Modern Sixth and which served as a model for the school in both *Metroland* and *The Sense of an Ending*. One of them was called Adrian Thorne and arrived at the school in sixth form. When the book was published, Adrian Thorne's son told his father, a musician, that he was in the book and Adrian Thorne contacted Barnes and suggested they meet.[3] When they did, he told the novelist his entire life story which had not turned out as he had planned.[4] In an early draft, the first sentence was 'His name was Adrian Thorne' (3.3) but Barnes noted: 'I knew it wasn't going to be the first sentence as Adrian Thorne was the name of a boy I was at school with.'[5]

The second source of inspiration was a boy called Alex Brilliant. In the green notebook in which Barnes took early notes for *The Sense of an Ending*, a first version of the incipit is preceded by the words 'Alex B.' (3.4). Barnes mentions this gifted boy in a 2007 non-fictional text entitled 'I Remember', a pastiche of and homage to Georges Perec's 1978 pointillist autobiography *I Remember*. In the course of forty-two short statements starting with 'I remember' or 'I don't remember', Barnes conjures up memories of deaths and funerals of family and friends. The eleventh item reads:

> I remember my schoolfriend Alex Brilliant, who was much better than me at English, whom I lost touch with after he went to Cambridge, and whose parallel existence, presumably in one of the liberal professions, I occasionally went on imagining for the next twenty-five years. I remember not knowing how to think about the matter when I learnt that he had killed himself almost half a lifetime back.[6]

Barnes also evokes the memory of this young man in the first pages of *Nothing to Be Frightened Of*:

> Alex Brilliant. The son of a tobacconist, Alex was reading Wittgenstein at sixteen, and writing poetry which pulsed with ambiguities – double, triple, quadruple, like heart bypasses. He was better than me at English, and took a scholarship to Cambridge, after which I lost sight of him. Down the years I would occasionally imagine his presumed success in one of the liberal professions. I was over fifty when I learnt that such biography-giving was an idle fantasy. Alex had killed himself – with pills, over a woman – in his late twenties, half my life ago. (13)[7]

---

[3] Annotations, 22–27 March 2018.
[4] Private email correspondence with the author, 27 April 2012.
[5] Interview by Lee, 'An Evening with Julian Barnes'.
[6] Barnes, 'I Remember', 56.
[7] Later in the book, Barnes refers to Alex Brilliant again when remembering that their English master had already scripted his last word which would be simply 'Damn!' and that he and Brilliant were determined not to live their own lives so they would come 'to the same verbal conclusion'. Barnes

In *The Sense of an Ending*, the fictional teenager named Adrian Finn (who later wins a scholarship to Cambridge) prefers Camus and Nietzsche while his friend Alex is the one who reads Wittgenstein but is dislodged from his position as the philosopher of the group by the arrival of Adrian (9). After the latter dies, his friends realize they never knew what his father did (53), although in the first draft, he 'ran a chemist's shop' (3.3). The manner of death also differs for the real and the fictional students as Adrian in *The Sense of an Ending* dies not 'with pills' but in the Roman way, cutting his wrists in the bath (48), a method Barnes sadly envisaged for himself after the death of his wife as he recalls in *Levels of Life*: 'I knew soon enough my preferred method – a hot bath, a glass of wine next to the taps, and an exceptionally sharp Japanese carving knife' (80).

In December 2006, Barnes published a slightly condensed version of the first fifteen pages of *Nothing to Be Frightened Of* in the *New Yorker* in a piece entitled 'The Past Conditional', with a notable difference in the reference to Alex Brilliant as the cause of his death was said to be unknown: 'Brilliant had killed himself in his twenties, for no reason my informant could determine.'[8] Barnes was able to provide a specific reason in the completed book because a fact checker at the *New Yorker*, Mike Peed, had done some research after finding that the young man's death had been registered in the spring of 1973.[9] He learnt that Brilliant graduated from Selwyn College, Cambridge (where he studied English) in 1967, having come up in 1964 with a scholarship from the City of London School, and then went to York University to do a PhD. Peed's informant Antoni Marianski added: 'He did commit suicide while there, i.e. as a young adult. It was over a girl. Pills were involved' (3.5). Unlike Tony Webster in *The Sense of an Ending*, Barnes only learnt about Brilliant's death several decades later and it would take two more decades before he turned him into a fictional character in his eleventh novel.

Another echo between *Nothing to Be Frightened Of* and *The Sense of an Ending* which points to the intertwining of memories and fiction, and the brooding or slow burning of ideas, concerns the young English master at the school Barnes and Brilliant attended. This teacher (unnamed in *Nothing to Be Frightened Of*) quoted to his pupils Eliot's 'bleak summary of human life: birth, and copulation, and death' (*Nothing* 17), just like his fictional counterpart Phil Dixon in *The Sense of an Ending* (6), but only the non-fictional book reveals that this zestful English master, like Alex Brilliant, later killed himself 'in a pills-and-drink suicide pact with his wife' (*Nothing* 17). Barnes also refers to him in the non-fictional text 'I Remember', just after reminiscing about Alex Brilliant: 'I remember Christopher J Dixon, the English master who taught us both and left to take up a post at Eton, and who killed himself there in a drink-and-pills pact with his wife.'[10] In *The Sense of an Ending*, the narrator recalls how Phil Dixon, when the class was discussing Ted Hughes's poetry, murmured: 'Of course, we're all wondering

---

adds: 'I hope that Alex had forgotten this by the time he was killing himself, with pills, over a woman, a decade or so later' (170).
[8] Barnes, 'The Past Conditional', 64.
[9] Five months later on 1 May 2007, Barnes's research assistant, Sumaya Partner, wrote that she found 'an Alexander Neil Brilliant whose death was registered in Derby between April–June 1973. He was born in Paddington on 30 August 1945' (3.5).
[10] Barnes, 'I Remember', 56.

what will happen when he runs out of animals' (6), and at the beginning of the second part, notes: 'I occasionally remember Ted Hughes and smile at the fact that, actually, he never did run out of animals' (61). This was an authentic statement by Barnes's English master Christopher Dixon as the novelist noted in his 1987 review of Philip Roth's *The Counterlife*: 'I remember my English master, twenty-five years ago, asking our class provokingly, "But what happens when Ted Hughes runs out of animals?"'[11] These echoes not only indicate that Christopher Dixon left a lasting impression on Barnes but also that some specific incidents or phrases remained lodged in the novelist's mind for several decades before the appropriate fictional context for their use presented itself.[12]

Another tragic episode from Barnes's youth – a teenager's suicide – became fictional material in both *Metroland* and *The Sense of an Ending*. The first paragraph of the chapter entitled 'Big D' in Part One of *Metroland* mentions Lucas, a schoolboy who was 'found one morning by his mother, gassed' (53), which leads the 16-year-old narrator to comment: 'we were more interested in the rumours than in the fact of his death. A girl friend? The family way? Unable to face parents?' (53). This passing reference led to a longer development in the report of a teenager's suicide in *The Sense of an Ending*, which drew the attention of his schoolfriends because of the rumours around it: 'a few days later rumour … supplied what the authorities couldn't, or wouldn't. Robson had got his girlfriend pregnant, hanged himself in the attic, and not been found for two days' (13); 'according to rumour', 'Robson of the Science Sixth' (12) left a disappointing suicide note. While the passing mention of Lucas's death in *Metroland* is the spark which leads Chris to muse about his 'fear of Big D' (53), three decades later in *The Sense of an Ending*, Robson's suicide is discussed at length from a philosophical point of view by Tony Webster and his teenage friends who declare that '[h]is action had been unphilosophical, self-indulgent and inartistic: in other words, wrong' (15), a conclusion that was to be reconsidered several years later when Adrian Finn killed himself.

These two fictional accounts of a teenager's suicide found their origin in a similar development which occurred when Barnes was in secondary school. In the annotated copy of *Metroland*, Barnes wrote in 2012: 'There was one such boy, named ----, who was in the same rugby team as me for several years. (Morgan Library 53). The writer also referred to him in the non-fictional piece 'I Remember': 'I remember two members of the school rugby team I played in dying while still in the sixth form, one in a car accident, one supposedly by his own hand after getting a girl pregnant; both of them were called Smith.'[13] The six-formers named Smith in real life, Lucas in *Metroland* and Robson in *The Sense of an Ending*, met in the early 1960s, remembered or reinvented in

---

[11] Barnes, 'Philip Roth in Israel', 3. The novelist also recalled the anecdote in an interview in 2000 and concluded like his fictional narrator: 'of course Ted Hughes never did run out of animals'. Interview by Guppy, *Conversations*, ed. Guignery and Roberts, 73.

[12] The name of another teacher from the City of London School (who never taught Barnes) is used in *Talking It Over*, that of Vokins who was Stuart and Oliver's form-master in 5A (14, 18). In a letter of 15 January 1993 to Mr Vokins (known as Biff Vokins), Barnes wrote that 'there was nothing sinister or hidden' in his use of the name: 'I think I did it because it is a wonderfully schoolmasterly schoolmaster's name.' Todd, 'Endings and Beginnings', 9.

[13] Barnes, 'I Remember', 55.

the 1970s and 2000s, reveal by their presence in several fictional and non-fictional texts that their self-destructive act remained vivid in the writer's mind for several decades.

Overlappings between real life and fiction also bring Barnes and the narrator of *The Sense of an Ending* closer. In a deleted draft of *Nothing to Be Frightened Of*, Barnes refers to his student years in Oxford and to his 'bookshelf which, as a fellow student who called round observed in amazement, "has more blue Penguins than orange ones". (Blue Penguins were Pelicans – brainy non-fiction – while orange was for fiction. I did not confess that I often struggled with the blue ones.)' (3.5). In *The Sense of an Ending*, the narrator Tony Webster likewise mentions the right balance of his bookshelves: 'In those days, paperbacks came in their traditional liveries: orange Penguins for fiction, blue Pelicans for nonfiction. To have more blue than orange on your shelf was proof of seriousness. And overall, I had enough of the right titles' (23–4). These common points between Barnes's early life and his characters' trajectories may indicate part of the origin of *The Sense of an Ending* but the writer also said that the novel really came out of *Nothing to Be Frightened Of* and the discussions he was having with his brother about the fallibility of memory, a central theme in the novel.[14] In addition, some of the characters in *The Sense of Ending* had a fictional origin as in the first drafts they were called by the same names as the characters in Barnes's first novel, *Metroland*.

2. A sequel to *Metroland*?

In early notes for *The Sense of an Ending*, Barnes wrote: 'perhaps revive the M/Land b[ack]/g[round] & reuse', and he asked himself: 'Are you going to base it on M/land, or somewhere else?' (3.4). And indeed, in the first drafts, the writer included details, anecdotes and almost exact quotes from *Metroland*. In the early notes, in the first draft in longhand and in the first typescript, the narrator was called Christopher Lloyd (rather than Tony Webster in the book) and his friends were Adrian, Alex and Toni Barbarowski as in *Metroland* (Toni became Colin Simpson in the published book while Alex kept his name, maybe as an indirect nod to the real Alex Brilliant).[15] As in the third part of *Metroland*, in the first draft of *The Sense of an Ending*, the narrator's ex-wife was called Marion (then turned into Margaret) and his daughter Amy (then renamed Susie) while he himself first worked for Ewart Porter, the advertising agency referred to in *Metroland* (139),[16] and then for Harlow Tewson (also in *Metroland*, 139) – in the published book, Tony simply works in arts administration (54).[17]

In addition to names and occupations, the first drafts contain direct echoes of conversations and reflections from *Metroland*, which were later deleted. For instance,

---

[14] In Lawson, 'Mark Lawson'.
[15] In the notes of the green notebook, Barnes listed the '4 friends' he wanted to write about and named them: 'me / Alex / Toni / Adrian Thorne'; on the next page, he wrote: 'Just call them Alex, Toni, Adrian & Chris to be going in with' (3.4).
[16] In the annotated copy of *Metroland*, Barnes wrote that the company was 'named after two poets who had been copywriters – Garin Ewart, & my friend Peter Porter' (Morgan Library 139).
[17] In the early notes in the green notebook, Barnes had thought of the narrator as 'an easily reachable (because known) person – is he not a writer – perhaps an academic on telly sometimes, w[ith] website?' (3.4).

the narrator remembers a conversation he had had with Marion (later Margaret) about the 'perfect age' to which one aspires and how, at that time, he had longed to be 'a sprightly sixty-five' when it would be 'all country walks & muffins by the fire and reading Peacock', a discussion which appears in *Metroland* (114). The narrator also refers to an old project of his of writing 'a kind of social history of travel around London', mentioned in *Metroland* (153), which, in the book, was replaced by the vague term 'projects' (55). Still in the first draft, the narrator recalls his wife's one-night stand (Marion confesses it in *Metroland*, 163) and notes that he used to make lists when he was younger (i.e. when Chris was in his early thirties in *Metroland*, 133), especially a list of the reasons why he loved his wife (in *Metroland*, 140–1), one of them being that 'there would be compensations, even to falling out of love with her' (3.3), an echo of *Metroland*'s characterization of Marion as 'a person with whom even falling out of love would have its compensations' (141).

When the narrator of *The Sense of an Ending* remembers how his teenage mind would 'make itself drunk with images of adventurousness' (93), the book remains vague about those images while the first draft referred to a vision, taken from Russian fiction, 'of driving a sled through a snowy birch wood and heroically escaping from a murderous pack of pursuing wolves', leading to the narrator's comment: 'I thought that adulthood must contain some version of this' (3.3). The same image appeared in *Metroland* (174) but was debunked by the pragmatic lawn-mowing 30-year-old narrator: 'As for that sled-and-wolves stuff: there isn't any evidence of a wolf ever killing a man, anywhere. Fancy metaphors can't all be trusted' (174). The first draft of *The Sense of an Ending* repeated the same words to demystify the sled-and-wolves image – adding 'Instead, I mowed my lawn, I had my life' (3.3) – but it also went one step further as the retired narrator admitted to having been wrong about the wolves when he was in his thirties: 'It was quite common for packs of hungry wolves to hunt and kill human beings. So driving that sled would have had an extra exhilaration. And later – provided that you escaped the wolves, that is – there would be less remorse about the unlived life, the paths not taken' (3.3). The draft therefore added another layer of awareness on the part of the narrator now in his sixties and although the specific image was cut, the final version retained the idea of adults being 'cowardly' and replaced the concrete example of the wolves by a more philosophical statement: 'What we called realism turned out to be a way of avoiding things rather than facing them' (93).

In the first draft, the narrator also refers to Uncle Arthur (a colourful character in *Metroland*) and to the 'pilot study of lying', called the 'Mendacity Curve', which he devised with Toni and according to which lying peaks at the ages of 16 and 60, a theory referred to in *Metroland* (47) in which Chapter Seven is entitled 'Mendacity Curves'. The theory is much more developed in the first draft of *The Sense of an Ending* (twenty-two lines against five in *Metroland*), with the narrator explaining the reasons why, as teenagers, he and his friends thought lying diminished after the age of 16,[18] and noting

---

[18] 'On our parts, we imagined that the constructions of bourgeois society – in other words, our parents – obliged us to lie in order to preserve our existential integrity, and that when we left home and were autonomous beings acting out of free will and – just as important – financially independent of our parents we would of course speak truth not only to power but to everything else from bus conductors to girlfriends' (3.3).

how he later realized 'the cleansing process never seemed to occur' and 'formulated a different theory instead: marriage moves you further away from the examination of truth, not nearer to it' (3.3).[19] He concludes with a readjustment of the lying theory:

> So now, if asked, I would say that our Mendacity Curve theory was almost exactly, diametrically wrong: that you probably tell most truth at 16 when you first begin to see life clearly, and have yet to make compromises with it; and then later at 60 or so, when your investment in the world is inevitably in decline, and there are fewer professional and social consequences at speaking your mind. (3.3)

Next to this paragraph, Barnes wrote 'cut' in the margin and later on, he deleted the whole passage, but as with the metaphor of the wolves, this example shows that *The Sense of an Ending* added a third stage to the narrator's reflections as it gave access to his thoughts as a retired man in his sixties, which contradicted his theories as a teenager (when he was 16 in the first part of *Metroland*) and as a young adult (when he was 30 in the third part of *Metroland*). Barnes himself was 34 when he published his first novel and 65 when *The Sense of an Ending* appeared.

As Barnes moved on in his writing and revising of the later novel, he became aware of the risk of inconsistencies if the book was to take up the same characters as in *Metroland*, particularly in relation to the narrator's sex life. Early in the handwritten draft of Part II, he wrote in the margin:

> If you're going to make it fit in entirely w[ith] m/land, then need to change who he first goes to bed with?
> Also how that he is remeeting Marion before they marry – V.[eronica] in between Paris (yes, it wd be, he at univ. where is M[arion] at this time?) (3.3)

In *Metroland*, Chris loses his virginity to Annick in Paris in 1968[20] and meets his future wife Marion in the same city shortly afterwards. In *The Sense of an Ending*, Tony's first 'proper girlfriend' (69) is Veronica with whom he goes out for about a year, followed by Annie in the United States (46) and then Margaret (called Marion in the first draft) whom he marries. The first draft does not include a passage, later added, which clarifies that the narrator did not lose his virginity with Veronica – 'I wasn't exactly a virgin …. Between school and university I had a couple of instructive episodes' (23) – which could thus account for his relationship with Annick in Paris in 1968. And indeed, later on, the draft makes the chronology of the narrator's girlfriends clear: 'I had three main relationships in my life – with Annick in Paris, with Veronica in Bristol (not to mention Chislehurst) and with Marion [later Margaret] in the suburbs of London' (3.3) – a passage then deleted. The first draft also includes a passage (cut later on) in which the narrator remembers his time in Paris with Marion who was to become his

---

[19] This last sentence in the form of a maxim appears at the end of the first chapter of Part Three in *Metroland* (141).
[20] In the annotated copy of *Metroland*, Barnes circled the name 'Annick' and wrote: 'I knew a young woman with this name, a schoolteacher in Brittany … but there all similarity alas ends' (Morgan Library 83).

wife: 'We had been having a sandwich lunch at a little café-restaurant in Paris. The nearest metro station, I remember, was called Filles du Calvaire. ... That day – our third or fourth meeting – I remember noting how she must have washed her hair that morning; she had a pinky-brown dress on, which went with her fresh, pinkish complexion and brown freckles' (3.3). This echoes a passage in *Metroland* about Chris and Marion meeting 'at a little café-restaurant called Le Petit Coq near République (Métro: Filles du Calvaire)' (112), the conversation they have over their 'third or fourth lunch' and his noting 'her boyishly cropped hair newly washed, and a pinky-brown dress' (113). In a later draft of *The Sense of an Ending*, the Paris episode was deleted and Tony merely notes that Margaret, now in her sixties, is no longer wearing the 'peasanty frocks she used to wear' (73) while some of her freckles are 'now closer to liver spots' (74).

When Barnes moved from handwritten draft to typescript, he was still conscious of possible inconsistencies, as evidenced by his comment in the margin next to the paragraph relating the narrator's time in the United States: 'but, again, this isn't Chris's m/land life post univ?' – there is indeed no mention of a trip to North America in *Metroland* – and then 'Do you, perhaps, simply change all the names?' Barnes therefore wondered whether he should really envisage *The Sense of an Ending* as a 'sequel' to *Metroland* or make it independent from the earlier novel, and he wrote down a 'Pro change' column and a 'Pro – stet' column in his blue notebook. The first column included the following arguments:

> Pro change
> 1) Hark back / 'sequel'; better stand alone
> 2) Sexlife now doesn't match: Annick was first --- easy to take her out
> Now you have a) girl pre-uni
>   b) v[eronica] gives in
>   c) girl during finals year
> 3) Easy to change names & markers
> So change e.g. Marion's name / backstory
> but use same character
> 4) Don't have to worry about e.g. Toni's subsequent history in M/Land (3.3)

The column in favour of keeping the novel as it was in the first draft included fewer arguments:

> Pro – stet
> 1) Useful to have Marion / school / life in place – & theme of M/land – ending in compromises / disappointment as backstory
> 2) The Chris/Marion relationship is strong/useful + This is how you've written it (3.3)

Barnes even imagined a 'semi-change?' which, however, did not pass muster:

> e.g. Chris not central, but one of the 3/4

Alex or Toni the narrator
But Marion in place (3.3)

The writer eventually decided to let go of the *Metroland* references and therefore of the characters and echoes. He wrote down: 'All the M/land stuff is of secondary importance to the story' and made a list of what should be deleted and what should be kept:

	So take out M/land stuff like?
keep	Marion's affair (but useful for his withholding)
lose	Mendacity Curve
lose	Wolves myth
lose	Perfect Age
lose, have another woman/girl	Annick, Paris
change/keep	Marion physically (3.3)

The mention of Marion's affair was eventually deleted, as were the 'Mendacity Curve', the 'Wolves myth' and the 'Perfect Age' developments, while the French Annick became the American Annie. What is not mentioned in the list above is that Barnes kept a reference to an episode from *Metroland* when 30-year-old Chris goes to a party by himself and flirts with a girl but declines her blunt invitation to go and have sex because he is married (154). In *The Sense of an Ending*, Tony remembers a party in the early years of his marriage to Margaret, to which he went alone and where he 'flirted with a girl', insisting it was 'way below even infra-sex', but adding also that he 'put a lid on it as soon as [he] sobered up' (118).

Barnes's suppression of most echoes with *Metroland* freed him from the constraints of plot and character consistency and enabled him to invent more freely in this darker novel whose original title was *Unrest* and whose incipit exists in several versions.

3. Getting started: The title and the incipit

The title *Unrest* appears in the early green notebook (3.4) as well as in the first handwritten draft (and the first typescript), where it was changed in pen to 'The Sense of an Ending', but this second title was also crossed out (3.3). After the end of the first full draft in longhand, Barnes wrote four possible titles, of which the first three were crossed out and the fourth deemed inadequate:

~~Unrest~~
~~The Sense of an Ending~~
~~The Colour of their Eyes~~
The River Tide – no – sounds like the name of the river (3.3)

The word 'unrest' – or the alternative the narrator refers to as 'Unrest v. Great Unrest' (10) – is central to the book and in the first draft, the phrases 'There was unrest' and 'there was great unrest' to describe Henry VIII's reign were uttered by Adrian (rather than by another schoolboy named Marshall in the published book, 5), while Adrian's suggestion of 'something happened' (5) to refer to any historical event did not appear in the original draft. Barnes said in an interview that he borrowed the 'rest/unrest' phrases from a schoolboy he met when teaching in Lawrence Beesley's crammer at the age of 18:[21]

> I once taught at a crammer between school and university, and there was a boy called Marshall who, whenever he wrote an essay about history, would start with 'There was unrest'. And when he was confident that there were wars or revolutions of other violent events going on in the period he was being asked to write about, he would begin his essay with: 'There was great unrest'.[22]

In the novel, the historical context is then displaced to a personal one, that of the narrator's own state of mind. In Barnes's first notes about the book (3.4), next to a reference to the narrator's girlfriend, the following sentence appears: 'when friends ask how it's going, he says "There is unrest"', a line which made it neither to the first full draft nor to the final book. The novelist also reflects about the distribution of rest and great unrest in the two parts of the novel: '1) Unrest – mainly then 2) Great Unrest – mainly now' (3.4). In the same green notebook, he writes about the narrator being shown his own letter forty years later and told of Adrian's diary, and adds: 'What it all leaves [Tony] in is a state of <u>un</u>rest, great <u>un</u>rest. You hope at the end of life, to have rest' (3.4). A similar version of this fragment appears in Barnes's notes when he starts thinking about the beginning of Part Two: 'Opening – towards the end of life, you expect rest. You think you deserve it. You get unrest, sometimes great unrest' (3.4), but he only kept the first two sentences in the published novel – 'Later on in life, you expect a bit of rest, don't you? You think you deserve it' (59) – maybe because he no longer needed to echo the title of the novel which had, by then, been changed to *The Sense of an Ending*.

Finally, the first full draft in longhand ends with two isolated sentences – 'There is unrest. There is great unrest' (3.3) – which also appear on the first page of notes in the green notebook after the words 'Last line:' (3.4), thus suggesting that the novelist had decided very early on to end the novel with these two powerful sentences. However, the published version is more developed as it doubles the anaphora of 'There is' by concluding the novel with a single paragraph of four balanced (and accumulating) sentences: 'There is accumulation. There is responsibility. And beyond these, there is unrest. There is great unrest' (150). This final version deliberately complicates the message by repeating words which appear in Adrian's diary (85–6) and on which the narrator regularly reflects, eventually understanding the accumulation of 'the integers b, a^1, a^2, s, v' (baby, Adrian, Anthony, Sarah, Veronica) and 'the chain of responsibility' of which he is part (149) – which all resulted in great unrest. The fact that *Unrest* was not retained as a title for the book might explain why Barnes gave the word slightly

---

[21] Barnes refers to his time in this crammer in the first of the 'Three Simple Stories' in *A History of the World in 10½ Chapters* (171). See p. 138.
[22] Interview by Lee, 'An Evening with Julian Barnes'.

less prominence within the final text even if its positioning at the closure of the book testifies to its centrality.[23]

While the last words of the novel were only slightly modified, the incipit exists in three main different versions (3.3), to which one should add a first attempt at an incipit in the early notes of the green notebook (3.4). This notebook mainly contains notes in longhand on the future novel, but on the second page, Barnes wrote 'Short novel' at the top and then drafted an incipit which was later discarded and is here transcribed in full:

> You have to understand that all this was/happened a long time ago. At the other end of my life. Or, to put it more exactly, at a distance from my birth which is about the same as the distance now to my probable death. What does that mean, you may reasonably ask. Well, it started when I was about fifteen and I am now 65, and expect to live – this is a calculation based on the death years of my immediate male ancestors – at around the age of 80.
>
> Why not say that more simply, you may – again reasonably – ask? Because … well, because each of us has only one way of telling a story, and this happens to be mine. And I am trying to give you precision, something I never had at the time.
>
> And though I start with the element of time, there is also the nature of time to be factored in. The physicists have many confusing/erudite things to say about time, but even the ordinary amateur – the person who lives inside time, as it were – knows that time does not unroll at a regular pace. Anyone who has been involved in a catastrophe knows that. Time – or our experience of time – slows down, speeds up, goes missing for a while, sometimes never to return.
>
> And history, which time controls, does the same. Occasionally it hurtles, often it stagnates and those who live in it are hard pressed to work out its natural pace. If, indeed, it has one.
>
> Let me try & give an example of that. (3.4)

Above this incipit, Barnes wrote 'Not like this – it's too Dowell – but use ideas' (3.4), a reference to the recognizable voice of the narrator John Dowell in Ford Madox Ford's *The Good Soldier* (1915), a book Barnes considers one of the greatest English novels of the twentieth century. According to Barnes, Dowell is 'the most perfectly deployed example of the unreliable narrator'[24] and the way he addresses the reader makes for 'the conversational talky and diversionary tone'[25] of Ford's novel which can also be perceived in this discarded incipit of *The Sense of an Ending*. In *The Good Soldier*, the bumbling narrator defers telling his story, 'goes backwards, forwards, sideways'[26] and

---

[23] Jonathan Coe noted in December 2013 that two of his novels (*The Rain Before It Falls* and *Expo 58*) and three of his short stories were part of a major literary project called *Unrest*, in which he aims to 'trace the history of a fictional middle-class Midlands family throughout the twentieth century'. Jonathan Coe, 'Author's Note', *Loggerheads and Other Stories* (London: Penguin ebook, 2014).

[24] Julian Barnes, 'The Saddest Story', *Guardian*, 7 June 2008, https://www.theguardian.com/books/2008/jun/07/fiction.julianbarnes. Accessed on 19 January 2019.

[25] Barnes, interview with Guignery, *Novelists in the New Millennium*, ed. Guignery, 21.

[26] Barnes, *Through the Window*, 48.

the detours taken by Barnes's narrator in the passage above resemble Dowell's own diversions. Barnes wrote that *The Good Soldier* proceeds 'by moments of disorienting readjustment, some sly and secretive, others dazzlingly brazen'[27] and the same might be said of *The Sense of an Ending*. Although Barnes did not retain the first two paragraphs of this first incipit which included precise details about the narrator's age and an insistent direct address to the reader, he kept the meditation on time and its irregular pace which can be found in the second paragraph of the published version: 'Some emotions speed it up, others slow it down; occasionally, it seems to go missing – until the eventual point when it really does go missing, never to return' (3). As for the deleted sentence 'each of us has only one way of telling a story, and this happens to be mine', it found a distant echo seven years later in the incipit of *The Only Story* in which a narrator in his seventies also tells a story that happened 'more than fifty years ago' (4). On the first page, he announces: 'Most of us have only one story to tell. ... This is mine' (3) and refers to all the retellings of that story over the years, thus suggesting that there is not only one way of telling a story, which is confirmed by the shift in the novel from first- to second- to third-person narration.

The incipit of the first full draft of *The Sense of an Ending* written by hand in the blue notebook differs not only from this early 'Fordian' attempt but also from the final published version. It includes neither the first paragraph of the published version which presents a list of watery elements the narrator remembers (1) – this would be added in longhand on the first typescript –, nor the memory of the teenagers' habit of wearing their watches with the face on the inside of the wrist (something Barnes himself used to do), 'next to where the pulse lies' (122), as a way of making time feel personal and secret (6, 25). Instead, the novel started in the following way:

> His name was Adrian Thorne.
> There were three of us, and he made the fourth. We didn't expect to add to our tight number. We didn't expect that anyone else would come along with a similar cast of mind.
> He arrived at the start of the second term: a tall, shy, nervous boy who looked at the lid of his desk unless obliged to answer a master's question. (3.3)

In *Metroland*, Thorne is the name of one of the former schoolfriends who does not come to the old boys' dinner in the third part ('Thorne had dropped out of sight', 169), and as mentioned earlier, Adrian Thorne was a boy who arrived into Barnes's sixth-form class at the City of London School and, because of that, 'was an outsider'.[28] In the first typescript, Adrian's family name was changed to 'Horne', and then in longhand to Webster (which was to become the narrator's family name).[29] Webster was also crossed

---

[27] Barnes, 'The Saddest Story'.
[28] Annotations, 22–27 March 2018.
[29] When Hermione Lee read the novel in the typescript and saw the names of Tony Webster and Veronica Ford, she commented: 'I wondered if Webster & Ford was a coincidence, or a deliberate literary ref to REVENGE TRAGEDY???)' (3.3) – an allusion to seventeenth-century playwrights John Webster and John Ford. Barnes confirmed it was a coincidence as he 'would never make that sort of literary reference'. Annotations, 22–27 March 2018.

out and replaced with Finn, an interesting echo of the French noun 'fin' which means 'ending', but actually inspired by the surname of British cricketer Steve Finn.[30]

The second sentence in the draft in longhand ('There were three of us, and he made the fourth') opens the third paragraph in the published book and the modified name of the character appears in the middle of that paragraph rather than at the beginning: 'His name was Adrian Finn' (4). While Adrian's joining the school in the autumn term is only referred to in the third paragraph of the novel, it was mentioned from the start in the draft and in a way which faintly echoed the incipit of Gustave Flaubert's *Madame Bovary*. In Flaubert's novel, the young Charles Bovary is said to be taller than any of the other boys in the class and looks uncomfortable, and in Barnes's draft Adrian is presented as 'a tall, shy, nervous boy who looked at the lid of his desk' (3.3). However, the British writer diverged from the potent French hypotext as, unlike Charles who suffers the sneers and jokes of the other schoolboys, Adrian is not put through any 'punitive induction' or 'welcoming ceremony' (4) and is barely noticed. In addition, Barnes later deleted the adjective 'nervous' which qualified the boy in the first full draft, thus making him less vulnerable than Charles Bovary.[31]

After the list of liquid elements remembered by the narrator, the second paragraph of the published book starts with 'We live in time' and includes a meditation on time's malleability. This paragraph did not appear on the first page of the handwritten draft but its first half (from 'We live in time' to 'it really does go missing, never to return', 3) was added at the top of the second page of the blue notebook, isolated from the rest of the page and followed by 'His name was Adrian Thorne', thus suggesting that this meditative paragraph on time was meant to be the revised incipit. However, Barnes recalls that he was unhappy with this beginning:

> I wanted the novel as a book with meditative passages on time and memory. I had first started with the second paragraph 'We live in time', and then I thought: 'Of course we bloody live in time!' These words would seem portentous if they came as the opening line of the book, so I switched the first two paragraphs round. When they start the second paragraph, they have less of a false impact.[32]

The second half of that paragraph in the published novel starts with 'I'm not very interested in my schooldays' (4) and introduces the narrator's memories of that period. It did not exist in the first draft which included instead a general development on history, which was close to the first attempt at an incipit in the green notebook quoted above:

> And history, which time appears to measure, does the same occasionally: it hurtles, often it stagnates; happiness & misery affect its speed, though rarely in the way

---

[30] Veronica's family name in the first typescript was Ward and not Ford. Lee asked Barnes if the name Ford was a deliberate homage to Ford Madox Ford, but the novelist said it was not. Interview by Lee, 'An Evening with Julian Barnes'.
[31] In a later draft, Adrian is presented as 'a tall, shy boy who initially kept his eyes down and his mind to himself' (3.3).
[32] Interview by Lee, 'An Evening with Julian Barnes'.

we hope. We are hard pressed to sense, let alone work out, time's natural pace. If indeed it has one. In our later years, we may look back & wonder if we have had too much history in our lives, or too little. No-one ever seems to think they have had the right amount. (3.3)

When Barnes moved from handwritten draft to typescript, he wrote in front of this paragraph that it should be used 'later (if at all)', probably because the shift from time to history in this philosophical disquisition came too early in the book. The passage was displaced (in the typescript but not in the last draft in which it does not appear) to the end of the first part when the narrator abruptly jumps forty years ahead, referring to his marriage, child, divorce and retirement within the length of a few paragraphs (54–6), an example of time hurtling or speeding up in the narrative.[33] Barnes commented upon this major leap: 'As a young writer, you have a great sense of nowness. As you get older, you allow yourself a bolder treatment of time, with such jump cuts.'[34] He compared this handling of time to the way Alice Munro or John Updike in his later stories give the sense of an entire life in a short space of time.

In the typescript, Tony, after mentioning that he is retired, adds that he still reads history but is 'only interested in history that happened before [he] was born' and wonders why that is (3.3). This remark was followed by a revised version of the paragraph above, emphasizing the impossibility to work out the speed of history ('whether it's hurtling, whether it's stagnating') while it is happening (hence the narrator's preference for past history). This passage was yet again rephrased as questions: 'But if we can't understand time, can't grasp its mysteries of pace & progress, how can we do the same with history? Let alone work out as they happen which are the important parts?' (3.3). Although the development was cut altogether, its re-positioning at the end of Part One in the typescript, after a prodigious temporal ellipsis and speeding up of a life story, granted it greater resonance.

It has been shown that the first handwritten full draft in the blue notebook started with 'His name was Adrian Thorne' followed by a description of the boy's arrival in school, but that this incipit was rapidly modified on the next page of the notebook so that the book would start with a philosophical discussion on time instead. When Barnes moved from handwritten draft to typescript, he tried another (later deleted) incipit:

My three schoolfriends all had brown eyes.

They didn't, of course, but that's how it seems to me now. And there is no corroboration of the contrary. All the photographic evidence that remains to me comes in black and white. And memory's default setting for eyes, I have discovered,

---

[33] A similar prodigious proleptic leap can be found at the end of the first part of *The Only Story* when the narrator, after recalling the first two years of his relationship with Susan for some eighty pages, condenses the next fifty years in a few sentences: 'We were together – under the same roof, that is – for ten or more years. Afterwards, I continued to see her regularly. In later years, less often. When she died, a few years ago, I acknowledged that the most vital part of my life had finally come to a close' (83).

[34] Interview by Lee, 'An Evening with Julian Barnes'.

is brown. At least, that's how it is for me. And my own eyes? They're also brown, as it happens. But at least, I've just verified this in the mirror, so you can believe me. (3.3)

This new attempt at an incipit is marked by a different tone which neither belongs to the narrative mode of the 'His name was Adrian Thorne' incipit nor to the reflexive mode of the meditation on time. Instead, this new incipit highlights the elusiveness of memory through the shift from the first unwavering assertion ('[they] all had') to its immediate negation ('They didn't'), and the focus on the fragility of the retrospective process ('how it seems to me now'). This paragraph also introduces a crucial word and concept early in the novel, that of 'corroboration', a word used thirteen times by the narrator in the book, either to deplore the lack of evidence and therefore the lessening of certainties about his past (pointing to the fallibility of memory) or to refer to snippets of unwelcome corroboration of who he was and how he behaved in his youth. Next to the passage where the retired Tony decides against contacting Alex and Colin to ask 'for their memories and their corroboration' (108), Barnes noted in the margin: 'EXPAND – it's a key contradiction in his "seeking corroboration" line' (3.3), and although he did not expand, this comment points to the centrality (and deceitfulness) of Tony's quest for corroboration, which explains why it appears so early in the new incipit.[35]

In that version, the focus on eye colour explains why one discarded title for the novel was 'The Colour of their Eyes'. Later in the novel, the eyes are presented by the narrator as an agent of permanence over time when he reflects on how people may change but their eyes remain the same (74). Thus, it will be in the gangly fellow's 'brown and gentle eyes' (136), 'their colour and expression' (137) that Tony will find the corroboration that he is Adrian's son. The emphasis on eye colour in the incipit recalls the heated discussion, in *Flaubert's Parrot*, about the uncertain (or inconsistent) colour of Emma Bovary's eyes in Flaubert's novel. Barnes's narrator, Geoffrey Braithwaite, also refers to his own eyes – 'you know I've got brown eyes; make of that what you will' (96) – and then immediately draws attention to the fact that he is 'honest', 'reliable' (97), 'aiming to tell the truth' (96). Braithwaite's appeals to the narratee echoes Tony Webster's concluding affirmation 'you can believe me' in the early draft of *The Sense of an Ending*, which paradoxically casts doubt on Tony's reliability as we may trust him on the colour of his eyes but not on his slippery memory. This incipit was cut, but in the second paragraph of the book, the narrator refers to the 'approximate memories which time has deformed into certainty' (4) and confesses that 'the best [he] can manage' is to 'be true to the impressions' past facts have left (4). The final version of the incipit (containing the list of liquid elements) appears for the first time in longhand on the typescript below the 'brown eyes' incipit, preceded by '<u>START</u>' in the margin, and places the process of recollection at the forefront through the opening words 'I remember' (3). As in the case of the wolves myth referred to earlier, Barnes did not

---

[35] In the third section of *Levels of Life*, Barnes returns to the theme of corroboration when referring to the greater uncertainty of memories when one member of a couple dies: '[the memory] can no longer be corroborated by the one who was there at the time' (109).

retain the detail or anecdote of the eyes, but he kept the main message it conveyed about memory.

The examination of the changes between the first drafts of the novel and the final version reveals that Barnes not only thoroughly revised the incipit, as well as cut echoes from *Metroland* or specific examples, but also deleted or greatly reduced philosophical or meditative passages.

4. A denser text

The archives for *The Sense of an Ending* show that the final version of the book includes fewer meditative or explanatory passages and is denser than the original versions. When asked about the slimness of the novel, Barnes explained that one reason for this was that the book has to do with holes in the narrator's memory and life that he cannot pin down, 'things that he doesn't know and can't find'. He also remarked that he is 'one of those writers who started off writing novels and came to writing short stories later' and that 'learning to write short stories ... made [him] attracted toward a paring down of the novel form', a tendency which can be noticed in later books, in particular *Levels of Life* and *The Noise of Time*.[36] When *The Only Story* was published (a book of 213 pages), Barnes remarked: 'maybe I'm compressing more as I'm getting older'.[37]

In the typescript of *The Sense of an Ending*, while Barnes added a few scenes about Adrian, as an answer to his self-recommendation: 'A bit <u>more</u> school stuff needed'; 'establish Adrian better', he removed some reflective passages, commenting next to a meditation on memory: 'Still too theoretical – let memory happen – then try & explain it?' (3.3). Among the passages which were slimmed down is one early on in the novel when Tony notes that as schoolboys, they 'waited to be released' into their lives, not realizing that their lives had already begun and that they would leave the holding pen they were kept in only to be released into 'a larger holding pen' (9). In the first draft, the meditation went on for longer in three successive paragraphs:

> However, being convinced that we weren't living but just existing, stuck in some kind of preliminary observation post, we observed. We judged. We pronounced. Our social sample was narrow/restricted, but this made judgment the easier.
>
> At that age, you believe most securely in the application of general ideas to life, in the notion that principles guide actions.[38] But when that illusory release [from the holding pen] occurs, you find that life doesn't merely speed up, but takes over. Life directs, and you accept its terms and conditions; ideas about life dwindle into a series of pragmatic decisions based on temperament. And since temperament is

---

[36] Jeffrey Brown, 'Conversation: Julian Barnes, Winner of the 2011 Man Booker Prize', PBS Newshour Art, 8 November 2011, https://www.pbs.org/newshour/arts/conversation-julian-barnes-winner-of-the-2011-man-booker-prize. Accessed on 19 January 2019.
[37] Interview by Lee, 'Julian Barnes'.
[38] Only this sentence was kept in the book to describe what Adrian encouraged his friends to do: 'Adrian, however, pushed us to believe in the application of thought to life, in the notion that principles should guide actions' (9).

given rather than self-created, the realization slowly comes that many things have already been decided [for you]. And then at the end you reach the place where I am now – the final holding pen, the one before the grave. Here, you find that life has slowed down again; also, that looking back you can now sometimes construe general ideas from your lived experience. But whether these late-arriving ideas are any better, any truer, than the ones you had when you were sixteen, whether deduction or induction is superior, remains debatable: who can say if our ideas are better or worse for a lifetime's experience? They ought to be, but there is little 'ought' in life.

[Of course, this is only how it has been for me. It might be different for you.] (3.3)

This meditative development may have been deleted because it shifted the perspective to that of the older narrator too early in the first part (which focuses on his life as a teenager and then a student) and for longer than the novelist probably wished for. The passage above draws attention to the fact that the narrator is elderly, having reached the 'final holding pen, the one before the grave' while the published book reveals the point at which the retrospective tale is told only in the last pages of Part One, when Tony writes that he is retired (55). The very last one-line paragraph was placed between square brackets before being deleted, maybe because it gave a visibility to the implied reader through the direct address – recalling a similar technique in *Flaubert's Parrot*, *Talking It Over* and *Love, etc* – while *The Sense of an Ending* more rarely involves the reader directly.[39] The whole passage above was kept in the first typescript but then deleted, and Barnes wrote after it ends: 'Hunt INSERT', and indeed the discussion in class with Joe Hunt about the origins of the First World War was added in place of the meditation above (10–12) – a passage which gives insight into Adrian's personality and introduces the crucial question of responsibility.

In the final history class with Joe Hunt, the schoolboys are asked to offer their own definitions of history, which Barnes had already written down in his first set of notes in the green notebook (3.4). Tony's hasty suggestion of 'the lies of the victors' (16) echoes Chris and Toni's own definition in *Metroland* ('The lays of the victors. Quite', 146), but the master of *The Sense of an Ending* pithily comments that it is also 'the self-delusions of the defeated' (16). Tony's friend Colin offers a provocative definition ('a raw onion sandwich .... It just repeats, sir. It burps', 16) which had already appeared in 'Parenthesis' of *A History of the World in 10½ Chapters*, a book which exposes the repetitions of historical tragedies and errors: 'History just burps, and we taste again that raw-onion sandwich it swallowed centuries ago' (241), but Barnes's notes reveal that he was well aware of that case of intratextuality as Colin was to add: 'I got it from a book, sir' (3.4), a remark which did not make it to the first draft however. The third more elaborate definition offered by Adrian ('History is that certainty produced at the point where the imperfections of memory meet the inadequacies of documentation',

---

[39] Tony nevertheless addresses the reader through a self-reflexive remark when he postpones revealing the content of Adrian's letter: 'You can probably guess that I'm putting off telling you the next bit' (40–1).

17) and attributed to the apocryphal French historian 'Patrick Lagrange' (the second given name of Barnes followed by the translation of his family name into French) originally appeared in his notes as 'History is where the unreliability of memory meets the unreliability of documentation'. Next to it, Barnes added 'epigraph? if too pretentious, give it to Adrian' (3.4), and indeed he opted for the lack of any epigraph and let the schoolboy expatiate on the clever formula.

The 'documentation' referred to in Adrian's definition can refer not only to historical sources but also, in the case of Tony's story, to Adrian's cryptic and partial diary (Barnes wrote in his notes that after Veronica says she burnt it, Tony could think: 'but w/out it, where is truth/certainty?', 3.4), as well as Tony's own spiteful letter to Adrian. Barnes described the letter in his early notes as 'another "document" that doesn't necessarily prove anything' (3.4), adding: 'the <u>documentation</u> must also be unreliable, e.g. Chris's letter – he <u>now</u> thinks he didn't mean it – he wrote what he thought Adrian/Alex needed/wanted him to say about her' (3.4). If the novel keeps the reader in the dark as to the exact chronology of events, some of Barnes's early notes were more explicit as he imagined that Adrian/Alex broke up with Veronica a few days after receiving the letter, which explains why she blames Chris (then renamed Tony) for what happened later: 'she finds the letter and then discovers Alex is sleeping w[ith] her mother' (3.4). The novel deliberately refrains from giving such precise details, thus complicating the narrator's and the reader's responses.

Among the deleted passages, Barnes cut a comic one which demonstrated the schoolboys' whimsical behaviour and probably belonged more to the tone of *Metroland* than to the later novel. The comic anecdote appears in the first typescript (but not in the handwritten draft) after the narrator provides a list of the serious authors and philosophers each teenager had read – Russell and Wittgenstein, Camus and Nietzsche, Orwell and Huxley, Baudelaire and Dostoevsky (9–10):

> One morning, at the top of the blackboard in the maths sixth form room, a line of chalked numbers appeared. The master inquired what they referred to. He was told how they represented a mathematical progression, and you had to work out the next number in the sequence. He spent some time on the problem, but without success. He was also surprised when boys from other classes came & copied down the numbers, seemingly eager to try the test themselves. It took a week before the master was tipped off and the numbers erased: they were a list of the page numbers in Lady Chatterley's Lover of greatest interest to adolescents. (3.3)

Barnes referred to this episode in his annotations on *Metroland* next to the passage in which the narrator remembers how he and his friends had 'pored over Lady C. and dreamed of breasts hanging down above [their] heads like bells, and raindrops glistening during atavistic entwinings' (98). In 2007, he wrote in the margin:

> When I was in the sixth form, Lady C was published in Penguin. The Maths sixth had on their blackboard for some days a succession of numbers which, the boys assured the master, were a mathematical progression: the problem was to work out

the next number in the sequence. In fact, they were the page numbers of the 'hot bits' in Lady C. (Morgan Library 98)

The passage in *The Sense of an Ending* was eventually cut, maybe because it shifted the topic to the boys' sexual needs at a time when the narrator was still discussing their intellectual pretentions.

A crucial memory of Tony's university years is that of the Severn Bore, the mysterious phenomenon of the tidal river rushing upstream. In the book, it is one of the items in the list that opens the novel (3) and it is described in detail after Tony and Veronica break up and before they sleep together (35–6). In the first draft, the passage occurred later, after the narrator receives Adrian's letter asking for his permission to go out with Veronica and Tony sends a postcard back (42). In this original version, the significance of the metaphor of the Severn surging upstream was made much more explicit for the reader as it appeared after a (later deleted) paragraph describing the narrator's psychological collapse – despite his 'instinct for survival, for self-preservation' (42) – and the way emotions came surging back, which led to his writing the shameful letter to Adrian:

> I think I underestimated the strain I was putting on myself. I worked ever longer hours, drank coffee late into the night, covered the walls of my room with notes, quotations, and key words written in capital letters. I dreamt about examinations, woke up muttering phrases I needed to remember, ate my meals with a book in front of me. I became desocialised, avoiding people with whom I had a perfectly normal, friendly relationship. But then I assumed they were doing the same as me, so perhaps they were avoiding me too. If I had been of a different temperament, I might have had a nervous ~~breakdown~~/collapse, or gone in for destructive behavior – self-destructive even. But as I say, I have an instinct for survival. However, after the exams were over, it was as if all the emotions I'd been holding back came swinging out. Have you ever seen footage of the Severn Bore? (3.3)

This early draft showed the narrator more emotionally devastated by the separation from Veronica and her taking up with Adrian than in the published book, thereby maybe offering a greater justification for his sending the angry letter to his friend. The parallel between his own reaction and the running upstream of the Severn was emphasized both before his description of the unsettling natural surge – 'it was as if all the emotions I'd been holding back came swinging out' – and after the detailed account of that 'mysterious, unfathomable, atavistic' phenomenon, through an explicit simile: 'Like some of those moments in the emotional life. And now what had been held back for several months came suddenly surging through my head' (3.3). In the first drafts, the reader was thus offered a fairly high level of guidance as to the interpretation of the Severn Bore metaphor while the published book demands a more active participation. In the typescript, Barnes wrote 'separate' in front of the passage about the river and indeed the description was moved seven pages earlier and disconnected from the return of Tony's strong emotions. In the margin of the typescript, in front of 'what had been held back for several months came suddenly surging through my head' – which was crossed out –, Barnes wrote a comment for himself: 'general dérèglement de tous les sens – & it includes writing letter' (3.3). The French expression is a quote from Arthur Rimbaud's notorious letter of 15 May 1871 addressed to his friend Paul Demeny, in which the 16-year-old poet defines his vision of poetic creativity: 'Le Poète se fait voyant par un long, immense et raisonné dérèglement de tous les sens.'[40] Applied to the narrator of *The Sense of an Ending*, the 'dérèglement de tous les sens' implied a release of violent emotions and therefore the writing of the infamous letter.

The first draft offered a much longer paraphrase of Tony's memory of his letter than the final version which sums up his remembrance of the content in just a few lines:

> As far as I remember, I told him pretty much what I thought of their joint moral scruples. I also advised him to be prudent, because in my opinion Veronica had suffered damage a long way back. Then I wished him good luck, burnt his letter in an empty grate … and decided that the two of them were now out of my life for ever. (42–3)

The early handwritten version (including corrections in pen) was much more detailed and gave an idea of the fierceness of the narrator's tone in the letter:

> I told him in simple terms that I quite understood that his letter was a joint one, from him & Veronica, and so he should consider that my reply was meant for both of them too, even if it was couched/addressed to him in the second person singular. I told him that he was overscrupulous in offering to reconsider his position, given that Veronica & I had broken up. So I had no power of veto over her actions, still less over his. I told him that she had doubtless given him her version of events, & that – since he must, as a trainee philosopher, be interested in truth – he deserved to hear my version too. I told him that – based admittedly only on my experience – Veronica was a cock teaser, also happy to be masturbated but reluctant to return the favour, who had only given it away in a final attempt to keep me; that she was someone who withheld her inner self from you and simultaneously manipulated you. I told him how she had singlehandedly disabused me of my naïve assumption that women could be wholly calculating; how even her own mother had warned me against her; how she was a snob, who would look down on him as much as she had on me and furthermore a quasi-psychopath insofar as she seemed unable or unwilling to imagine someone else's emotions. I concluded in a more measured tone that in my view – not that it in any way excused her actions, which I thought were fully preconceived – she had probably suffered damage a long way back, and it was this that made her a dangerous person to get involved with. And then I wished him luck, and told him to fuck off, and burnt his letter. (3.3)

---

[40] 'The Poet makes himself a seer by a long, gigantic and rational derangement of all the senses.' Arthur Rimbaud, *Complete Works, Selected Letters*, trans., intro. and notes by Wallace Fowlie (Chicago: University of Chicago Press, 1966), 307.

The great many details, the sense of accumulation conveyed by the anaphora of 'I told him' and the abrasive tone suggest that the narrator's memory of his feelings and of the letter was still fresh and stinging more than forty years after the event. If this long and detailed description had been kept, it might have been more difficult to insist on the fallibility of the narrator's memory. Later in the draft, when the narrator's letter is offered in full after Veronica gives him a copy (95–7), Barnes wrote in the margin: 'change/water down p.31 to make the impact here' (3.3) – 'p.31' being a reference to the early long paraphrase of the letter quoted above. Therefore, Barnes crossed out many passages in the typescript to slim down the references to the letter, but then commented in the margin: 'if this is no longer mad & violent, does the Bore image work?' (3.3). Indeed, as seen earlier, the aim was to provide a parallel between the river's counterintuitive movement upstream and the surging back of strong emotions. In the book, the interpretative key to the Severn Bore metaphor, instead of appearing early in the first part, is provided fairly late in the second part, just before Tony is to see Adrian's son for the first time and at a moment when he is 'trying to liberate new memories of Veronica' (121): 'these new memories suddenly came upon me – it was as if, for that moment, time had been placed in reverse. As if, for that moment, the river ran upstream' (122). The book thus keeps the significance of the image enigmatic for longer, thereby challenging the reader's interpretative skills.

Another significant change between the first draft and published book concerns a crucial sentence in Tony's letter. In the first draft, the narrator wrote in his letter: 'The only thing I don't wish is that you have a child' (3.3), but Barnes noted in the margin: 'possibly change the curse', and it was indeed transformed into its opposite – 'Part of me hopes you'll have a child' (95) –, which made the curse more terrifying with Tony wishing time would take its revenge on the child. The first draft therefore showed the narrator as being slightly less relentless but also more prone to reflecting on issues of guilt and responsibility. In the published book, after sharing with his ex-wife the content of his letter to Adrian and his feelings of remorse, Tony asks her: 'Did you leave me because of me?', to which she replies 'No .... I left you because of us' (102). In the original draft, the narrator wondered about this at the beginning of the second part: 'Maybe she just left me because of me', which led him to ponder over the apportionment of blame:

> So it's all your fault? This is one of the things you find yourself thinking as you look back over your life. Was everything that went wrong my fault? By the law of probability, almost certainly not. But no-one can really tell you, not least because the only witnesses have their own questions of guilt and responsibility to deal with. (3.3)

This passage (later deleted) not only echoes the discussion in class about the distribution of responsibility for the start of the First World War (10–2) – which was absent from the original draft – but also anticipates the narrator's suppositions as to what his daughter may think: 'At some level, she blames me for the divorce. ... it was obviously all her father's fault' (103). In the draft, this later passage was followed by a (then deleted) introspective reflection on the narrator's three main relationships in his life (with Annick – later renamed Annie, Veronica and his wife):

> All three of them failed. Oh yes, I know we're not supposed to say that nowadays. Not 'the marriage failed' but 'the marriage ended.' I still prefer the old terminology. Where else but in our intimate behaviour, are we most answerable for our own lives? So where better do questions of guilt & responsibility, blame and fault apply? And for that reason, where are we most likely to deceive ourselves. (3.3)

This self-examination showed the narrator as more willing to accept responsibility for the failure of his relationships. His insistence on using the blunt verb 'failed' rather than the euphemistic 'ended' recalls Geoffrey Braithwaite's stance in *Flaubert's Parrot*: 'Use the short, simple, true words. *Dead*, I say, and *dying*, and *mad*, and *adultery*. I don't say *passed on*, or *slipping away*, or *terminal*' (91).[41] However, just as Braithwaite himself found refuge in sidestepping traumatic issues, Tony in the final version of *The Sense of an Ending* proves reluctant to confront his responsibility and frequently gives in to self-deception.

Although *The Sense of an Ending* was marked by significant changes from the first draft to final version (especially the later disconnection from *Metroland*), what is remarkable is that the first handwritten draft seems to have been written with a great fluidity and was not submitted to a great amount of rewriting. Compared to the archives for other books, this novel is accompanied by a lighter load of notes and self-addressed comments, as if the author had very early on a precise idea of where he was heading and how he was going to get there.

---

[41] In the third part of *Levels of Life*, Barnes writes: 'One euphemistic verb I especially loathed was "pass". "I'm sorry to hear your wife has passed" (as in "passed water"? "passed blood"?)' (78).

Conclusion

Novels are like cities: some are organised and laid out with the colour-coded clarity of public transport maps, with each chapter marking a progress from one station to the next, until all the characters have been successfully carried to their thematic terminus. Others, the subtler, wiser ones, offer no such immediately readable route maps. Instead of a journey through the city, they throw you into the city itself, and life itself: you are expected to find your own way.[1]

Thus does Julian Barnes conclude his essay on Penelope Fitzgerald, adding that her novels are pre-eminent examples of the second kind. It can be argued that Barnes's novels belong to the same category of books with no 'immediately readable route maps' as the examination of his archives has testified to the sinuous paths sometimes taken by the writer to reach his final destination.

In an interview in 2014, Barnes told Mark Lawson: 'For a long time, I certainly had a notion of what the next [book] would be', but after publishing *Levels of Life* in 2013, he was unsure as to the direction his next work would take: 'I know there will be one, but I'm just sort of looking around, mooching.'[2] Three years later, he published *The Noise of Time* and remarked: 'I think it's true that with each new book, you make new mistakes.' He gave the example of the incipit of this novel based on key incidents in the life of the Russian composer Dmitri Shostakovich:

> it started with a line of Flaubert's, which says modern life has no heroes and no monsters and literature should therefore have no heroes and no monsters, and so the book began with a riff that the monsters had come back, and the monsters had killed all the heroes, so we live in a world that is monster full, and hero free. But I eventually scrapped it because it was too declamatory, it was too un-novelistic.[3]

The analysis of Barnes's archives has shown that he often writes several versions of incipits for his novels and that this type of false start is not rare. However, deletions of whole passages are less frequent in the typescripts of his more recent work than earlier

---

[1] Barnes, *Through the Window*, 13.
[2] In Lawson, 'Mark Lawson'.
[3] Freeman, 'How the Writer Edits'.

on in his career, which is part of the gains of being an experienced writer as Barnes remarked in an interview: 'I know more what I'm doing, so there are fewer false trails that have to be abandoned.'[4] On the other hand, the relentless quest for the right tone, voice, word and structural balance has remained unchanged. At the time of finishing this exploration, the writer's archives at the Harry Ransom Center do not yet include the typescripts and notes for *The Noise of Time* and *The Only Story* (and the novels that will come afterwards), but they no doubt will testify to an assiduous and meticulous combing of the prose, with words and sentences written, crossed out, amended, revised, and written again and crossed out again. These passages under erasure, which archives give access to and which offer an understanding of the genesis and intricate palimpsest of a writer's work, may be compared to the narrator's notebook in *The Only Story*, in which he writes down entries on love and crosses them out when he judges them incorrect: 'That was there for a few years; then he crossed it out. Then he wrote it in again; then he crossed it out again. Now he had both entries side by side, one clear and true, the other crossed out and false' (165). One might read in this passage an indirect description of the writer's own craft.

The future archives are bound to reveal more secrets of fabrication and this book is therefore condemned to partiality and foretold obsolescence. One of the original ambitions of this study was to try and 'know everything' about Barnes's writing process (*Flaubert's Parrot* 127) – just as Barnes himself wants 'to hear every opera that's ever been written, and drink every wine that's ever been made'[5] – but sifting through the writer's papers has confirmed what Geoffrey Braithwaite had already surmised, namely that 'Everything confuses' (102). It is therefore fitting that some areas should remain in the shadows, protected from a too intrusive glare.

---

[4] Bhattacharya, 'Julian Barnes', 41.
[5] Annotations, 22–27 March 2018.

Works Cited

Texts by Julian Barnes

Novels

Metroland. London: Jonathan Cape, 1980. The Morgan Library & Museum, New York. PML 194959. Gift of Alyce Toonk, 2013.
Before She Met Me. London: Picador, [1982] 1983.
Flaubert's Parrot. London: Picador, [1984] 1985.
Staring at the Sun. London: Picador, [1986] 1987.
A History of the World in 10½ Chapters. London: Picador, [1989] 1990.
Talking It Over. London: Picador, [1991] 1992.
The Porcupine. London: Picador, [1992] 1993.
England, England. London: Jonathan Cape, 1998.
Love, etc. London: Jonathan Cape, 2000.
Arthur & George. London: Jonathan Cape, 2005.
The Sense of an Ending. London: Jonathan Cape, 2011.
The Noise of Time. London: Jonathan Cape, 2016.
The Only Story. London: Jonathan Cape, 2018.

Short stories

'A Self-Possessed Woman'. In *The Times Anthology of Ghost Stories*, 132–49. London: Jonathan Cape, 1975.
'One of a Kind'. *London Review of Books* 4, no. 3 (18 February 1982–3 March 1982): 23.
Cross Channel. London: Jonathan Cape, 1996.
The Lemon Table. London: Jonathan Cape, 2004.
Pulse. London: Jonathan Cape, 2011.

Non-fiction (books)

Letters from London 1990–1995. London: Picador, 1995.
Something to Declare. London: Jonathan Cape, 2002.
The Pedant in the Kitchen. London: Atlantic, 2003.
Nothing to Be Frightened Of. London: Jonathan Cape, 2008.
Through the Window: Seventeen Essays and a Short Story. London: Jonathan Cape, 2012.
Levels of Life. London: Jonathan Cape, 2013.
Keeping an Eye Open: Essays on Art. London: Jonathan Cape, 2015.
The Man in the Red Coat. London: Jonathan Cape, 2019.

Non-fiction (individual pieces)

'Scraping and Grimthorping'. *Times Educational Supplement*, 25 May 1973, 24.
[unsigned] 'The Big Yawn'. *Times Literary Supplement*, 29 March 1974, 313.
'Conservational'. *New Statesman*, 9 January 1976, 45.
'Ductile'. *New Statesman*, 12 March 1976, 334.
'Nice and Nasty'. *New Statesman*, 18 June 1976, 822.
'Any Old Irony'. *New Statesman*, 30 July 1976, 152.
'Many a Snip'. *New Statesman*, 10 December 1976, 846.
'Comic Cuts'. *New Statesman*, 28 January 1977, 134–5.
[Paddy Beesley, pseud.]. 'Just Like Us'. *New Statesman*, 4 February 1977, 163.
[Paddy Beesley, pseud.]. 'Be Bad'. *New Statesman*, 25 March 1977, 407.
'Decent Exposure'. *New Statesman*, 22 April 1977, 537.
[Edward Pygge, pseud.]. 'Untitled'. *New Review* 4, no. 38 (May 1977): 1–2, 64.
'Rousing Stuff'. *New Statesman*, 1 July 1977, 22.
[Edward Pygge, pseud.]. 'Greek Street'. *New Review* 4, no. 42 (September 1977): 1–2, 64.
[Edward Pygge, pseud.]. 'Greek Street'. *New Review* 4, no. 43 (October 1977): 1–2, 64.
'Farce Talking'. *New Statesman*, 24 March 1978, 407.
'Don't Quote Me'. *New Statesman*, 16 November 1979, 771–2.
[Paddy Beesley, pseud.]. 'Weekend Competition. No 2606'. *New Statesman*, 29 February 1980, 334.
[Basil Seal, pseud.]. 'Tatler Restaurants'. *Tatler*, June 1980, 15–16.
[Basil Seal, pseud.]. 'Tatler Restaurants: Basil Seal Goes Back to School'. *Tatler*, September 1980, 15–16.
'Television. Devilish Cunning'. *Observer*, 18 April 1982, 40.
'Television. The Fatal Web'. *Observer*, 25 April 1982, 40.
'A Complex Heart: Gustave Flaubert (1821–80)'. [TV documentary] BBC2 *Writers and Places*, 14 August 1983. Producer: David F. Turnbull.
'Flaubert and Rouen'. *Listener*, 18 August 1983, 14–15.
'Flaubert's Parrot – A Story'. *London Review of Books* 5, no. 15 (18–31 August 1983): 20–1.
'Television. The Afternoon of Vietnam'. *Observer*, 21 October 1984, 26.
'The Follies of Writer Worship'. *New York Times Book Review*, 17 February 1985, 1, 16, 17.
'Philip Roth in Israel'. *London Review of Books* 9, no. 5 (5 March 1987): 3–7.
'Diary'. *London Review of Books* 9, no. 20 (12 November 1987): 21.
'Letters'. *London Review of Books* 10, no. 1 (7 January 1988): 5.
'Playing Chess with Arthur Koestler'. *Yale Review* 77, no. 4 (Summer 1988): 478–91.
[Translation]. *The Truth about Dogs*, by Volker Kriegel. London: Bloomsbury, [1986] 1988.
'Books'. *Harpers & Queen*, March 1989, 60, 62.
'Flaubert's Bottle'. *London Review of Books* 11, no. 9 (4 May 1989): 10.
'My Hero: Julian Barnes on Jacques Brel'. *Independent Magazine*, 10 June 1989, 46.
'Diary. Ambushed in Streets of the Sneaky Pun'. *Guardian*, 17 June 1989 (Barnes's papers 2.5.3).
'Bin End: A Highly Personal View of the World of Wines and Spirits'. *Decanter*, November 1989, 144.
'Dirty Story: The Making of *Madame Bovary*'. In *Soho Square II*, edited by Alberto Manguel, 62–5. London: Bloomsbury, 1990.
'Candles for the Living'. *London Review of Books* 12, no. 22 (22 November 1990): 6–7.
'U'. In *Hockney's Alphabet*, edited Stephen Spender with drawings by David Hockney, n.p. London: Faber & Faber, 1991.

'Short Story/Essay. Shipwreck'. In *The Writer in You: A Writing Process Reader*, edited by Barbara Lounsberry, 174–95. New York: HarperCollins, 1992.
'How Much Is That in Porcupines?' *Times*, 24 October 1992, 4–6.
'*Last Poems*, XII, A.E. Housman'. In *Lifelines. An Anthology of Poems Chosen by Famous People*, edited by Niall Macmonagle, 150–1. London: Penguin, 1993.
'Acceptance Speech for the Shakespeare Prize'. Stiftung F.V.S zu Hamburg, 12 June 1993, 21–6. Reproduced in *Shakespeare Prize 1937–2006*, edited by Jürgen Schlaeger, 206–13. Trier: Wissenschaftlicher Verlag Trier, 2013.
'Preface'. In *Dictionary of Accepted Ideas*, by Gustave Flaubert, v–xi. London: Syrens, 1994.
'Grand Illusion'. *New York Times*, 28 January 1996, section 7, 9.
Desert Island Discs. BBC Radio 4, 28 January 1996.
'"Merci de m'avoir trahi"'. *Nouvel Observateur*, 12 December 1996, 114.
'Back to the Future'. *New York Times Book Review*, 26 January 1997, 4.
'Out of Place'. *Architectural Digest* 54, no. 5 (April 1997): 36, 38.
'A Game Which Demands a Saintly Letting Go'. *Literary Review*, May 1997, 43–4.
'The Wise Woman'. *New York Review of Books* 45, no. 16 (22 October 1998): 15.
'Pilgrimage to Rayas'. *Appellation Magazine* 6, no. 6 (November 1998–31 December 1998): 34–5, 83.
'The Bitter Lemon Days'. In *Another Round at the Pillars: Essays, Poems, & Reflections on Ian Hamilton*, edited by David Harsent, 15–21. Tregarne, Manaccan: Cargo Press, 1999.
'A London View'. *Granta* 65 (Spring 1999): 176.
'Days I'll Remember'. In *Changing Times: Being Young in Britain in the '60s*, by Alison Pressley, 65. London: Michael O'Mara, 2000.
'Introduction'. In *Reliable Essays: The Best of Clive James*, by Clive James, xv–xviii. London: Picador, 2001.
'Influences – Single-Handed'. *New Yorker*, 25 December 2000–1 January 2001, 114–15.
'Foreword'. In *Dear Dodie. The Life of Dodie Smith*, by Valerie Grove, vii–viii. London: Pimlico, [1996] 2002.
'Literary Executions'. [19 May 1996] In *The Writing Life: Writers on How They Think and Work*, edited by Marie Arana, 380–6. New York: Public Affairs, 2003.
'Lost for Words'. In *Mortification, Writers' Stories of Their Public Shame*, edited by Robin Robertson, 36–8. London: 4th Estate, 2003.
'Sentimental Journeys'. *Guardian*, 11 January 2003, Review 4–6.
'Holy Hysteria'. *New York Review of Books*, 10 April 2003, 32–4.
'This War Was Not Worth a Child's Finger'. *Guardian*, 11 April 2003, 2–4.
'The Pedant in the Kitchen. Picture Perfect'. *Guardian*, 11 April 2003. https://www.theguardian.com/books/2003/apr/12/julianbarnes.houseandgarden. Accessed on 19 January 2019.
'Union Blues'. *New Yorker*, 21–28 April 2003, 145.
'Hate and Hedonism. The Insolent Art of Michel Houellebecq'. *New Yorker*, 7 July 2003, 72–5.
'The Proper Vehicle of Passion'. BBC Radio 4. 29 April 2004 and 6 May 2004 (with Hermione Lee).
'Kipling and France'. BBC Radio 4. 10 and 17 November 2005 (with Hermione Lee).
'When Flaubert Took Wing'. *Guardian*, 5 March 2005, 20.
'Soul Brothers'. *Guardian*, 5 November 2005. https://www.theguardian.com/books/2005/nov/05/fiction.classics. Accessed on 19 January 2019.
'Blood and Nerves'. *Guardian*, 25 November 2006. https://www.theguardian.com/stage/2006/nov/25/theatre.stage. Accessed on 19 January 2019.

'The Past Conditional'. *New Yorker*, 25 December 2006/1 January 2007, 56–64.
'Alan Raitt Remembered'. *The Royal Society of Literature*, 6 January 2007. https://rsliterature.org/fellow/alan-raitt/. Accessed on 19 January 2019.
'The Case of Inspector Campbell's Red Hair'. In *The Anthology of New Writing, Volume 15*, edited by Maggie Gee and Bernardine Evaristo, 289–99. London: Granta Books, 2007.
'I Remember'. *Areté* 23 (Summer/Autumn 2007): 55–8.
'Christmas Books. Past, Present and Future'. *Guardian Weekly*, 21 December 2007, 50.
'The Saddest Story'. *Guardian*, 7 June 2008. https://www.theguardian.com/books/2008/jun/07/fiction.julianbarnes. Accessed on 19 January 2019.
'Remembering Updike'. *New Yorker*, 27 January 2009. http://www.newyorker.com/online/blogs/books/2009/01/remembering-upd.html. Accessed on 19 January 2019.
'Such, Such Was Eric Blair'. *New York Review of Books* 56, no. 4 (12 March 2009): 17–19.
'Flights'. *New York Review of Books* 56, no. 10 (11 June 2009): 8, 10.
'Running Away'. *Guardian*, 17 October 2009, R20.
'Writer's Writer and Writer's Writer's Writer'. *London Review of Books* 32, no. 22 (18 November 2010): 7–11.
'Carcassonne'. *The Spectator*, 18/25 December 2010, 53–7.
'For Sorrow There Is No Remedy'. *New York Review of Books* 58, no. 6 (7 April 2011): 10–14.
'Badger Claws'. *London Review of Books* 33, no. 13 (30 June 2011): 23–4.
'A Candid View of *Candide*'. *Guardian*, 1 July 2011. https://www.theguardian.com/books/2011/jul/01/candide-voltaire-rereading-julian-barnes. Accessed on 19 January 2019.
'Where Sibelius Fell Silent'. *The Economist 1843*, January/February 2012. https://www.1843magazine.com/content/arts/house-sibelius-fell-silent. Accessed on 19 January 2019. Reproduced in *Treasure Palaces: Great Writers Visit Great Museums*, edited by Maggie Fergusson, 145–51. London: Economist Books, 2016.
'The Defence of the Book'. *Guardian*, 3 February 2012. Reproduced in *The Library Book*, edited by Rebecca Gray, 9–13. London: Profile Books, 2012.
'A Life with Books'. London: Jonathan Cape, 2012.
'Listener, They Wore It: Charles's Cap (*Madame Bovary*)'. BBC Radio 3. 11 February 2013. http://www.bbc.co.uk/programmes/b01qkw6j. Accessed on 19 January 2019.
'The Big Question: What's the Best Sense? Julian Barnes: A Sense of Self'. *Intelligent Life*, July/August 2015. http://www.intelligentlifemagazine.com/intelligence/the-big-question/whats-the-best-sense. Accessed on 19 January 2019.
'The Real Thing!' *London Review of Books* 37, no. 24 (17 December 2015): 15–16.
'Lucy Mackenzie: Showing the World in a Particular Light'. In *Lucy Mackenzie: Quiet*, n.p. New York: Nancy Hoffman Gallery, 2015.
'Introduction'. In *Metroland*, 1–5. London: Vintage, 2016.
'My Mother Before I Knew Her'. *Guardian*, 5 March 2016. http://www.theguardian.com/books/2016/mar/05/writers-mothers-photographs-carol-ann-duffy. Accessed on 19 January 2019.
'Julian Barnes Remembers His Friend Anita Brookner: "There Was No One Remotely Like Her"'. *Guardian*, 18 March 2016. http://www.theguardian.com/books/2016/mar/18/julian-barnes-remembers-anita-brookner. Accessed on 19 January 2019.
'My Stupid Leicester City Love'. *Guardian*, 6 May 2016. http://www.theguardian.com/football/2016/may/06/julian-barnes-leicester-city-premier-league-stupid-love. Accessed on 19 January 2019.

'Changing My Mind. Words'. *BBC Radio 3*, 6 December 2016. https://www.bbc.co.uk/programmes/b084fvlv. Accessed on 19 January 2019.
'Changing My Mind. Politics'. *BBC Radio 3*, 7 December 2016. https://www.bbc.co.uk/programmes/b084fvlx. Accessed on 19 January 2019.
'Diary'. *London Review of Books* 39, no. 8 (20 April 2017): 41–3.
'Foreword'. In *Simon Leys: Navigator between Worlds*, by Philippe Paquet, translated by Julie Rose, xi–xiii. Carlton, Australia: La Trobe University Press, 2017.

Other sources

Adeane, Olinda. 'Barnestorming'. *Harpers & Queen*, April 1982, 150–1.
Allardice, Lisa. 'Barnes, Lively, Holroyd, Moggach and Self Talk about Their Relationships with Their Typewriters'. *Guardian*, 1 December 2009. https://www.theguardian.com/books/2009/dec/01/barnes-authors-typewriters. Accessed on 19 January 2019.
Amis, Martin. *The Rachel Papers*. London: Jonathan Cape, 1973.
Amis, Martin. 'Books of the Year'. *Observer*, 2 December 1984, 19.
Amis, Martin. *Einstein's Monsters*. London: Jonathan Cape, 1987.
Amis, Martin. *London Fields*. London: Jonathan Cape, 1989.
Amis, Martin. *Information*. London: Flamingo, [1995] 1996.
Amis, Martin. *Night Train*. London: Vintage, [1997] 1998.
Anonymous. 'You Ask the Questions: Julian Barnes'. *Independent*, 16 January 2002, 8.
Anonymous. 'Julian Barnes: "Some of My Best Friends Are Biographers"'. *Oxford Centre for Life-Writing*, 2 March 2016. https://oxlifewriting.wordpress.com/2016/03/02/julian-barnes-some-of-my-best-friends-are-biographers. Accessed on 19 January 2019.
Atanasova, Poliana. 'Englishman Writes a Novel about Zhivkov's Darned Socks'. *Democracy* (Sofia), 18 September 1992 (Barnes's papers 1.18).
'Audio Discussion: Julian Barnes and Jay McInerney'. 7 March 2001, New York Public Library. http://movies2.nytimes.com/books/01/04/01/specials/barnes.html. Accessed on 19 January 2019.
Bailey, Paul. 'Settling for Suburbia'. *Times Literary Supplement*, 28 March 1980, 345.
Barnard, Megan, ed. *Collecting the Imagination: The First Fifty Years of the Ransom Center*. Austin: University of Texas Press, 2007.
Baron, Scarlett. '*Nothing to Be Frightened Of*: An Interview with Julian Barnes'. *The Oxonian Review of Books* 7, no. 3 (Summer 2008). http://www.oxonianreview.org/wp/nothing-to-be-frightened-of-an-interview-with-julian-barnes/. Accessed on 15 October 2019.
Baudelaire, Charles. *The Flowers of Evil*. Translated by James McGowan. Oxford: Oxford University Press, [1857] 1993.
Bech, Henry. 'Henry Bech Redux'. *New York Times Book Review*, 14 November 1971, section 3, 3.
Best, Jason. 'Parroting On'. *Due South*, Christmas 1985–January 1986 (Barnes's papers 1.18).
Bhattacharya, Soumya. 'Julian Barnes: "I Do Believe in Grudge-Bearing"'. *New Statesman*, 12–25 April 2013, 38–41.
Blaine, Garth. 'Books. Mutual Admiration Society'. *Queen's Counsel*, 1984, 300–2 (Barnes's papers 1.18).
Braine, John. 'Letters to the Editor'. *New Statesman*, 25 June 1976, 848.

Brooks, Xan. 'Julian Barnes: "I Told the Film-Makers to Throw My Book against a Wall"'. *Guardian*, 1 April 2017. https://www.theguardian.com/film/2017/apr/01/julian-barnes-i-told-the-film-makers-to-throw-my-book-against-a-wall-. Accessed on 19 January 2019.
Brown, Craig. 'The Critic Has Three Lives'. *Over 21*, August 1980, 87–8.
Brown, Jeffrey. 'Conversation: Julian Barnes, Winner of the 2011 Man Booker Prize'. PBS Newshour Art, 8 November 2011. https://www.pbs.org/newshour/arts/conversation-julian-barnes-winner-of-the-2011-man-booker-prize. Accessed on 19 January 2019.
Bruckner, D. J. R. 'Planned Parenthood and the Novel'. *New York Times*, 12 April 1987, section 7, 3.
Burton, Peter. 'Dan Kavanagh / Julian Barnes'. *Gay News* 196 (24 July–20 August 1980): 16.
Camus, Albert. *The Myth of Sisyphus and Other Essays*. Translated by Justin O'Brien. New York: Vintage Books, [1955] 1960.
Carey, John. 'Land of Make-Believe'. *Sunday Times*, 23 August 1998, section 8, 1–2.
Carr, John Dickson. *The Life of Arthur Conan Doyle*. New York: Harper & Brothers, 1949.
Carter, Angela. 'Love in Two Climates'. *Vogue* 1980, 21–2 (Barnes's papers 1.18).
Childs, Peter. *Julian Barnes*. Manchester: Manchester University Press, 2011.
Coe, Jonathan. 'Author's Note'. In *Loggerheads and Other Stories*. London: Penguin ebook, 2014.
Collins, Lauren. 'An Evening with Julian Barnes'. *New Yorker*, 12 December 2011. https://www.newyorker.com/news/lauren-collins/an-evening-with-julian-barnes#ixzz1gPFJqR4o. Accessed on 19 January 2019.
The Conan Doyle Collection. Wednesday 19 May 2004. London: Christie's International Media Division, 2004.
Contat Michel, Denis Hollier and Jacques Neefs. 'Editors' Preface'. *Drafts*. Special issue of *Yale French Studies* 89 (1996): 1–5.
Cooke, Rachel. 'Julian Barnes: "Flaubert could have written a great novel about contemporary America"'. *Guardian*, 29 January 2018. https://www.theguardian.com/books/2018/jan/29/julian-barnes-interview-the-only-story. Accessed on 19 January 2019.
Daniel, Caroline. 'Lunch with FT: Ian McEwan'. *Financial Times*, 24 August 2012. http://www.ft.com/intl/cms/s/2/a54cd796-eba3-11e1-9356-00144feab49a.html. Accessed on 19 January 2019.
Daniel, Caroline. 'Interview: Clive James'. *Financial Times*, 27 August 2015. http://www.ft.com/intl/cms/s/0/a6393156-4c33-11e5-9b5d-89a026fda5c9.html. Accessed on 19 January 2019.
Davis, Edward B. 'A Whale of a Tale: Fundamentalist Fish Stories'. *Perspectives on Science and Christian Faith* 43 (1991): 224–37.
de Biasi, Pierre-Marc. 'What Is a Literary Draft? Towards a Functional Typology of Genetic Documentation'. *Drafts*, edited by Michel Contat, Denis Hollier and Jacques Neefs. Special issue of *Yale French Studies* 89 (1996): 26–58.
Depmann, Jed, Daniel Ferrer and Michael Groden, eds. *Genetic Criticism: Texts and Avant-Textes*. Philadelphia: University of Pennsylvania Press, 2004.
Dinnage, Rosemary. *A Ruffian on the Stair. Reflections on Death*. London: Viking, 1990.
Doyle, Arthur Conan. *Memories & Adventures*. 1924. Ware, Hertfordshire: Wordsworth Editions, 2007.
Doyle, Dame Jean Conan. 'Foreword'. *The Quest for Sir Arthur Conan Doyle: Thirteen Biographers in Search of a Life*, edited by Jon L. Lellenberg, xi–xv. Carbondale: Southern Illinois University Press, 1987.

Du Camp, Maxime. *Souvenirs littéraires*. Paris: Hachette, 1892.
Eco, Umberto. *The Role of the Reader. Explorations in the Semiotics of Texts*. Bloomington: Indiana University Press, 1979.
Eco, Umberto, Richard Rorty, Jonathan Culler and Christine Brooke-Rose. *Interpretation and Overinterpretation*. Edited by Stefan Collini. Cambridge: Cambridge University Press, 1992.
Edgar, David. *Stage Adaptation of* Arthur & George *by Julian Barnes*. London: Nick Hern Books, 2010.
Edgar, David. 'Ways of Seeing'. *Guardian*, 13 March 2010, 16–7.
Eliot, T. S. *The Waste Land. A Facsimile and Transcript of the Original Drafts Including the Annotations of Ezra Pound*. Edited by Valerie Eliot. San Diego: A Harvest Book, Harcourt, 1971.
Eliot, T. S. *Collected Poems 1909–1962*. London: Faber & Faber, 1974.
Elkin, Judith Laikin. 'The Reception of the Muses in the Circum-Caribbean'. In *The Muses Flee Hitler: Cultural Transfer and Adaptation 1930–1945*, edited by Jarrell C. Jackman and Carla M. Borden, 294–8. Washington, DC: Smithsonian Institution Press, 1983.
Enright, D. J., ed. *The Oxford Book of Death*. Oxford: Oxford University Press, 1983.
Fenton, James. 'A Novelist with an Experiment: Discuss'. *Times*, 4 October 1984, 13.
Field, Michele. 'From a Sat-Upon Son to an Honorary Frog'. *Sydney Morning Herald*, 27 February 1988, 72.
Flaubert, Gustave. *Dictionary of Accepted Ideas*. Translated by Geoffrey Wall. London: Syrens, [1913] 1994.
Flaubert, Gustave. *Correspondance III. 1859–1868*. Edited by Jean Bruneau. Paris: Gallimard, 1991.
Flood, Alice. 'Arthur Conan Doyle was the Victim of a Police Conspiracy'. *Guardian*, 18 March 2015. https://www.theguardian.com/books/2015/mar/18/arthur-conan-doyle-set-up-by-police-fabricated-letters. Accessed on 19 January 2019.
Fox, William, dir. *Sir Arthur Conan Doyle*. Filmed October 1928 in Windlesham, Crowborough, Sussex. Screened May 1929 (Fox story 2–616). https://www.arthur-conan-doyle.com/index.php?title=Sir_Arthur_Conan_Doyle_(movie_1928). Accessed on 19 January 2019.
Freeman, John. 'How the Writer Edits: Julian Barnes'. *Literary Hub*, 26 May 2016. http://lithub.com/how-the-writer-edits-julian-barnes/. Accessed on 19 January 2019.
French, Mike. 'Mike Interviews: Julian Barnes'. *View from Here*, 4 April 2008. http://www.viewfromheremagazine.com/2008/04/mike-interviews-julian-barnes-part-1-of.html. Accessed on 19 January 2019.
'From the archive'. *Metroland*, by Julian Barnes, n.p. London: Vintage, 2016.
Fudge, Thomas A. *Medieval Religion and its Anxieties: History and Mystery in the Other Middle Ages*. New York: Palgrave Macmillan, 2016.
Fuentes, Carlos. 'The Enchanting Blue Yonder'. *New York Times Book Review*, 12 April 1987, 3, 43.
Gilbert, Harriett. 'Julian Barnes. *Flaubert's Parrot*'. [Radio] BBC World Book Club. 31 July 2003. https://www.bbc.co.uk/programmes/p02r846w. Accessed on 19 January 2019.
Gompertz, Will. 'Barnes: "Novels Tell Truth About Life." ' BBC Arts, 2 November 2012. https://www.bbc.com/news/entertainment-arts-20179787. Accessed on 19 January 2019.
Goncourt, Edmond et Jules de. *Journal des Goncourt: Mémoire de la vie littéraire. 1895–1896*. Tome XXI. Edited by Robert Ricatte. Monaco: Éditions de l'imprimerie nationale de Monaco, 1956.

Groes, Sebastian and Peter Childs, eds. *Julian Barnes*. New York: Continuum, 2011.
Grove, Valerie. *Dear Dodie. The Life of Dodie Smith*. London: Pimlico, [1996] 2002.
Guignery, Vanessa. 'Julian Barnes in Conversation. 9th November 2001'. In *Flaubert's Parrot de Julian Barnes 'Un symbole du logos?'*, edited by Antoine Capet, Philippe Romanski, Nicole Terrien and Aïssatou Sy-Wonyu, 119–33. Rouen: Publications de l'Université de Rouen, 2002.
Guignery, Vanessa. *The Fiction of Julian Barnes*. Basingstoke: Palgrave Macmillan, 2006.
Guignery, Vanessa. 'Untangling the Intertwined Threads of Fiction and Reality in *The Porcupine* (1992) by Julian Barnes'. In *Pre- and Post-Publication Itineraries of the Contemporary Novel in English*, edited by Vanessa Guignery and François Gallix, 49–71. Paris: Éditions Publibook Université, 2007.
Guignery, Vanessa, ed. *Worlds within Words: Twenty-first Century Visions on the Work of Julian Barnes*. Special issue. *American, British and Canadian Studies* 13 (Dec. 2009). Sibiu: Lucian Blaga University Press, 2009.
Guignery, Vanessa, ed. *Novelists in New Millennium. Conversations with Writers*. Basingstoke: Palgrave Macmillan, 2013.
Guignery, Vanessa and Ryan Roberts, eds. *Conversations with Julian Barnes*. Mississippi: University of Mississippi Press, 2009.
Gunston, David. 'The Man Who Lived in a Whale. And His Name Was Not Jonah'. *The Compass. A Magazine of the Sea* 42, no. 2 (Spring 1972): 9–11.
Harris, Robert. 'Full of Prickles'. *Literary Review*, November 1992, 26.
Hay, Louis. 'Does "Text" Exist?' Translated by Matthew Jocelyn and Hans Walter. *Studies in Bibliography* 41 (1988): 64–76.
Hay, Louis. *La littérature des écrivains. Questions de critique génétique*. Paris: José Corti, 2002.
Heaney, Seamus. *Opened Ground: Selected Poems, 1966–1996*. New York: Farrar, Straus and Giroux, 1998.
Hill, Peter. 'A Student Dreamer Who Woke to Fame'. *Oxford Journal*, 9 April 1982, 13.
Holmes, Frederick M. *Julian Barnes*. Basingstoke: Palgrave Macmillan, 2008.
James, Clive. 'Clive James and Julian Barnes Talking in the Library'. 2001. https://www.youtube.com/watch?v=XZfIBIBD6No. Accessed on 19 January 2019.
Johnson, Douglas. *France and the Dreyfus Affair*. London: Blanford Press, 1966.
Kastor, Elizabeth. 'Julian Barnes' Big Questions'. *Washington Post Book World*, 18 May 1987, B1, B9.
Knowles, Elizabeth M. *The Oxford Dictionary of Quotations*. Oxford: Oxford University Press, 1999.
Kondeva, Dimitrina. 'Непредвиден Предговор [Unplanned Introduction]'. In *Bodlivo Svinche*, by Julian Barnes, translated by Dimitrina Kondeva, 7–8. Sofia: Obsidian Press, 1992.
Kondeva, Dimitrina. 'The Story of Julian Barnes's *The Porcupine*: an Epistolary ½ Chapter'. In *Julian Barnes*, edited by Sebastian Groes and Peter Childs, 81–91. New York: Continuum, 2011.
Larkin, Philip. 'Books of the Year'. *Observer*, 5 December 1982, 25.
Larkin, Philip. *Collected Poems*. Edited by Anthony Thwaite. London: Faber & Faber, 1988.
Lawson, Mark. 'A Short History of Julian Barnes'. *Independent Magazine*, 13 July 1991, 34–6.
Lawson, Mark. 'Front Row. *Levels of Life*'. BBC Radio 4. 3 April 2013.
Lawson, Mark. 'Mark Lawson Talks to Julian Barnes'. BBC Four Television. 30 March 2014.

Leader, Zachary, ed. *The Letters of Kingsley Amis*. London: HarperCollins, 2000.
Lee, Hermione. *Edith Wharton*. New York: Knopf, 2007.
Lee, Hermione. 'An Evening with Julian Barnes, Talking to Hermione Lee'. 8 December 2011. The Institute of Engineering and Technology, London. (For a partial transcription, see Collins).
Lee, Hermione. *Guardian Live*. 16 March 2016. Islington Assembly Hall, London.
Lee, Hermione. 'Julian Barnes in Conversation with Hermione Lee'. 21 February 2018. Royal Institute, London.
Leith, William. 'Too Clever by 10½'. *Tatler*, July 1989, 90–3.
Lellenberg, Jon, Daniel Stashower and Charles Foley, eds. *Arthur Conan Doyle. A Life in Letters*. New York: Penguin Press, 2007.
Lewis, Georgie. 'Julian and Arthur and George'. *Powells.com*, 13 February 2006. https://www.powells.com/post/interviews/julian-and-arthur-and-george-by-georgie/. Accessed on 1 March 2014.
Lloyd, Chris. 'Chris Lloyd Talks to Julian Barnes'. *Club* 1986: 52–4 (Barnes's papers 1.18).
Lodge, David. 'The Home Front'. *New York Review of Books* 34, no. 8 (7 May 1987): 10.
Lycett, Andrew. 'Adultery, my dear Watson'. *Guardian*, 15 September 2007. https://www.theguardian.com/books/2007/sep/15/history.biography. Accessed on 19 January 2019.
Mackenzie, Compton. *My Life and Times. Octave Three (1900–1907)*. London: Chatto & Windus, 1964.
Marrus, Michael R. *The Unwanted: European Refugees in the Twentieth Century*. Oxford: Oxford University Press, 1985.
Maschler, Tom. *Publisher*. London: Picador, 2005.
Masterman, J. C. *To Teach the Senators Wisdom or an Oxford Guide-Book*. London: Hodder and Stoughton, 1952.
McCloskey, James. 'In Conversation: Julian Barnes with James McCloskey'. *The Brooklyn Rail*, 1 September 2005. https://brooklynrail.org/2005/09/books/julian-barnes-in-conversation-with-james. Accessed on 19 January 2019.
McGrath, Patrick. 'Julian Barnes'. *Bomb* 21 (Fall 1987): 20–3.
McHale, Brian. *Postmodernist Fiction*. New York: Methuen, 1987.
McInerney, Jay. *A Hedonist in the Cellar: Adventures in Wine*. New York: Knopf, 2006.
McInerney, Jay. 'Good Wine and Fax Machines Brought Jay McInerney and Julian Barnes Together'. *Town & Country*, 17 August 2017. https://www.townandcountrymag.com/leisure/drinks/a10364108/argument-for-letter-writing/. Accessed on 19 January 2019.
Meades, Jonathan. 'Parrot Fashion'. *Time Out*, 27 September/3 October 1984, 27–8.
Mikhail, Kate. 'Life Support'. *Observer*, 24 February 2002. https://www.theguardian.com/theobserver/2002/feb/24/julianbarnes. Accessed on 19 January 2019.
Minns, Rainer. *Bombers and Mash: The Domestic Front 1939–45*. London: Virago, 1980.
Moseley, Merritt. *Understanding Julian Barnes*. Columbia: University of South Carolina Press, 1997.
Mourthé, Claude. 'Julian Barnes: un savoureux éclectisme'. *Magazine Littéraire* 315 (November 1993): 96–102.
Nordon, Pierre. *Sir Arthur Conan Doyle. L'homme et l'œuvre*. Paris: Marcel Didier, 1964.
———. *Conan Doyle*. Translated by Frances Partridge. London: Murray, 1966.
O'Connell, John. 'Julian Barnes: Interview'. *Time Out*, 18 September 2008. https://www.timeout.com/london/things-to-do/julian-barnes-interview. Accessed on 15 October 2019.
Parker, Ian. 'Print'. *Blitz* 57 (September 1987): 104–6.

Pateman, Matthew. 'The Trials of Barnes'. *Leeds Student Independent Newspaper*, 29 October 1993, 16.
Pateman, Matthew. *Julian Barnes*. Tavistock: Northcote House, 2002.
Pearson, Hesketh. *Conan Doyle: His Life and Art*. London: Methuen, 1943.
Porter, Henry. 'The Heart of a Man of Letters'. *Independent on Sunday*, 2 April 1995, 4–6.
Raine, Craig. 'Letters'. *London Review of Books* 9, no. 22 (10 December 1987): 4.
Rees, Jasper. 'The Inscrutable Mr Barnes'. *The Telegraph*, 23 September 2006. http://www.telegraph.co.uk/culture/books/3655483/The-inscrutable-Mr-Barnes.html. Accessed on 19 January 2019.
Rice, Leslie. 'Giving Teaching A Go'. *The Gazette. The Newspaper of the John Hopkins University*, October/December 1995. http://pages.jh.edu/gazette/octdec95/oct2395/23barnes.html. Accessed on 19 January 2019.
Rimbaud, Arthur. *Complete Works, Selected Letters*. Translated, with introduction and notes by Wallace Fowlie. Chicago: University of Chicago Press, 1966.
Rimmer, Louise. 'Shelf Life: Julian Barnes'. *Scotland on Sunday*, 13 January 2002. http://news.scotsman.com/index.cfm?id=44002002. Accessed on 19 January 2002.
Risinger, D. Michael. 'Boxes in Boxes: Julian Barnes, Conan Doyle, Sherlock Holmes and the Edalji Case'. *International Commentary on Evidence* 4, no. 2 (published online 27 February 2007). https://law.shu.edu/faculty/fulltime_faculty/risingmi/articles/ICE.pdf. Accessed on 15 October 2019.
Robb, Nancy. 'The Novel Diversions of Julian Barnes'. *Quill & Quire*, June 1989, 50.
Roberts, Ryan. *Pseudonym as Character: The Development of Julian Barnes's Multiple Aliases*. MA diss., Department of English, University of Illinois at Springfield, 2011.
Roberts, Ryan. 'Inventing a Way to the Truth: Life and Fiction in *Flaubert's Parrot*'. In *Julian Barnes*, edited by Sebastian Groes and Peter Childs, 24–36. New York: Continuum, 2011.
Roberts, Ryan, ed. *Conversations with Ian McEwan*. Mississippi: University of Mississippi Press, 2010.
Rushdie, Salman. *Shame*. 1983. London: Picador, 1984.
Salgas, Jean-Pierre. 'Julian Barnes n'en a pas fini avec Flaubert'. *Quinzaine Littéraire* 463 (16–31 May 1986): 13.
Scammell, Michael. 'Trial and Error'. *New Republic*, 4–11 January 1993, 35–8.
Skvorecky, Josef. 'In the Court of Memory'. *Washington Post Book World*, 15 November 1996, 6.
Stashower, Daniel. *Teller of Tales. The Life of Arthur Conan Doyle*. New York: Henry Holt and Company, 1999.
Stuart, Alexander. 'Barnes Storm'. *Time Out*, 21–28 June 1989, 26–7.
Sutherland, John. 'Looking Back'. *London Review of Books* 2, no. 10 (22 May 1980): 27–8.
Thwaite, Anthony, ed. *Selected Letters of Philip Larkin. 1940–1985*. London: Faber & Faber, 1992.
Todd, Bruce. 'Endings and Beginnings: The Success of Author Julian Barnes'. *The Gazette (Magazine of City of London alumni association, The John Carpenter Club)* 303 (Summer 2012): 8–9.
Toledo, Pablo. 'Interview with Julian Barnes, Part I: "I like the idea of chance having an effect"'. *Buenos Aires Herald*, 12 February 2008, 1.
Toledo, Pablo. 'Interview with Julian Barnes, Part II: "Art tells more truth than anything else"'. *Buenos Aires Herald*, 13 February 2008, 16.

Tory, Eszter and Janina Vesztergom, eds. *Stunned into Uncertainty: Essays on Julian Barnes's Fiction*. Budapest, 2014. http://www.eltereader.hu/media/2015/01/Book-Barnes_READER1.pdf. Accessed on 19 January 2019.
Turnbull, William. 'Essential Icon. Julian Barnes'. *Equator*, Fall 1987, 20, 22, 23.
Twain, Mark. *The American Claimant*. 1892. New York: Oxford University Press, 1996.
Updike, John. 'A Pair of Parrots'. *New Yorker*, 22 July 1985, 86–90.
Vianu, Lidia. 'Giving up Criticism is Much Easier Than Giving Up Alcohol or Tobacco. Interview with Julian Barnes. 8 November 2000'. *Desperado Essay-Interviews*. Bucharest: Editura Universitatii din Bucuresti, 2006. http://lidiavianu.scriptmania.com/julian_barnes.htm. Accessed on 19 January 2019.
Walsh, John. 'Faction, Fiction and Flaubert'. *Books and Bookmen*, October 1984, 20–1.
Waugh, Auberon. 'Pseuds' Progress'. *Evening Standard*, 1980 (Barnes's papers 1.18).
Waugh, Evelyn. *Black Mischief*. 1932. Boston: Back Bay Books, 2002.
Wroe, Nicholas. 'Literature's Mister Cool'. *Guardian*, 29 July 2000, 6–7.
Yalom, Irvin. *Staring at the Sun: Overcoming the Terror of Death*. San Francisco: Jossey-Bass, 2008.
Zalewski, Daniel. 'The Background Hum. Ian McEwan's Art of Unease'. *New Yorker*, 23 February 2009, 46–61.
Website: www.julianbarnes.com (Webmaster: Ryan Roberts).

Index

Amis, Kingsley 11, 39, 40, 44, 46, 47, 53 n.44, 55, 72, 92–3, 97, 100, 143, 165
Amis, Martin 40, 47, 52, 64, 67, 93, 107, 136, 143, 148 n.5, 168, 174
   Dead Babies 52
   Einstein's Monsters 136, 143
   Information 143 n.29
   London Fields 143 n.29
   Money 106
   Night Train 123
   Other People 52
   The Rachel Papers 22, 98
autobiographical/autobiography 14, 136, 137, 138, 141, 201, 204–5, 207–12

Bailey, Paul 43–4
Barnes, Julian
   Arthur & George 4, 10, 13, 72 n.97, 88, 103 n.16, 104, 172, 177–99
   Before She Met Me 7, 9, 10, 14, 36, 43, 45–57, 88, 103, 105–6, 117, 128
   brother (Jonathan) 17, 60, 68, 70, 71, 91, 166, 167 n.12, 204, 206–7, 219
   Cross Channel 59, 61 n.14, 62 n.28, 63 n.36, 206
   England, England 4, 6, 9, 13 n.12, 45, 54, 60, 69, 70, 72 n.97, 107, 110 n.41, 112, 118–19, 127, 167, 175, 177, 191
   father 46, 59, 60, 64, 65, 68, 166, 207–8
   Flaubert's Parrot 2, 5, 7, 9, 10, 12, 13, 14, 36, 39, 40, 50, 53, 54, 57, 67, 73 n.103, 75–94, 102, 103, 104, 106, 108, 109, 112, 113, 114 n.49, 115, 117, 121, 122, 127, 131, 136, 137, 148, 149, 166, 169 n.26, 173, 175, 182, 190, 199, 201, 109, 211, 213, 229, 231, 236, 238
   A History of the World in 10½ Chapters 3, 7, 10, 67, 68, 73, 105, 107, 108–9, 122, 131–45, 148 n.5, 181, 192, 201, 203, 231

Keeping an Eye Open 62, 132, 174
The Lemon Table 40 n.6, 54, 70, 110, 111, 140, 152 n.22, 166, 205, 207
Letters from London 1990–1995 15, 46, 68, 148 n.5
Levels of Life 36, 65, 72, 114–15, 118, 119 n.5, 137, 201, 209, 210–12, 217, 229 n.35, 230, 237
A Literary Guide to Oxford 22 n.37, 64, 95–103, 138, 139 n.23
Love, etc 6–7, 9, 104, 105, 114, 134 n.9, 191, 231
The Man in the Red Coat 148 n.5, 208 n.17
Metroland 2, 7, 9, 11–37, 42–5, 46, 48, 54, 61 n.16, 62, 63, 65, 66, 100, 103, 104, 105, 113, 118–19, 121, 123 n.15, 125, 127, 132, 138, 139 n.23, 148 n.5, 165, 172, 191, 203, 204, 207, 215, 216, 218–23, 226, 230, 231, 232–3, 236
mother 17, 46, 48, 49, 59, 60, 61, 65, 70, 207–8
The Noise of Time 14, 19, 36, 42, 57, 118–19, 120, 127, 164, 181, 182, 194, 199, 214, 230, 237, 238
Nothing to Be Frightened Of 2, 10, 14–15, 16 n.23, 17, 25, 27, 28–9, 46, 49, 54, 60, 61, 62, 63, 65, 67 n.69, 68, 70, 103, 110 n.43, 112, 113, 115, 121, 122, 125, 126 n.20, 130, 140, 168 n.18, 171, 172, 191, 201–9, 211, 212–14, 216, 217, 219
The Only Story 1, 13 n.12, 15, 22, 49–50, 52 n.40, 91 n.39, 91 n.40, 105, 111, 113, 118, 141 n.24, 148 n.5, 172, 201, 203 n.8, 208, 211, 212–14, 226, 228 n.33, 230, 238
The Pedant in the Kitchen 71, 80, 166, 168, 170
The Porcupine 7, 9, 68, 107, 147–64

Pulse 17, 40 n.3, 54 n.48, 110, 152 n.22, 209–10, 215 n.2
'A Self-Possessed Woman' 11, 64, 138
The Sense of an Ending 2, 4, 6, 7, 9, 10, 13, 15, 18, 20, 33, 36, 57, 72, 73, 104, 105, 114, 125, 127, 134 n.8, 194, 206, 211, 212, 215–36
Something to Declare 16 n.23, 42, 61, 66, 85–6, 125, 148 n.5, 170
Staring at the Sun 4, 10, 13, 14, 23–4, 51, 61, 103, 105–6, 111, 112, 117–30, 131, 148 n.5, 202
Talking It Over 4, 5, 6, 9, 67, 101–2, 104–5, 106, 114, 127, 134 n.9, 143 n.29, 165, 172, 191, 218 n.12, 231
Through the Window 65, 92 n.44, 92 n.45, 173 n.49, 203 n.8, 210–11, 225, 237
Baudelaire, Charles 109, 122 n.14, 232
Beesley, Laurien 96, 139 n.23, 148 n.5
Beesley, Lawrence 138, 139–40
Beesley, Paddy 65, 138–9
beginnings, *see* incipits
biography 1, 2, 76, 85–6, 182–5, 199, 211, 214
    Amis, Kingsley 165
    Doyle, Arthur Conan 181
    Flaubert, Gustave 85–6
Bragg, Melvyn 46
Braine, John 46–8
Brel, Jacques 66, 69, 124–5
Brexit 65, 167
Brookner, Anita 67, 165
Buford, Bill 70

Calder, Liz 7, 12–13, 21, 29, 30, 33, 34–5, 44, 79, 83, 86, 91
Camus, Albert 67, 85, 112, 125, 217, 232
Carter, Angela 28–9, 138–9
characters (*see also* names of characters) 4–5, 35, 60, 104, 122, 140, 153, 162, 165, 169–70, 213, 237
    Arthur & George 182, 196, 199
    Before She Met Me 46–51
    Flaubert's Parrot 79–80, 86, 88, 90
    The Sense of an Ending 217, 221, 222, 223, 227
Coe, Jonathan 225 n.23
correspondence, *see* letters

Daudet, Alphonse 70, 91–2, 104, 109, 173
death 9, 61, 66, 68, 70, 72, 73, 111, 112, 115, 136
    Arthur & George 181, 185–92
    Before She Met Me 51–2, 56 n.52
    Flaubert's Parrot 81 n.21, 87, 89, 112, 209, 236
    Levels of Life 114, 115, 201, 209–11, 217
    'Marriage Lines' 209–10,
    Metroland 21–9, 65, 203–4, 218–19
    notebooks 202–3
    Nothing to Be Frightened Of 112, 201–5, 209, 214, 217,
    The Only Story 22, 52 n.40
    The Sense of an Ending 216–19
    Staring at the Sun 106, 117, 119, 121–3, 124, 125–6, 129 n.27, 130
    Through the Window 210–11
dedications 54, 96, 139 n.23, 148, 209
diaries 8–9, 68, 71, 133–4, 184, 196, 201, 202, 210, 224, 232
Didion, Joan 42, 203 n.8, 210–11
Doyle, Arthur Conan 177, 179–86, 188, 191, 199

Edgar, David 104, 188 n.32, 198 n.45
Eliot, T. S. 56, 98, 208 n.16, 217
ending
    Arthur & George 178–9, 192, 193, 194
    Before She Met Me 51
    'The Fruit Cage' 207–8
    A History of the World in 10½ Chapters 133
    Metroland 34–5
    The Porcupine 154–60
    The Sense of an Ending 227
epigraphs 15, 55, 61, 122, 124, 125, 127 n.25, 128, 232
Europe 62, 70, 72, 107, 150, 167

Fenton, James 65, 85
film adaptations 73, 104
Fitzgerald, Penelope 11, 237
Flaubert, Gustave 40, 73, 75–91, 104, 109, 115, 117, 166, 175, 201
    Madame Bovary 12, 59, 71, 76, 77, 78, 79, 82, 89, 172, 173, 227
food 56, 98, 110, 171
football 60, 67, 73, 166, 167, 170

Ford, Ford Madox 65, 225–6, 227
Fuentes, Carlos 130

genre 10, 104, 106, 214
  Arthur & George 183, 199
  Before She Met Me 51, 52, 53
  Flaubert's Parrot 76, 85
  A History of the World in 10½ Chapters 134, 136–7
  Levels of Life 50
  Nothing to Be Frightened Of 204, 211

Harry Ransom Center 2, 8, 71
Heaney, Seamus 11, 142
Hitchens, Christopher 64–5, 168
Hockney, David 80, 100, 174

incipits 10, 22, 112–13, 127, 202–3, 237
  Arthur & George 13, 185–92
  Before She Met Me 52–3
  'The Fruit Cage' 207
  Metroland 13–16
  The Noise of Time 14, 237
  Nothing to Be Frightened Of 202
  The Porcupine 152, 158, 164
  The Sense of an Ending 13, 18, 127, 216, 225–30
  Staring at the Sun 13, 128–9

James, Clive 43 n.24, 66, 168

Kipling, Rudyard 56, 92
Kavanagh, Dan (pseudonym) 29, 52, 66, 103
Kavanagh, Pat (wife), 54 n.48, 65, 83, 93, 95, 148, 149, 169, 194, 201, 208–12
Koestler, Arthur 66, 75, 117, 150, 203
Kondeva, Dimitrina 7, 147–60

Larkin, Philip 53, 85, 93–4, 100, 126, 165
Lee, Hermione 5, 7, 43, 45–6, 48–53, 54, 55, 70, 73, 83, 92, 102, 111, 115, 121, 123, 124, 130, 134, 135, 136, 145, 148 n.5, 150, 177, 179, 180, 193 n.37, 196, 205, 208, 209, 226 n.29, 227 n.30
Leicester City Football Club 60, 72, 73
letters 8, 61, 64, 85, 95, 100–1, 105, 139–40, 148–60, 161–3, 166, 169, 172, 218, 232–5
  Amis, Kingsley 53 n.44, 93, 143

Banks, Russell 143
Calder, Liz 29–30, 33, 34–5, 79, 81, 86, 91
Doyle, Arthur Conan 180, 183, 184–5
Ellmann, Richard 165
Flaubert, Gustave 40, 69, 79 n.14, 80 n.17, 80 n.18, 81, 82, 89
Larkin, Philip 44, 53, 85, 93, 165
O'Hanlon, Redmond 144
Raine, Craig 170–1
Smith, Dodie 104
Steegmuller, Francis 166
Updike, John 40 n.3, 173
lexicographer 63 n.36, 76–7, 95, 134 n.9
Lodge, David 11, 40, 53, 85

Maschler, Tom 11, 64, 174
McEwan, Ian 6, 11, 47, 52, 64, 67, 68, 72, 168, 174, 194
McInerney, Jay 67, 69, 143, 148 n.5
memory 17, 59, 60, 127, 185–6, 191, 192, 206–7, 212–3, 215, 219, 227, 229–30, 231–2, 235

names of characters 5, 134
  Arthur & George 192, 193–4
  Before She Met Me 48
  England, England 13 n.12
  Flaubert's Parrot 90–1
  A History of the World in 10½ Chapters 134, 138
  'Knowing French' 166
  Metroland 13, 15, 18, 19
  The Only Story 13 n.12
  The Porcupine 152–3
  The Sense of an Ending 134 n.8, 216, 219, 222, 226–7, 232
  Staring at the Sun 127
  Talking It Over 134 n.9, 218 n.12
New Statesman 43 n.24, 45, 47, 64–5, 66, 100, 138, 171

Oates, Joyce Carol 42, 203 n.8, 210–11
O'Hanlon, Redmond 67, 95, 144, 174
old age 111, 140, 207
order of chapters 10
  Flaubert's Parrot 77–9, 82
  A History of the World in 10½ Chapters 135–6
  Metroland 21

painters/paintings 24, 68, 80, 121, 122, 131–2, 135, 169, 174
Pygge, Edward 3–4, 40–1, 65, 69

Raine, Craig 12, 46, 103, 148 n.5, 170–1
Raitt, Alan 62, 83
reader 1, 2, 4, 12, 15 n.18, 20, 31, 40, 45, 49, 51, 81, 89, 90, 91, 98–9, 108, 113, 122, 128, 130, 134, 147, 150–1, 152–3, 154, 155, 159–60, 163, 169, 172, 197, 199, 201, 225–6, 231, 233, 235
Reid, Christopher 12
Renard, Jules 171, 204, 214
research 1, 2
   Arthur & George 10, 179–85
   A History of the World in 10½ Chapters 137–8
   A Literary Guide to Oxford 96, 99–100, 102
reviewing 39–45, 47, 48 n.39, 64, 65, 66, 67, 77, 85–6, 98, 100, 102, 109, 136, 138–9, 160 n.51, 165, 166, 167, 177 n.1, 203 n.8, 210, 214
Rimbaud, Arthur 15 n.18, 234
Roberts, Ryan 3 n.14, 75, 76, 138
Roth, Philip 41, 106, 218
rugby 17, 61, 71, 218
Rushdie, Salman 67, 68, 150, 154

Seal, Basil 66, 97–8, 123, 171
Shostakovich, Dmitri 14, 42, 214 n.32, 237
Sillitoe, Alan 46, 47
smells 13, 15, 18, 20
Smith, Dodie 68, 104, 139 n.23
sounds 18–20
Spender, Stephen 21 n.34, 92, 99, 100

stage adaptations 104–5, 188 n.32, 198 n.45
structure (*see also* order of chapters) 4
   Arthur & George 178–9
   Flaubert's Parrot 87
   A History of the World in 10½ Chapters 132, 136
   A Literary Guide to Oxford 96–7, 99
   Metroland 15, 28 n.42, 30, 118
   The Noise of Time 118, 120–1
   Nothing to Be Frightened Of 208
   The Sense of an Ending 215
   Staring at the Sun 118, 120, 128

tenses 5, 13, 30, 35, 186, 189, 196–9
titles 1, 10, 64, 112, 205 n.11
   Arthur & George 186, 192–5
   Before She Met Me 54–7, 106
   Flaubert's Parrot 79, 82, 87, 88
   A History of the World in 10½ Chapters 131, 133, 135, 140
   The Lemon Table 111 n.44, 207 n.14
   A Literary Guide to Oxford 95, 99
   Metroland 15, 17, 19, 21, 22, 113
   The Sense of an Ending 223–5, 229
   Staring at the Sun 106, 117–21, 123–4, 126
translation 70, 73 n.103, 77, 92, 109, 148, 155, 166, 173
Twain, Mark 113
typewriter 6

Updike, John 39–40, 85, 173, 228

Waugh, Auberon 44
Waugh, Evelyn 97–8, 99, 175